MASTERS OF CRAFT

MASTERS OF CRAFT

Old Jobs in the New Urban Economy

RICHARD E. OCEJO

PRINCETON UNIVERSITY PRESS

Princeton & Oxford

Published by Princeton University Press, 41 William Street,
Princeton, New Jersey 08540
In the United Kingdom: Princeton University Press, 6 Oxford Street,
Woodstock, Oxfordshire OX20 1TR

press.princeton.edu

Jacket art courtesy of Shutterstock

ISBN 978-0-691-16549-3

British Library Cataloging-in-Publication Data is available

This book has been composed in Whitman, Burford and Helvetica Neue

Printed on acid-free paper. ∞

Printed in the United States of America

1 3 5 7 9 10 8 6 4 2

For Chantal, my heart, and for Rita, the answer to every question

CONTENTS

ACKNOWLEDGMENTS

Before I begin I have a few people I would like to thank. First, I reserve the biggest thanks for the people in these jobs, workplaces, and industries who opened up their lives to me. This book would not exist without your generosity. I'll never forget the six years I spent in your company, and I remain fascinated by your work.

Although initially skeptical when all I talked about was the importance of ice in cocktails instead of finishing my dissertation, Sharon Zukin encouraged me to start a side project on cocktail bars. I truly appreciated her early support and guidance. Similarly, Eric Schwartz showed tremendous support for this project as it expanded and evolved (while probably wishing I was focusing more on my first book). I thank him for always believing in me and getting this book under way. When Eric left Princeton University Press to work at Columbia, I was pretty sure I was going to stay at Princeton for this book, because I enjoyed the overall experience so much the first time around. Still, I wanted to meet Eric's replacement before I made a final decision. I'm so lucky Princeton hired Meagan Levinson, who has been the perfect person to work with through the bulk of the writing. Her editorial skills are remarkable, and I've benefited tremendously from her ability to see both the forest and the trees, and to know how they relate to each other. I would also like to thank Sara Lerner and Samantha Nader at Princeton for guiding this book through production, and Jennifer Harris for her helpful copyediting corrections and suggestions.

I'm blessed to have colleagues who are also good friends. Always first are my CUNY boys, who have offered wonderful comments on this project and joined me in many a cocktail over the years, especially Alex Frenette, Jon Wynn, and Jeff London. I've always written in solitude, but for some reason I joined a writing group a few years ago, when I first started thinking about what the book would actually look like. (And somehow that group turned into an editorial board for a journal.) For their insightful thoughts at a key step in the process I would like to thank Greg Smithsimon, John Krinsky, and Debbie Becher. I had the pleasure of attending two of the Experiencing the Creative Economy conferences at the University of Toronto's Martin Prosperity Institute at important junctures in this project. From these experiences I want to especially thank Kevin Stolarick, Brian Hracs, Doreen Jakob, Pacey Foster, Oli Mould, and Atle Hauge. I must also thank the following folks for their feedback, encouragement, and friendship during this journey: Michaela DeSoucey, Andrew Deener, Black Hawk Hancock, Damian Williams, Tim Dowd, Yasemin Besen-Cassino, Japonica Brown-Saracino, Richard Lloyd, Randol Contreras, Wendy Guastaferro, Jen Johnson, and Shyon Baumann. Finally, thank you to the three reviewers who gave so much of their time to offer so many wonderful thoughts on how to improve this book (and sorry the first draft was so long).

Thanks to the work-study students who helped me transcribe some of the audio recordings over the years. Other than their services, my small annual amount of departmental travel funding, and a highly appreciated award from John Jay's Office for the Advancement of Research to pay for the index, I received no other formal support (financial or otherwise) for this project and book.

No one's story of how they met their romantic partner is better than the one of how I met my amazing wife, Chantal. We met at 4 a.m. on Bourbon Street in New Orleans, outside the Old Absinthe House, while I was conducting research at Tales of the Cocktail, and she was covering it for the *Village Voice*. A smoke-filled conversation on a humid night, while surrounded by cocktail people, turned into a few dates back in New York, which became the relationship that defines my world. Chantal, you saw almost every step of this project, the highs and lows, and always had an open ear, a piece of advice (always from the heart), and a warm embrace for me. Shortly after I finished my fieldwork our daughter, Rita, was born. Rita, I'm thrilled I've gotten to see so much of you as you have grown from a baby to a toddler to a little girl (in part because of your love of steak). I'm already so proud of you, and I can't wait to see what else you have in store. I love you both.

PREFACE | THE DAILY GRIND

> Thus a man's work is one of the things by which he is judged, and certainly
> one of the more significant things by which he judges himself.
>
> —*Everett Cherrington Hughes*[1]

The subway is never too crowded when Joaquin goes to and from work.[2] A bartender by trade, Joaquin, 29, works at Death & Co., one of the most popular cocktail bars in New York City. His shift runs from 6 p.m. to 2 a.m. on Tuesdays, Thursdays, Fridays, and Sundays, but he arrives a couple of hours before the bar opens, and leaves an hour or so after last call (sometimes stopping at another cocktail bar nearby for a nightcap or two before heading home). So he commutes to work in the late afternoon and returns home around 3 a.m., waiting bleary-eyed on a near-empty platform for the F train back to Brooklyn. But the hours are worth it to make and serve cocktails for a living. "I walk into work feeling good, I walk out of work feeling way better. Tired as hell, but it's a satisfying tired. I sleep well."

Born in Ecuador, raised in Miami, and educated at Boston University, Joaquin moved to New York City in 2005, at the age of 27. Uncertain of his career path, he started bartending to pay the bills, as he did after college. After early stints at beer and shot joints, he moved on to places where the quality of the drinks only sometimes mattered, until he got his job at Death & Co. This Friday Joaquin wakes up around noon, gets out of bed, and spends a couple of hours trolling various food and drink websites and blogs to stay abreast of the latest trends. Today he is most interested in learning about new ingredients that chefs are using, for inspiration. Last month, Joaquin worked at a dinner for a supper club and paired five cocktails with five courses.

The next month's dinner sold out quickly. "So now I know the pressure's on, and I gotta do it better," he says.

Joaquin understands his role behind the bar to be like a performance on a stage. He waits to shower and shave until just before he leaves for work, to look as fresh and awake as possible. Light-skinned with light brown hair, he maintains a fashionable amount of stubble. Wearing blue-gray pants with cuffs rolled just above the ankle, boat shoes, and a white V-neck t-shirt, Joaquin walks from the sunny downtown streets of the East Village into the windowless bar. He goes downstairs to change into his work clothes: a button-down dress shirt, tie, vest, arm garters, slacks, and dress shoes. In uniform, he checks himself in the mirror to make sure everything is on just right. He ties on an apron and starts prepping the backbar by filling bins with five different varieties of ice, juicing lemons and limes by hand, and making sure the dozen or so bitters bottles the bar uses are full. By 6, he is ready for his audience.

The tiny town of Gardiner, in Ulster County, is a two-hour drive north of New York City. Along with the natural beauty of the mid–Hudson Valley region, one of the town's attractions is Tuthilltown Spirits, on the site of a historic landmark gristmill, which turned grain into flour for over two hundred years with waterpower from the Shawangunk Kill. The distillery is down a short, dead-end dirt path off Tuthilltown Road called Grist Mill Lane. Ralph, the company's co-owner, purchased the property in 2001, and with his partner, Brian, renovated the two granaries into a craft distillery operation and a rickhouse, or a warehouse for storing whiskey barrels as their contents slowly age. In addition to the converted granaries, Ralph's house, some storage facilities, and a port-a-potty, the property consists of a large field with patches of overgrown grass. The people at Tuthilltown are considering growing crops (heirloom varieties of apple, corn, and rye) for making spirits. For now, some of its employees use the field for recreational camping over the summer. Their rent is to mow the grass.

Liam wakes up in his teepee at the break of dawn. He puts on a pair of thick khaki-colored work pants and worn brown boots. With the temperature already approaching ninety degrees, and a long day ahead of making whiskey amid the steaming hot stills, he does not bother to put on a shirt. Twenty-seven years old and over six feet tall with a thick mustache, a stubbly beard, shaggy brown hair, and an upper body chiseled by more than a year of lifting heavy barrels and equipment, Liam resembles a rugged character from American folklore. Born and raised in nearby Rhinebeck, he bartended locally for a few years after he graduated from SUNY New Paltz, a town close to Gardiner, with a degree in geology. Wanting a change, but wanting to still work with his hands, he responded to an ad on Craigslist for a job at a small distillery that makes handcrafted spirits from local ingredients. Although he had never distilled before, the job appealed to several of his interests and sensibilities—manual labor, spirits, and sustainability—and the chief distiller, Joel, happened to be an old customer from his bartending days.

Liam and I walk behind the distillery to finish priming six-gallon barrels for today's barreling, and prepare more for tomorrow. Two sets of six sit stacked in pyramids from yesterday, each one full with water. We remove the wooden bungs from the holes with a hammer, drain the barrels into a cistern, and then place them upright on a wooden pallet to be forklifted into the distillery. We take twelve more, stack them and fill them with water from the hose, and hammer the bungs in with a rubber mallet. Letting barrels sit for a day or so with water primes them by causing the wood to expand, thereby closing any possible leaks. "You would rather lose water than whiskey," says Liam. By 10 a.m., we are ready to start barreling.

Miles usually takes a car service to his job as a barber from his apartment in Park Slope, Brooklyn. Half African American and half Puerto Rican, Miles grew up in various apartments (some in public housing projects) throughout all five boroughs, but mainly in the Bronx. As usual, Miles arrives ten minutes or so before 11 a.m., when Freemans Sporting Club opens. Seven young men waiting for haircuts stand outside the gated front door, which opens to a high-end men's clothing store. Past shelves, tables, and rails of handmade shirts, pants, suits, vests, jackets, shoes, and ties (and some samples of taxidermy) is the entrance to the barbershop. Miles, who started cutting his friends' hair at age 15, was drawn to the barbershop/clothing combo. "I was always into fashion, menswear. If anything, I'm just kind of like a creative dude. I'm into art. I just like creative things."

Barbers stand on their feet with their arms half-elevated and have to be "on" for clients and attend to their needs for nine hours a day. Some can start "banging out" haircuts immediately, but others prefer easing into the day gradually, at their own pace. After entering the shop through the building's side door in Freemans Alley, Miles takes his tools out of his locker and lays them out on a towel at his station. He checks his spray bottle's water level and chats for a few minutes with the other barbers as they also set up. More men have arrived as the shop opens. Freemans is a walk-in shop without appointments, which leads clients to come early. Clients can request a specific barber, which may mean a longer wait, or just see the next available one. As one of the shop's more popular barbers, and someone his colleagues recognize as an expert on fades (from having worked in " 'hood" shops in black neighborhoods), Miles already has three customers who put their names in with the receptionist to have him cut their hair. He greets a regular client with a handshake into a half-hug, and tells him to sit in his chair and he will be right back. Miles then goes to the restaurant next door that operates an espresso bar during the day and orders an iced Americano. He flips through a men's fashion magazine he picked up in the window of the clothing shop, takes a few sips, and sits on the bench outside. At 11:15 he goes in and cuts his client's hair. At 12:30 he finishes a second one, and then goes back outside to check his phone and chat with Mark, another barber, who is having a cigarette, while two other clients on his list continue to wait. Meanwhile, Van, whose station is next to his, has started on his fourth haircut of the day. The clients do not complain. They simply sit quietly and take in the atmosphere. As the day goes on Miles settles into his rhythm and starts banging out cuts every half hour.

Five days a week, from Sunday through Thursday, Giancarlo leaves his Harlem apartment, which he shares with three strangers, and rides the A train down to 14th Street, to his job as a butcher at Dickson's Farmstand Meats in Chelsea Market, an indoor food center. Thirty years old, Giancarlo moved to New York from Colorado last year. "I was tired of working in a box," he says about his former post-college job as a manager of a medical center. He decided to pursue his true passion, food and meat, and after stints at a charcuterie shop, slaughterhouse, and butchery program at an upstate university, ended up in the city at Dickson's. Giancarlo goes through the back door by the loading dock on 16th Street instead of the main entrance most people use on 9th Avenue.

He greets Junior, the kitchen's sandwich maker, and goes into the bathroom to change into his uniform of black clogs, white snap-button shirt, white butcher coat, and white apron, all of which will get redder throughout the day. He keeps on the old black jeans he wore to the shop, since he does not have any special plans after work. He hangs a side towel from the shoelace tie of the apron. Like all employees in the cutting room he wears a baseball hat, but he keeps on his "Neil Young and Crazy Horse" hat instead of putting on the black and white "Dickson's" trucker hat. Finally, he puts on a pair of white disposable powderless latex gloves, and a pair of thicker off-white cloth "cut" gloves. The sharp knives the butchers use will easily slice and pierce right through both sets. But if they are working slowly enough, the cut gloves at least provide a warning.

With no customers in sight for another two hours, Giancarlo goes over to the laptop and puts on music by the heavy metal band Pantera. Music aside, the prep period is a peaceful time in the shop. The butchers spend most of it filling the 15-foot-long, two-tiered refrigerated display case. "We do a complete overhaul," Giancarlo says as I follow him. "We go tray by tray and anything that looks old we replace with something new."

They also replace anything that got sold, or, if they are completely out of a cut, add something different. The "old"-looking cuts are still perfectly edible. The people at the shop just feel customers will not want to buy cuts of meat that look less red than others. So either the staff will take home old cuts, or the kitchen will prepare them in a lunch dish, for the "family" lunch.

Giancarlo removes the strips of butcher paper that the crew who closed the shop last night placed on top of all the meat in the display. He takes out a long metal tray with nothing left on it but a fifth of a whole cut of beef tenderloin, about three inches in length, and a rolled up skirt steak. Brian, another butcher, takes a top blade, one of many primal cuts, or subsections, on a cow, out of the walk-in and starts making flatiron steaks. Giancarlo takes out another tenderloin from the walk-in, cleans it of fat, sinew, and silvery skin until it resembles a small meat log, and ties it. He stands the older tenderloin on its end next to the skirt at the top-right corner of the tray, which will be farthest from customers, and lays the new one behind it. He then takes out the short rib section from the walk-in and begins sawing it into even pieces with the electric bandsaw. Two-by-two, standing upright like columns, he arrays them next to the tenderloin. Giancarlo then cleans another skirt he grabbed from the walk-in, rolls it up, and places it in the top-left corner, with the old one in between it and the short ribs (counter workers know to try to sell the cut closest to them first, which is often the oldest). One empty corner remains on the tray, for the flatiron steaks that Brian is preparing at the other butcher table. He brings four of them, stacked staircase-like on a white ceramic plate, over to the tray. Giancarlo squishes and scrunches the soft tenderloin a bit to fit them, then brings the tray over to the display and slides it in.

Today is also pork day. Six pigs hang in the walk-in, sawed in half down the spine. Once the beef display is complete, Giancarlo and the two other butchers prepare the cutting area for breaking them down. By noon, with the shop now buzzing and full of customers, they are ready to start the day's main event.

Perhaps because my own job requires me to work with and within my head I have always been drawn to people who work with their hands. I have always liked the performance aspect of being a professor: using my body and facial expressions to make points while standing in front of a classroom full of students, or telling a story from my field notes at a conference. But still it is not the same feeling as harmonizing the body and brain to make something tangible, something people can instantly determine the quality of, and something you can satisfyingly hold up as your own.

My interest in these workers also stems from my own background. My parents grew up in white ethnic neighborhoods in Brooklyn in the decades after World War II: Bay Ridge (my mother) and Bensonhurst (my father). Places like bars, barbershops, and butcher shops were community institutions in these neighborhoods. They were local meeting places, part of the rhythm of daily life. Growing up, my parents and extended family regaled me with stories of their lives as kids and young adults. Residents walked to the greengrocer, the cheesemonger, the fishmonger, the baker, and the butcher shop, all on the same few blocks, sometimes daily. Men went to the local bar after work with co-workers and neighbors. And fathers and sons went to the same barber each month. People dealt with the same personnel at these shops, who watched their children grow up, saw the same neighbors, and never had to leave a few-block radius to satisfy their basic needs. In my mother's case, the shop owners, workers, and customers spoke Norwegian. In my father's, they spoke Italian and Brooklyn-accented English (although my father was Spanish). Where I grew up, the more suburban Staten Island, we went to the butcher shop and bakery only for special meals and holidays. Our regular food came from the supermarket. We always drove to buy anything. When he first moved to Staten Island, my father lamented not being able to walk for his needs, not even to a corner bar, because one didn't exist. He stocked a home bar and learned how to make his own Martinis: stirred with London dry gin and a hint of vermouth, served on the rocks with olives.

My father's father was a barber from Spain. He came to the United States in the late 1920s, and eventually owned a barbershop in Chelsea and a house in Bensonhurst. He died of cancer at 45 when my father was just 9, and my father started working at a young age to help support his mother, aunts, and cousins. College was not an option for a family of immigrants who lost the main breadwinner. He inherited my grandfather's tools and became a hairdresser for a time. But cutting hair in his working-class family and neighborhood was a *good, honest* job for a son to have.

Never did my parents think I would enter a trade, or get a manual labor job, as their parents and so many of their peers from working-class Brooklyn did. They both worked in offices in Manhattan, and we lived a comfortable, middle-class life. College was always in my future, because they felt it was the best way to move up. Manual labor and "blue-collar" professions were honest and respectful, but not for me. The message sunk in. A few degrees later, I'm now a knowledge worker.

Despite my basic interest and personal background, I came to study these workers and their workplaces by accident. I first learned about cocktail bars like Death & Co. while I was conducting research for my previous book.[3] I was drawn to the people of what I learned was a cocktail-based "taste community" of national and even global scale: owners, serious cocktail enthusiasts, members of the liquor industry and lifestyle media, PR representatives, casual consumers, and, of course, the bartenders.[4] Of all these groups, they intrigued me the most. Most had gone to college. Some at one time worked full-time jobs in other industries. Some had bartended to earn money while in school, or while they worked toward a creative pursuit, like acting or music (their "real" passion).[5] All had a lot of cultural capital, or hip, cool tastes for food, fashion, and music found in today's city. But at some point they all decided on bartending—specifically bartending in specialized cocktail bars— as their job, career path, and professional identity. Like Joaquin, these young workers did not turn away from drink service—they ran toward it. In today's "new economy," with its slew of knowledge-, creativity-, and technology-based jobs for well-educated and culturally savvy workers, they wanted to bartend, in spite of other job options and, in some cases, the expectations their families had for them. As a sociologist with an interest in the cultural economy of cities, and as someone who came from a background similar to theirs, I was fascinated and began studying the cocktail community.

Since at first I wanted to look at the entire extended cocktail world, I chose to also study the craft distilling industry.[6] Many small companies opened in the 2000s and made new spirits, which cocktail bartenders embraced. Some bartenders even started working at these craft distilleries or for liquor companies as "brand ambassadors," a fancy term for a PR representative. To learn about craft distilling firsthand, I worked as an intern at Tuthilltown Spirits, where I toiled alongside Liam and the crew to help make several varieties of whiskey and vodka.[7] But my fieldwork there reinforced my interest in the workers themselves.

I began to come up with several interrelated research questions. Why do people with options in the labor market pursue service, manual labor, and light manufacturing jobs like bartending and distilling, which have never required advanced degrees or hip tastes to get, as careers? Why have some traditionally low-status service, manual labor, retail, and light manufacturing jobs become "cool?" Why have they transformed in this manner today? How do these workers come to understand these typically low-status jobs as respectable rather than as yielders of downward social mobility? What meanings do they create from their work? What impacts, if any, are they having on their larger industries? What do these masculine-coded jobs reveal about the gendered nature of work?[8] And how can we understand this transformation and where do these workers fit in the larger context of today's "new economy?"

To choose more occupations to study and answer these questions, I relied on the commonalities between bartending and distilling beyond alcohol.[9] I also used my knowledge of the work and culture literature in sociology and other disciplines, and my own knowledge of the zeitgeist of cultural trends among the postindustrial city's gentrifying neighborhoods and well-educated, creative young adults. I noted how bartending and distilling shared several elements. They were old, classic, manual labor jobs. They had gone through a "deskilling" phase and are now being "reskilled."[10] Most importantly, young people took these jobs seriously as occupations (not as cool lifestyles) and even pursued them as careers. And, by doing so, these workers were injecting these jobs with a new set of meanings and values that underlie the work they do. In effect, they were forming a unique "occupational community" and making a specialized niche for themselves within their larger industries.[11] They were, to build from a concept I engaged with in my previous book, "upscaling" these common occupations, or ascribing an exclusive status on them based on a new cultural understanding of how professionals in these fields *should* work.

I sought out two more occupations that fit these criteria to study and chose upscale men's barbers and whole-animal butchers. As with the first two workplaces, I used participant observation research in the shops to get close to the workers and the work. I sat, watched, and spoke with barbers like Miles as they worked, as I did at the cocktail bars, and worked shoulder-to-shoulder with such butchers as Giancarlo as an intern at the butcher shop, like I did at the craft distillery. By the end of my fieldwork I realized I had studied three jobs that combine service and manual labor in retail workplaces that people regard as community institutions (bartenders, barbers, and butchers) and one that focuses on light manufacturing with less of a retail, service, and neighborhood-oriented component (distillers). But I contend there are more similarities than differences between the new workers in these two types of industries. And I only exclude craft distillers in chapter 7, on service work practices, because distiller is not a service job, and distilleries are wholesale, not retail, businesses.

Perhaps the most interesting commonality among these four occupations is their status in today's cities as "cool" jobs. In-the-know, middle-class urbanites, the lifestyle media, and hip consumers all regard young people who want to make exquisite cocktails and small batches of booze, coif retro hairstyles, and break down whole animals into unusual cuts of meat as being on the cutting edge of the postindustrial city's cultural cornucopia, and at the vanguard of what makes a city worth living in as a provider of cool amenities. So much of today's postindustrial city revolves around consuming, particularly in gentrifying neighborhoods. Well-educated urbanites who move to and explore these neighborhoods for new and authentic products and experiences are exactly who city leaders aim to attract as residents and visitors.[12] They are "cultural omnivores," or people with the cultural and economic capital to consume a broad range of products and genres, from the highbrow to the low, without threatening their own status.[13] Most significantly, these consumers look to these workers in the industries of nightlife, alcohol, style, and food for guidance in their pursuits.

In this book I argue that the upscale, new elite versions of these classic, common occupations have become cultural tastemakers, specifically producers of omnivorous tastes, in the gentrifying city and legitimate employment options for young, well-educated, and/or culturally savvy workers at a time in urban history when the meanings behind "good" tastes and "good" jobs are changing.[14] This view differs tremendously from how people in mainstream society have typically viewed these jobs: honest, respectable, and necessary, but low-status, dirty, physically demanding, for people with few other work options, not jobs people would want their children to do if they want them to move up in the world, and certainly not culturally hip.[15] These jobs have also been traditionally viewed as "man's work," requiring physical labor and done in workplaces not suitable for women. These images still exist, but not in contexts of the cool quarters and social circles of today's city.

Most importantly, people pursue these jobs as careers not because they're cool, but because they provide meaningful work with many intrinsic rewards, which is not easy to obtain in today's volatile economy of precarious work conditions.[16] In an economy in which high-status jobs revolve around knowledge and ideas, these workers seek out knowledge-based manual labor that combines thinking, serving, and making. But these new workers and their work present an intriguing paradox. While they do not pursue these jobs as careers because they are "cool," once they get them they must show they *get* them, or can put them all into practice, in part by acting cool. They must competently, confidently, and convincingly enact a set of "cultural repertoires," or use cultural "toolkits," that combine physical and technical skills based on a sense of craft and craftsmanship with an ability to understand and communicate specialized cultural knowledge.[17] Not everyone succeeds. Doing so not only defines them and their work professionally but also separates them as upscale versions of these classic jobs.

Covering the period from February 20, 2007, when I first walked into Death & Co. to see what all the fuss was about with craft cocktails, to August 28, 2013, my emotional last day as an intern at Dickson's Farmstand Meats, in this book I document what I learned from these workers and their work.[18] In part I, I introduce each job and explore a number of themes found in them: the new "elite" in service work, the logics of authenticity, the role of masculinity in the new economy, and the production of omnivorousness. In part II, I examine how people pursue these careers (paths) and how they perform in them (practices). I show how high-status work in today's knowledge- and service-based urban postindustrial economy includes a pattern of young workers who choose to enter manual labor jobs because they derive meaning from what they do. They construct this meaning through a set of performances based on these cultural repertoires: the services they provide, interactions they have, and products they make. By fusing mental and manual labor, head and hand, cultural taste and physical skill, they form a new elite tier in the retail, service, and light manufacturing industries, or a niche occupational community in the new economy.[19] While people from certain social backgrounds would have once dismissed, overlooked, or shunned the low status of these occupations, the presence of these cultural repertoires leads these workers to pursue and take pride in them. And by plying their trade publicly, in the service of others, they transform traditional community institutions—the local bar, barbershop, and butcher shop—and manufacturing businesses—distilleries—into examples of the new elite in retail and craft production, complete with validated notions of "quality taste" and "good work" in the gentrifying city. This book tells their stories.

MASTERS OF CRAFT

"Hey, doctor, didn't you study barbers before working here?" Giancarlo asks me after returning to the butcher shop from getting everyone coffee.

I was in the middle of my yearlong internship at Dickson's Farmstand Meats in Chelsea Market when Giancarlo asked me this question. Chelsea Market is located in the former Nabisco factory. It takes up an entire city block, between 9th and 10th Avenues and 15th and 16th Streets in Manhattan. Chelsea Market is actually twenty-two separate structures, seamlessly sutured together. In the late nineteenth century Chelsea was a manufacturing area for many products, including baked goods. After a series of consolidations the National Biscuit Company officially formed in 1898, and at its peak Nabisco produced half of the baked goods in the United States, including such products as Premium Saltines, Fig Newtons, Barnum's Animal Crackers, and, most famously, the Oreo. By the 1930s new technology, specifically long, continuous "band ovens," was remaking the baking industry by replacing the old vertical ovens. Nabisco installed some band ovens in its complex, but assembly line–style manufacturing is better suited for long, single-story buildings. As a small island Manhattan does verticality quite well; horizontality, not so much. To stay competitive Nabisco moved all of its production to New Jersey in 1958, and sold its Chelsea buildings in 1959. Some light manufacturing companies occupied the buildings in the ensuing decades, but for the most part they fell into disuse, along with most of the neighborhood's industrial buildings.[1]

In the 1990s real estate investor Irwin B. Cohen assembled a group to buy the Nabisco buildings and convert the upper floors into one million square feet of office space and the ground floor and basement into 225,000 square feet of retail space. With this plan Cohen extended the idea of repurposing old industrial buildings into more contemporary and profitable uses, which had already been happening in the city for new housing, such as lofts in former manufacturing buildings.[2] Completed in 1997 the market's crowning achievement was the conversion of the back lots of each individual building into a ground-level concourse. With entrances on either end on 9th and 10th Avenues, the serpentine concourse creates an arcade-like experience for visitors, themed around food. Initially, the shops did mainly wholesale business for restaurants and hotels around the city, with some local retail. Chelsea was still gentrifying in the late 1990s, and the idea of a food destination in the neighborhood had yet to blossom.

Today Chelsea Market resembles the upscale nature of its surrounding neighborhood, with a mix of repurposed industrial hardware and sleek add-ons, and fits quite well into the foundations of New York City's postindustrial economy. The market itself is a high-priced mart, mostly for food, with nearly fifty shops, stands, eateries, and restaurants selling products with labels like "handmade" and "authentic." The arcade is like a postindustrial theme park. The architects and designers retained the corrugated metal and rusted girders from the complex's factory days. They also added industrial-metal motifs to the walls and signage; revealed more brickwork; and used granite, drill bits, and an exposed pipe to create a central fountain, as one would find at any mall. Chelsea Market invites visitors to experience the industrial past through a lens of modern urban consumerism.

The upstairs offices have several prominent companies of the new economy as tenants, such as Google, the Food Network, the Oxygen Network, MLB.com, and NY1, a local TV station. In 2010 Google purchased the massive three-million-square-foot Port Authority Building, which it had been leasing since 2006, located directly across the street from Chelsea Market on 9th Avenue, for $1.9 billion (the company paid for the building in cash). In doing so Google joined Lower Manhattan's expanding base of IT and media companies permanently.[3] Along with nearby fashion companies and the boutique Maritime and Standard hotels, these models of today's economy bring numerous young professionals to the market on a regular basis.

The collection of so many food-related businesses in one enclosed place, the pedigree of some (like Masaharu Morimoto and Mario Batali, who own restaurants there), and the market's location near the High Line, an abandoned railway repurposed into a public park, and in the exclusively hip neighborhood of Chelsea have made it a popular destination for New Yorkers and tourists alike. The market receives six million visitors every year. Tour buses regularly drop

Figure 1. The concourse at Chelsea Market. Photo by the author.

off passengers to explore the market (and use the public bathrooms), shop, and walk the High Line, while local companies offer food-centered walking tours.[4]

I first learned about Chelsea Market from my research on New York City's craft cocktail community. Tad Carducci, a bartender and half of the bar and beverage consulting duo the Tippling Bros., opened the Tippler bar in its basement in 2011. By then Chelsea was a popular neighborhood for luxury shopping and hip nightlife and the word on the Chelsea Market was out. With so many young, well-educated people with disposable income living and working in Chelsea, and so many more visiting the neighborhood to shop and go out at night, opening a craft cocktail bar there made sense for the Tippling Bros. On the backbar at the Tippler sit several bottles of Hudson whiskeys (Baby Bourbon, Four Grain, Manhattan Rye), Tuthilltown's most famous line of small-batch spirits. It also made as much sense to Jake Dickson to open his whole-animal butcher shop there in 2009, to appeal to the city's growing foodie scene.

And on his coffee run, my co-worker Giancarlo noticed a new barbershop, Decatur & Sons, had just opened by Ninth Street Espresso, a fancy espresso bar, just down the concourse from Dickson's. Offering quality men's haircuts in an array of cool styles—undercuts, fades—as well as straight razor shaves in a classic-looking environment, the shop joins an expanding industry of men's grooming and high-end fashion. Coincidentally, I knew its owner, Thorin, from his old shop, where he was just a barber. Thorin told me a few times he wanted to open his own shop, and a year prior he mentioned he was looking at spaces. He chose the Chelsea Market, right next to an old-fashioned shoeshine stand.

Here, then, was my entire project, in one form or another, under one roof: cocktail bartenders, spirits from craft distilleries, men's barbers at a high-service shop, and whole-animal butchers. Bars, barbershops, and butcher shops were neighborhood cornerstones in the industrial city. Today, new versions of them catering to knowledgeable and wealthy consumers have been opening in gentrifying neighborhoods in cities across the country (for example, Wicker Park in Chicago, the Tenderloin and Dogpatch in San Francisco). While not always tightly clustered in hubs like Chelsea Market, they tend to be located near one another. Professionals in high-profile economic sectors (like Google employees), members of the city's "foodie" taste community, and tourists—all key consumer groups in today's urban economy—support them. These businesses are more upscale than their predecessors and peers, like the corner bar, the neighborhood barbershop or butcher shop, and the meat counter at the supermarket. Craft cocktails cost $13 to $15, squat 375-milliliter bottles of small-batch bourbon go for $42 in liquor stores, stylish haircuts start at $40, and meat from whole-animal shops can be quadruple the cost at a supermarket. They're clearly for people with financial means. Price, however, is not the sole basis for their exclusivity, nor are they exclusive in the same way as traditional luxury goods like expensive watches or cars. These products and services are loaded with unique cultural meanings, and these workplaces put workers in a knowledge-sharing relationship with consumers.

We can trace the rise of these new elite occupations, workplaces, products, and forms of consumption like those at the Chelsea Market to three key cultural, urban, and economic changes happening in society today: reconfigured understandings of taste, the new role of community institutions in gentrifying neighborhoods, and work in the "new economy" of postindustrial cities like New York. Looking at these three distinct changes in concert lets us see how they are producing the conditions under which these jobs are seen as among the new elite in service, retail, and light manufacturing, and under which these workers find themselves pursuing these jobs as careers without experiencing them as downward social mobility.

The Rise of the Cultural Omnivore

Taste used to seem rather simple. People "knew" some examples of modern culture were superior to others. Opera was a higher form of art than rock music, wine was a more refined drink than beer, and filet mignon was better than hot dogs. Of course, there is nothing natural about taste. Both high and low cultures are social constructions. History, politics, and forms of power (economic, cultural) have shaped their statuses. Nothing makes any cultural products inherently "better" or "worse" than others, and they are valuable and meaningful to the people who consume them regardless of their status in wider society. Still, people regularly associate cultural tastes as being highbrow or lowbrow, often based on how they are made and distributed, and on who consumes them. People usually see elite culture as noncommercial and nonstandardized. Fine art, for instance, meets these criteria. But popular culture is mass-produced and standardized, like Hollywood blockbusters: open and understandable to everyone, with little depth or effort required.[5]

Most importantly, people have regularly linked taste with social class. "High" culture was considered not just superior, but the domain of the wealthy and powerful. Wealthy people went to the opera, took in priceless art, drank fine wines, and dined on French cuisine. They were also able to speak in detail about what they were consuming. Growing up with wealth essentially gave them the keys to not just buying but also understanding these elite art forms and products, and to acting like they belonged in elite company. Meanwhile, the working classes listened to pop music, read trashy novels, drank beer, and ate basic stews or their own ethnic foods at home, and they never really thought about what they were consuming on an intellectual level. Since they had relatively few resources, like money and time, to reflect on culture or give their children the tools to do so, cultural products like film and music were merely entertainment, and food and drink were merely nourishment, not sources for intellectual engagement. The working class's lower status kept their cultural preferences within the province of the body, the common, and the necessary, while the wealthy class's higher status elevated their cultural preferences to the province of the mental, the rarefied, and the all-enriching. And people from these different backgrounds, the elite and the blue collar, reinforced their own social status by consuming their respective cultures.[6] There have been many examples of people from wealthier backgrounds "slumming" among the working classes and of folks from blue-collar backgrounds moving up the social ladder and adopting upscale tastes, and certainly "midbrow" culture complicates the model somewhat. But this system of cultural stratification still conforms to a strong idea of how Americans consume.

New consumption and lifestyle patterns have disrupted this imagination. Specifically, society's elites have been consuming low- and middlebrow culture, which they may have once shunned, in addition to or in place of traditionally upscale offerings, without compromising their status as elites.[7] Today's young and future leaders in business and culture are as likely to be appreciative of and well versed in hip-hop and beer as they are classical music and wine. In fact, outright snobbery has no place among these elites, who do not accept the arbitrary reasons given for why highbrow culture has been accepted as high quality.[8] No longer discriminating from their own social class position, these people are "cultural omnivores" in search of variety. The world is their oyster, and nothing is off limits to their appreciation because of its origins or who else shares in it. By virtue of consuming it, they do much to elevate low culture in status. Hip-hop, with origins in the inner city among poor African Americans, takes its place alongside classical music as a valid art form. Even once-abandoned factories like the Chelsea Market, with some major revamping and basic food choices like tacos and hot dogs in a mall-like environment, take a place alongside classic landmarks and fancy restaurants as integral destinations.

This shift in cultural consumption has launched a debate over whether culture has become truly democratized, or if it still signifies distinction. Is the old order of what is "high" and what is "low" culture, or what is "elite" and what is for the "masses," over—in which case everyone can now equally access and appreciate all cultures and cultural products? Or does the old stratifying order persist today, only in new forms, and therefore does what people buy (or listen to, or see, or eat, or drink, or wear) still distinguish them from others in ways that reinforce their own social backgrounds? In other words, is difference erased when elites listen to and talk about hip-hop, or does it somehow remain? Despite the potential of cultural omnivorousness to remove distinction from people's tastes, most research supports the latter claim: people still reproduce inequality when they consume low culture, they simply do so along new lines.[9] They are simply new elites.

For example, today's "foodies," or everyday people who love talking, reading, and writing about food along with eating and cooking it, face a contradiction. On the one hand, they earnestly seek out and praise a wide range of foods and cultures regardless of their origins, while rejecting the exclusive snobbery from traditional but arbitrary elite food cultures, such as French haute cuisine.[10] Everyone should get to eat good food, and everyone can be a foodie, their democratic thinking goes. On the other hand, foodies also make new definitions for what is and is not "good" food. They create and police the "symbolic boundaries" surrounding these definitions.[11] They ask a number of questions about food to determine its quality: Is it "authentic?" Or does it have geographic specificity? Was it made simply, by hand? Is there a clear personal link between the product and its maker or makers? Does it signify history and tradition? And is it "exotic?" Or does it come from a distant culture? Does it break common eating or cooking norms? Foodie culture promotes these meanings through various traditional and new media outlets, while foodies debate them in conversations and online. Most importantly, the "authentic" and "exotic" foods foodies typically laud as "good" are hardly accessible to most people in terms of both their cost and the complex understandings behind their "good-ness." While they champion democratic and multicultural eating, these new elites still seek out and obtain greater cultural status through consumption, but by different means from the traditional model.[12]

A dimension to this shift identifies culture not merely as knowledge to be known or a product to be consumed, but as behavior to be performed.[13] At one point, elites looking to show their status and distance themselves from mere aspirants through consumption could simply name fine distinctions in the cultural products they liked, such as knowing specific details in high-quality men's suits, the subtle variations in multiple performances of classical musical pieces, or the differences between wine vintages.[14] But with so much cultural knowledge openly and easily available on the Internet, and with the risk of coming off as an elitist snob, people show their status by acting out their cultural bona fides, but casually, and with ease. Pushing fine distinctions is forceful showing off. New elites want to show their multicultural tastes as a normal aspect of who they are, and as something others can obtain. Such performances, which must be casual and convincing, are sources of cultural power in an era of omnivorousness.

This shift in cultural consumption and taste is important because it permeates the social worlds of craft cocktail bars, craft distilleries, upscale men's barbershops, and whole-animal butcher shops. In one sense, the products they sell and the services they provide are very ordinary. People order cocktails and booze at bars all the time, everyone gets a haircut at some point, and meat is a dietary staple. People are highly aware of these basic, neighborhood businesses, and someone has to provide the services and make these items for customers. These workers often frame their special products and services as basic and mundane, like any other version of them. In other words, they take a very democratic approach to what they offer.

But what they make, do, and sell is neither ordinary nor broadly accessible. Each workplace and its workers elevate their products and services above the common and into a rarefied cultural realm through particular work practices, applied cultural knowledge, and philosophical underpinnings.[15] While we know much about how cultural omnivores consume, a look on the ground at these new elite culture workers reveals where and how these tastes get made and spread.

A number of philosophies undergird the work practices and professional identities of these workers. Cocktail bartenders use the philosophy of "mixology," which includes following precise recipes, using specific ingredients, and employing certain tools and techniques, to make what they think are "great" drinks the "right" way. Craft distillers use ideas like "sustainable" and "local" to undergird their production of "authentic" small batches of spirits. Men's barbers at upscale shops rely on a sense of style and masculinity rooted in hip, downtown urban cultural scenes and use both traditional and new haircutting techniques to provide stylish haircuts for professional men in a deliberately masculine setting. And whole-animal butchers use a "meat philosophy" that determines ethical and sustainable meat and artisanal butchery techniques to make rare cuts of meat and meat products. These workers imbue their products and services with these meanings while inculcating these values of "good" taste to consumers.

Using craft-based techniques and applying cultural knowledge make these workers and businesses among the new cultural elite in retail and light manufacturing. They are where savvy consumers can find items and services that appear rather normal, and a part of everyday life in the city. But they really contain complex meanings that make them unique, "authentic," and special to these consumers. Most importantly, these businesses are places where workers create and teach "good," omnivorous tastes.

Cocktail bartenders use their own tastes and those of their taste community to choose ingredients for their drinks. They often favor less prestigious spirit categories (rye) and inexpensive, unknown brands (Rittenhouse) over highly regarded (aged scotch and cognac) and popular ones (Grey Goose vodka). Similarly, craft distillers often use local and rare ingredients different from what popular liquor brands use (heritage ryes, corns, apples) and adjust recipes (reducing the juniper content in gin) to make products with unique flavor profiles. And distilling in small batches ("artisanally") leads to inconsistent flavors compared to mass-produced and blended spirits. These decisions of cocktail bartenders and craft distillers and the techniques they use to make their products help restructure taste in the drinks world. They elevate certain products, lower others, and create new "good" ones based on the philosophies and work practices behind them.

Barbers in upscale men's shops use a sense of style and detailed service within the confines of a masculine-coded space, where professional urbanites can get stylish haircuts without compromising their manhood while also consuming working-class culture. And whole-animal butcher shop workers butcher and sell cuts of meat that are both unusual (feather steak, boneless chuck short rib) and popular (tenderloin, strip steaks). But they ignore popular ideas of what makes meats cuts and meat products "good" and "bad," such as fat content, and instead use their own tastes to distinguish cuts from each other. In short, today's upending of tradition and restructuring of cultural taste have influenced all four of these industries, with a small segment of workers leading the charge of creating and teaching "quality" taste in unique workplaces.

Shifting Community Institutions in Gentrifying Neighborhoods

Many popular images of neighborhood life in the industrial city are of self-contained "urban villages."[16] These are the Little Italys, Little Polands, Greek-towns, and other enclaves for ethnic groups (mainly of European descent), as well as neighborhoods for Jews and blacks (or shtetls and ghettos). To their residents these areas were like safe havens, intimate places of familiarity in the anonymous city. Residents defined their neighborhood's culture and uses, and the more a single group dominated a neighborhood's population, the stronger its boundaries dividing insiders and outsiders. Like Main Street in Small Town, USA, these neighborhoods had everything for residents' daily needs: native cuisines and groceries, social hangouts, and mother tongues in the streets. The businesses were community institutions, provided the basics, and got people out of their cramped apartments and together in public. Of course, these pictures of the urban village are often romantic. Life in them wasn't always harmonious. Conflicts regularly emerged between different groups over such issues as jobs, housing, and the use of public space; some groups were essentially forced to live in these areas, and they sometimes lacked adequate services and/or became victims of "urban renewal" programs.[17]

Its founders based Chelsea Market's concept on the romantic urban village idea. It is the shopping street of the old neighborhood except indoors and in microcosm. Inside shoppers can go to the butcher, baker, greengrocer, chocolatier, cheesemonger, and fishmonger. They can buy a bottle of wine or booze, or milk at the dairy. They can browse in the bookstore; stop in the ice cream parlor; get a haircut, shave, and shoeshine; and then pop downstairs for a beer or cocktail. And because it's the twenty-first century and the foodie movement is in full swing, they can also get Cambodian sandwiches, crepes, vegan sushi, "authentic" tacos, fancy espressos, and oysters. The workers often know and are passionate about the items they sell. It is the anti-supermarket. But there are big differences between it and the urban village. Chelsea Market is a repurposed factory in a wealthy destination area, not the streets of a neighborhood. Shoppers are usually professionals who work nearby, visitors from around the city, and tourists, not necessarily neighbors. And the workers celebrate the sense of craft and cultural knowledge undergirding these businesses rather than any sense of local community or group identity.

The actual and romanticized urban villages gradually declined in the decades after World War II. Manufacturing industries began to leave cities for less expensive land and labor in rural areas and overseas and for more efficient production, as Nabisco did when it left Chelsea.[18] With factory jobs disappearing in cities, people, mainly of European descent, and retail businesses, such as their community institutions, began moving to suburbs (known as suburbanization, or "white flight"). Some workers began commuting to white-collar jobs in offices for companies in the service industries, such as finance, accounting, and advertising, or in suburban office parks. Real estate and business investment in the central areas of cities declined, while crime and inner city poverty increased. Some groups, most especially African Americans, were essentially left behind. Urban renewal programs, such as the building of public housing projects, concentrated poverty and joblessness in dense clusters. By the late 1970s old industrial cities seemed all but dead, while suburban living thrived.

The moving of the white, well-educated middle class to the urban core since the 1980s has helped revive the urban village model for city neighborhoods in the postindustrial era. Critical of suburban living and in search of an urban lifestyle, this group of college students and recent graduates, creative workers, and young professionals often shows a desire to put down roots in "authentic" neighborhoods, such as by shopping at local, independent stores. Of course, most of the neighborhoods available to young newcomers in terms of having affordable vacancies and a vibrant street life have been in recent history working class and low income, with people from minority populations or the remaining white ethnic groups still living in them. Rents gradually increase and new businesses catering to this population open as these neighborhoods gain reputations for being up-and-coming.

A well-known term for these events is "gentrification," which continues in urban neighborhoods around the country today. Each of the businesses in this book has opened in gentrifying neighborhoods. The most successful of these neighborhoods, which have been gentrifying for decades, such as Chelsea and those in lower Manhattan, are now becoming upscale destinations, with increasingly more expensive housing, shopping, and nightlife.[19] But gentrification potentially displaces existing low-income groups and their businesses from their neighborhood and effectively denies access to it for any future ones.[20]

As in the industrial era, new businesses open in today's gentrifying neighborhoods to serve the local community, which is markedly different from the existing communities or those of the past. Young, well-educated residents often have discerning, omnivorous tastes and senses of style, and/or disposable income and curiosity to check out trends, which these new elite culture workers seek to satisfy. These consumers are often knowledge and culture workers who respect creativity and uniqueness, and who admire craft and artisanality in an age of digital formats and mass production.

Cocktail bars, upscale men's barbershops, and whole-animal butcher shops all draw on the romantic imagery of classic community institutions and on vintage versions of their businesses through their themes and motifs. Many cocktail bars model themselves on Prohibition-era speakeasies or swanky hotel bars. New men's barbershops look like classic shops or hunting lodges with vintage barber chairs and stations, where men can hang out with each other and talk in comfort. Well-lighted and white-tiled with large display cases and service counters, whole-animal butcher shops evoke simple meat-and-potatoes American food. The owners of these businesses strive to provide these environments and services for their communities.[21]

For the most part, however, these businesses attract narrow slivers of their local populations—specifically, those who see the value in spending a lot of money on basics like alcohol, haircuts, and meat, and, obviously, those who can afford to do so with regularity. Some have become destinations for curious consumers who like the novelty of drinking cocktails in a bar with a hidden entrance, of getting a straight razor shave, and of watching a butcher separating their steak from a whole animal.[22] And some consumers are "in the know," or members of their industries' rarefied taste communities. Sharing knowledge of and passion for the products and philosophies of these businesses binds these consumers together, although they often do not live near the establishments, or each other.[23]

Most importantly, in practice these new businesses do not serve as community institutions in the same ways as their forebears or contemporary peers in minority and immigrant neighborhoods do. Taste, of the physical (craft spirits taste better) or philosophical (meat "should" be raised a certain way) variety, or both, unites them with their customers. Socially, these businesses structure interactions and conversations between workers and customers around the products they sell, techniques they use, and philosophies they promote. There are exceptions, such as regular customers who become friendly with a bartender, barber, or butcher. Rarely, however, do relationships grow between customers, and rarely do customers feel a sense of community greater than themselves while at these establishments. They are not bound together culturally, racially, or ethnically as people are at the working-class bar, African American barbershop, or Halal butcher shop, nor do they sense sharing a common fate or set of circumstances as people in these groups do. These businesses merely meet a lifestyle-based need. While boasting a community orientation, they are in effect individually oriented.

Meanwhile, as examples of the city's "old order" institutions of luxury consumption and service struggle to survive (opera houses), renovate to adapt (high-end hotels), and disappear (haute French restaurants) in today's era of taste, these new establishments increasingly occupy their former positions among the cultural elite. In part these new businesses have reached this point of exclusivity by both adopting omnivorousness and borrowing a sense of high-end, personalized service from the old elite.[24] Quality service lies at the heart of each of these business types, but what separates the new cultural elites from their older peers and makes them part of a new form of luxury is how their workers intertwine interactive service with cultural knowledge and omnivorous tastes, and highlight a sense of craft in their work. These elements elevate these businesses to a new level of cultural status in gentrifying neighborhoods, and make them attractive places to work and build a career. We already know much about consumption and retail outlets as both signposts and catalysts of gentrification.[25] These businesses further our knowledge of this complex process by showing the important role that work practices of craft and craftsmanship are playing in transforming community institutions in these neighborhoods.

The New Economy: Segmented Industries, Masculinity, and Craft

Economic foundations help shape how cities grow and change, and cities change most dramatically when their economy's foundation shifts underneath them. The United States prospered in the early twentieth century and after World War II because of urban manufacturing, with the industrial sector reaching a peak of nearly twenty million workers in 1978.[26] These "blue-collar" jobs were well-paid with benefits, and did not require more than a high school diploma. And as companies grew, so did their administrative support staff, or "white-collar" workers, in office buildings.[27] Blue- and white-collar workers could generally expect long-term employment in their companies, and opportunities to get promoted and retire on generous pensions. With high productivity lowering prices on consumer goods and the growth of inexpensive housing in city outskirts and suburbs, these jobs allowed millions of American families to enter the middle class. Having a good, stable job, owning a home and a car, and parents giving children more than they had: many of these popular staples of the American Dream emerged during this period.

At its peak, however, manufacturing jobs represented only about 30 percent of the American labor force, but they were the engines of urban economies. Factory workers and those administrative white-collar workers in the increasingly complex bureaucracies for these and connected industries (legal, accounting, finance, insurance, advertising) drove their growth. These workers bought cars and televisions, went food shopping, and ate out at restaurants. They built, expanded, and repaired homes, went on vacations, and saw movies at theaters. They went to bars and liquor stores, got haircuts, and bought meat. Steady employment at the blue- and white-collar levels in manufacturing and connected industries supported these and many other jobs in the service sector. And all of these workers and businesses, in both manufacturing and service, paid taxes to their local municipalities and states, which supported more jobs in the public sector (teachers, firefighters, government employees). Manufacturing workers, such as those in the Nabisco factory and larger factories in more lucrative industries than baking (for example, steel, automobiles) around the country, were important for being 30 percent of the workforce (at its highest) and because of their impact on the other 70 percent.[28]

Then the economy began to slowly shift during the 1970s as manufacturing declined. Increased globalization and free trade since this time has meant companies could move their factories abroad to countries with cheaper land and labor, raising their profits. Technological innovations have also made manufacturing more efficient, which means companies have gradually needed fewer workers to produce even more products than they did before. As a result of these twin factors, employment in manufacturing has steadily declined since its peak, while production has increased and the price of consumer goods has remained affordable.[29] Today approximately 12.3 million people work in the manufacturing sector, which is only about 8.8 percent of the workforce.[30] These jobs have also diverged in terms of quality. Some high-end ones, such as in aeronautics, pay very well and require considerable skill and advanced degrees. But most workers in the manufacturing sector have seen their wages drop, their benefits slashed, and their stable jobs grow more precarious as competition from abroad and the next technological innovation loom.

Perhaps most importantly, when manufacturing jobs vanished, so did jobs in the service and public sectors. The loss harmed some places worse than others. Smaller cities that depended on a small factory (Galesburg, Illinois: Maytag) and larger cities that depended on a single industry (Detroit:

automobiles; Akron: rubber; Youngstown and Pittsburgh: steel) were hit the hardest by this shift.[31] Cities like New York, which had a more diverse manufacturing sector and a more dynamic economy overall than cities like Detroit, certainly suffered through deindustrialization, but not as uniformly and for not as long. Spatially, New York City experienced large pockets of poverty, especially in neighborhoods and communities dependent on manufacturing work. In Chelsea, for instance, manufacturing gradually disappeared, warehouses emptied, and shipping ended, while employment and rents declined. These conditions primed the neighborhood for gentrification, but the city still needed a new economic foundation for that process to begin.

The shift that began in the 1970s led to the postindustrial era of today. Rather than material goods, the production and distribution of ideas drive today's successful urban economies. This "new economy" is a knowledge economy.[32] The most successful industries with the greatest potential for growth create ideas that can become usable, and sellable, products and services. These industries include information technology, finance, telecommunications, nanotechnology, health (pharmaceutical, biomedicine, and other life science research), and culture. Many fall under the general categories of "high-tech" and "high-end service." A product's value lies in the idea behind it, such as its function or design, while the product itself gets made elsewhere (like Apple products in China) or nowhere except in digital code (computer software, phone apps). Driven by human intelligence, creativity, and ingenuity, or "human capital," companies in the new economy must constantly innovate and come up with new ideas to succeed.

As in the industrial era, the majority of jobs today are in local services, which are still, most importantly, an effect of economic growth in the innovation sector, not a cause.[33] Workers in the knowledge-based industries support service industries like beverage, grooming, and food. As the former grow in a city, so do the latter. People in the services cannot support each other without outside help. Bartenders, craft distillers, barbers, and butchers cannot buy products and services from each other unless someone else, someone who generates exchange value from what they make in their work, does so first.[34] The key difference is between what generates exchange value in the postindustrial era versus what did in the industrial era—namely, knowledge and ideas versus material goods.

Work in any sector and industry today looks very different from yesterday. While "stable" and "stability" may have once described jobs and work conditions in the industrial era, when people often stayed at one company their whole careers (or at least had the option to do so), many scholars use the term "precarious" to describe work in the new economy.[35] Jobs have become less stable and secure than they were in the past because of how both companies and workers have responded to the forces of postindustrialism. The United States has significantly deregulated many sectors of the economy since the 1970s, such as the finance, transportation, communication, and energy industries. A key goal of removing limits on how companies can act has been to increase competition between them domestically and abroad, which in theory makes them more productive and flexible and lowers prices on goods and services for consumers.[36] But giving companies greater autonomy over their behavior has led to such common uncertainties as mass layoffs during financial strains and outsourcing work abroad and to freelance, temporary, and part-time workers, which reduces the need for full-time employees and, by extension, reduces costs due to lower pay and few, if any, benefits.[37] Meanwhile, people also face greater job insecurity because of competition from well-educated, highly skilled workers who move to the United States from abroad. The impacts of these changes vary by industry, but they have become common aspects of work in the new economy.[38] As a result of this precarious, unstable economic environment, many people today feel significant stress and uncertainty in their work lives, which they must increasingly cope with on their own and often experience as a personal failing.[39] The age of certainty and stability has given way to an age of risk.[40]

On the other hand, some workers relish the enormous potential of work in the new economy. While the "stable" industrial era meant people often stayed at one company, with security but also with limits on their earnings, today they are freer to work on their own terms. Temps, freelancers, consultants, and contract employees all fall under today's "gig economy."[41] These workers trade security and stability for autonomy.[42] If knowledge, ideas, and information drive the economy, then people's abilities to be creative and innovative make *them* the most valuable commodity on the market.[43] Companies need talented people because talented people generate ideas, goes the reasoning. Talented people should therefore not sell themselves short, limit themselves, or deny their potential by staying in one place. And advanced communication technology allows people to work from nearly anywhere while being active in their business networks and communities. While risk defines today's economy and industries create the conditions for the gig economy by preferring short-term, temporary, and freelance employees, many workers see these opportunities as personal choices.[44] Whether force or choice, the results of these activities is precariousness and insecurity in the job market.[45]

Jobs in the new economy in general fall somewhere on a spectrum between "good" and "bad" based on such criteria as salary, benefits, stability, status, autonomy over work, and time spent working.[46] Most importantly, education usually serves as the great divider between whether a job is "good" or "bad." A college degree has almost always meant a higher salary, but today, with fewer well-paying and stable manufacturing jobs, a lack of a college degree is even more harmful to one's chances of getting a good job.

Following from this breakdown, not all service jobs in the new economy are created equal. As the service sector has expanded to accommodate workers in the knowledge industries it has also become more segmented. Elite service jobs, like those in finance and the law, require advanced degrees and generally offer people the chance to earn high incomes with a good amount of stability and status. But most jobs in this overall sector, the ones in local services, are in a lower tier in terms of salary, autonomy over work, stability, and the status the job confers. A lot of research has been conducted on "emotional labor," or those service jobs, like flight attendants and waitresses, that require workers to control their emotions to elicit an emotional response out of their customers and clients.[47] While emotionally draining, these interactive service practices also further reinforce much service work as "bad." In addition, the work in these jobs is often physically draining and not mentally challenging, like knowledge work is. These include most jobs in retail and food and beverage service, housecleaners, and health care aides, none of which require advanced degrees.[48]

At first glance, bartender, distiller, barber, and butcher are not "good" jobs in the new economy, if we compare them with other ones. They are not at the forefront of innovation, like high-tech entrepreneurs and software engineers, but are basic manual labor and retail jobs in service industries and manufacturing. They do not offer job security, and the incomes are low on average compared to college graduates in other occupations.[49] They still require workers to get their hands dirty, stand on their feet all day, do heavy lifting, sweat, and deal with various splashes, spills, and stains. These jobs require people to know how to interact with consumers and engage in emotional labor (with the exception of distilling), and they are not known for requiring workers to use much special knowledge or creativity, or at least only a basic amount, and not enough to rank them among today's vaunted knowledge-based or creative jobs.[50] And they do not bring much status. The people in this book often describe having to justify what they do to their families, who imagined a nice, clean, stable office job for their kids. When people with college degrees become low-level service workers, they often find ways to justify doing so, such as by saying it's a means to an end. Their "real" job is something else: artist, actor, musician, or student. They're just trying to pay the bills.[51]

But these workers love these "bad" jobs. The idea of taking pleasure in and deriving meaning from one's job underlies work in the postindustrial era. Work has become a path to happiness, not a duty or simply a way to earn a living.[52] Or, work should be pleasurable and meaningful. With its emphasis on human abilities and personal autonomy, the new economy promises the achievement of happiness through work. The workers in this book believe in this idea. They have sought out work that provides meaning for them. And they have found occupational communities whose members recognize them and their work as good.[53] More importantly, most were in privileged positions to do so, as people with many options in the job market are. They are young and free to choose whatever job they wanted, in most cases without any responsibilities such as a family to care for, and often with college degrees in hand to give them choices.

A key argument in this book is that today's expanded service sector has not just segmented in terms of "upper" and "lower" tiers, with high-skilled knowledge-based jobs in one and unskilled manual labor-based jobs in the other. The picture is more complicated. Good versions of typically low-status, manual labor jobs also exist in small segments, or niches, within service and manufacturing industries. The jobs in this book have been recoded as "cool," creative ones, with opportunities for young workers to shape tastes, innovate, and achieve higher status. They seek out these jobs as careers instead of other jobs in the new economy with higher profiles. For them, these jobs are vocations, or callings, providing meaning through materially oriented, craft-based manual labor, in front of knowing peers and an accepting public. While emotional labor is present in these occupations, it does not best explain the nature of the interactions these workers have with consumers. Cultural knowledge and craft-based technical skill structure both the work these workers engage in and much of the interactive service work they provide. Their work is omnivorous cultural production and dissemination: they sell the ideas behind their products and services as much as they sell the products and services themselves. These jobs, then, show how the new economy has expanded into non-knowledge-based businesses of retail, service, and light manufacturing, leading to the segmentation of their larger industries.

We can also understand the new economy, and the transformation of these occupations, through a gender lens. Most of the workers in these occupations and book are men. For cocktail bartenders and upscale men's barbers, the ratio of men to women is greater than national statistics of these occupations show. According to the U.S. Bureau of Labor Statistics (BLS), women are nearly 60 percent of all bartenders and 22 percent of all barbers, while cocktail bartenders who are men outnumber women and upscale men's barbers who are men have an even greater majority than barbers in general. The BLS does not keep records of distillers, and butchers are categorized with "other meat, poultry, and fish processing workers," and 25 percent of these workers are women. Anecdotal evidence that I have obtained from people in these industries shows that women are rarely distillers at large liquor companies, and even more rarely butchers at butcher shops and slaughterhouses.[54] While still minorities compared to men, I believe women have greater representation in these niche occupations than in their mainstream versions. Still, men tend to dominate these niche industries as both workers and owners.

Work and workplaces have always been important loci for men to determine their own worth and that of others, as well as to achieve masculinity.[55] Men, specifically white men, throughout American history have often struggled in these endeavors in work settings amid regular economic shifts and the gradual inclusion of other groups, such as women, nonwhite men, and immigrants, into their industries. For instance, as offices came to characterize elite work settings in the mid-twentieth century, men, who saw them as gendered, feminizing spaces that restricted their opportunity to perform masculinity, experienced a decline of independence and autonomy over their work, compromising their goal of becoming "self-made" men. The growing presence of women in the office setting and their perceived threat to men's power during this time increased men's anxiety over their ability to perform their manhood.[56]

The stable manufacturing jobs in the industrial era were masculine-coded and mostly filled by men. They allowed men to show their manhood through manual labor, while these workplaces fostered male camaraderie. These jobs also gave men incomes to support their families and serve in the important role as breadwinners. The coming of postindustrialism and the new economy has meant the gradual transformation of this dynamic. Women are increasingly becoming breadwinners and household heads as the new economy favors jobs either historically filled by women or that require feminine-coded skills and abilities (for example, communication, empathy).[57] In short, men perceive fewer opportunities to display their manhood through work in today's economy when a "good" job typically lacks a comfortable homosocial environment to perform masculinity, involves intangible knowledge work, consists of precariousness, and includes women and workers from diverse groups.

But these new elite manual labor jobs give men—mainly those of a certain race and social class standing—the chance to use their bodies directly in their work, as men did in the industrial era but do so less often today, as well as their minds, which grants them greater status in these jobs than they would otherwise have. They are simultaneously respected knowledge workers and skilled manual laborers, and perform their work in public. Men are thus able to use these jobs to achieve a lost sense of middle-class, heterosexual masculinity in their work. Women in these new elite manual labor jobs, however, experience threats to their pursuit of a professional identity in these male-dominated, masculine-coded jobs in spite of the lessened role emotional labor plays in them. These threats specifically come from male consumers, who sometimes question their expertise. While the voices of women are present, this book mainly features men, who get to uniquely perform masculinity through intertwined forms of physical and mental labor.[58]

A final aspect of the new economy in the postindustrial city playing a role in the rise of cool manual labor jobs is an expanding "artisan economy" of small-scale manufacturing.[59] Businesses in the artisan economy, such as craft brewers, coffee roasters, and knitters, are based on shared understandings of quality, authenticity, and the importance of "localness." They thrive on cultural omnivorousness and the idea of connecting people with the products they buy and the people who make them. Of the four jobs in this book, craft distillers best fall under this category. They make a new product out of raw materials, just like major industry, except on a very small scale and with an emphasis on craft. The other three are primarily service jobs. But common to each of them is how people practice and promote a sense of craft in their work.

I smiled to myself on the day Giancarlo returned to the butcher shop from getting artisanal coffee and told me about the new barbershop. I had already thought of Chelsea Market as an excellent example of these cultural, urban, and economic transformations. The barbershop simply completed the circle. The market is unique for combining these workplaces, jobs, products, and services, and for grounding these cultural and economic shifts happening in today's postindustrial city, in one enclosed place. A former complex of manufacturing in a formerly industrial neighborhood, Chelsea Market and Chelsea's gentrification mirror the rebirth of New York City and other cities from the industrial era. Where workers once toiled by hot ovens and packed Oreos into boxes for mass consumption, today they make and distribute ideas and cultural content in upstairs and nearby offices for elite businesses in the new economy, while tourists and shoppers stroll through and consume in the arcade. They go because of its unique shops, where a different set of workers not only make and sell special products and services but also the ideas behind those products and services that make them special.

The three transformations that frame the content of this book—the restructuring of elite taste around omnivorousness, the changing of traditional community institutions into destinations of the new cultural elite in retail, and the recoding of work in the new economy—combine to explain how these jobs and businesses have become upscale, cool, and desired. Examining these cultural, urban, and economic changes together through the cases of these new elite jobs pushes forward our understanding of each.

PART I

Each chapter in part I examines one of these four occupations (bartender, distiller, barber, butcher). My goal is to outline the foundations of the cultural repertoires of each job. I provide a brief history and discuss the philosophical underpinnings of each industry, job, and workplace, and explain their revival in today's cities, the symbolic boundaries that divide them from other versions of these jobs in their industries, and the moral boundaries within their occupational communities. Each chapter contains a mix of historical facts, stories of key behaviors in these workplaces, interviews with workers and owners, and discussions of the social contexts these workers find themselves in.

Most importantly, each chapter focuses on a specific theme. While we can see each of these four themes in each occupation in some form, I base the discussions in these chapters on the theme the occupation best represents. Chapter 1, on cocktail bartenders, deals most directly with new elite service work. Chapter 2, on craft distillers, deals with the logics of authenticity. Chapter 3, on upscale men's barbers, deals with the role of masculinity in the new economy. And chapter 4, on whole-animal butchers, deals with the production of omnivorousness.

I present all excerpts from recorded interviews and conversations from the field in paragraph form. I also aim to provide readers with a glossary of terms for understanding these work cultures (many definitions and explanations are in footnotes and endnotes). While I focus each chapter on a single occupation and its unique characteristics and conditions, occasionally I refer to similarities or differences between it and the others. I show the commonalities between these four jobs in the chapters in part II. Readers will also note several undeveloped and underdiscussed topics in part I (for example, how these workers came to pursue these jobs as careers, the role of service, and definitions of craft). I also analyze these and other topics in part II.

1 | THE COCKTAIL RENAISSANCE

Recalling certain gentlemen of other days, who made of drinking one of the pleasures of life—not one of its evils; and who, whatever they drank, proved able to carry it, keep their heads, and remain gentlemen, even in their cups. Their example is commended to their posterity.

—*A framed sign in the bathroom at Milk and Honey, excerpted from* The Old Waldorf-Astoria Bar Book, *by A. S. Crockett, from 1935*

In 1919 the Volstead Act brought a swift end to nightlife, and the refined craft of the American bartender was outlawed. It was thought that to drink alcohol was to live a life shadowed by death. It was thought that these were death and company. It's taken us nearly a century to restore flavor to the drink and class to specialty cocktails. In our time, a night to celebrate life's simple pleasures with fine wine, exquisitely crafted cocktails, beautifully prepared food, and impeccable sipping spirits is a rare gift. To those who shun the night, we tip our hat. To those who shine after dusk, we offer a warm embrace. Welcome to the new golden age. Welcome to Death & Co.

—*A framed sign in the bathroom at Death & Co.*

The July air in New Orleans is like thick soup. Every year at this time the extended world of craft cocktails descends on the French Quarter for the annual Tales of the Cocktail festival. They are bartenders and bar owners, people in the liquor industry like brand owners and ambassadors, drinks writers and bloggers, lifestyle media members, restaurateurs, hoteliers, people who sell highly specialized products like vintage barware, ice machines, and bottled ingredients for tiki drinks, and the PR reps for each of these groups. Many members of the lay public, such as cocktail enthusiasts and casual consumers, attend (and pay the full price), but the real festival—the networking, the hotel room parties, the secret stashes of homemade hooch—is for community members only. Tales is the global craft cocktail community's largest event. At it they rejoice the cocktail renaissance, see old friends and make new ones, share drink ideas, consider business plans, and regale themselves with awards and praise. The people in New York who do not attend joke that the city's cocktail bars may as well shut down during Tales, due to lack of staff. Some do.

A nocturnal bunch, cocktail people huddle inside the historic (and air-conditioned) Hotel Monteleone with its rooftop pool and rotating Carousel Bar (where the classic Vieux Carré cocktail was invented) during the day.[1] They attend and host panel talks and demonstrations, tastings and seminars, book signings, broadcasts and podcasts, until the sun goes down. Then they hit the city, and stay out all night. They repeat this same day five times in a row.

I spend a Friday afternoon in the Monteleone, at seminars. In one, named "Twenty-first Century Gin," four brand ambassadors for different gin companies discuss the history and current state of the spirit. Audience members in the packed room sit in rows behind tables with plastic cups filled with clear liquids. Charlotte, a former bartender from London who works for Hendrick's Gin, introduces the panel and the topic. She tells the audience about the seven different types of gin on the tables in front of them, each representing a particular style. The panelists will refer to them in their talks, and audience members can taste each one as they go along. Charlotte then provides a brief history of gin, from its roots in Holland as genever in the 1500s to its migration to London, where the Old Tom and London dry styles took shape. While gin remained a popular spirit in the twentieth century, she explains, not many producers innovated within the category, until recently.

"Five years ago we couldn't have done this seminar and had this many gins on the table," says Charlotte. "I certainly couldn't have named four or five gin brands ten years ago. So things are definitely changing. And with that in mind, with all these new gins that we have, we're very pleased to have them, what do we call them? Do we need to call them anything? Is it appropriate to call these new gins new? Or do we need to find some way to distinguish them from the London dry and the Old Tom that we heard about before? Ryan, would you possibly have any thoughts on this matter?"

A bartender and consultant from Portland, Oregon, Ryan Magarian cofounded Aviation American Gin in 2006. The audience, knowing Ryan has strong opinions on classifying gin, laughs at Charlotte's lead-in.

When me and my partners developed [Aviation] three and a half years ago, I thought, "Let's just be obnoxious. Let's take it right to the edge of the gin universe." And we were really excited. We thought we could make a gin that didn't fall within any of the acknowledged designations that were around today. And gin, when we looked at the definition, it seemed to me that there was a lot of room for artistic freedom. And when we looked at the gin category, it seemed relatively monochromatic. People weren't, in our opinion, getting far enough away from the traditional London dry. And when I talk about London dry gin, I talk about any neutral spirit-based gin where the juniper is without a doubt the first thing that you get. It's like somebody puts a steak dish in front of you and it's a forty-eight ounce porterhouse, a little bit of broccoli, and a touch of au gratin, but it's the steak that defines that spirit.

Ryan then explains how he and his partners wanted Aviation to represent the region (specifically Oregon) well, such as by using organic products and having a savory and rich flavors and a "damp" taste. Since his partners were whiskey makers, they wanted a gin people could sip neat, which is uncommon for London dry styles.* They also had cocktails in mind. Since Aviation has a different flavor profile from London dry gins, it doesn't always work with classic recipes, and Ryan has had to train bartenders how to use it in drinks. He concludes by proposing a new name for his style of gin.

This is something new, I think "new Western" style is fun and sexy. I don't know if it's going to stick, but by gosh, I'm going to use it until someone comes up with something better—perhaps "twenty-first century" gin—we'll find out. I would also use [this] key word in new Westerns: balance. You're finding a lot more balance. Like I talked about the forty-eight ounce porterhouse steak dish? Well, think about an equal steak dish, but the new Western is an eight-ounce filet, a large mound of orange-scented couscous, some sautéed kale with rendered bacon fat and chopped bacon, and maybe a little bit of scallions or something funky on the side. It's still a steak dish, but it's not this steak dish. Having this kind of style protects gin, by separating these new gins from old gins. We don't do this, next thing you know vodka and gin are going to meld, and the whole gin category is going to be a total debacle.

* Drinking a spirit "neat" means drinking it completely on its own, without ice, water, or a mixer (bitters, a sweetener, and so on).

A former bartender originally from England, today Angus Winchester is a consultant and the global brand ambassador for Tanqueray. Quiet and looking smug for most of the panel, he chimes in on Ryan's argument.

"Well, I find it interesting. Everybody talks about 'Let's have less rules and regulations from the government' and things like that, and here's Ryan saying we should have some more. I mean, we have a knowledgeable group of people here, how many styles—legally—of American whiskey are there?"

He pauses as the room mumbles.

"Twenty-six. There are twenty-six legal styles of American whiskey. So these all exist, but we all talk about there just being five styles. You see that with a lot of things. And we're seeing now gins that don't really taste like gin, which is why you have to start adapting the recipes to be able to use them in classic gin drinks. And I feel some of these are multiflavored vodkas. If the juniper is not immediately discernable, which I think, if you try Tanqueray Ten, put your nose on that, there is juniper there, front and center. There is refreshing citrus, things like that as well, but it is obviously juniper.

"I'm conflicted with it. Sometimes I think, yes, we should perhaps recategorize. But I think on the whole they've worked quite well for us, and the bartender should be the one explaining both. Miller's and Hendrick's are not your typical style of gin. And as we start to make gin that doesn't taste like gin to get people into gin, we're not doing the right thing, are we? It's obviously so radically different to what our customers expect from gin. We don't need everything to be called gin. If everybody drank the same thing life would be rather boring. You don't like gin? Well, sorry. I'm not going to make a wrong gin so you could now say to your friends you do like gin."

"To call Aviation a London dry gin or even put it in the same category is wrong," replies Ryan. "Think about genever, I mean, genever isn't anything like London dry. Gin is a story of evolution. So to me, stopping at just dry gin and not being able to articulate more succinct styles to people doesn't make sense to me."

Ryan and Angus both speak on behalf of their brands: the newcomer and the old standard.[2] An audience member, Simon Difford, then speaks up. Simon owns a bar in London and writes a series of drinks guides both online and in print. Others in the room who know his guides get excited to hear him speak in person. He directs his comment at Ryan.

"We went from genever to gin, but they didn't call gin genever, they came up with another name for it, because it's different. It was a progression. What you've created is not a gin. It's a flavored other spirit."

FIGURE 2. David Wondrich, cocktail and drinks writer,
speaking at a Tales seminar. Photo by the author.

"But you call it a gin in your book," says Ryan. "And you gave us four-and-a-half stars!"

Enjoying the start of a duel, the audience approves Ryan's zinger with applause.

"And I commented under that that it's not a gin. What's happened is that we haven't got a gin police. There's no one testing gin saying that there's not so many milligrams per liter of juniper to be classified gin. So that's the trouble. You can call whatever you like gin. Yours is still a dry style. It hasn't got juniper, but it is a dry style of spirit. It's a delicate spirit. I'd like it if you called it 'new Western spirit.' The reason it's called gin in my book is because you put 'gin' on the label. That's what you've branded it."

"Would you like 'new Western botanical spirits'?"

"Fine, that's a great term."

"But this is gin," says Ryan, pointing at his own bottle.

"Gin is predominantly juniper. It's not predominantly juniper, it's not gin."

"My point about using the steak dish example, they're both steak dishes, whether it's a forty-eight ounce porterhouse or the eight-ounce filet."

"That's like calling a burger a steak. It's a different product."

Tales seminars and the public sides of the festival and cocktail community in general are remarkably harmonious. Critical comments and back-and-forth debates barely exist out in the open. The traditional London dry style (like the heavy pine flavor of Tanqueray, Beefeater, and Gordon's) dominated the spirit category for decades and shaped the general public's idea of what gin tastes like. But along with demonstrating the significance of history and an expanding palate of flavors for cocktail bartenders, the lengthy discussion in this seminar reveals the tensions that sometimes arise between the community members over definitions and categories. Since new gin products reach the market and do not conform to convention, the gin category has become turf for wars of taste, and marketing. People in the craft cocktail community constantly discuss such questions as what is and what is not "proper" gin, or the merits of any new product, or the influence of big brands on the public's taste. These debates and contestations are part of a common discourse for the cocktail community.

After the gin panel I attend a seminar called "Sugar," on the science of sweetness in cocktails, and another called "The Fine Art of Tending Bar," led by Stanislav Vadrna, a Polish bartender who trained for a time with Kazuo Ueda, a renowned veteran bartender in Tokyo. With the sun setting I walk over to the W Hotel, a few blocks outside the Quarter, for the Bar Chef Competition, an annual Tales event. Modeled on the television show *Iron Chef*, bartender contestants from around the country have to make two cocktails, one for before dinner and one for during. They must use the sponsor's product and a secret ingredient, revealed only seconds before the competition starts, in both. Grand Marnier and Navan—an orange and a vanilla liqueur, respectively—sponsor the event, and a cocktail called The Perfect Storm (a variation on the classic Dark and Stormy, with the sponsored ingredients) gets passed around to the crowd. An elevated stage in the large ballroom features eight identical bar stations with full backbars, bar equipment, and a stovetop for sautéing (recommended for culinary cocktails). The contestants come from New York, Miami, Boston, Seattle, San Francisco, Virginia, Los Angeles, and New Orleans. The panel of seven judges consists of more experienced bartenders, chefs, and people in food and wine media. The host is none other than Dale DeGroff, the "King of the Cocktail," a living legend, and the man people in the United States consider the founder of today's cocktail renaissance.

After explaining the rules (45 minutes to make two original cocktails) Dale reveals the secret ingredient: ginger marmalade. The timer starts and the bartenders get to work. One takes advantage of the stovetop and sautés some rosemary while smelling and tasting a bottle of sherry. People in the crowd cheer them on while Dale offers commentary on what each contestant seems to be trying. Mickey and Sammy, the famed bartending pair at Milk and Honey—considered the first of New York City's new craft cocktail bars—shout teases at their friends Giuseppe and Eric, two contestants from New York (though Eric moved and opened a bar in LA the previous year). It's their way of supporting them. I spot Steve Olson, a veteran in the industry as a bartender and consultant, and a founder and director of the Beverage Alcohol Resource (BAR) Program, an education and training course in the craft cocktail community. He is elated.

"Look at all the people on stage right now! One is Dave, but all but one has been through the BAR course, and that person is enrolled to do it in the fall.[3] Few of us who have been doing this for twenty-five, thirty years would have ever believed that this time would come, but now it has happened and it has expanded the way we could only have dreamed. It used to be so insular, and it still is, but it's much larger and is starting to have impacts outside of the community. I love it that people come up to me and say that they want to become bartenders."

The urgency picks up on stage as the clock ticks down. The bartenders abandon any early experiments in favor of well-established flavor combinations from their taste memories. Only the judges will try the drinks they come up with, and the corporate sponsors will likely use the winning recipes in their promotional materials. There is no bar for these bartenders tonight—no service or conversation with customers—just drinks and the act of making them, on display, in front of a knowing audience.

As the buzzer sounds, Dale, with a tremendous grin on his face and his eyes closed, tilts his head back, holds a fist to the sky, and screams into the mike, "The craft is back!"[4]

The past looms large for people in today's cocktail world. Of the four occupations in this book, cocktail bartenders are most likely to respect, discuss, and debate the history of their craft and its culture, and recognize its importance in the work they do. (The gin discussants at Tales, for instance, referenced genever's transition into gin, and considered whether it represented an evolution of gin or the creation of a new spirit category.) Classic cocktail culture appears in their recipes and personal style, the motifs of their bars, and their professional identity. To them, the spread of craft cocktails throughout the nightlife industry and the rise of bartending to what they see as its rightful place as a respected trade are true revivals and rebirths. Cocktail bartenders build on and reshape the past, for their own livelihood and for a drinking public who want special bar experiences and crave a story behind their drink. As bars, cocktail bars have become more like restaurants, behind the bar more like a kitchen, and cocktail bartenders more like a combination of chefs and servers. Bringing their cocktail knowledge to bear on their service helps to elevate their work to an elite level.

The New Golden Age

People have been mixing alcoholic drinks together with other ingredients for thousands of years and for many reasons. At various times and in different places, some groups have done so for medicinal or religious purposes. The English mixed citrus and quinine (an ingredient in tonic water) in gin to ward off scurvy and malaria, respectively, and many aromatic bitters, which became the salt and pepper of cocktail making, began as healthful elixirs.[5] Others have done so to preserve products. Fortified wines like vermouths, for instance, last longer than their base beverage on its own, which suits long-distance travel. And some groups have mixed ingredients in spirits to mask the harsh taste of poorly made distillates.[6] In each case, people used local products and resources, while customs shaped their drinking habits.

Punch, an English cultural invention from the sixteenth century, stands out among the cocktail's mixed-drink predecessors. It represents among the first recorded drinks consisting of spirits and mixers that people drank for social, rather than medicinal or religious, reasons. Already fond of flavoring their alcohol, the English boasted ingredients from around the world due to Britain's vast trade routes. Originally a drink for seamen and sailors, punch came to symbolize gentility and conviviality. People drank punch communally, and slowly, around a bowl, for enjoyment. Cocktails, by contrast, which bartenders make in individual servings, for individual drinkers, take less time to prepare, promoting individualism and efficiency—two reasons why the cocktail is considered an American invention.[7]

The first use of the word "cocktail" in print in the United States was in 1803.[8] The author wrote, "Drank a glass of cocktail—excellent for the head. . . . Call'd at the Doct's. found Burnham—he looked very wise—drank another glass of cocktail." At this point in history people still saw alcoholic drinks as good for one's health. The first definition came in 1806.[9] In a letter to the editor, the author replies to the question "What is a cocktail?": "*Cocktail is a stimulating liquor, composed of spirits of any kind, sugar, water, and bitters—it is vulgarly called bittered sling*." The author describes what bartenders today call an Old Fashioned, but does not give a precise recipe or directions for how to make it. Bartenders used ad hoc techniques (and local ingredients), which was the state of drinking at the time.

This tradition changed during the course of the nineteenth century as the United States became modern and industrialized. The rise of a national media and publishing industry helped spread a universal cocktail culture. The first book of cocktail recipes was *The Bar-Tender's Guide: How to Mix Drinks or, The Bon Vivant's Companion*, written by Jerry Thomas, also known as "the Professor," in 1862. Thomas traveled widely across the United States as a bartender, picking up local recipes, techniques, and ideas along the way. Historically, bars and restaurants may have had some of their own guarded recipes, but bartenders did not write a lot down about their work. His book was the first to codify what had mostly been oral traditions and professional secrets. Thomas provides drink names, ingredients, and measurements for others to follow.[10] He replaced local customs and arbitrary bartending practices with universal standards and a rational order for making drinks.

Popular for its time, Thomas's book ushered in several more of its kind. These books were bartenders' guides, meaning recipes represented only a part of their content. The rest gave instructions on how to actually be a bartender, including "Rules for Bartenders in Entering and Going Off Duty," "Treatment of Patrons—Behavior toward Them," "How to Improve the Appearance of Bar and Toilet Rooms," and "To Know How a Customer Desires His Drink to Be Mixed."[11] Bartenders at the time were considered tradesmen. Bartending required apprenticing, knowing hundreds of cocktail recipes from memory as well as inventing new ones, mastering drink-making skills and techniques, and making unique bitters and liqueurs. These guides served as professional manuals. While at the beginning of the nineteenth century people may not have known what a cocktail was or defined it the same way, by century's end someone could probably order a Manhattan in New York City and know with confidence they would get the same drink if they ordered it in San Francisco.[12]

New technology and social changes of the nineteenth century also played roles in the maturation of cocktails and bartending. Steam replaced fire in distillation, making the process easier to control. Column stills joined pot stills, making it possible to distill continuously, and therefore to mass-produce spirits. Combined, these technological advances made more consistent and predictable products. Transportation technology, chiefly the railroad, gave bartenders better access to nonlocal ingredients, and expanded the public's palates. Refrigeration technology meant farmers could ship such ingredients as fruits long distances, while bartenders did not have to rely on winter or cold northern regions for ice. Meanwhile, the industrial revolution led to the growth of large cities, with swarms of newcomers in search of new beginnings in a changing economy. Who people were often meant not just what they did or where they came from, but what they bought.[13] The working class and immigrants had their beers and whiskeys, while the old wealth had their wines and brandies. Cocktails matured at a time when the city's new elites, like the professionals of industry, wanted to show off their new status in public, such as in the grand bars of luxury hotels. The cocktail became a symbol of urbanity and sophistication, of a status one could obtain by drinking right.[14]

These gradual changes in American society culminated in the classical era, or the "golden age," of cocktail culture, which lasted from around 1870 until 1920. During this period, cocktails existed firmly in the national consciousness, people regarded bartenders at high-class establishments as professionals of their trade, and "mixology" became the standard for making cocktails.[15] Mixology refers to an array of principles for making drinks. These include using precise measurements, standard ingredients, freshly squeezed juices, and various drink-making techniques like shaking and stirring (as well as when to shake versus when to stir) and muddling.* Some of these principles are implied, and some are explicitly stated in bartenders' guides from

* While arbitrary in some cases, cocktail bartenders generally follow the rule of shaking drinks that have citrus, and stirring drinks that do not. Besides ensuring that the ingredients get mixed, a key reason, they say, is mouth feel. Cocktails with citrus tend to be more refreshing than more spirit-forward cocktails. People also tend to drink them faster. Bartenders therefore want these drinks to be bright in the mouth. By contrast, people tend to sip boozier drinks more slowly. Bartenders want these drinks to be smooth. The big example is the Martini, which cocktail bartenders do not shake. They want the gin to be smooth, not bubbly or a bit frothy, which shaking would cause. However, letting a shaken Martini sit for a short time will cause it to settle, and a customer would probably not be able to tell the difference.

Muddling entails using a small, smooth stick (called a muddler), usually made of wood, to mash ingredients (usually fruits and their peels) and extract their juices and oils.

the classical era. Bartenders at higher-class bars used these principles to make drinks that were balanced, or with fresh, quality ingredients acting in harmony (that is, without a single ingredient overpowering the others, or an ingredient not serving a purpose).[16]

The basic principles of mixology are the philosophical foundation for today's cocktail renaissance. Cocktail bartenders regularly cite the golden age as an inspiration for the craft cocktail's revival as well as for the work they do. Dave opened the world-renowned craft cocktail bar Death & Co. with a partner in 2007.[17] He cites the past as fundamental to the cocktail revival and to his bar: "I've always said that we're still trying to regain what we had one hundred years ago. Before Prohibition things were just crazy. The bartender was making their own bitters, every bartender had his house cocktail, and every place had well over one hundred drinks and it was insane. The garnishes were so elaborate, so over the top, the fresh fruit was just all over the place, different types of ice—it was amazing! And we're not back there yet, so it's important to go back there to figure out what we should do next. So I would say, if anything, that's definitely our school of thought."

For cocktail bartenders, reviving the golden age lays the foundation for the culture's growth. Brian, in his mid-thirties, is a bartender at Death & Co. and a consultant for liquor companies and other bars. Originally from Seattle, at 18 he fell in love with New York City after visiting his brother the summer before starting college, and moved there right after graduating, without any job prospects. He worked in food and beverage service to pay the bills until he got exposed to the cocktail world and began building a career. For him the people and culture from the classical era serve as a guide for the drinks he makes: "It's like life: you can't know where you're going unless you know where you've been. Know your history to know your future. We have a tremendous amount of respect for the elders that were there before us, and I'm not talking about Dale [DeGroff]. I'm talking about Jerry Thomas, Charles Baker, people that were there before us making really great drinks.[18] And it's like, 'OK, cool, we're just going to take that and riff on it.' I think Gary [Regan] calls it 'pimping the classics.'[19] I've done something as simple as taking the 20th Century: gin, Lillet, lemon juice, and white crème de cacao. I took out the gin, put in bourbon, and took Lillet blanc and put in Lillet rouge, crème de cacao, and lemon. And it's just another drink that works."[20]

Classic texts serve as references for cocktail bartenders not just for recipes but also for techniques. Brian discusses his shaking technique: "Audrey

[Saunders] gave me the book when I started working at Pegu [Club].[21] She had like a list of required reading, and one of them was, she was incredibly kind enough to loan me a copy of David Embry's book, *How to Mix Drinks*.[22] And the line he had in that book it was basically, 'Shake like seven demons are chasing after you.' So you just shake the hell out of a drink."

As Dave mentions in his quote, national Prohibition ended the cocktail's golden age. Also known as the Volstead Act, the Eighteenth Amendment to the U.S. Constitution made the manufacture, distribution, and sale of alcohol illegal.[23] On January 1, 1920, when the law took effect, drinking went behind closed doors and underground. Prohibition saw the rise of the speakeasy, so named because people had to "speak easy," or carefully with a password or code, to gain entrance. While some speakeasies offered genuine products of quality, such as New York City's Jack and Charlie's (also known as the 21 Club), most did not.[24] Proprietors often mixed flavoring agents into cheap neutral grain spirits to make them palatable, such as with bathtub gin, and bootleggers added food coloring to make clear spirits look like whiskey. Most speakeasy customers were more concerned with just being able to drink in public than with the quality of what they drank. Bartenders no longer mixed ingredients to enhance flavor, but to hide it, as they did during distillation's primitive days.[25] Left without the means to ply their trade, skilled bartenders slummed in the speakeasies, went into other professions (such as soda jerks), or went to work abroad, where talented bartenders who could make "American drinks," as cocktails were often known in Europe, were in demand.[26] In short, the golden age ended.

The Twenty-first Amendment to the U.S. Constitution repealed the Eighteenth on December 5, 1933, amid the Great Depression, becoming the only amendment to repeal a previous one. Legal employment in alcohol sales, shipping, and manufacturing returned, and tax dollars on alcohol started flowing into state and federal coffers once again. Cocktails reentered nightlife and regained their status as symbols of sophistication, but this point in the twentieth century differed from the golden age. Venues gradually became more efficient at serving customers.[27] Highballs, like vodka and soda, gained popularity for their simplicity: a spirit and mixer with ice, and no measuring. Technological innovations further simplified bartending. Machines replaced the need to chip ice from large blocks, soda guns eliminated the need to mix syrups with liquid, and packaged juices meant bartenders did not have to squeeze lemons and limes. And bartenders stopped using measuring devices, relying on free pouring instead of following recipes precisely. Bartending did not regain much of the technical aspects that the occupation had required.

Members of today's cocktail community refer to the declining quality in bars and the "deskilling" of the bartender profession during this period, both of which continue into the twenty-first century in a majority of cases.[28] They use classic mixology to draw lines around what they do and label it as the "right" way of making drinks. Knowing recipes, drink-making techniques, and the flavor profiles of their ingredients; using dense, cold ice in multiple shapes; and squeezing juice to ensure freshness at the expense of efficiency all underlie their notion of bartending as a skilled trade. Sasha opened Milk and Honey on the Lower East Side on New Year's Day 2000.[29] The cocktail community generally considers Milk and Honey to be the first of the craft cocktail bars in New York City. When Sasha opened it, he deliberately swapped standard elements of today's bars with those of the golden age, most especially ice: "American bartenders who because of Prohibition just, you know, life being what it is, everything went downhill. So the stuff that was standard in the 1910s—squeezing juice to order, having ice from a big block—all of these things were kind of forgotten in America, because of Prohibition, because of technical innovations like the soda gun, if you want to call that an innovation. Basically, if I couldn't have the big ice I wouldn't be in the business at all. There's no point, to my mind. Cocktails taste good because of the recipe, but also because of temperature and mouth feel. And without that, without the temperature and without the little bits of ice crystals and stuff like for these shaken drinks, I'd just rather have a glass of wine. What we can do is impossible to do with ice machine ice. You need a large piece of ice that's very cold in the shaker. We use the terminology 'alive' and 'dead': a dead drink would look like a glass of wine, or a dead shaken cocktail looks like a stirred cocktail. Basically, we do things right."

Throughout the night Milk and Honey's bartenders squeeze juice by hand, use bottled soda water, and, before their shifts, saw and chip giant blocks of ice into large chunks for shaking and for cocktails that call for rocks. (A specialized ice machine also makes pellet ice, for such drinks as juleps and swizzles.) For cocktail bartenders, standard ice-machine ice (the common square, flat chips) is too warm and small, and features too high a surface area ratio with the drink for the goal they are after. It does not get the cocktail cold enough, and dilutes the drink because it melts too quickly. To them, efficiency through technology has decreased quality. Perhaps more importantly, most bartenders no longer know the flavor profiles of their ingredients, nor do they have to in order to do their jobs.

"There's so few bartenders who actually know how to use a spirit," says Phil, the head bartender at Death & Co., "that's why a lot of spirits are dumbed down to where any moron bartender—most bartenders don't know what the hell they're doing—can use it. Stoli orange and soda, you have your orange-flavored vodka, you have your citrus in there, they don't have to add anything."*

"The Jose Cuervo margarita mix," says Brian.

"Yeah. It's dumbing everything down, and the level of spirits is going down to compensate for the lack of skill that bartenders have."

Cocktail bartenders who are reviving the golden age lament this current state of affairs, which they say originated after Prohibition.

The post-Prohibition era also saw the rise of vodka in the United States. Americans scarcely drank vodka in the golden age, and the first vodka company to succeed in the American market was Smirnoff (it had already dropped the Russian "v" for the Western "ff" when it tried breaking into the French market in the early 1900s). After nearly twenty years of failing to appeal to the American palate, which favored domestic whiskeys, Smirnoff finally broke through in the 1950s, aided by savvy advertising campaigns. "No Smell, No Taste" and "Smirnoff Leaves You Breathless" became popular slogans, and the company invented a promotional cocktail, the Moscow Mule, to go along with its endless highball combinations.[30] Odorless, colorless, and tasteless (by federal law), vodka mixed with anything and packed a silent punch. In line with the deskilling claim, bartenders did not need to know much about flavor profiles or measuring when making vodka drinks.[31] Vodka became a simple, flexible spirit in an age of increasing efficiency behind the bar.

Vodka is often a spirit non grata in today's cocktail bars and among bartenders. Many keep a bottle or two behind the bar, but not on display on the backbar, and not a well-known brand. As it's the most popular spirit in the country, selling vodka makes financial sense for a bar. "Vodka tonics pay the bills," as Jim, a bartender and bar owner, puts it simply. But they very rarely put a vodka-based cocktail on their menu, or they do not stock ingredients like cranberry juice, to avoid having to make popular vodka drinks like the Cosmopolitan. Joaquin, at Death & Co., provides a common sentiment toward vodka among bartenders: "Well, we like to tell people, we don't have anything

* Here Phil refers to the popular Russian vodka brand Stolichnaya.

against vodka. We love vodka. We clean everything with it. A little kosher salt, a little vodka, it cleans the inside of a bottle like nobody's business. No, I mean, there's nothing *wrong* with vodka, but it doesn't bring anything to the party except proof. You don't ever drink a vodka drink and you're like, '*Damn*, that's a *good* vodka.' No, you taste everything else that they put in the drink. So if you're using really fresh herbs and fresh juices you're going to really taste those. But then the quality of your drink is going to depend on the quality of your mixers. If you have really good mixers you're going to make a great vodka drink, and that's great, but if we're going to put an ingredient into a cocktail we want each ingredient to be special, we want each ingredient to bring something flavor-wise, aroma-wise, color-wise, something, to each drink, and vodka doesn't do it. It's designed by nature to be odorless, colorless, and flavorless. That's by definition vodka. So why are going to throw an ounce or two of something that just ups the proof? I'm sure we can find another spirit that has a complimentary taste or smell or something, that'll make it taste more interesting. So why not use that? Why not use a rum or a gin or a tequila in that? It's going to be a more interesting drink. So that's why we shy away from using vodka. You're basically limiting the taste of the cocktail to the mixers. That's not very interesting."

Bartenders will serve customers who ask for a vodka drink if they work at a bar that carries it.[32] But they prefer to showcase the classic mixology of the golden age, which includes balancing flavors among its basic tenets.[33] Vodka does not allow them to use such skill. Thereby it has a tenuous place in the craft cocktail world.[34]

Like the Visigoths sacking Rome, ending the classical era and ushering in an uncertain time, cocktail bartenders call the collective period of Prohibition's passing to around the mid-1980s and 1990s the "dark ages." Darkness here refers to the lack of craftsmanship, creativity, and knowledge among bartenders (or the abandonment of mixology), and to the general drinking habits of Americans. Some quality cocktail activity took place during the dark ages, such as the creation of tiki drinks, and some classic cocktails survived through this era, such as the Martini and Manhattan.* Most did not. New

---

* The name Martini remained, but the drink went down several paths from its origins, which are fairly obscure in themselves. Most significantly, vodka replaced gin as the base ingredient, dry vermouth disappeared from the cocktail, and shaking replaced stirring. We can likely attribute these changes to vodka's rising popularity and easy-to-drink nature, the fact that you can taste vermouth more distinctly when it is mixed with vodka (and perhaps because vermouth

cocktails to enter the American drinkscape, like the Margarita, succumbed to the same forces of efficiency as the classics did. People cared more about drinking these and other drinks rather than how bartenders made them.

Bartenders as professionals and we as a country lost something because of Prohibition, the narrative goes, and we needed to be shown the light.[35] Allen is a prominent member of the cocktail community. He is the director of mixology and spirits education for Southern Wine and Spirits, the largest wine and spirits distributor in the United States, for which he holds events. He is an owner of the New York Distilling Company. And he hosts a weekly radio program on cocktails on Martha Stewart's station on Sirius Satellite Radio. Allen came to cocktails from food, specifically the Slow Food movement, which led him to learn more about the "gastronomic heritage," as he puts it, of the United States. He often makes parallels between food and cocktails when he discusses the dark ages and today's revival: "What comes with [the rise of cocktails] is an evolution and—I mean this with total respect—a maturation of taste, as well. I look at things like sweetness. As a huge generalization, we love sugary things in America. Great, fine. Where is the willingness to then eat broccoli rabe and breakfast radish and other radish or other herbs that heretofore we've not been familiar with? Our willingness to accept and ultimately enjoy these bitter flavors, I think, is also translatable to the types of cocktails that you now see coming and the types of spirits that have become popular in varying degrees: certainly whiskeys, not just light rum but aged rum that has nuance, and not just sugar and caramel but even some notes of bitter citrus or cooked fruit. You have elements like amaro and Chartreuse that are almost imperative in a contemporary cocktail culture in New York now that are not overly sweet products. These are herbal flavors and tastes that all of a sudden people are curious about, but there's an open door that allows people to accept these flavors, which, if you go back twenty years ago, it was the sweeter drinks, that are not in and of themselves bad. A Cosmopolitan can be just a fine cocktail in and of its own, but is a more or

––––––––

started tasting bad as a result of poor storage in bars—another lost aspect of cocktail culture), and the greater efficiency of shaking compared to stirring drinks. The transformation of the Martini runs parallel to the James Bond character, who in the original books by Ian Fleming ordered his Martinis with gin or vodka, and once with gin and vodka (known as a Vesper, after the character Vesper Lynd in the book and film *Casino Royale*). Gin and vermouth soon disappear from his order, and Mr. Bond started essentially drinking cold vodka with a little water from melted ice in a glass.

less, not overtly, but a sweeter cocktail that comes out of a nature of overly, frankly, sugary or artificially sugared, cocktails, [with] artificial ingredients."

The job of bartender acquired a mixed reputation during this era. Nationally people saw bartending as low-status service work.[36] Perhaps bartenders in upscale places, like swanky restaurants and the bars of luxury hotels, earned higher wages and had greater prestige, but they were still basic members of the service industry. Some bartenders, such as those in ethnic or working-class bars, boasted high status among their clientele, but their authority and the respect they received generally did not extend beyond the bar's doors or the boundaries of their community.[37] Like waiting tables, bartending became seen as a job for people who were just making ends meet while aspiring to something else (for example, actors, artists, musicians, and students). For these young folks early in their careers, the hours are flexible, the pay is decent and in cash, and, for some, they get to meet other people in their fields and maybe even land gigs.[38] But most people who hope to build a career, achieve respect, and derive meaning from work see it as a temporary step, not an end.

For these workers, the bartending occupation has entered the light, because they have once again embraced the principles of mixology. And the public duly rewards bartenders for doing so.

"One question that I got constantly when I [worked at other bars] was, 'What do you really do?'" explains Joaquin. "I got that a lot, because everyone's an actor, everyone's a writer, everyone's a playwright, a director, a stage-hand, a painter, a sculptor, and they're just doing this to pay the bills. I don't get asked that at Death & Co. People understand that if you're working there you're a bartender. You're a professional, you obviously have a lot of knowledge and a lot of skill, and this is what you're getting into. It takes a lot of time outside of the job in order to do our job. And you don't ever get that question, and it's really, really nice. This is what I do. You're looking at what I'm doing and how I'm doing it. I'm not moonlighting doing this; this is really what I do. You get that validation in your work and it's certainly a nice ego booster. People are telling you it's the greatest drink they ever had or this is the most perfect, so yeah, it makes you feel great."

Cocktail bartenders see themselves, and want others to see them, as professionals. The emotional tip they receive from customers about the quality of their work supports and confirms these needs.[39] But they disavow labels like "bar chefs" or "mixologists," popular terms the media and public use. They feel these labels overemphasize the cocktail-making aspect of their work and improperly place it at the center of their professional identity.[40] Cocktail bartenders fiercely promote the bartender identity. To them, being a professional bartender literally means being skilled at tending the bar.

"I'm a bartender," Brian explains. "I'm not a mixologist. I *hate* that term. I hate it with a passion. It's something you read in *Cosmopolitan*: [in a pretentious voice] 'Ohh, this mixologist . . . ' It's like calling a janitor a refuse engineer. He's a janitor, he's probably happy being a janitor. I'm happy being a bartender. That's what I *want* to be. I want to be somebody that can do it all: make drinks, serve drinks, do it fast, count cash, create things, do inventory, be a manager. Like a baseball player, I want to be a five-tool baseball player. I want to be able to do it all, I don't want to just concentrate on making drinks."

Mixology serves as the basis for the professional identity, but to them it is not the identity itself. Cocktail bartenders see their bartending as multifaceted. Being a good bartender means combining the knowledge and craft of mixology with the interpersonal skills necessary for quality service and the temperament to perform basic and even menial tasks behind the bar. Tom makes a novel distinction: "The obvious crossover occurs in pastry making. Cooking has soul to it. It has emotion to it, in a way that baking doesn't. Baking is a science. It has proper ratios. I think bartending has soul to it. At the end of the day, the term I'm most comfortable with is bartender, because that's what I do. I don't mix in a vacuum."

In this analogy, mixology is the science, but bartending is the art.[41] Like bread that doesn't rise because of improper measurements, a bartender can ruin a drink's balance by adding a quarter-ounce more of an ingredient. That drink won't be what they wanted to make; it won't rise. But learning how to make drinks, cocktail bartenders assert, is simple. As Joaquin puts it, "It's just a matter of doing it enough so that it looks easy and it looks natural, but it's not rocket science. It's really not. You're just making drinks; you're following recipes." The soul, or the art, is the ability to make drinks while also interacting with people and being in charge of the bar. The notion of the bartender as more than just a maker of drinks, as a tradesman, emerged in the golden age, and today's cocktail bartenders have latched onto it.[42]

Still, cocktail bartenders recognize the importance of knowing and practicing mixology for the attention and opportunities it gives them. Jason, a bartender at Death & Co., makes this point very succinctly: "As a cocktail bartender, you get paid for what you know and what you do. But you're *respected* for what you know. That was very appealing to me. But, like, as a professional

FIGURE 3. A cocktail bartender pouring out a drink, with bottles of ingredients.
Photo by Chantal Martineau.

bartender, the customers are more important. As important, if not more important than the actual cocktails themselves" (emphasis added).

Without their abilities in mixology, cocktail bartenders would not get the media coverage they do. They would not get the validation in their work from customers who express their love for their drinks. They would not get a chance to consult for other bars on their drink program or menus or train their staff, run events, educate the public, enter competitions, or work with brands. And they would probably struggle answering the question "what do you really do?" or perhaps at least struggle to cope with the judgments they might receive if their answer is "I'm just a bartender." Unlike janitors, who do not have such opportunities to expand beyond their own pails and brooms and reach a higher status as "refuse engineers," cocktail bartenders have the means to gain status for their work and branch out from behind the bar, but they use mixology to do so. While cocktail bartenders downplay cocktail-making as part of their professional identity in conversation away from the bar, their actions suggest a different story. They devote much more of their time to cultivating mixology-related knowledge and skills than to interpersonal skills or learning how to improve their service. Most of the seminars, education programs, and activities in the cocktail community, around New

York City and at big events like Tales, revolve around discussing and learning more about cocktails and spirits in some way. Furthermore, cocktails structure most interactions between bartenders and customers at cocktail bars.

Cocktail Cathedrals

Death & Co. is located in the middle of the block on East 6th Street, between 1st Avenue and Avenue A, in New York City's hip East Village. Like most of the first generation of craft cocktail bars to open in New York City, people always walk past Death & Co. without knowing it's a bar. Milk and Honey has a gray steel door with a rusty grate in front of its black-curtained window (which has the letters "M & H" between "Tailors and Alterations" on it), and only takes reservations. PDT (Please Don't Tell) is only accessible through a fake phone booth with a false wall in Crif Dogs, a fast-food joint, and only takes reservations for tables. Raines Law Room is behind an unmarked door in a basement, and is "first come, first served" on most nights. Little Branch and Pegu Club are in the basement and on the second floor, respectively, of nondescript buildings on major streets. Bathtub Gin is only accessible through a false wall in the back of Stone Street, a place for fancy coffees, and only takes reservations for tables. Keeping with this pattern, Death & Co. has no windows and no real sign (just a small plaque with the bar's name, next to the door).[43] The façade resembles segments of a dark horizontal plank fence, with an elaborately designed bronze handle on the heavy wooden door.

Considering Prohibition marked the end of the golden age cocktail bartenders celebrate, the use of the secretive speakeasy as a key motif is odd. But the hiddenness of craft cocktail bars only adds to the specialness, mystique, and exclusivity of them and their drinks. While they are almost always located in popular nightlife scenes, they try to set themselves apart from the fray of noise-filled revelry. Cocktail bars are unique destinations amid a wealth of nightlife options. They add touches of gentility and sophistication in a nightlife culture of quick consumption. Getting through the door transports customers from typical nightspots into a different world of nightlife experience.[44]

Upon entering Death & Co., customers meet a thick, heavy black velvet curtain. If it is still dusk outside (the bar opens at 6, so it only serves a nighttime crowd, like all cocktail bars), they are immediately disoriented as their eyes adjust to the sudden darkness. Low lights and candles, a low ceiling, and cement walls make for an encompassed environment. The sounds are a din of jazz, light conversation between seated customers and with their servers, and bartenders making cocktails: ice cracking, bottles clanking, and vigorous shaking. Aromas from the fresh juices and garnishes from the bar wrestle with scents from the kitchen.[45] On the marble-topped bar and backbar shelves sit accoutrements galore: ice-chilled bins with tiny cups of mint, olives, and brandied cherries; baskets of lemons and oranges; dozens of cheater bottles and bottles of bitters; mixing glassware; tools (jiggers, bar spoons, Hawthorne and julep strainers, wooden muddlers, swizzle sticks); and rows upon rows of spirits and liqueurs, most of which are unfamiliar to customers.* When customers sit with a menu, they are in their seat for the night. There are no televisions, no jukebox, no switching tables or moving chairs, no mingling, and little chance for conversation with other customers besides the people they came with (although sitting at the bar gives customers a greater chance to interact with strangers). The feeling is more fancy restaurant than bar.

Craft cocktail bars resemble taste cathedrals, sacred places for making and consuming cocktails. The seriousness of practicing mixology structures the fun of public drinking. Owners design them with making cocktails and providing a specific drinking experience in mind. An owner must be behind the idea of making craft cocktails using mixology. Otherwise, the idea, and business, won't work. As Sasha puts it, "You simply make a lot less money when you do things right." Doing it "right" means customers must wait longer for their drinks than they would at another type of bar. The bar must stock a wide array of spirits and liqueurs, some of which will be very expensive (such as craft spirits and scotches) and most of which other bars don't carry, as well as a wide variety of bitters. The bar must have an ice program of some sort (expensive machines, block ice, or both) and dedicated staff for juicing, cleaning glassware and tools, and making syrups. And the bar must usually

---

* Cheater bottles: Bartenders often fill clear glass bottles with some of their most used ingredients, such as simple syrup and lemon and lime juice, to increase efficiency. If Green Chartreuse, for instance, is an ingredient in a few popular cocktails on the menu, bartenders will put some in a cheater bottle and refill it throughout the night. They label these bottles and keep them on the bar or in the well (a rack behind the bar at a bartender's knees), for easy access.

Jigger: Bartenders use this small metal tool that measures liquids in ounces or milliliters to ensure precise pours. In profile most jiggers look like two pyramids stacked and glued together at their apexes, with one larger than the other (measuring 2 ounces and 1 ounce, say). Cocktail bars stock multiple jiggers for a variety of amounts.

limit the number of people it serves at a time, hence reservation, "first-come, first-served," and no standing policies; otherwise, the volume will overburden bartenders. Owners have to deal with each of these matters so their bartenders can make good cocktails the "right" way. They have to set their bartenders up to succeed. Death & Co. meets each of these objectives.

One night I take a seat at the bar and order a Red Baron off the menu, a stirred cocktail with Aviation Gin, Carpano Antica vermouth, Ramazzotti Amaro, and Maraska Maraschino liqueur. It's a spirit-forward, stirred cocktail, essentially a variation on a Martini. A small group of two young men and a young woman watch Kate, tonight's bartender, make my drink. Wearing a white button-down shirt, an apron over black dress pants, and a vest, her movements are precise as she sets down the mixing glass and precisely measures each ingredient with a jigger. Kate then takes the back of a bar spoon and whacks a few large ice cubes to break them up, and fills the glass to the brim. After a minute of staring, the young woman asks a question.

"Does breaking the ice make a difference?"

"Yeah," says Kate. "It just depends on what drink you're making. We have this big ice [holds up a cube] so you want to break it up to get the right dilution."

"Do you have special machines?" asks one of the men.

"Yeah, we have different types, and crushed ice for certain drinks and tall ice for tall glasses."

After filling the glass, Kate then stands about a foot away from the bar with her arm extended, back straight, and other arm behind her back. Using the same bar spoon, she stirs my drink, forcefully, but steadily and smoothly. She barely moves her arm, but toggles and rotates the spoon with her first two fingers and thumb. The glass remains in place. After thirty seconds or so the ice has melted down some, and Kate takes a julep strainer and pours out my cocktail into a chilled coupe. After she has set down my cocktail on a napkin, the group goes back to their conversation.

As it does for these customers, making cocktails at craft cocktail bars inspires questions for people who have not seen such techniques or ingredients before. Most bartenders who make, say, a vodka soda, simply take a glass (sometimes using it as a scoop for typical ice-machine chip ice to save time), and then build the drink without measuring, usually by pouring the vodka straight from the bottle into the glass while simultaneously pressing a button on the soda gun. Kate does the opposite. She starts by measuring her modifiers (typically cocktail bartenders start with the least expensive ingredients first, such as simple syrup or juice, in case they make a mistake), and then the spirit before adding the ice last, to prevent excessive dilution before achieving the appropriate coldness. She stirs to achieve this dilution and coldness, doing so far longer and more concertedly than most bartenders (if they stir at all). Finally, Kate uses a strainer to pour out the drink into a separate glass.

Customers sitting at the bar regularly ask questions like these about the drink-making process. People with more mixology knowledge ask bartenders more advanced questions, such as why they use a particular brand of rye over another in a cocktail's recipe. And cocktail bar owners and bartenders purposefully add several elements to the experience to prompt conversation. Menus list each drink's ingredients, assuming there will be one that a customer has never heard of and ask about, and break drinks down into categories. For instance, people at the Raines Law Room use such categories as "Tall and Fizzy" and "Stirred and Strong" to distinguish some of their drinks, and Pouring Ribbons' menu has a "flavor matrix" of "Refreshing" and "Spiritous" as the two ends on the x-axis, and "Comforting" and "Adventurous" as two ends on the y-axis. They then map their drinks somewhere on the matrix, so a drink in the "Refreshing" and "Comforting" quadrant is likely to be fruity, fizzy, and not very spirit-forward, whereas a spirit-driven drink with complex ingredients like scotch and vermouth would likely fall in the "Spiritous" and "Adventurous" quadrant. Along with guiding customers toward an understanding of their own taste, a goal of these categories is to get customers to think differently about what they drink and to give them a set of terms to use when discussing them.[46] Most bars change their menus a few times a year, often to reflect the season. In spring and summer they feature light spirits, like gin, unaged tequila, and unaged rum, as well as refreshing cocktail styles like juleps and swizzles, and in fall and winter they feature darker spirits, like bourbon, brandy, and aged rum, and more boozy drink styles, like Old Fashioned variations.

The Cocktail Community

Of the four occupations, cocktail bartenders are members of the largest and tightest community (both occupational and taste community), which extends throughout the city and country and around the world. While large compared to those in other cities, the New York City cocktail community is still small, and most members know each other personally or at least by reputation. They regularly visit each other's bars and those in other cities, and call on each other with work opportunities, such as when someone gets hired to bartend at an event for a liquor company. Big events like Tales of the Cocktail and the Manhattan Cocktail Classic introduce them to bartenders from around the world (although being in New York City means people from the global cocktail community often come to their bars and introduce themselves). And bartenders sometimes engage in informal "bartender exchange programs," whereby bartenders in different cities swap bars for a few weeks. The aim is to spread the word about their bars at home and to exchange cocktail knowledge.

They also have their own formal membership group, the United States Bartenders' Guild (USBG; representative of the International Bartenders Association) and educational and accreditation programs. The USBG has several certification exams, and the elders of the cocktail community developed the Beverage Alcohol Resource (BAR) Educational Program, which provides a five-day intensive course on spirits, cocktails, and mixology principles, with both written and blind tasting exams.[47] People do not legally need these certifications to bartend in a cocktail bar or any other type of bar, and most of the participants are already either cocktail bartenders or members of the extended community (for example, employees at liquor companies). But the program serves as a form of socialization, showing members how to taste and talk about tasting and teaching them some of the finer details and historical facts about the ingredients they use and products they serve.[48]

As the cocktail community has expanded, more and more people have flocked to the industry in some capacity. For cocktail bartenders, tensions emerge when people enter the occupation because they love mixology, rather than tending the bar. Often times, they bartend for a short period of time, and then become consultants or brand ambassador for brands. I spoke with Joaquin once about people who become cocktail bartenders because of their interest in the culture, but who had never bartended in their lives.

"That's definitely an issue," he says. "The difference is between serving guests and serving drinks. [New bartenders are] very good at serving drinks. It's very, very hard when you have someone who went from being a cocktail geek to being a bartender for them to get anything beyond that. Sometimes it's really, really challenging to get them to talk intelligently or passionately about anything other than bitters. It's like, alright, what happens when the guest wants to know what the score of the game was? Do you even know who is playing? Did you know that the Knicks and the Nets were playing each other on Martin Luther King Day? Are you even aware of the fact that two local teams were squaring off? You know?"

"Right. What if the customer just doesn't care about bitters?"

"Right! Exactly. What if they want to know what shows opened? What if they want to know what is at MoMA? Are you reading the *Village Voice* to know what shows opened? Are you reading this stuff to find what else is going on in the city? Do you have six recommendations for bars or restaurants that are within four blocks of you that you can give them no matter what it is that they're in the mood for? How well do you know this area? How well do you know the tourist areas, even? If you are expecting to have a lot of people come in from out of town, you should know places to recommend in Midtown, you should know places to recommend near the World Trade Center. Those are those little nuances that they never pick up on."

"Right. That's the best service."

"When someone walks into a bar wearing glasses, like you are, and it's a cold, frosty day. You come in, what happens?"

"It fogs up all the time."

"Knowing this, because I wear glasses, and I do those things, the first thing I do when I see a guest walk in wearing glasses and I see them walk to the bar is I grab a napkin. As they're standing there I'm like, 'Here you go, for your glasses.' It's a very simple thing. Right off the bat I'm showing that guest, 'I see what your needs are.'"

"'I'm here to take care of you.'"

"You don't have to ask. I already know you needed this. Before you try to find some dry spot on a layer underneath the four layers you have on in order to wipe your glasses, I'm already acknowledging that. And here's a glass of water and a menu. And that's the difference, I think. When you have someone who has bartended for a brief period of time, less than a year, when they make that jump from having bartended for that amount of time into brand work, when they make that jump into trying to do their own programs and consulting on places, that's where these things go horribly awry."

By underscoring the importance of service in cocktail bartending, Joaquin and other cocktail bartenders with prior bartending experience distinguish themselves from those without it who pursue the occupation for the culture ("mixologists"). Here Joaquin also echoes Tom's earlier comment about mixology as the science and bartending as the art. When the science becomes popular (and marketable), the bartender artists trumpet the true essence of their service work: the soul-filled human touch.

DISTILLING AUTHENTICITY

Prohibition is over!

—*Tuthilltown slogan, written on shipping boxes and t-shirts*

Nick is a college student at SUNY New Paltz, near the Tuthilltown distillery. When he moved to the area for school, his uncle, Ralph, a co-owner, asked him if he wanted a job. Nearly three years later, Nick has done just about every task at the distillery, but mainly he does bottling and maintains the database. His schedule varies throughout the year to accommodate school. On my first day working at Tuthilltown Nick picks me up from the bus station in a white SUV. The inside's a mess. A spare battery and set of jumper cables sit on the backseat, in case it needs a jump. We pick up breakfast for the guys from a deli and head to the distillery in the rural town of Gardiner.

Tuthilltown Spirits Distillery formally began in 2005, making it New York State's first licensed whiskey distillery since national Prohibition, a gap of eighty years. The facilities largely consist of two historic mill granaries that date from 1788 and have been retrofitted for light manufacturing. One is a combined store, visitor center, and rickhouse.* The other holds the action. On the first floor is a simple electric mill for grinding grain, a cooking tank for making the mash, and several 200-gallon, open-top plastic fermenters, which look like tiny topless silos, for holding the products.† Cloth sheets loosely

---

* A rickhouse is a warehouse for storing barrels. Aging spirits is a complex practice. A barrel's wood variety, sawn nature, size, and char and/or toast levels (that is, how much it is burned and/or toasted on the inside), its location in the rickhouse (bottom, middle, or upper floors), and external conditions (that is, outside temperature and moisture levels in the air) all influence how a spirit ages, and thereby how it will taste. I will discuss more about distillation and aging throughout this chapter.

† Tuthilltown makes 400 gallons of mash per batch, which they split between two fermenters.

FIGURE 4. The converted granary building with Tuthilltown's
main operation. Photo by the author.

cover the openings to keep dust and debris from falling in. Paper forms taped
to their sides list the exact contents and date of fermentation. Inside the tanks
some products actively bubble like soda as the yeast breaks down the sugars
in the mash and turn it alcoholic, while others are fairly dormant, with an
occasional bubble, which indicates the yeast is about done.* The room smells
like a rich sour corn mixed with baked bread.

Once fermenting is complete, pumps hooked up to the fermenters push
the product up through a pipe leading to the stills on the second floor, where
the actual distillation—the act of purifying a liquid through heating and
cooling—happens. Tuthilltown has two custom-made copper and stainless
steel pot stills, made by the German company Christian Carl, which look like
old-fashioned submersibles and make up one end of the large room with a
barreled ceiling. A small tasting area and office at the top of the stairs divide
the floor. Next to them are double-doors leading to the outside for forklifts to

* Fermentation takes about five days.

move pallets of freshly filled barrels to the rickhouse for storage. At the other end of the floor are the bottling and shipping stations and a storage area.

After I put on the "uniform" (a brown t-shirt with "Distilleryman" written across the chest), Nick brings me over to the bottling station. First he shows me how to blow the dust and debris from the packaging out of each bottle by using a machine that shoots compressed air. Nick grabs two squat 375-milliliter bottles, holds them facedown, and lowers them over the upturned nozzles. He steps down on a pedal and the air makes a sharp, piercing sound. He removes them and puts them down on the counter.

"Now you try," he tells me.

I take two bottles and mimic Nick, but my foot lacks his light touch, and I end up shooting a lot of unnecessary air and making a loud, shrill noise. After watching me overshoot for a bit, Joel, the "chief distiller" and head of operations, says, "You can just do two shots," and then shows me how to step quickly on the foot pedal while moving the bottles up and down the nozzle.[1] A bit different from Nick's, his technique is very efficient. After a dozen or so bottles I get the hang of it and find my own technique.

Continuing with the lesson, Nick takes me to another table of bottles, each filled with rye and stopped with a plastic-topped cork.

"I did these yesterday, but just bang on the corks with this mallet to make sure they're in," he instructs.

I take the rubber mallet and start tapping them slowly and carefully, trying not to damage the bottles. Nick says, "Nah, dude. Like this."

He then takes the mallet and quickly strikes the tops hard and fast, like a lightning round of whack-a-mole.

"You can bang the shit out of them. They won't break."

He also shows me the best way to line them up on the table, for maximum banging efficiency.

Nick and Joel then take me through the inspecting process. Once they fill and cork the bottles, the distillers hold them up to a fluorescent light, to check for any debris that may still be in the spirit after filtration.

"It's easier with the corn whiskey and the vodka, because they're clear," says Joel. "It's tough to see things floating around with the bubbles in the dark spirits. Look for things that are falling faster than others. The most important thing to look for is shards of glass. We've been having a problem with glass shards since we switched bottle companies. They reflect light a bit as they fall. You may see some debris, but a little bit is OK. Just give it a quick determination and use your judgment, as if you were a consumer in the liquor store. Would you buy this bottle if it had that amount of debris in it? A little bit is OK, but too much is not good. Any bottles that don't make the cut, just dump them back in the drum for refiltering and rebottling."

Finally, Nick and Joel take me through the waxing process. Tuthilltown applies red, black, or green wax (depending on the spirit) around the cork to seal their bottles. They have set up a rather basic system: a pot of wax steaming on a hot plate and a metal rack that holds four bottles on their sides above it, next to a bucket of water for cooling.

"Literally, a really crappy system," as Joel describes it. "But, ya know, we'll try to refine it. It does work, that's the thing."[2]

The wax has been on the hotplate for nearly an hour and is ready for dipping. The task is to take the bottles and dip them neck first into the wax, only submerging them to where the neck meets the bottle. Joel shows me his style, whereby his hands are always moving. He takes two bottles and dips them, then takes two more. He then dips the first two in water and wipes them, and then takes two more. He repeats the process over and over.

"Liam does it differently," says Joel. "He combines the inspecting with the waxing. He does both more or less at the same time and establishes a rhythm that he is comfortable with and is efficient. You can experiment and do it however you want, as long as it is done properly."

Not ready to go at Joel's speed, I do one at a time. I submerge a bottle for three seconds and then take it out and rest it on the rack to let the excess wax drip down back into the pot. I do it again three more times until four bottles sit on the metal rack. After resting the fourth one I then take the first one and submerge its top in the water to cool and harden the wax. Drying the bottle with a paper towel, I notice the wax came out uneven. A bit has dripped onto the top of the bottle and some has dried mid-drip while coming off of the cork, forming a little wave-like bubble. Joel comes over and sees me staring at the wax, my brow a little furrowed.

"Let me see," he says, taking the bottle. He inspects it and says, "That's OK, that's authenticity. They don't all have to be perfect."

Nick and I then quietly get into a rhythm, as he fills up and puts corks on the bottles I cleaned out earlier, while I wax their tops. We form a simple, small assembly line. I ask him, "So large distilleries have machines that do this, right?"

He nods and says, "Yeah, but we have two sophisticated machines that they don't have."

"Oh yeah?"

"You and me."

Craft distillers are unique among these four occupations. They work in factories. They manufacture material goods, which they do not serve, and thereby have less exposure to consumers.[3] Compared to the other three occupations, their case reveals similarities in terms of who becomes a distiller and opens a distillery and how a distinct philosophy underpins their motivations, and differences in terms of the work they do and how they communicate the meanings behind their products to consumers.

Craft distilleries are part of a groundswell of small-batch, "artisanal" light manufacturing businesses that have recently emerged in the United States.[4] Their closest cousin is the craft beer, or microbrewery, movement.[5] Along with their small size, businesses like craft distilleries have a number of attributes. They have respect for handmade products and all the subtle variations they contain. They promote a strong sense of localness in terms of where they source their ingredients, the regions where they sell their products, and/or how they use place as a basis of their brand's identity. Perhaps most importantly, they create and promote a sense of authenticity, or the idea of a product as full of integrity, truth, and real-ness as markers of its quality. And a product can be authentic because it is handmade and comes from a unique place.[6] Many scholars have examined how consumers determine the authenticity of what they consume.[7] We know less about how workers who make authentic products think about their work of imbuing material products with authentic qualities.[8]

From Grain to Glass

Distilling refers to both a multistep manufacturing process of making spirits and a specific moment in that process (the reaction taking place in the still). At its core craft distilling is based on an ancient practice. Distillation has been around for thousands of years, and nearly every ancient culture engaged in some form of it. Most societies originally distilled to make essences, balms, and perfumes for medicinal and religious purposes. The alembic still, or two vessels connected by a tube, dates from the third century CE, in Egypt. (Today it is more commonly called a pot still.) One vessel containing the base liquid is placed on a heat source (an open fire, originally), and the vapors float up through the tube and collect in the other vessel. It was (and usually is) made out of copper.[9]

Some Europeans in the Middle Ages likely distilled alcohol for consumption, but contact with the Arab world in the Near East, where distillation technology and practices matured, led to its rise.[10] Early spirits were called "aqua vitae" or "eau de vie," meaning "water of life," and were distilled from wines and fermented fruits and grains.[11] Basically, people distilled what was available to them, including the waste from wine- and beer-making. Many of the traditional spirits from Europe—vodka, brandy, gin, akvavit, whiskey—date from this period of the late Middle Ages and Renaissance. With primitive technology, low-quality ingredients, and few practices of refinement, most early spirits were rather harsh. For instance, there is no indication on record of distillers cutting "heads" and "tails" until the nineteenth century.[12] The "head" is the first liquid to come out of the still during a run. Essentially methyl alcohol, the heads are high in acetone and other toxic aldehydes, and have a highly potent taste, while the tails are highly bitter. "Cutting" the heads and tails, or separating them from the "hearts," or the middle and most flavorful portion of the run, into different containers, has become standard practice in distilling. The pot still would also improve over time, such as through the addition of cooling pipes inside the tube, which helped the vapors condense into liquid in the second vessel, and through more controllable heating systems than direct flame.[13]

European settlers regularly made beer and cider and drank imported wine in the New World. They also brought stills from Europe and made gin and rum with native ingredients.[14] Both spirits gradually lost popularity as citizens of the new United States associated them with the old European order, and as westward expansion led people away from cities along the eastern seaboard. Farmers distilled their crops—namely, grains like corn, rye, and, in some cases, wheat. These products became American whiskeys, chiefly bourbon, which is mostly corn-based, and rye. Most Americans drank whatever whiskey their local farmer made, and farmers saw whiskey as a basic product, like any other product they sold. In fact, whiskey was more valuable than the grains it was made from because it was easier to transport and could be sold at a higher price than these ingredients. In Kentucky, distillers used barreling practices—as brandy and scotch producers in Europe did—and bourbon was born.[15] Technological advancements during the nineteenth century, such as steam-powered heat (first used in distilling in 1816) and the invention of the column still (1831) as an alternative to the pot still, gave distillers greater control over production quality and allowed them to mass-produce their spirits, respectively.* And the transcontinental railroad made shipping efficient. Distilling became industrialized, and whiskey became a widespread commodity. Many farmers expanded to become whiskey companies, but most whiskey distillers were still small-scale farmers.[16]

As was true for cocktail culture, national Prohibition destroyed the distilling industry and distilling culture in the United States. More than five hundred distillery businesses closed, most sold their copper stills and equipment for profit, while many thousands, such as farmers who profited nicely from distilling their crops, stopped.[17] Some companies kept distilling secretively, while some were allowed to legally manufacture alcohol under medicinal-use licenses, since doctors at the time still prescribed whiskey for certain ailments (a remnant of the Middle Ages, when people regularly took distillates for medicinal purposes).[18] While always present in the country in some form, bootlegging and moonshining operations boomed during Prohibition, giving the period its romantic palette of colorful characters: dapper gangsters in double-breasted suits, Tommy Gun–wielding getaway drivers, and hillbillies outrunning the cops. Previously a whiskey nation—bourbon and rye—the spirits that bootleggers brought in from abroad, such as Canadian whisky,[†] scotch, and rum, found an audience in the United States during Prohibition. These imports were usually the real McCoy, while native spirits were scarce or of dubious quality.[19] Locally (and illegally) made gin also became popular, given the ease of adding botanicals and other flavorings to a neutral grain spirit (think adding tea bags to hot water, and think doing so in bathtubs, as in "bathtub gin").

The Twenty-first Amendment ended Prohibition in 1933. But the distilling industry did not immediately return to its pre-Prohibition numbers after

---

* A distiller must remove the solids from the beer mash before distilling it in a pot still and then clean the leftover beer mash (that is, the remaining grains that have been stripped of their alcohol) from the still after a distillation run. Both take time. In a column still, which consists of several tall towers, a distiller can distill continuously, with the beer mash entering and exiting the machine in different places, and can leave the solids in the mash. In short, column stills are far more efficient.

† Americans and the Irish spell their versions of the spirit "whiskey" ("whiskeys" plural), while Canadians and the Scottish spell theirs "whisky" ("whiskies" plural). The difference is merely a minor variation in how the original Gaelic word has been translated into English and does not denote two different categories.

repeal for many reasons. In 1933 the United States was in the middle of the Great Depression. Investment capital was scarce, and many distilleries had already sold their facilities and stills. Spirits-drinking Americans before Prohibition preferred aged whiskey. So even if companies got up and running quickly, they had to wait for their product to age before bringing it to market (meanwhile, fewer consumers had disposable income, given the economic climate). A few years later, during World War II, the federal government required distilleries to make industrial alcohol for the war effort, which limited the distilling industry's growth. Tastes from Prohibition—for blended whisky (from Canada and Scotland), gin, and rum—remained, while vodka gradually became popular. And unlike in the United States, the distilling industries in these countries had more than enough product to export.[20] The vast majority of whiskey companies that disappeared when Prohibition began did not return.

Of these four occupations, the law has had the biggest impact on craft distilleries and the craft distilling movement, specifically through licensing. Along with repealing the Eighteenth, the Twenty-first Amendment also gave each state the power to decide how to handle the manufacturing, distribution, and sale of alcohol within its borders. As with the beer industry, most of the liquor companies that survived Prohibition and were able to get back up and running, such as Jim Beam, Jack Daniel's, and the companies that would eventually make Wild Turkey and Maker's Mark, were fairly large and had deep pockets. As such, they were able to influence many state laws for alcohol manufacturing in their favor, such as by placing minimums on annual production and making licenses prohibitively expensive. In New York State, for instance, prior to 2000 a distiller's license cost $65,000 a year, regardless of level of production. Some craft distilleries began operating on the West Coast, in California and Oregon, in the 1980s.[21] But in most states restrictive laws prevented growth.[22] In 2001 there were only twenty-four craft distilleries in the United States.[23] Americans for the most part only consumed spirits from several multinational companies.

The craft distilling industry in New York State grew out of a combination of luck and small business advocacy. In his late fifties, Ralph, Tuthilltown's co-owner, bought the property with the unused mill granaries and moved into the adjoining house in 2001. An avid mountain climber, he previously owned several indoor climbing gyms in Manhattan and built climbing walls for trade shows. Wanting to start a new business, he bought the upstate property, just two hours north of the city, with the intention of starting a climbing park and retreat. His neighbors vehemently fought him on the idea ("They feared another Woodstock-type situation, with visitors coming up there and taking over the town," he recalls), which he eventually scrapped. With these historic buildings and the property, Ralph began to think of other business ideas: "In the course of doing research, I discovered that the year [before] New York State introduced the A-1 distiller's license, which was the first microdistilling license in New York since Prohibition. It dropped the fee from sixty grand a year for a distillery down to about $1,250 for two years, and they capped production at 35,000 [proof] gallons a year.[24] After I did the right math, I figured out that's about $3.5 million worth of sale if you could get it, if you could sell it. I thought that was a good idea."

The A-1 license became available in 2000. A winery owner in the Finger Lakes region who wanted to also make spirits proposed the idea to his state legislator, who then pushed it through in Albany. The intention of the legal change was not to start a small local movement, increase jobs, or boost tourism in the state, as proponents for future changes to liquor license law would claim as goals. But this significant fee reduction made it possible for small distilleries to exist in the state and potentially turn a profit. Ralph still saw opportunities to improve it. "It was short on a couple of matters," he says. "For instance, it did not come with the ability to sell the goods at the distillery like wineries and breweries can do. Once we got our license it was the first thing I went after."

After several years of advocacy from Ralph and other craft distillers in the state, in 2007 New York passed the Farm Distillery Act, which allows distilleries to sell their products directly to consumers and to have tastings, provided 75 percent of the product's ingredients come from New York State. Most craft distilleries were already using ingredients from within the state as part of their desire to support local agriculture and promote their businesses as "local." The new law gave them and prospective owners financial incentives to source their ingredients from within the state, since selling products directly to consumers, such as in tasting rooms, is more lucrative than selling them through retailers. Ralph and other distillery owners around the state then got the Farm Distillery law amended shortly after its passing, to allow a single distillery to hold more than one license. With two licenses, a distillery could produce up to 70,000 proof gallons of product per year without paying a prohibitive fee.[25] Similar legal changes and grassroots efforts in states around the country had similar impacts.[26]

Along with legal changes, cultural factors also played a role in the expansion of craft distilling in New York State, most significantly the rise of cocktail culture.[27] The growth of New York City's cocktail scene exposed consumers to new spirits and flavors. Rye, for instance, recovered more slowly than bourbon after Prohibition. While bourbon is often smooth and sweet, rye is usually spicy and grassy, and thereby tougher to consume neat.[28] Craft cocktails have served as vehicles for rye and other spirits and ingredients with strong flavors. Additionally, cocktail bartenders are constantly in search of new flavors and products with a story. Craft spirits provide such flavors and stories.

Craft distillers also began speaking to cocktail bartenders while coming up with their product's recipe. Tom, a co-owner of the New York Distilling Company, in Brooklyn, says of their origins, "[We started] talking to other cocktail experts. What did they like? What didn't they like? What was missing? What did they wish was there? Historically, what should come back?" Given their knowledge and interest in new products, cocktail bartenders became important resources for craft distillers. Cocktail bartenders also serve important roles for craft distilleries as spokespeople for the brand, either informally as supporters who use or talk about their product to customers, or formally as hired "brand ambassadors." Ralph's son Gable handles sales and marketing for Tuthilltown. After graduating from college Gable worked in marketing for a media company in New York City. He made decent money and could have turned it into a career, but he didn't see himself working there his whole life. After a few years Gable quit to join the Peace Corps. He gave up his apartment and moved back home for a short time before leaving, but his assignment was canceled due to internal strife in the country he was going to. With nothing else to do, he started working around the new distillery. After helping get the company up and running and doing every distilling task, he moved over to sales. Gable speaks about the importance of their relationships with cocktail bartenders: "We've been really fortunate to be introduced to a lot of the really key bartenders in that community. I've become really close friends with a lot of them and they're huge supporters. We're on all of their [shelves] regardless of whether they're using us for cocktails or not. For us it's really important to get in touch with those guys and build a sound reputation with them as a stand-up brand, a quality brand that is attentive to the details, such as working with local farmers and being as ecologically friendly as possible. These guys, the whole bartending community now, this mixology movement to career bartenders, they take it seriously. They want to learn as much as they can about the products that they're pouring. Any opportunity to talk about it they take it. Without their support we'd just be another local brand, local product, that doesn't really make it outside your general region. Also, we're just regular guys who can sit and have a beer with them, sit and have fun."

And given its close proximity to New York City, it's easy for Tuthilltown to host bartenders at the distillery ("I've gotten a number of the top bartenders in the country sleeping on my floor on an air mattress," says Gable). In short, the craft distilling industry and cocktail world have a close relationship, with members from each regularly interacting with, supporting, and even working for each other and switching industries (bartenders becoming distillers and distillers becoming bartenders).

The Craft Distilling Industry

Each of these four occupations has a similar pattern in terms of the backgrounds of business owners and workers in the first generation of their existence.[29] In short, the first wave of owners usually did not previously work in these occupations or businesses.[30] Rather, they had an entrepreneurial spirit, and an idea. Neither Ralph nor his co-owner, Brian, knew anything about cocktails or the cocktail movement in New York City, or even about distilling, when they started Tuthilltown (neither really drinks alcohol, either). As mentioned, Ralph had been in the climbing business, which he wanted to operate on his upstate property, and Brian had been an engineering consultant for the television industry. He went back to school in his fifties to earn an MBA (from Columbia University) and start a business. He did a class project on Samuel Adams, the beer company, and how they used the existing beer manufacturing infrastructure to build a brand while giving the appearance of being a small microbrewery. The case introduced him to the alcohol industry and small-batch production. Brian had worked at the previous flour business at Ralph's gristmills, and he contacted Ralph with the proposal of restarting it. "I convinced him that making flour was like making Coca-Cola," says Ralph. "It's already been done. It's cheap and it's available everywhere and why would you want to bust your back doing that kind of work." He told Brian about New York State's new license category and about his distilling idea. After making some calculations, and recalling his Samuel Adams project, Brian agreed to partner with Ralph on a craft distillery.

They had the business and engineering backgrounds, but neither knew anything about distilling or making whiskey, which also involves aging. They were not concerned. "I mean we looked at each other and went 'this ain't rocket science,'" recalls Ralph. "There are guys with no teeth and a kinder-garten education back in the mountains and they're making whiskey. We're an engineer and a producer and developer and businessmen having worked at the highest levels of the industries we were in. We figured [we] were smart enough to do this. We just started. We just did it. Half the job is showing up."

Like many people in the craft distilling world, Ralph uses common stereo-types of uneducated, unhygienic, backwoods distillers as both a reference and point of comparison. Brian has a similar memory of their company's distilling origins: "[We learned by] the seat of the pants. We just started. Ian Smiley wrote a book that talked about grain and distillation.[31] There was a lot of technical detail inside this one relatively simple way to making grain whis-key. So he dealt with all the aspects of making it from picking the grain to the enzymes to the cooking parameters and all of that—how to run it. It's pretty well defined. There's not much out there in terms of a cookbook or manual. There's no 'Distilling for Dummies' book. Ian Smiley's book is good because it really defines a lot of it. It gives you enough of a grounding to be able to create a spirit. Whether it's gonna be good is something else."[32]

Many other craft distillery owners followed a similar path of leaving one industry to start a business. Since home distilling is illegal throughout the United States and the legal industry was small, there were few opportunities at the start of the craft distilling movement for people to learn how to distill small batches of spirits. Only one owner I met had distilled before. Colin, co-owner of Kings County Distilling Company, in Brooklyn, is in his early thir-ties. He grew up in a dry county in southeastern Kentucky, and as a teenager would sometimes buy moonshine with his friends from men in the woods.* Usually he would drive across the border into Tennessee, to a county where buying alcohol was legal. Colin moved to New York City after graduating from Yale University with the hopes of working in the film industry. He even-tually got a job as a publications manager at an architecture firm (he majored in architecture). When he would visit family in Kentucky he would bring

---

* Moonshine is also known as "corn whiskey" and "white whiskey." It is basically unaged bourbon. And since the Twenty-first Amendment gives states the power to determine their own licensing systems, after Prohibition many counties throughout the country decided to remain dry. Many still are today.

moonshine back with him for his friends in New York to try. Eventually, he bought a still online and began experimenting at his apartment in Brooklyn.

"I was into it just from a, not as a hobby necessarily, but just I guess more of an intellectual curiosity," he says. "How to learn how to do this thing that nobody can teach you how to do because it's illegal? So I would say that aspect of it was very interesting." His day job paid the bills, but wasn't his main passion. Aware of a general interest in craft spirits among culturally attuned New Yorkers, he saw an opportunity to start the first craft distillery in the city, which opened in 2010.

Geographically, craft distilling began in rural areas upstate, where property is cheaper and distillers have easier access to farms and ingredients. Derek, owner of Harvest Spirits, is a third-generation apple farmer in upstate New York. An already difficult business for turning a profit, over the years Derek noticed how he couldn't bring more and more apples to market because they had already fallen off their trees (he attributes recent abnormal weather patterns due to climate change as a factor in the increase), which added to his surplus. If he couldn't sell these apples directly, he thought of what to do with them.

"I wanted to have a value-added product," says Derek. "We have a bakery at the orchard, but there are only so many apples that go into a pie. Then a friend of mine told me, 'Hey, you know you can make vodka from apples,' and a light went off. Not that I like vodka, but I saw the potential to have a value-added product."

As with thousands of farmers before Prohibition, for Derek distilling helped him subsidize his farm's main operation. Other upstate craft distillers also see a direct connection with farmers as integral to both businesses. Dealing with each other directly avoids the need to pay a broker, who normally sources ingredients for distilleries. But most importantly craft distillers help support local agriculture and can thereby benefit from promoting their products as "local" and part of a "sustainable" system.

Since its rural origins in the 2000s, many craft distilleries have opened in New York City. These companies can offset the added cost of operating in the city, such as higher rents, by being more accessible to visitors who want to see the distillery and learn about the products and how they are made. The zoning code limits them to manufacturing areas of the city, which are often located relatively far from residential and commercial areas. Craft distilleries in the city have mainly opened in such places as Red Hook, Williamsburg,

Gowanus, and Bushwick, all gentrifying neighborhoods with industrial pasts, and in the Brooklyn Navy Yard, a former government-owned and -operated single-industry giant that now features dozens of small, private light manufacturing businesses. As mentioned, the farm distiller's license gave craft distilleries the opportunity to have tasting rooms and sell their products directly to consumers. Located in the hip, gentrified neighborhood of Williamsburg with a large nightlife scene, the New York Distilling Company used its license to open a cocktail bar, the Shanty, on its premises. Large glass windows divide the distillery from the bar. Even without going on a tour, customers can see the operation and learn about the spirits (the distillery makes two gins and a rye whiskey) from knowledgeable cocktail bartenders. They chose the location for this reason.

"It's fantastic," explains Tom. "Part of the reason that we're here instead of someplace else in the city, the reason why we chose this building and not the other fifty that we looked at, is because we felt that this had the best access to public transportation and people would come. Both the consumer public and the trade public. It has definitely worked out that way. The bar draws people, that has worked out really well. Our location has really helped."

Since so few craft distillers had ever distilled before, they came to the occupation for a variety of reasons. Most common is a desire to make a unique material product from raw ingredients with their hands. Introduced in the preface, Liam was bartending at a craft beer bar in New Paltz after graduating from college, unsure of what else he wanted to do for work. The ad's description fit his idea of an ideal job in several ways: "This job, it goes in the line with everything I like to do. One, it's beyond the point of just mindless labor. I just like working with my hands. And I really like the spirits industry. Having everything revolve around the whole aspect [of] sustainability, working for a company that isn't concerned with mass production and mass consumption. And stepping away from everything corporate is really a dream come true—to find a place like that that's as cool as this."

Like other craft distillers, Liam contrasts his work at Tuthilltown with that at more corporate spirits companies with automated processes. One day, while Liam and I were removing bungs (wooden plugs) from barrels with hammers to fill them with whiskey, he explains the difference between Tuthilltown and other, larger distilleries: "Jack Daniel's does, I think, 20,000 fifty-five-gallon drums a day, or something like that, ridiculous. That's on the larger end of the spectrum, you have huge to small. Four Roses [a smaller distillery] had one guy that did the work of myself and Steve [another Tuthilltown distiller], but they're very automated. They have history and time and refinement behind them. They have tracks that their barrels roll down. The barrels, what I'm doing right now, they have automatically done. The guy pulls the barrel in the places, puts the nozzle in, it fills until it hits the cutoff switch, and that's it. Their process would be, this much whiskey would be filled in a matter of minutes. As opposed to what we're doing is by hand. In a matter of an hour or two we can get that same sort of volume. That's one difference."

Important to the identity of craft distillers is how and when in the process they use their hands, or what personal elements they add to the production of spirits and how they distinguish their products. For Liam, the distinction of their products is not simply their taste compared to other spirits, but also the fact that he filled the barrels with whiskey by hand. While this practice will not change the taste or flavor of the final product, to craft distillers it signifies its overall quality and justifies the work they do.

As with the craft beer industry, the rise of the craft distilling industry has created an infrastructure for the manufacturing of small brands of spirits.[33] In short, there are a lot more spirits brands than there are distilleries because companies contract out the manufacturing of their product, and brand owners' involvement in the production process ranges from active to nonexistent. These differences are often hidden behind marketing.

The Manhattan Cocktail Classic is an annual consumer and industry event held in the spring at a variety of venues—mostly hotels and bars—around the city. It's New York City's answer to Tales of the Cocktail, and like at Tales, craft distillers have a strong presence at it. In 2010 I walk through the spirits exhibit, where about twenty small companies provide people in the industry, the press, and consumers with samples of and stories behind their products. Some of the company representatives are distillers or distiller-owners, while some are brand owners or brand ambassadors. I stand near the Prohibition Distillery table, which sells Bootlegger 21 Vodka. The name is misleading, since they're not a distillery and technically don't make anything. Tuthilltown makes it. They base their marketing on Prohibition and all of its allure and mystery. On the table is an informational flyer made to look like an aged newspaper from the 1920s. Posters with old, grainy, and sepia-toned photos of outlaws and moonshiners announce that "Prohibition is on!" The marketing campaign is somewhat anachronistic considering vodka was barely in the United States during Prohibition (moonshine wouldn't have had promotional materials, either).[34] Bootlegger 21 doesn't officially hit the market until June 1, 2010, and so far they have been sponsoring underground parties and spreading the news of their product through word of mouth.[35] While I was helping make the vodka at the distillery, I had yet to meet the brand owners. I introduce myself to Brian, a co-owner, and ask him about the company.*

"My partner and I are history nerds and we were finally able to put our history knowledge to good use. [My partner] had the idea for the company and asked me to go in on it. I was in HR/payroll and decided to give it a shot. As you know, Tuthilltown is producing it and we think we're a good fit for each other. And by going through Tuthilltown we're using the handcraft distilling infrastructure. We're going to be distributed through Domaine Select."[36]

Notepad and recorder in hand, a reporter standing next to me asks Brian, "What distinguishes your corn vodka from corn whiskey?"

"Um, I really don't know," he replies. "I don't really handle that end of the business."

Tuthilltown has taken on contract work before. For craft distilleries that do not produce up to the amount allowed under the license (35,000 proof gallons per license), making another brand's product adds to their bottom line. But not all craft distilleries will make anything just for the money. Tuthilltown did not continue a relationship with Edward III, an absinthe brand, when it was first starting out, because the distillery wouldn't compromise its production values.

One day Joel asks me to do an absinthe tasting with him. He takes down a bottle of Edward III and another clear bottle with something scribbled on a blank white label. Its contents are the result of Joel's own experimenting with Edward III's recipe. He pours them into separate glasses and then slowly pours water in each from a slender glass measurer. They both begin to louche, but the second one does so more quickly, and turns more opaque and whiter, almost like milk. Joel takes a sip of the first one. His face stays neutral. He then sips from the second one, makes a sound of satisfaction, and holds the glass up to the light.

"I was never happy with the original Edward III recipe. This one's much better. Too bad it won't ever go to market."

"Why?"

---

* There are two Brians in this chapter. One is Tuthilltown's co-owner, and this one is a co-owner of the company Prohibition Distillery.

"I refused to do the original recipe they sent me. They approached me with a crappy recipe and dried, powdered herbs. They wanted us to make it quick. Take some herbs and alcohol, throw it in the still, put it in bottles, and you're done. But it's not so easy. They wanted it on shelves by September. I changed it a bit and presented it back to them, and they accepted. But later on I said that we are not the distillers that they're looking for."

"Why?" I ask.

"We're not an herbs distillery."

"Could you be?"

"Only if I grow it [the herbs]. I would only do fresh herbs if I were to ever make an absinthe. [The dried herbs] are over there, on the shelf.[37] I would never have the first one again; I was just making it [for them]. But this one [the second one] is something I would actually drink."

Joel perceived the Edward III owners were only interested in making money and owning a spirit brand—in this case, one with a unique history and cachet for being illegal for a time and having psychoactive properties. The brand went against the values of the distillery, and he wouldn't compromise their process.

At first, Joel thought the same of Prohibition Distillery when John, Brian's co-owner, approached him. "I thought that he was just someone who was looking to make money and throw a recipe at us, but I learned he wasn't looking to do that and appreciated the work we do." In their mid- and early forties, respectively, John and Brian had come from the corporate world, specifically a company called ADP, which provides outsourced services for businesses (human resources, payroll, and so on). But they grew tired of corporate work, where "everything is about making the numbers," as John puts it. They had originally considered opening their own distillery, but they recognized their lack of distilling knowledge made it unwise and, in any case, their financing fell through. John got a list of craft distilleries from New York to Maine, and he set out to visit them all, learn about distilling, and talk about their idea. "We decided to tap into the microdistilling infrastructure that has developed recently," says John. He and Brian would focus on marketing. Six months separated his two visits to Tuthilltown, and Joel was impressed with how much John had learned in the interim from his research. John respected their process, while Joel respected their desire to learn. And while a form of marketing, John and Brian's Prohibition references are detailed: the label is based on a federal prescription ticket for medicinal alcohol during Prohibition, the bottle is based on an old medicine bottle from the period, "21" references the Constitutional amendment, and an old alcohol tax stamp covers the cork.[38]

People in the craft distilling industry also support serious aspirants, such as by offering them use of their stills to come up with their recipes. Bill, before becoming the head distiller of the New York Distilling Company, had no experience distilling when he started. Before they got their still, he went to the Warwick Valley Winery and Distillery, in upstate New York, to work on recipes and learn.

"That was the whole idea," says Bill, "that we were up there trying to figure out what our gins were going to be. We did about thirty test batches. I did probably about twenty of them. At first we were watching the first couple of batches. We watched Jason [Grizzanti, Warwick's master distiller] do it and helped him out. Then it got to we were doing it, [and] Jason was helping us and watching. Eventually it got to the point where we were doing it [ourselves]. Mostly running the equipment with Jason checking up on me."

"Was that just to really learn the steps?" I ask.

"Yeah, [and] to figure out what our recipe was. We did some whiskey up there as well, maybe about another ten small batches of whiskey. We were aging them in small, five gallon barrels. I guess I just found myself doing the production. That was the role that I fell into as we were building up the company and as we were playing to our individual strengths. We learned just by doing it."

Producing and Showing Authenticity

The handmade nature of craft distilling represents a significant part of the industry and of brands' identities. Craft distillers want the product to reflect their process. Debris and excess wax in and on Tuthilltown's bottles, as shown in this chapter's opening vignette, are neither imperfections nor errors. They signify authenticity, or that people made and bottled the whiskey by hand, and therefore it cannot and should not be perfect.[39] Waxing "properly" allows for a range of practices and outcomes, just as a "proper" inspection allows a range of debris to remain. Tuthilltown uses a number of other methods to create authentic products. One day I watch as Joel pitches yeast into a batch

Figure 5. Four bottles dripping wax on the drying rack. Photo by the author.

of rye in a plastic fermenter while also checking the other fermentations. I ask him if there are any differences between how they ferment compared to larger distilleries.

"[A] main thing is this is open-top fermentation. There is no lid [on the fermenter]. We do use these little carton caps, shower cap things, but that's really just to keep things like dust and crap out. We do an open fermentation, [but] in beer it would totally ruin it. If this was beer, it would be shot by now. No one would want to drink it ever. But for whiskey we want to actually encourage some contaminations because they'll add flavors that will come over in the final product that will actually contribute to it. Whereas in beer it would be too much flavor, it would be too aggressive and ruin the character of the beer. Most beer and wine are much more delicate products of fermentation. [With] beer and wine, you're drinking the actual juice and the grain juice. But with this we're drinking the distilled [juice], so it's a much different process. None of what you see here is standard practice, across the industry. Everybody has their own techniques. There are some things that are the same but for the most part everybody is doing it their own way which is why you have more diversity in what you taste out of barrels."

"What would be a different way of doing this?"

"Closed-top fermentation. Steel fermenters, really nice, efficient, clean fermentation. We're much more rustic. The thing is, without disparaging anybody else, this is as close to authenticity as frontier bourbon as you'll ever see. People aren't doing this. [Big distilleries are] getting $10,000 fermenters and these [Tuthilltown's] are $200 and they're what we could afford and they work really well. That's really dictated the type of product we make and that's why it's so unique. The biggest flaw, I think, in the mentality of the industry is that things can and should be the same. You know *Mondovino*? Did you see that movie?"[40]

"Yeah."

"This guy is saying that great wine can be made anywhere.[41] It can be forced to be made anywhere. But really, the expression of the spirit or the wine or the beer should be an expression of the location."[42]

"The place where it comes from."

"That's pretty much the opposite mentality. For us, I can't say that it's some normal pursuit; it's a functional necessity. Like, we had to do it this way. We had to use cheaper equipment; we had to find ways to make it work with what we had."

Here Joel raises an important point about craft and the production of authenticity—namely, the notion of making a virtue out of necessity. How much of what craft distillers do is a conscious decision to engage in authentic production, and how much of it is because it's all they can afford? Cutting edge distilling equipment and bottling systems that would make more consistent products—neatly affixed labels, evenly coated wax—at much greater speeds and volumes cost a lot of money. Does using more expensive equipment make a product less handmade, and thereby less authentic? Debates surrounding this type of question permeate the craft distilling industry. Like with cultural consumption, authenticity in craft production is a social construction and represents a sliding scale.[43] People in the industry use the conditions of their business—the source of their ingredients, their production methods—to make authenticity claims. The decisions craft distillers make, whether deliberately or because they have no other option, become part of their brand's story.

A final example concerns Tuthilltown's barrels. According to federal law, many whiskeys must be aged in certain types of barrels for specific amounts of time before heading to market under certain labels. To be legally called bourbon, a whiskey must be mostly corn-based (that is, more than 50 percent of its base ingredients must be corn) and age for at least two years in a new (that is, unused), charred American oak barrel. Corn whiskey, off the still, is a clear liquid. As it rests in the barrel it absorbs the sugars and materials from the charred wood, which changes its flavor and color. The aging standard of two years is for a full barrel, or a barrel that holds approximately fifty-five gallons of liquid. The chemical processes that naturally occur when alcohol touches wood are modified by the amount of alcohol by volume, or how much spirit comes into contact with the wood. In other words, corn whiskey in smaller-sized barrels, with lower surface area ratio, will yield bourbon in less time than in full-sized ones (as a large tea bag would steep faster when placed in a smaller cup of hot water). Tuthilltown, for instance, started using three- and ten-gallon barrels early on.

"We spent the first winter making vodka and corn whiskey," recalls Ralph, "and by spring we had product. Then six months later we had aged whiskey. We started using small barrels and discovered very quickly the smaller the barrel, the faster it cures the whiskey. Cure is not the right word. Matures I would say, more softens and colors and flavors, because we're not interested in how old it is. We've taken that position from the beginning, because if a small distiller is bent on making whiskey the way whiskey has been made for the last eighty years they're going to spend the first five or six years not making money but spending a lot of it on one product."

"It just takes too much time to age, right?" I ask.

"If age was really the important thing, then what we discovered quickly was it wasn't. There were other methods that could be used to get the same quality spirit and the same taste profiles as the best whiskeys in the world, but it could be done in, instead of six years, in six months."

As it does in many decisions that craft distillers make, cost factors into their choice for small barrels. Two years is a long time to wait to sell a product, when a barrel is only sitting in the rickhouse and not generating revenue. Big brands can afford such time and space. Small barrels allow craft distillers to bring their brand to market faster as well as to control the production process by manipulating time and to distinguish themselves from larger companies that use more conventional production methods.[44] This economic imperative also explains why many brand owners start their business by first selling light spirits like gin (New York Distilling Company) and vodka (Prohibition Distillery, Tuthilltown) or unaged spirits like corn whiskey (Kings County Distillery, Tuthilltown). In demonstrating the sliding scale of authenticity in craft distilling, Allen, of New York Distilling Company, distinguishes his barreling decisions with those of other distilleries: "Our first ryes are currently aging. I do not want to use small barrels, which I disagree with, with respect to those [companies] who do it. We are experimenting with small barrels but they will not be the products that we will be rolling out. We are going to let them age in the thirty-gallon and in full barrels for at least two years before we bottle and sell them. Other distilleries do the small barrels to get the product out faster—they combine affordability with experimentation—or they make moonshine. But we have gins to sell while we wait for our ryes to come out. I just prefer respecting the full aging process. Legally the straight rye must be at least two years, although we think that it will be between two and three years. It will be ready when it's ready, but that will have at least two years on it."

While craft distilleries are manufacturing businesses, the Farm Distillery Act allowed craft distilleries to sell their products directly to consumers, which incentivized them to also open tasting rooms and give tours of their facilities. People in each of these four occupations promote transparency in the work process. They want to show and teach consumers about the work they do, often contrasting it with that of other versions of their jobs. Tours are mainly how craft distilleries achieve this goal.

Kings County Distillery is located in Bushwick, a gentrifying former industrial neighborhood in northeastern Brooklyn. They lease two small rooms in an old factory building that has been converted to spaces for artists and artisans. One room serves a triple function: it is where they store barrels of aging bourbon, sell bottles directly to consumers, and lead visitors in tastings. The other room is for actual distilling. There they cook and ferment the corn mash, strain it out, and distill it twice. They have five eight-gallon, stainless steel stills with copper-lined interiors, which they heat with induction cooktops. From this highly primitive operation they collect about a gallon-and-a-half of distillate per shift. With two shifts a day, and by operating seven days a week, they manufacture approximately twenty-one gallons of whiskey a week. However modest, they run weekly tours of their distillery to consumers.

On a Saturday in March, Colin leads a tour for one of his co-workers at his day job and a married couple, both of whom are bourbon fans who heard about the distillery in a local magazine. He starts by making connections between his distillery and two key themes for craft distillers: history and locality.

"So, welcome to Kings County Distillery," Colin begins. "We are the oldest distillery in New York City, at about eleven months," he pauses for laughter, "and the first distillery in the city since Prohibition, which is remarkable that there hasn't been a distillery in New York. There used to be a lot of distilleries, both in this neighborhood, [also] around Gowanus, and sort of in the Vinegar Hill neighborhood—a big distilling culture, particularly, well, during the Civil War they levied a tax on whiskey for the first time since the Whiskey Rebellion, and they actually had to call in merchant marines to go break up illegal stills to get the taxes out of people, and it was like a big, horrible battle against alcohol that was in Vinegar Hill.

"But after Prohibition the tradition basically died, and like a lot of industries in a lot of cities it just became consolidated, mostly in Kentucky, and distilling wasn't a part of urban culture, and it seems strange to think of it, even though for the majority of the country's history it was certainly an urban phenomenon."

By opening and operating in Bushwick, Colin makes the point that Kings County Distillery restores this lost connection between the manufacturing of craft spirits and cities. These opening comments demonstrate how craft distillers promote their brands as revivals of lost culture and situate themselves within the context—historical and contemporary—of their local environments. Colin then describes their two products—moonshine and bourbon—and their base ingredients—namely, corn and barley.

"The corn is over there on the far side of the room. That's an organic, cracked corn from the Finger Lakes [in upstate New York]. The moonshine's 80 percent corn and the bourbon's 70 percent corn. The barley comes from Scotland; it's a particular strain of barley that's grown for whiskey. And it's been malted, which means the grains have been allowed to germinate slightly. And then, before the leaves pop out, they dry it in a kiln, and that gives the seeds a different enzyme profile, which at one point was a nutritional supplement, which is how you get malted milkshakes and malted milk balls and things like that. But distillers and brewers have always used malted grains because those enzymes are capable of converting the starch in grain to sugar, which is then consumed by yeast to make alcohol, which is what we're into."

"Wow," says the woman to her husband, who replies, "I didn't know that."

Sometimes craft distillers have no choice but to buy nonlocal ingredients, as in the case of barley (there are no malting operators in New York State) as well as many of the botanicals used in gin that are not grown locally. But overall they try to buy local when they can, and emphasize the localness of their products to their consumers and tour participants. Colin then says that they are also experimenting with rye, which they happen to be distilling today (he admits a recent failed attempt).

"So wait, what does the rye make?" asks his co-worker. "I'm dumb."

"Whiskey," says Colin. "To be called . . ."

"One hundred percent?"

"It doesn't have to be one hundred. It has to just be more than 50 percent rye grain to be called rye whiskey. Bourbon is basically corn whiskey that's been aged; rye is, you already know, rye whiskey. There's also wheat whiskey, malt whiskey, which is made entirely with malted barley."

"Is that what scotch is?" asks the man.

"Scotch is, yes, I believe it's always . . . there's a lot of different types of scotch, but a single malt will have grain that has been all malted in the same distillery, I believe—I could be wrong about that. And then I believe Irish whisky is made with unmalted, or majority unmalted [barley]. But American whiskey is usually made with corn, because that's what grows here."

These exchanges allow craft distillers to provide even more information about the production process and their products. Experiments, like with rye, are important to the creative process, and craft distillers often share information on their ongoing projects with tours. After this exchange, Colin takes the group into the distillery room, which is just around the corner and down the hall.

"It looks like a science lab!" says the woman upon entering.

Colin warns them to be careful because the stills are very hot. He then tells them about the actual production.

"So I'll walk you a little bit through the process. So this in front of you is the beginning of a mash [points to pots boiling on cooktops]. We just heat water up to a boil, add in the corn, and turn it into like a corn porridge. And then when it cools to 155 degrees we'll add barley, and that's the right temperature at which those enzymes are more efficient to convert the starch and corn to sugar. And then when it cools to room temperature it'll be like a sweet, corn pudding. And that's when we add yeast, and it goes into one of these tubs along the wall to undergo a weeklong fermentation process [points to a corner with a bunch of plastic buckets]. And I'll actually pop the lid of one of these things, and you could see sort of what it looks like."

Colin opens a container and points out how the mash inside is slightly bubbling, which represents the yeast converting the oxygen that has dissolved in the water and sugar to carbon dioxide and ethanol.

"Oh, *that's* the yeast," says the woman.

Colin then says that it is essentially at this point corn-based beer, but explains the difference between making beer and whiskey.

"It's got all this stuff in it. It's a lot easier to ferment than beer, because beer has to be very sanitary, because you're actually drinking the wort, you're actually drinking what you're fermenting.* Whereas with this we're going to turn into steam, and refine it twice over, before we actually let it go anywhere near our palates. So it's more forgiving than making beer."

Craft distillers try to explain the distillation process to their tours in as simple terms as possible. Some stick to scientific language and some provide more colloquial analogies. Colin here uses a combination of the two by referring to enzymes as well as corn porridge and corn beer. But craft distillers make effective use of the hands-on display of the production process in the distillery. Colin continues through the process, leading up to the actual distillation.

"At the end of a week, it will be about 6 percent alcohol, and we'll strain out the corn and barley that's left over with a laundry bag, and the liquid's just dripping into this tub over here. The corn we collect in these big yellow tubs and send to a farmer, who's at Union Square's farmers' market, so when he's done every day, he comes over here, picks up six of those things, and brings them back to his pigs. And there's plenty of residual alcohol left in the corn, so the pigs are like stumbling around. But they're very happy.

"We're interested in the liquid that's left over. And we'll put it into one of the four stills on the left, which will do the first distillation, and the still on the right for the second distillation. So the still is just a hot plate and a kettle, and the kettle is boiling the steam into the column, and in this plastic set of tubes are all just cold water reservoir. So there's an aquarium pump that's pumping cold water through these jackets, so that when the steam hits the inside of this pipe, it'll condense to droplets and then drip into the jugs below."

After explaining the distillation process and answering questions from the group, he leads them back into the first room for the tasting with David, the brand's other owner. Their license allows them to provide three free tastings to visitors. Since they only make two products, they came up with a way to educate people further about the process.

---

* The wort is the actual liquid from the mash that distillers distill after it finishes fermenting. As Colin explains (and as Joel explained earlier), it must be kept clean and pure when making beer because people will actually consume it.

"We created a third for the purpose of the tasting so you can kind of see how the whiskey evolves from one to the other," says David. "Because really, as you heard before, there's a slight change of percentage, but basically moonshine and the bourbon are the same thing, just the bourbon ages in barrels."

Being in the first room, where the bourbon is aging in small barrels, enhances the effect of the tasting. David then pours each tour participant some of the clear moonshine in a shot-sized clear plastic cup. As they try it he explains how they wanted a more flavorful corn whiskey instead of "fire water" that moonshine is known to taste like; hence, they brought the alcohol level down to 40 percent to make it easier to sip. The group members point out the corn flavor as they taste. David then pours them the unique product.

"This bourbon is an immature bourbon that was barreled a month ago. And you can see that it's already pretty dark."

"So it's well before halfway?" asks Colin's co-worker.

"Yeah. But the maturation process is sort of like an asymptote. Within a month it's already turned this color and you'll be able to taste the kind of architecture, so to speak, of the bourbon flavor. But what's missing is the sort of robustness that'll take place as it ages."

The group then samples the "halfway" product, and point out the difference in flavor compared to the corn whiskey. David then pours them each a cup of the proper bourbon, which they aged for eight and a half months (in a small barrel). After trying it, they all go back to the original corn whiskey and the in-between whiskey, to compare the three.

While the media plays an important role in circulating these meanings, tours allow craft distillers to show their authentic production directly to consumers. For craft distillers, the tasting is the culmination of the tour, when participants can taste the distinctiveness of the product after having been exposed to the handmade production process. Through tastings they aim to make direct connections between ingredients, process, and product. Consumers get to first see the handmade process and then experience the result. Tours and tastings reveal the work that goes into bottles of spirits, which is usually done behind the scenes. They allow people to experience authentic production.

3 | WORKING ON MEN

presentable: adj.: clean, well-dressed, or decent enough to be seen in public.

—*From a chalkboard in Freemans Sporting Club*

The barbers have been busy all day, and the client list has been long. All five chairs are filled and six clients are waiting their turn. Two sit reading—one a magazine and the other something on his phone—while the other four alternate between staring around the room and at the floor and following the group conversation. Throughout the day the barbers keep the atmosphere lively with a constant stream of chatter. They start swapping marijuana stories about themselves and people they know. Ruben talks about how he doesn't smoke anymore because he gets too paranoid. He explains how one time he woke up and was holding a knife, and how twice he fell asleep while holding a knife. His stories lead Miles to pose a hypothetical question to the group.

"Would you ever stab somebody?" Miles asks the shop.

"I couldn't do it, that's personal," says Joey.

"You're screaming at the top of your lungs—Ahh!" exclaims Miles, excitedly.

"That's fucked up," says Ruben.

"What do you mean?" says Miles.

Ruben pauses slightly. "I've thought about this a thousand times . . ."

"So you're waiting for it to happen!" interrupts Miles.

". . . a thousand times I've thought about what it would really be like. It would suck balls after, but if the guy is walking into my house through my window at night, guess what, it's pretty personal."

"You can't plan anything out, dude," says Miles.

"What's this guy look like?" asks Joey, to laughter from the barbers and some snickers from clients.

"Let me ask you a question," says Miles above the din, "this guy's in your house—you've been in fights, right? Be honest, do you hit people as hard as you can?"

"Umm, no," says Ruben.

"Yep, then you can't stab somebody."

"Yeah, but, this is . . . dude . . . I don't feel like, as much danger from you, as if you were . . . dude . . . first of all, I never had this happen where somebody actually walked in through my fucking window. But if you did, I think I'd be pretty fucking angry, dude. I'd be way angrier than I've ever been before."

"I know I could stab somebody."

"You're Puerto Rican, that shit's in your blood," says Ruben, to laughter from all the barbers and most of the clients.

Hypothetical questions, challenges, teases, calling people out, showing bravado. Such exchanges are typical at Freemans Sporting Club, an upscale men's barbershop on the Lower East Side. A client walking into Freemans for the first time may have his images of what a barbershop should be like—a place where "men can be men"—confirmed. Group banter fulfills the ideal promise of the men's barbershop as a place for fraternity. But if a new client paid attention, he would notice something missing: barbers talk, clients remain silent. The banter is an unplanned performance, based on the idea of the ideal barbershop, for the benefit of clients, who consume this masculine, typically working-class, culture. Barbers do not deliberately exclude them from their group conversations. The social dynamics of the shop, and the societal conditions under which these new upscale shops have opened, influence how the banter plays out.

Manhood, or what it means to be a man, is in a state of crisis today. It always is. Men are always worried if they are acting as a man should, whether in their family, romantic, or work lives, or in relationships with other men. The reason is society's expectations of proper male behavior constantly change and present men with challenges and mixed signals about how to act. Men are often looking to past times, of their youth or fabled ones told to them by their elders or shown in popular culture, when men were somehow better—stronger, tougher, more responsible—than they are now, for guidance. "How should I be acting right now? What are others doing? How did men used to act?" they ask themselves. If the enduring ideal masculine image in the United States is of the "self-made man," or the man who earns his living independently and is in control of his own life, then being a man means constantly struggling to live up to it. The question is not whether men feel like manhood is in crisis, but what the crisis looks like in any given era, what is causing men to feel like it is, and how they respond to it.[1]

In the face of such crises, men have historically retreated to homosocial environments, or places where people from the same gender interact, such as social clubs and bars, to achieve masculinity.[2] These places have always been important because men primarily seek to show their masculinity in front of other men, who they feel are the best judges of their own manhood.[3] They are where men go to be and become men, or to "do masculinity."[4] And the masculinity men feel pressure to do, or perform, often represents a "hegemonic," or dominant, ideal form.[5] In other words, while it seems natural and normal, gender doesn't just happen. People make it happen through behavior. They try to act as women and as men according to societal expectations of how women and how men *should* act. And such factors as race, ethnicity, religion, social class, and sexuality all shape how people determine what this performance looks like. The work of "doing gender" is never done; it is an ongoing process. People constantly try to "accomplish" or "achieve" a successful gender performance in their everyday lives.

If gender is something people always "do," barbershops are homosocial environments where men go as part of this continuous quest to be "like men." Not only are they where men go to have their bodies (specifically the hair on their head and face) changed to accomplish this goal and look how they think they should, they are also where men have gone for centuries to be around other men and put their masculine performance on display. But the barbershop has changed as the expectations of how men *should* be, the settings where they can behave like men, and the societal conditions surrounding them have shifted, creating an array of threats.[6]

Style without the Fuss

For millennia people across the world often considered barbers to be spiritual leaders, playing valuable roles in religious rituals. In the Middle Ages they were skilled tradesmen and craftsmen, forming guilds under an apprenticeship system. At this time barbers were called "barber-surgeons" because medical and dental care (for example, bloodletting, herbal treatments for cuts, tooth extractions) were part of their work along with cutting hair.[7] As medical knowledge and skills became specialized and physicians and dentists emerged as professions of their own, barbers gradually came to focus solely on hair. While they retained some of their medical roles at the start of European colonization, by the 1700s barbers in the United States were seen as a working-class occupation, akin to servants. In the nineteenth and early twentieth centuries, American barbers began professionalizing, such as by adopting work standards, forming unions, and creating licensing and educational requirements, while barbershops fell under more and more government regulations for cleanliness and disease prevention.[8]

The golden age of the American barbershop lasted from around the Civil War until World War I.[9] Much of the imagery of the barbershop as a place for fraternity and relaxation comes from this time. Aligning roughly with the Victorian era, well-to-do men in cities and towns sought to maintain a clean, prim, and proper look, with short and well-kept hairstyles and either clean-shaven faces or well-groomed facial hair. Men would go to barbershops regularly, and those who couldn't be bothered shaving themselves with a straight razor went several times a week to maintain their appearance. Styling products, like pomades and tonics, and shaving soaps and lotions, proliferated. Barbershops became all-service establishments, where men could not only get a shave and a haircut but also get their shoes shined, mustaches waxed, hair perfumed, and clothes ironed (some also offered beer and cigars) while hearing about politics, business, and local gossip.

A few events led to the gradual decline of barbers and men's barbershops during the twentieth century. First came the widespread use of the safety razor. While versions were around in the nineteenth century, the safety razor took off when King Gillette, a salesman, made a disposable razor (the common double-edged razor blade) in 1903. The blades were easy to mass produce, provided as close a shave as a straight razor, and unlike straight razors required no upkeep, since they were discarded, and did not require as much skill to use. Sensing a potential backlash from men who would link shaving themselves at home with feminine beauty rituals, Gillette's ads equated self-shaving with masculinity, a symbol of rugged individuality as well as convenience. Sales grew, and then, during World War I, the United States equipped soldiers with Gillette razors, giving the company sales of 3.5 million safety razors and over 36 million blades, plus remarkable publicity at home and abroad. Daily (or at least regular) shaving at home in Western countries has been a norm ever since. But shaving at home meant men no longer had to go to barbershops as often. Meanwhile, the Great Depression caused many barbershops to close. With unemployment at 25 percent, fewer men had the income to get regular haircuts.

Short, conservative haircuts and such fancy styles as the pompadour and wave kept barbershops popular during the 1940s and 1950s. Returning soldiers from World War II popularized certain short styles like crew cuts and flattops, which require regular upkeep. But the 1960s really signaled the decline of professional and public men's grooming. Wearing shaggy mops, the Beatles appeared on *The Ed Sullivan Show* in 1964, sparking a youth revolution in popular culture. Long hair became trendy for members of the counterculture and staid professionals alike. A visit to the barbershop went from a biweekly ritual to a rarity. Barbershops closed, and thousands of barbers lost their jobs. Some of them left the industry, while others took up hairstyling and cutting women's hair.* Women's and unisex salons expanded, and many long-haired men began going to them.

The coming of the postindustrial era has marked a change in men's grooming. Like in the industrial era, achieving manhood today (specifically among white-collar men) means conforming to certain looks and styles. Today, however, they have more options (that is, a wide array of styles) and less guidance (that is, fewer dress codes and more nontraditional ideas of what is masculine).[10] Professional men in the new economy feel pressure to "look good" at work and consider their appearance an important part of their career success.[11] Sales of men's beauty products, which companies and consumers refer to more gender-neutrally as "grooming products," have grown in recent years, with nonshaving toiletries recently surpassing shaving items (which have also experienced growth) in sales for the first time in 2013.[12]

---

* The difference between a barber and a hairstylist is not just that the former works on men's hair and the latter works on women's hair, although that is usually the case. (And for this reason, barbers are often more comfortable working on short hair and using clippers, while hairstylists are often more comfortable working on long hair.) They also require different licenses, and licensing guidelines, such as how many hours of instruction are required (usually completed in a school), the nature of the exam, and the services each can provide, vary by state. Barbers, for instance, usually do not learn how to give manicures and pedicures or apply wax in school, are not tested on these skills in their exam, and are not legally allowed to provide these services. Hairstylists with a cosmetology license can provide these and other services, but usually cannot legally remove hair with a razor. Again, the precise differences vary by state.

Perhaps no other term captures the phenomena of straight men who are concerned with their appearance than "metrosexual," which refers to men who groom and treat their bodies like beauty projects.[13] Since the care and obsessiveness over one's body are often seen as feminine acts or aspects of gay culture, people and the media often use the term humorously or derogatorily against straight men.[14] It's funny, or wrong, because "real" men shouldn't be fussing over themselves. (Gillette addressed this dilemma by promoting shaving as a manly act.) The acts of too much personal grooming, concern for clothing, and worry about hair (on one's head or body—the removal of which is sometimes called "manscaping," with equal parts humor and scorn) take away from the "normal" and dominant forms of masculinity a man "should" be trying to achieve in everyday life.[15] They threaten "doing masculinity" right.

At first barbershops did not change to meet the styling needs of urban professional men. In response to the pressure to "look good," many white, professional men go to women's hair salons. Hairdressers at salons offer the quality and style they need, which the ordinary barbershop, with its imagery of an out-of-touch old man with shaky hands, lacks. But salons present their own problems for these men. Most obviously, they are feminine spaces, places for women. They are where beauty work gets done, where women gossip about anything and everything and express their insecurities for their hair, bodies, and lives (as the stereotypes have it). A man's manhood is at risk in the salon, surrounded by women, and his masculinity is under threat when he gets beauty and bodywork done. These men use a number of strategies to maintain their masculinity to counter the threat. They specifically frame the work stylists do on their bodies as something other than feminine beauty work. They're not gay for going to a salon, but have normal heterosexual interactions with a straight woman. They don't pay some stranger for beauty work, which would be turning their bodies into beauty projects, but have a personal, friendly relationship with a women stylist. The work is incidental. Finally, they're not indulging themselves, but actually *need* to look "stylish" as part of their professional identity. They can't achieve the manly look they *must* have to be successful in the masculine and homosocial but unstylish barbershop with poor service. In other words, they receive pleasure out of a genuine relationship with a woman and also get to "look good" and help advance their careers.[16] They thus control the threat, disavow the metrosexual claim, and preserve their sense of manhood.

New upscale men's barbershops like Freemans are direct responses to the threats and pressures of today's crisis of masculinity. Owners deliberately open them as alternatives to the high-quality but feminine salon and the masculine but low-quality barbershop. These shops seek to combine the skill, style, and service of women's hair salons and the homosocial, highly masculine environment of traditional men's barbershops.[17] Clients get the style they need in their professional and personal lives without the fuss of having to go to a women's space. They are a remedy for an era when men feel pressure to look good.

Van was the first barber hired by Sam, the owner of Freemans Sporting Club, who is not a barber. Now in his mid-thirties, he had been working at a high-end women's salon for eight years, and he worked at other neighborhood barbershops in the years before working there. Van met Sam through a mutual friend and loved his barbershop idea. He became the head barber when Freemans opened, in 2006. Van describes the shop's philosophy: "That's our ethos, that's what we stand on: you get the skill of a hairstylist matched with the sensibility of a barber. Like a hairdresser's going to charge you, and I used to charge $75 for men's haircuts, I would stand here and act like [starts making deliberate gestures with a serious look on his face], put on the act that all this shit's going on to justify that I'm doing a $48 haircut for $75. But you feel confident going to a hair salon that you're going to get a consultation, you're not going to be rushed in and out, and you feel like you're getting a higher skill set, which you are in some cases, but not in all cases. But you don't want to be in a fucking hair salon. You want to be around guys, not all the women, the shitty techno music, all the hoo-ha, the inter-fighting, the two women hating on a third for some reason—you know what I mean? This is, what we're working on, is the in-between: you get the attention and the detail and all the time you want, like a hair salon. If [a client] tells me, when I'm done with this [haircut], that [he] wants it shorter, cool. I got no complaints, you got it, [I'll] do whatever you want. It kind of fits into our price point. But, again, we're barbers, we're just guys."

In line with Van's comments, barbers at upscale shops feel men should not have to deal with the threats of a salon, or spend a lot of money for a quality, stylish haircut. These shops thereby target young, appearance-conscious men who need and/or want style in a safe place, without compromising their manhood or straining their performance of masculinity. Upscale men's barbershops explicitly attempt to reclaim hegemonic masculinity for men, and implicitly for professional men. As clients these men get to consume a working-class masculinity found in traditional barbershops, as well as the communality found in the much-researched African American or ethnic barbershop.[18]

Their business models, décor, and themes, which provide a heterosexually coded backdrop for the work and interactions inside, help them achieve these goals.[19]

Freemans is part of a mini-empire for a hip downtown urban lifestyle. Along with the Lower East Side shop on Rivington Street, the ownership group also owns another barbershop in the city, in the West Village, as well as one in San Francisco, two high-end men's clothing stores, a bar, and two restaurants.[20] (The restaurant, clothing store, and barbershop are all called Freemans Sporting Club.) Rivington Street, between Chrystie Street and Bowery, is the heart of the empire. One of the clothing stores is in the middle of the block, at a "corner" created by Freeman Alley, which gives the businesses their name.[21] The barbershop is through the clothing store, with windows facing out onto the alley. An old-fashioned wooden barber pole and sign tell passersby it's there, but otherwise people need to know about it. Clients pass the pricey clothes and arrive at the reception desk next to the entrance to the barbershop. A glass window and door separate the two shops. At the end of the alley, past some art galleries, is the restaurant, with administrative offices and fitting and tailoring rooms upstairs. With locally hand-tailored men's clothes in the store, rustic Americana cuisine in the restaurant, a classic barbershop, and hunting lodge motifs of wood interiors and taxidermy adornment in each, the businesses aim to revive a lost sense of craftsmanship and manliness and promote a masculinized sense of cool.

Like other new upscale shops, Freemans adheres to the style of the traditional barbershop, with vintage barber chairs and stations, classic mirrors, and sepia-toned photographs on the wall (one is of a bareknuckle boxing match, another a bicycle race on a beach). The shop has eight wooden seats, four side-by-side on either wall upon entry, and two leather-padded chairs against the glass window in a small waiting area for clients. Right next to them are five barber chairs, two each on the left and right walls upon entry, with one in the back corner. Pieces of taxidermy (fish and some antlers) and a lodge-like motif of distressed wood explicitly call to mind such manly pursuits as hunting and fishing. The genres in the magazine rack appeal to the young, hip, and culturally conscious urbanite. They range from men's lifestyle (*GQ, Esquire*), cool downtown culture (*Vice, Edible Manhattan*), and the high-minded (*New Yorker, Wired*). While Freemans does not, some of these new shops also combine the traditional masculine space of the barbershop with that of the bar by offering complimentary alcoholic beverages with haircuts. (While they usually offer beer, one shop, the Blind Barber, is attached to a

FIGURE 6. Freemans Sporting Club, from the start of
Freemans Alley. Photo by the author.

proper bar, with a craft cocktail list.[22]) Others have an espresso machine and
premier brands of craft coffee, as at any of the new high-end cafés. The men
who pay $15 for a cocktail and $5 for a coffee drink are the same ones who
pay $45 for a haircut, their thinking goes.[23] They're largely right.

But these shops' efforts to provide a proper manly community space for
men have their contradictions and limits. For instance, unlike traditional barbershops, upscale shops sell men's "grooming products," such as pomades, lotions, and shaving creams, either under their own label or under those of small
companies. Barbers use these products on clients and often on themselves in
their daily lives. They risk making men's bodies seem "made up" rather than
"natural."[24] To reduce this risk they convey to clients their products' quality,

ease of use, and effectiveness for achieving a particular style for men. That is, they emphasize the practicality of products, lest the advice to use them comes off as overly feminine (or metrosexual) to clients.

One afternoon a first-time client named Charles sits in Joey's chair. Quiet for a few minutes after the consultation, Charles asks Joey a question.

"What do you use in your hair?"

"You mean like shampoo?"

"Yeah."

"I don't use shampoo. I keep it natural. And I only use products that wash out. You should only use water soluble products."

"I need to use shampoo. I'm a pretty sweaty guy."

"Sweat's just water," counters Joey.

"Salty water."

Joey shrugs and says, "It's still water. Salt's soluble. It washes right out. Do you use any pomades?"

"No," says Charles with some hesitation in his voice. "Should I?"

"Well, if you want your hair to look a certain way. I could show you one with a strong hold and not a lot of shine. No one will know you have anything in."

In my own conversations with him, Joey praises the shop's aims of giving men a natural look: "I like everything more natural, not as clean. I don't dig the whole perfect clean. Well, I like it, I could do it. But it's not what we're about. Even walking down the street I can tell sometimes [if someone] got cut by our shop. The way we finish a haircut, we never leave lines. You know how someone puts a line? Like a line, and then hair. Sometimes the big [high-volume] shops get those really sharp lines, so you know it's not from [us]. You can tell they don't know how to fade. For this shop, it picks this style over that. We don't leave sharp lines. We usually stay away, even if someone asks." For these barbers gradually fading hair into skin provides a more natural look for men.[25] But naturalness here doesn't come naturally. It must be achieved. Men must work to look natural, and barbers tell them what natural and a natural-looking style means (that is, a pomade that doesn't signal to people that they're using a product).

Another issue of new upscale barbershops is their goal of being a place for men to act like men. They pay homage and strive to be like traditional shops that serve as homosocial community institutions, like working-class, neighborhood, ethnic, and African American shops. They want to be local hangouts and places for community, but they do not play such a role for clients.

Located in gentrifying neighborhoods, and surrounded by other forms of high-priced and trendy businesses (for example, restaurants, bars, clothing boutiques), upscale shops draw clients from the city's population of young urban professionals and creative workers.[26] Nearly all are white and in their twenties, thirties, and forties.[27] They have the financial means to afford these shops' services, want to achieve a certain style (or feel the pressure to do so), and are also attuned to (or at least aware of) the hip forms of manly style they promote and offer. However, most clients travel to these shops from outside the neighborhood and do not use them as hangouts. Many of the barbers who have worked in other shops recognize this reality.

After cutting his friends' hair as a teenager, Miles began his career by working in African American barbershops, known among the barbers as "'hood" shops. He worked at a series of them throughout the city before coming to Freemans. Skin fades are a popular hairstyle among men of African ancestry, and given the clientele of 'hood shops, Miles became an expert at them. He went to Freemans to expand his repertoire, especially using scissors and cutting long hair (that is, white men's hair). But the clippers skills he learned at the 'hood shops served him well. "That theory is like the new way of barbering," he explains, referring to fade styles among white men. "Even though it has been happening for like the past twenty years at least, it's still like the newer way of barbering." As urban white men have begun wearing shorter hairstyles, fades have become an important part of their haircuts. Miles brings those skills and styles, which have been popular in black barbershops for a long time, to Freemans. But working there for him comes at a cost: "Every barbershop I've ever worked at it has always seemed like there were like two or three dudes [barbers] there who were really good and other ones kind of just picked up the rest that those three guys couldn't handle. I would work with a lot of people who I would feel didn't take the craft seriously. I didn't like it. But the conversation definitely was going on. It felt super community, like *really* community. Working here, I feel like, yeah, these guys I work here with are my family, but the connection with my clients isn't really there. I mean, I have a few that I have great connections with. But I think it's just that kind of Manhattan mentality: hustle and bustle, get in, get your hair cut, get the hell out, 'I'm not here for nonsense, I'm not here for bullshit' kind of thing."

New upscale barbershops are the opposite of the 'hood shops from Miles's youth. Group conversations involving clients, who are strangers to one another and usually to every barber except the one they see regularly, are re-

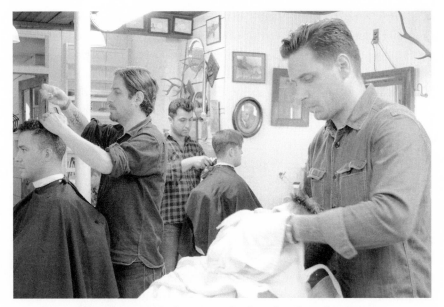

FIGURE 7. Freemans' barbers at work. Photo by Chantal Martineau.

markably rare. The actual social reality contradicts their claim of community, and contrasts with the idea of barbershops as places for community.

A final contradiction stems from this last point. Instead of socializing and community, clients go to these shops for their special services, new and traditional barbering techniques, and the promise of homosocial communality. Their services and techniques include longer-than-average (at least thirty minutes) and finely detailed haircuts, straight razor shaves (with hot towels, oils, and lotions), beard trims, head and face massages with a hot eucalyptus-soaked towel, and little services for certain clients, like trimming nose hair and eyebrows and singeing ear hair.* Although these shops do not offer shampooing or dying services, as salons do, these other high-touch personal services threaten the masculine environment with acts of intimacy, which can create feelings of

---

* Technically, new upscale barbershops, like any other barbershop in New York State, cannot legally use a proper straight razor on clients because of the risk of spreading a blood disease. The barbers at Freemans use a safety razor made to look like a straight razor with disposable blades that they replace after each use.

Singeing: Burning hair with a small, controlled flame. It originates in Turkey and is believed to last longer than trimming, and in the case of ears prevents loose hairs from getting in the ear canal.

insecurity. Instead of places where "men can be men"—that is, perform masculinity and achieve manhood in front of other men—without compromise, these shops both provide a space for achieving hegemonic masculinity and put this performance at risk. Despite not being a place of community for men, fraternizing still occurs at these shops. But it's between the barbers, who construct and regulate the homosocial environment and provide the services.

Men Are Easier

Nearly all of the barbers in this book are white men in their twenties and thirties who live outside their shop's neighborhood. They resemble their clientele in these regards. Of these four occupations, barbers are the most likely to have had family members who are barbers or stylists, which introduced them to the profession at a young age. (They are also the most likely of these four occupations to be from New York City or the metropolitan area.) But in most cases they did not want to become barbers, and/or their parents did not want them to cut hair for a living.

Most of the barbers have attended college and/or pursued a different career before deciding to cut hair for a living. A few started as barbers at upscale barbershops and have never worked anywhere else.[28] Most previously worked at either other kinds of barbershops (for example, local neighborhood mom and pop shops; "chop shops," their term for high-volume, high-speed shops; racial/ethnic shops with a homogeneous clientele, such as African American, Hispanic, or Russian shops) or women's salons. Those who worked at the former left because they wanted to work at a shop that focused on service and quality and provided stylish haircuts for a hipper and more discerning clientele. At their previous shops they often did similar hairstyles repeatedly and got treated like basic service workers. Joey compares Freemans with a neighborhood shop he used to work at: "People [at upscale shops] treat haircuts more like they *want* it, instead of it being like they *need* it. A lot of times, where I [used to work], [clients] were just getting a haircut to get a haircut; something you do because you need it. And they didn't treat you like you were a stylist or a barber. They would just be like, 'Oh, you're just doing a service for me.' As opposed to here, you get treated with more respect. You went to school for this, you trained for this."

The vast majority of men need to get a haircut at some point in their lives, but barbers see upscale shops as places men choose to go to because they either have a sense of personal style or are open to acquiring one, and they are concerned about their appearance and want to enjoy their haircut as an experience rather than a necessity.[29]

With a business model of high-quality service and attention to detail, up-scale shops also offered these barbers a chance to expand their technical skills. Miles alludes to this opportunity in his earlier quote. Ruben, who worked in a variety of shops earlier in his career, some of which emphasized speed over quality, says, "I decided that I have the skill, so I decided to take it to the full-est, like, be the best at it. That's my attitude. Certain things [in haircutting] need a little bit of attention." As with the other three occupations, when shops give their workers the resource of time to do their jobs, they can attend to their craft's finer details. Achieving mastery over the technical skills of the trade at an upscale shop among style-conscious consumers who respect them gives these workers the opportunity to gain status as hip professionals in today's ser-vice economy. As Joey stated earlier, they already feel respected by their clients, who regularly defer to them (sometimes by saying, "you're the expert").

Barbers who previously worked in women's salons, however, certainly used technical skills to provide meticulous haircuts. But they quit because they grew tired of working on women and in the feminine salon environment in general. These people wanted to cut men's hair and work in a barbershop in-stead. And they chose a new upscale shop instead of a neighborhood shop for similar reasons as the other barbers: at them they can use the full extent of their skills and knowledge of style and feel respected for what they do.

The brother of Joey's best friend owned a women's salon. Joey was in col-lege while his friend went to hairdressing school. After seeing how much money he was making (and all the women he was meeting), Joey dropped out of college, went to hairdressing school, and started working at the salon. After a few years there his feelings changed.

"Then I hated it because the salon environment's way different than a bar-ber shop. A lot of times it's really fake."

"You mean you've got to put on something for the people?" I ask.

"Yeah, and I never did do that ever in my life. It was hard to do that, es-pecially working with women all day. It's just a different vibe. They're more needy. You've got to make believe a lot. You have to make them feel better most of the time."

Like other barbers who previously worked at salons, Joey grew tired of the "emotional labor" he had to do to work on women.[30] He quit and finished col-lege. But he didn't have a clear idea of what he wanted to do with his degree.

Possessing the skills, he decided to try cutting hair again, but this time with men.

"It felt easier. Guys are just easier. It's simple. They almost always know what they want. You never have to pamper them. It just becomes a cool relationship with them, and I could be myself. It's good. I was doing the whole hair stuff for the wrong reasons: money, girls. I was trying to like it, but it never worked out."

Working at a salon made Joey be someone he wasn't.[31] Men, on the other hand, are easier for these barbers. They know what they want, and barbers can "be themselves," or "be men," when working on men in the barbershop. Haircutting techniques, however, are not what make cutting men's hair easier than cutting women's hair. "Hair is hair," as many say.[32] According to barbers who previously worked in salons, the key differences are social. Working on men's hair represents an ease and naturalness in terms of both the interaction ("We're just guys," as Van says) and the haircutting work. Van explains his decision to stop working at a salon: "As soon as I saw [Freemans] I was like, 'Yeah, I want to do that. I never want to cut a woman's hair again.' I would rather not be around another woman other than my wife again. I don't ever want to be around them at all. I can't engage in conversation with them anymore. So this [place] is the in between. It's the good parts of both. It's guys, so that is 50 percent of the equation, which is awesome. Guys are the best to deal with." By contrast, working on women's hair, with the need for putting on airs and spending emotional energy, as well as the extra products, treatments, and procedures, drifts toward being fake and unnatural.[33]

These barbers recognize the need for these men to achieve a certain look for their professional and personal lives. They share a familiarity with the city's cultural zeitgeist. Along with popular hairstyles, they also know about fashion, food, and music (and often personally know and cut the hair of people in these industries). Many also look like their shop's ideal client: young, stylishly dressed (Freemans barbers get discounts from the highly fashionable clothing store), with their own unique hairstyle and facial hair.[34] While they sometimes differ over specific definitions of and criteria for style, these barbers share an avid interest in men's style when it comes to hair and clothing. They each have a clear idea of what is a "good" appearance, with "good" possessing both functional properties (for example, haircuts that are balanced, sides that are neat, neck fades that taper evenly), and aesthetical considerations (for example, haircuts that are stylistically unconventional, cool, or unique for a client's personal look).[35] As they gain experience, they become better at discerning looks and more comfortable telling clients what they think would be "good" for them. Bret, in his early thirties, explains: "I think over time I've probably gotten better at that. At one point it used to be I'd have a client who would tell me what they want and I would say 'OK' and I would just give them what they want even if it's not the best thing for them. Now over time I've developed [an ability to] talk them out of something that I think doesn't benefit them. That's the difference between the shops in that past that I've worked and this place, more of the men's salon: trying to actually be an actual consultant to their look. They want a better look or [to know] if you think changing their look would actually benefit them."

Along with this notion of knowing what "benefits" clients and the professional desire to teach them such style, they also each hold the idea that men today "should" have a certain level of awareness of and pride in their bodies and appearance. In fact, they consider their role to not just be about hair, but the "doing masculinity" project. When I ask Thorin if teaching clients about their hair is an important part of his job, he agrees and adds: "[Also] how to be an adult, how to be a man, doing what a man should be doing. This is the way a mature adult male acts. A lot of people are not like that. It's also teaching people something about themselves they don't even know. Just investigating yourself, like how your hair is, what type of hair it is. Just put your hands to your hair, you know what type of hair you have, I'm just assuming that, you know? Smart guys, you know, probably growing up learning about themselves, and lack self-awareness."

Banter in the Male Preserve

The group banter between barbers is the most distinguishing feature of Freemans. The promise of fraternity is part of how the shop promotes itself as a masculine environment. Banter can originate between two barbers and then spread to the group, or start with a barber casually making a comment or posing a question to the group for discussion (as Miles did at the start of this chapter). For barbers at upscale shops, being a place for male bonding is integral to what barbershops *should* be like.

While it has the appearance of a performance before an audience, group banter in the shop is not an act that the barbers consciously put on for clients. It stems naturally from their personalities and relationships with each other, which several barbers (recall Miles's earlier quote) refer to as being "like a family."[36] Banter serves several interrelated functions in the shop. Barbers feel it sets their clients at ease and helps explain why they come to the shop (that is, to have an ideal barbershop experience). It also allows barbers to enjoy themselves while working, keep loose, and maintain their relationships with each other.

Another function of group banter is as a masculine cover for the more intimate, emotional, bodywork going on in the shop. Like hairdressers and stylists who mainly work on women, all barbers who mainly work on men engage in emotional labor. But emotional labor is usually seen as a feminine performance, and workers who perform it often find their work degraded. Hairdressers, who regularly work on women who earn more than they do, use emotional labor to bridge the social distance and nullify the status differences between them and their clients. But doing so comes at the expense of their technical expertise, which undermines their desire to be seen as professionals.[37] Barbers also touch their clients, listen to their problems, and offer them advice (on their hair and appearance as well as their personal lives). But the masculine-coded banter they conduct and the skills-based services they provide help to hide the emotional labor they perform.[38] In short, group talk bolsters the intended social environment of these shops, and shifts attention away from the regular touching and bodywork. And unlike men who work as women's hairdressers, they are not at risk of having their gendered performance "misunderstood" or "misinterpreted" as feminine.[39]

For barbers at upscale shops, banter reinforces the shop as a masculine environment by taking certain forms and expressing certain themes. At the start of this chapter, the banter shifts from storytelling (marijuana experiences) to a hypothetical situation ("Would you ever stab somebody?"), both of which are common forms that banter takes. Group banter also regularly shifts from one form to another as the conversation proceeds, rarely ending in the same form in which it began. In terms of its content, the barbers challenge one another ("I think you couldn't even do it") and joke around, including by making essentializing comments about ethnicity (Puerto Ricans are violent). Given their familiarity with each other and their different backgrounds (for example, Italian, Jewish, Puerto Rican), the barbers regularly make ethnicity and ethnic stereotypes a theme of their banter. While they do not cause offense among each other, it is possible their comments do for clients, who are not part of the shop's social circle or "in" on the jokes.[40] Among the other themes barbers cover are women and relationships, sports, cars, music, food, and personal manhood. And among the forms that group banter takes, teasing, or "talking shit," stands out the most.

I'm sitting in the shop on a Thursday afternoon when the barbers start talking generally about relationships. The conversation shifts to household responsibilities. Not all the barbers are married or living with a girlfriend, but they weigh in anyway on what men should do in a relationship. Van says he lets his wife handle a lot of their family's business, such as bills and the mortgage.

"Man, you're whipped," says Ruben.

"How am I whipped when I make my wife take care of my shit?" replies Van. "She's already been creating a file for our next truck."

"Wait, truck?" asks Mark.

"Yeah," says Van, somewhat embarrassedly, "my wife drives a truck."

"And you drive a Prius!" interjects Ruben.

"It has good gas mileage! I have to drive from Westchester! You know what says 'I have a giant penis?' A Prius."

"You know what says, 'I have a giant penis'?" asks Ruben, rhetorically. "A giant penis."

While he tries to defend himself, Van realizes he is now the target of teasing and that his argument is indefensible. Accepting defeat, he laughs it off. The banter then shifts along to the subject of cars as the barbers start talking about wheel rims.

In this episode the barbers see the opportunity to tease Van for not being the one in charge in his family. They jump on the idea that he is neither representing hegemonic masculinity nor a status as an independent, self-made man. Of the many options he has during this bout of "shit talking," Van chooses engagement.[41] In doing so, however, he accidentally opens himself up for further teasing. The threat to Van's masculinity is obvious to the barbers, who are well-versed in the basic ideas of what displaying true manhood should be about (for example, driving a certain type of car). But being the center of teasing does not have structural consequences within the social order of the barbershop. Van, the head barber, does not decline in status within the group; tomorrow he will do his share of teasing other barbers. He is not a "lesser" man or barber vis-à-vis the others because of these facts about his life that threaten his continuous pursuit of ideal manhood. By participating he remains an upstanding member of the group while also contributing to the notion of the barbershop as a space where such masculine-coded behaviors (being in charge of the family, driving trucks) are normative.

Like talk itself group banter has rules.[42] "Taking it" when being teased, as Van does, and not getting upset, is one. Barbers expect targets to not take offense when they get teased and recognize that it is essentially their turn. They label those who get upset as "insecure," because they are not comfortable enough to laugh at themselves, a true sign of being comfortable in one's own manhood, when others point out how they deviate from what is normative.

One afternoon the barbers start teasing Mark, exaggerating his New York accent, which they do often. Interestingly, he is not even in the shop, having gone to lunch. Van's client asks him who they are impersonating.

"It's a guy we all like, but he has a thick Long Island accent and says funny things. [To the other barbers] Hey, the other day he said to someone, 'You got nice, small feet. I wish I had little feet like that, eight-and-a-half. I like the petiteness,'" says Van, in a deep and scratchy baritone.

After laughing at the impression, Ruben says, "I'm going to be on him today. He's fucked."

"He gets upset when we make fun of him," adds Miles.

"That's because he's insecure," says Joey. "He should be able to take it."

The barbers know that Mark recently moved into his parents' house on Long Island temporarily while he finds a new apartment in the city. When he returns from lunch, they pick up this fact as a theme.

Van says in his "Mark voice," "Why'd you wash those jeans, Ma? They were just getting good."

Mark usually chooses "inaction" in response to teasing from his fellow barbers.[43] He often just shakes his head with an annoyed grin and ignores them. But after more teasing, Mark says, "Come on, I'm shaving a client."

"He's laughing too!" says Jason.

"I'd like to not laugh when I have a blade to his face."

"Oh, you won't cut him that bad."

"You're a retard," says an agitated Mark.

The barbers like Mark as a person and respect him as a barber. They regularly chat, go to lunch, and hang out outside of work. But in the group context while within the shop they expect him to accept their teasing of his quirks. It's part of the rules of group banter, and doing so demonstrates membership in the fraternity, or being a "part of the family."[44] Deviating from the shop's cultural script by complaining about being teased results in a condemnation of being insecure in his confidence and manhood. Meanwhile Mark's client, whom he does not know, chuckles along with the barbers' teasing as he gets a shave, but does not participate in it. He understands the playful displays and condemnations of behavior in spite of not knowing anyone personally.

There are limits, however, to group banter's adherence to the ideals of hegemonic masculinity. According to prior research, to display hegemonic masculinity in typical homosocial settings, men must compete with each other in some form.[45] When "talking shit" during banter, barbers regularly hype their abilities and sense of style as the best in the shop. In more personal dialogue, barbers honestly assess themselves and the talent level in the shop.

While running his fingers through his client's hair after the consultation, Van asks, "Where did you get your hair cut last?"

"Here."

"Who?"

"The guy over here next to you."

"Miles."

"It was good."

"Yeah, it's a good cut, that's why I asked."

Meanwhile, from the corner chair, Mark asks Jason, "Hey, will you shave me after work on Sunday?"

"Why?"

"A friend who's a hairstylist wants to learn while you do it."

"OK, but I'm not the best shaver here."

"You're good. You're better than me, and you could show him well."

While competition factors into banter as a mark of typical hegemonic masculine behavior and manifests in such exchanges as a form of "shit-talking," it disappears when honesty enters the conversation. Barbers have no problem admitting when they are not as good at something as someone else, as Jason does, pointing out who is better at it than they are, as Mark does, or openly complimenting each other, as Van and Mark do. They do so among each other and with their clients.

Along with such open admissions, barbers in upscale shops also sometimes discuss matters of a personal nature with each other while in the group context. They talk about relationship issues, family problems, health concerns, and other sensitive topics. Sometimes the barbers seek out advice, and sometimes they only want to vent their feelings. In short, they are not as emotionally detached as men are expected to be in a homosocial environment.[46]

One Friday Joey and Miles continue a conversation about a friend of Joey's that they began outside the shop while on a break. Their backs face each other as they work on clients, and their voices carry over the din of the shop. Joey has an old friend from childhood from whom he has grown apart. But while this friend originally included him in his wedding party, he removed him from it when Joey apparently wasn't as involved in the wedding planning and events as his friend would have liked. So Joey said he just wasn't going to go to the wedding at all.

"We've had some disagreements and I said I didn't want to be in the wedding party, but he insisted," says Joey.

"Well, it's probably his girl who's telling him to remove you," says Miles.

"Yeah."

"When is it?"

"It's next week. Now I'm not even going."

"He's basically saying that you could come, but he doesn't want you there."

"Right. I try to ask him to meet for dinner in the city, but he always turns me down. We've been texting each other to try to talk. You could tell how anal he is."

"Are you sure it's him, though?" says Miles, offering some analysis.

Visibly hurt, Joey nods a little to show he understands, but does not answer. He continues his preparation to shave a client, while Miles cuts someone's hair. They pause the conversation and continue working on their clients for a few minutes. Joey then breaks the silence.

"His mom used to always call my mom."

In short, while group banter comes off as maintaining and promoting the ideal of hegemonic masculinity in the homosocial barbershop, the barbers' segmented group behaviors show an environment with more differentiated meanings. The exclusion (or noninclusion) of clients betrays the individual-oriented nature of the shop, rather than the community-oriented goal owners seek to achieve. While not a fake performance put on by barbers, group banter and the male camaraderie it signifies nevertheless resemble a performed, nuanced masculinity before an audience.

There are two major exceptions to the group banter performance at Freemans Sporting Club, one based on gender and the other based on race. The role that women play in group banter furthers the shop's image as a homosocial space. Quite simply, the shop's one full-time woman barber, Coco, does not participate in it. In her mid-thirties, Coco is originally from Tokyo and decided to get into hairstyling after a dissatisfying career in accounting and a desire to work with people more directly. She always wanted to work with men ("Women are too much drama," she says), and first worked in a high-priced men's salon in Midtown before coming to Freemans because she preferred the barbershop environment. She gets along with the other barbers very well, and they regularly chat together one-on-one and in small groups. She has her own regular clients, with whom she has friendly conversations. When Coco has an interesting client, such as someone with an unusual haircut request or who talks loudly, the barbers regularly ask her how it went after he leaves, as they do with each other. But during group banter, Coco largely stays silent, offering no hypothetical situations or personal stories. She neither teases nor gets teased. The other barbers also do not tone down the overtly masculine content of their normal conversations with each other when speaking with her, another unexpected occurrence when a woman enters a man's homosocial environment.[47]

A competitive distance runner, Coco snacks on carbohydrate- and protein-rich foods during the course of the day. While sitting around on a break, Van notices Coco's large Tupperware full of snacks.

"Jesus Christ!" he says. "You have to eat all that by the end of the day?"

"Yes. You want some?"

"No, that makes me fart, but thank you. How was your trip, it was good?"

"Oh my God—"

"That's the first relaxing vacation you've taken."

"—I ran, but still."

"You ran a race?"

"No, but every morning."

Women are part of the social life of the barbershop as frequent topics of conversation. Barbers regularly discuss wives, girlfriends, dates, friends, and celebrities in personal and joking ways and to demonstrate and reinforce their own manhood. But Coco, a woman who is physically present in the shop, stays out and is kept out of the shop's masculine performance, which proceeds regardless of her presence.[48]

The second major exception concerns a client who goes to Miles.

Hugh is an African American man around 30 years old. He is husky, of average height, and has a slight widow's peak. Because of his experience with fades, most people of color go to Miles, and Hugh heard about him and Freemans from a friend. On his first visit Miles sits him down and stands facing him, leaning on one elbow against his station—his usual pose for consultations.

"So what do you want to do?" he asks.

"Well, I didn't like what they did to me at another shop. Now, I'm losing some [hair] over here [points to widow's peak], but I want to blend it into my hairline, you know?"

Miles listens and assesses his request. "I can do that, but *next* haircut. Right now it's like this is up [points to one side of the receding area], then it comes down, then it goes back up, and you just want it straight. I gotta even this out first, so I can do it, but in a month. Do you want to do that?"

"Do what you gotta do."

Miles puts on the apron, gets his tools ready, and begins the haircut while Hugh checks his phone. After a few minutes Hugh asks Miles, "You into boxing?"

"Yeah. In fact, I've been doing some training."

"Where?"

"Right down over here."

"Yo, that shit's crazy. You watching the Mayweather fight?"

Van then tells me to check out something he's doing with his client and I lose track of Miles and Hugh's conversation. After a few minutes talking with Van I notice the din in the shop has risen.

"Mike Tyson is the smartest and dumbest person," says Hugh, loudly and clearly to the group, as a barber would do.

"Yeah, but you saw that shit he did to Holyfield?" says Ruben.

"Holyfield? He's smart, he went to college," adds Mark, to some laughter.

"I don't trust any athlete that says they went to college," says Van.

"What I can't get into is that MMA [mixed martial arts] shit," says Hugh. "I'm too old school."

Agreeing, Miles says, "Those guys are standing for like three seconds, then some guy kicks and falls down and waits for the guy to jump on him."

"I don't know," says Ruben, "I have to disagree with you Miles. Check this out. You see this?"

Ruben stops working on his client and takes out his phone out of his pocket to show people a video of an intense MMA fight. He walks over to Miles's station to show him and Hugh.

"Whoa!" they both exclaim after watching a flurry of punches.

The conversation flows freely among the barbers and Hugh. He talks with them comfortably, as if he's been coming to the shop for years. Hugh returns the next month. When I walk into the shop I find him in the waiting area as

Miles finishes with a client. Miles remembers him and they slap hands into a half-hug.

"So what do you think? You wanna keep going?" he asks a seated Hugh.

"Yeah, let's do that."

A few minutes into the haircut, Miles and Hugh start talking about food and restaurants, particularly bagels, pizza, and Italian food in general.

"You ever go to Areo's, in Bay Ridge?" asks Hugh, loud enough for anyone to answer.

"Yep, but I like Lucchese," says Miles. "Also, Staten Island's got some good pizza places."

"Joey's parents ruined me on Italian food," says Ruben, joining in (Joey isn't here today). "They made me a homemade meal once. [Shakes head.] That shit was the fucking best, bro. But I like Cirelli's for Italian."

"That's not Italian Italian, though," says Hugh.

"No, but it's Italian influenced."

"Yo, you know a place called Ma Peche, where they use a lot of fat as an ingredient?" asks Miles.

Barbers almost always talk to their client through the mirror, while they stand behind the chair. They usually only face them directly when they have to go to the station to put down or get something. During this cut, Miles regularly stops what he's doing simply to walk around to the front of the chair, so he can face Hugh directly during the conversation, not to get anything. And at times he turns the chair around so he can face the shop rather than the mirror.

The conversation shifts to what kind of restaurant they would open if they had a chance, with Hugh saying he'd want to have a place for high-end Latin American food. At this point Miles is not even halfway done with the haircut, because he's been stopping so often to talk.

"What's the difference between a Caesar fade and a fadeup?" asks Hugh.

"A Caesar fade doesn't exist. I could do a fade, instead of a fadeup."

After a few minutes of the barbers just focusing on their clients, the conversation then turns to movies.

"I think Benicio Del Toro is one of the most underrated actors," says Ruben, who says he recently rewatched the movie *The Usual Suspects*.

"Oh! Benicio Del Toro!" says Hugh. "He's nice."

The group talks about movies and actors a bit more, with other barbers joining in, until the conversation dies down again. Hugh then reignites the group banter.

"I went to a Kanye [West] concert in Atlantic City, and there were all these smokers. Man, I'm not used to that."

"I know," says Ruben. "Even though I am a smoker, I appreciate that you can't smoke in restaurants in New York."

"I like cigars and weed, but not cigarettes. And I don't allow smoking in my apartment. That's why I bought a vaporizer."

"How's that work exactly?" asks Miles.

And so the conversations go. I observed a few clients make a loud comment to the group banter here and there, but it never lasted, and they never initiated it. But right from the jump, and without knowing anyone, Hugh starts small conversations that grow. Barbers at Freemans usually start their one-on-one conversations with clients, and usually they just make simple chitchat ("Any weekend plans?" "Crazy weather, isn't it?"). Hugh's simple statements can easily lead to a longer discussion about the topics.

Freemans becomes a community-oriented barbershop when Hugh comes in, a place where clients fulfill social needs as well as grooming needs. Given the racial backgrounds of him and Miles, the easiest comparison is the African American barbershop. But really, any barbershop that operates "for" a specific group, or "for" people who live nearby, compares well. These places are not just about getting a haircut. They are hangouts, male preserves. They are where men—both barbers and clients—can challenge each other, tease each other, call each other out, brag, and, most importantly, put their manhood on display in front of other men. In these cases, their masculinity intersects with their race and/or ethnicity. These shops are safe spaces not just where men can be men in front of other men, but where black men (or Dominican men, or Russian men, or Chinese men) can be black men in front of other black men. Perhaps because of his familiarity with the social dynamics of the black barbershop, the group banter among the barbers he heard before sitting in the chair, and his barber's appearance as a person of color, Hugh felt comfortable to treat Freemans as a communal space, where conversations flow and clients interact with other barbers and other clients. The barbers talk with as much enthusiasm when he's in the shop as they do among each other. He may think such open conversations involving clients are common at Freemans. But while they seem normal, his visits give the shop a rare communality its owners strive to achieve.

4 | SHOW THE ANIMAL

Local. Natural. Meaty.

—*Motto of Dickson's Farmstand Meats*

Eat Real Food.

—*Written in red-lettering on a billboard facing the eastbound Brooklyn-Queens Expressway, on top of the Brooklyn Kitchen, location of the Meat Hook butcher shop*

Tuesday is delivery day at Dickson's. Joe, the driver, goes to the Double L Ranch, about twelve miles west of Albany and two-and-a-half hours north of New York City, to pick up the animals and drive them down to the shop in a refrigerated truck. A small, family-owned and operated abattoir, Double L slaughters animals for Dickson's from its nearby farmers.[1] Depending on the week and season, the shop gets five to six steers, eight to ten pigs, and four to six lambs per week.[2] The pigs and lambs are slaughtered the day before delivery. These come sawed in half along the spine. The steers are slaughtered two weeks before. These dry age in Double L's refrigerator before delivery, and arrive quartered: sawed in half along the spine, and then split into shoulder and hind sections, with the rib section removed separately (imagine a giant chainsaw hanging from a high ceiling, which is what they use to accomplish this task).*

---

* Dry aging is a process that involves letting beef hang at near-freezing temperatures for several weeks, which allows water to evaporate from the muscles, leading to more highly concentrated flavor, and the enzymes to break down the tough connective tissue and muscle, leading to more tender meat. Dry aged meat costs more because the product is kept off the market that much longer (as with aged spirits), and because the meat weighs less after the water

One Tuesday at around 10:30 a.m. Joe backs the truck up to the loading dock on 16th Street. I help Giancarlo, Aldo, and JM (short for Jose Manuel) unpack it. We've mostly been preparing for the delivery all morning by printing labels for the bags and filling the display case with what remains from last week's delivery. Along with the hanging meat, in the truck are boxes of offal, removed from the animals after slaughter.* We carry the sections into the walk-in refrigerator, and the butchers will break them down over the next few days. After the weekend the walk-in is fairly empty. By the end of the day it will be bursting, the shelves loaded with vacuum-sealed bags of primal cuts and trim.† Delivery day is also beef day. We bring most of the beef sections into the walk-in, and take two out into the cutting area. The sections are very heavy, and despite being nearly frozen, very messy. Blood stains our white butcher coats, aprons, and gloves, and bits of fat stick to our hats. Small pools of blood form under the animals in the walk-in. With two hind quarters hanging from the rail, in full view of the shop, Aldo asks JM, "Ready?" Sharpening his scimitar knife, JM nods his head. They bump fists, grab their hooks, and get to work.

Meghan, the other intern, and I await the primal cuts the butchers will hurl in our direction after removing them from the carcasses. Tip-cap, eye round, shank, flank, sirloin, tenderloin, culotte. When the hindquarter is done, they bring out the shoulder. Brisket, Tiberio, chuck neck, platanillo, top blade, clod. Meghan and I stuff each of them in a bag, slap on a label, vacuum seal them, and set them aside to go in the walk-in. With so many cuts, we sometimes have trouble identifying them all correctly. I try to memorize the cuts' unique features: chuck neck (large, kind of ribbed on one side), top blade (long, flat, thick, with a fat cap on it), sierra (kind of shaped like a trapezoid), clod (large), brisket (also large, but with a lot of fat on it), complexus (small, so stuff a lot in one bag).‡ The labels have "WO" or "SWA" written on

---

evaporates from it, which means the customer would pay less for dry aged meat compared to freshly slaughtered meat without a price increase by the abattoirs and retail outlets.

* Offal is the internal organs of animals, such as liver and heart. While it sells these parts, Dickson's also uses them to make dog food.

† Primal cuts are the whole sections of an animal that butchers remove when breaking them down. Examples include the round (top, bottom), loin, chuck, and rib. These are large sections. Butchers then break these down into retail cuts, such as beef tenderloin or a rump roast.

Trim is the bits of meat and fat butchers remove from primal cuts when making retail cuts. The butchers set it aside and use it to make ground beef and hamburgers.

‡ The nomenclature varies in meat, particularly in beef, from country to country, region to region, and even shop to shop. Dickson's, for instance, calls a cut from the top blade a flat iron

them, short for Wrighteous Organics and Sir William Angus, or the animal's specific farm, as well as the letters "K" for when it was killed (with the date from two Tuesdays ago underneath it), "P" for when it was packaged (today's date), and "U" for when it has reached its use-by date (two weeks from today).

Customers who come in are drawn to the action. They all walk over to get a closer look and take pictures with their phones. Even people walking by in the Chelsea Market's concourse outside the shop stop, stare, and take pictures. Kids have awed expressions on their faces, as they often have when they see something they've never seen before.

An hour into breaking Ted walks up to JM with bad news.

---

steak, while the Meat Hook, another craft butcher shop in Brooklyn, calls it a blade steak. The latter calls the clod heart a flat iron steak. A popular example of this phenomenon is the Delmonico steak, named after the famous New York City restaurant. It's unclear where exactly on the cow the restaurant originally got its cut from, except that it's tender with good marbling, which suggests the rib or loin sections. Some shops call their boneless rib-eye a Delmonico steak, some call their strip steak a Delmonico steak, and some don't use the name Delmonico at all (or use it for a cut from another section of the cow). And then some use the name strip steak, some New York strip steak, and some Kansas City strip steak to refer to the same boneless cut off the short loin of the cow (keep it on the bone, and it's either a T-bone steak or a porterhouse steak, but there is disagreement over how much of the tenderloin one must leave on to differentiate between the two).

Differences emerge in craft butcher shops depending on the butchers' experience and preferences. Some butchers keep large cuts whole, while some seam them out (that is, divide them up) into many smaller cuts. Dickson's, for instance, gets it sierra and feather steaks from the shoulder, between the chuck and the rib sections, but many butchers at other shops either do not know they could remove these muscles and sell them as their own steaks or prefer to leave them on the chuck or rib, to give these sections more meat.

These variations extend to other countries. Animal anatomy obviously does not vary from place to place (wherever they are raised and whatever the breed all cows and pigs have four legs, a loin section, ribs, and so on), but different breeds have their own unique features (for example, fattier, longer legs) and different regions have their own special environments (for example, grasses, water, climate) that influence an animal's growth. Most importantly, with their own cuisines and traditions, different cultures have their own preferences for which cuts to use, how to break down primal cuts, how to use them (for example, as a main part of a dish or as an ingredient), and how to prepare them (for example, grilled or braised). Since JM, the head butcher at Dickson's, is Mexican, the shop's display case features cuts and names that are common in Mexico, such as the platanillo (the cow's biceps) and the bistec norteño (from the round section, popular in northern Mexico). As I discuss later in this chapter, JM has a lot of experience breaking down and deboning whole animals, and Mexican butchers in general seam out sections and primal cuts into many smaller pieces, hence the significant and unusual (to most Americans) variety in the shop's case. This combination of unique cuts and varying nomenclature creates special challenges for counter workers at craft butcher shops. I examine these issues in more detail in chapters 6 and 7.

Figure 8. Beef carcasses hanging in the walk-in. Photo by the author.

"A customer would like one pound of top sirloin, and two pounds of New York strip—tartared."

"Is he kidding?" asks JM, who stops cutting with a look of disgust on his face.

"No, he's not kidding."

"Fuck."

"That's a lot?" I ask.

"Yeah."

JM loves breaking down whole animals. He could do it all day long. The disruption to his routine for a time-consuming order bothers him. He goes to the display case and walk-in and gets the cuts. He grabs two knives, one smaller than the other. He rocks the large one in his right hand along the curved edge as if chopping vegetables. With his left hand he's holding the knife normally, but slicing away from him. The knives' tips are facing each other, and as he slices the meat the blades touch each other slightly, creating a chinking sound common in movie sword fights. The motions are very smooth and fluid, which captivates his audience.

"That's a wonderful technique!" says a woman who is with her husband. "I've never seen that before. How did you learn it?"

JM stops and looks around a little bit with a grin on his face.

"In Mexico."

"Oh, that's how they do it in Mexico? Wow."

"Yeah."

"It's really wonderful."

"Thank you."

New whole-animal butcher shops have emerged alongside the rise of the "foodie" movement. Indeed, the food industry in general is a leading locus in the United States for the emergence of "artisanal" and craft-based endeavors. Food is an indicator of social status, and haute French cuisine (including the tender filet mignon) used to have a stranglehold on highbrow taste in food.[3] But in today's age of cultural omnivorousness, when the boundaries surrounding high and low culture have become blurred, savvy consumers look deeper into a food item's provenance, such as who made it, how, and where, and how exactly it got on their plate, to demarcate taste.[4] Restaurateurs and specialty food store owners have adopted terms like "craft," "artisanal," "handmade," "authentic," "small batch," and "local" for their products, and the notions of "quality" that they all imply, as integral business strategies and identities and to signify taste. Whole-animal butcher shops, where the butcher trade is being redefined, is one among many retail outlets for observing these shifts in food production and taste.

From Nose to Tail

Since European colonists first came upon its shores, the United States has been a meat-eating nation. The imported livestock thrived on the vast, fertile land. Early on, meat consumption was largely seasonal and local, as pasture-raised animals only reached an optimal weight for slaughter when grass was plentiful. But farmers began to make good use of their corn surpluses. Instead of facing the uncertainty of selling their whole crop at market, they fed it to their animals to fatten them up and turn a quicker profit.[5] By the Civil War these year-round feeding operations were widespread. In times of relative scarcity people ate or found use for the whole of the animal. Headcheese, brains, pluck, feet, and calf head soup were common ingredients and dishes.* But as production grew more efficient and meat became abundant, and as people moved to cities and increased their wealth, tastes changed. Some animal cuts and parts, such as heads, organs, and feet, which often maintained their appearance on the plate, became seen as somehow "lower" foods than internal muscles, which were simply steaks and chops. Readily available porterhouse and strip steaks, hams, roast beef, and racks of lamb became "higher" cuts, for the sophisticated, and the tenderer the better.[†] (Hence the expression living "high on the hog," or well enough to eat pork loin, not knuckles, belly, and feet.[‡]) By the late nineteenth century many Americans had become accustomed to plentiful, good, and inexpensive meat.[6]

The growth of cities during the industrial era pushed livestock operations farther west, into the country's vast open prairies, where they could expand. The advent of the national railroad system and advances in refrigeration technology—specifically the refrigerated railcar—widened the distance between farmer and marketplace.[7] Farmers in the West could ship animals and/or carcasses to urban meatpackers, who broke them down for local sale. Given the dirty nature of their work—bloody streams, pungent waste—these companies usually clustered together in cities, forming their own unique industrial zones (for example, New York City's Meatpacking District, The Yards in Chicago, Butchertown in San Francisco). Meat became a basic commodity of the industrial era, part of an efficient national system. With animals being raised in the West and broken down in specialized areas of the city, most Americans at the start of the twentieth century were completely separated from the meat production process.

---

* Headcheese refers to meat from a pig's head. Pluck is often a synonym for offal. But sometimes it just refers to an animal's heart, liver, esophagus, trachea, and lungs.

† Tender cuts tend to come from muscles cows seldom use. Imagine a cow in a pasture. She walks around and lowers her heavy head to eat grass all day, putting the most weight on her forelegs, shoulders, and chest. These muscles are the strongest, and are therefore tougher cuts of meat. The muscles in the hind section do not get as much use, especially the loin section, which is between the rib and round sections. Hence the popularity of the tenderloin, which is where filet mignon steak comes from. (Since we humans walk upright and thereby use our loin sections, they are probably not as tender as a cow's.) Cows that do not eat grass in a pasture but get fed grains have weaker muscles overall, but are fatter, which makes for a different sort of meat quality. I discuss this point later in the chapter.

‡ Pork, particularly feet, belly, and intestines, or chitlins, also took on a racial connotation as whites associated it with the diet of African Americans, especially those in the South.

But a number of postwar innovations in technology and shifts within the industry changed this arrangement. Independently owned farms had already been declining since the early twentieth century with the rise of manufacturing as workers left farm life for factory jobs in big cities. The war effort led to advances in nitrogen-based chemical fertilizers and farming equipment, which in turn led to more scientific and technological farming practices, monoculture in crops, and enormous grain surpluses. Large farming corporations adopted the basic feeding operations smaller farmers innovated and had been using for two centuries: keeping animals clustered together on feedlots and feeding them cheap grains to fatten them up quickly. But with a growing population from the Baby Boom generation, an expanding national appetite for fast food and even cheaper meat, and the price of corn at historic lows, they enlarged and corporatized the model, industrialized the process, ramped up production, and reaped huge profits. Meat businesses became adept at husbandry, and thereby at selecting breeds that best fit their production process and met consumer demand, such as Angus cows and Yorkshire pigs, which are high-fat and low-fat animals, respectively, with good durability and tender meat. (Americans generally prefer lean pork, but associate quality beef with fat marbling.) They also began giving their animals antibiotics, to ward off potential illnesses resulting from prematurely feeding them grains and from being housed in close proximity to larger numbers of other animals, and growth hormones, to hasten the fattening process.[8]

Agribusiness leaders also shifted the meat industry's geographic locations and their business structure to become even more efficient. Companies moved meatpacking from cities to rural areas to be closer to feedlots, avoid strong labor unions, and completely remove "dirty work" from populated urban environments, which fit with new urban sensibilities.[9] They also concentrated all meat production activities (from slaughtering to butchering) within large factory-style processing plants. These places divide the work of killing and breaking down an animal into a series of repetitive tasks in an assembly-line fashion: one worker stands in one station and stuns the cow, another cuts its throat, another farther down the line removes the hide, and so on, until the most popular cuts are in boxes and the rest of the animal is divided up for its usable parts.[10] The result is greater yields in less time. Meanwhile, a decreasing number of companies increasingly own a larger share of the meat industry, and a shrinking number of slaughterhouses are becoming responsible for greater majorities of animals killed for consumption in the United States.[11]

Along with these shifts in the industry came changes to meat's point of sale. The rise of the supermarket as the most popular place to buy food in the United States led to a dramatic decrease in the number of neighborhood butcher shops. With supermarkets people began buying their meat in the same manner as other foods: packaged, labeled, and with largely unknown origins. "White flight" led to the decline of the ethnic neighborhood in industrial cities (for example, "Little Italys," "Little Polands," and Jewish districts), which also aided the closing of independent butcher shops. Some of these old ethnic shops, as well as old elite shops that sell expensive and Prime-grade meat, remain in urban areas, while new ones catering to more recent immigrants (for example, Latinos, Halal shops for Muslim groups) have joined them.* As a consequence of these changes, areas like New York City's Meatpacking District aren't at all what they used to be.[12] Abutting the wealthy neighborhoods of the West Village and Chelsea, today the district is gentrifying with boutiques for clothing and accessories, restaurants, and bars.

These changes in the industry have also significantly affected the American butcher trade, which has in some cases declined in skill and/or moved completely behind closed doors. Today, most meat arrives at retail outlets frozen and vacuum packed in boxes, as either primal cuts or, more commonly, as retail cuts, reducing the need for skilled butchers. Supermarkets without meat counters often have frozen prewrapped "commodity meat," or industrial meat, shipped directly to their stores. When supermarkets have a meat counter and employ butchers, their work is mostly hidden from customers, in a back area. They prepare the cuts they receive into retail cuts, such as by breaking down primal cuts, tying roasts, or simply trimming retail cuts of excess fat, which they present in their own style in their display cases. These butchers often do not interact with customers and only work with the supermarket's chosen items. Neighborhood ethnic butcher shops—Italian, Jewish, Halal—often specialize in cuts and products that suit their group members' tastes or their culture's cuisine. Both supermarkets and neighborhood shops generally sell cuts of meat that are popular among the local population. They neither receive whole animals nor sell unusual cuts. And their butchers do

* The U.S. Department of Agriculture (USDA) regulates all meat production in the United States. At a meatpacker's request, USDA inspectors will grade the quality of the meat it produces by using a system based primarily on the meat's fat content (known as marbling) and the physiological age (or physical maturity) of the animal. There are eight grades, and the highest are Prime, Choice, and Select.

not need to know the intricacies of breaking down a whole animal. In addition to retail, butchers also work in cities' remaining meat wholesale and packing companies, where they break down animals into primal and retail cuts, and dry age and distribute products to restaurants and supermarkets. Finally, butchers work in slaughterhouses. In these latter two cases, their work is highly repetitive and regimented and, especially in slaughterhouses, kept out of sight from public view.[13] Since they generally stand in place and break down animals all day, these butchers can work very quickly, but they do not share their knowledge with the consuming public, and the animals they butcher often come from feedlots.

Points of purchase have become central in today's environment of curious and concerned food consumers. For instance, farmers' markets have spread around the country, promoting a sense of localness in food and allowing consumers to interact with farmers, the actual growers of the food they eat.[14] In general, meeting the makers of products and even seeing where they make them (such as in craft distilleries) has become a popular form of consumer tourism. With food and other items, people have become more interested in finding out where exactly the products they consume come from, how they were made, and who made them. Combined with a growing fascination with food and the rise of celebrity food culture in the United States, the importance of provenance, transparency, and these new definitions of quality make places like whole-animal butcher shops perfect additions to today's upscale retail landscape.[15]

As with mixology for cocktails bartenders, authentic production for craft distillers, and masculine style for men's barbers, a distinct philosophy undergirds the work people at whole-animal butcher shops do. Workers at shops like Dickson's hold and promote a philosophy of good taste in meat. This philosophy encompasses several moral tenets of where meat "should" come from and how it "should" be produced, which refers to how animals should be raised and slaughtered, and promotes what "good" taste in meat is. No longer based on tradition, like the consecrated tender cuts of filet mignon or prime rib, meat's status is based on where the animal comes from, how it was slaughtered and butchered, and how unique the cut is. The philosophy of craft butcher shops reflects these ideals for meat, while the shops and their workers restructure the value system that determines meat quality.

In the spirit of this philosophy, artisanal butcher shops source their meat from small-scale, independent farmers who engage in certain ethical practices.

These include raising their animals in pastures, feeding them grass, and not giving them any unnecessary antibiotics or hormones. Shop owners also ensure the animals are slaughtered at small and humane abattoirs. And the process is usually "local." In short, they shun the industrialized meat system. Jake, the owner of Dickson's, explains the importance of localness for the craft butcher movement while considering its historical context: "Local food from a meat perspective is not an old school thing. New York City has been fed by Chicago slaughterhouses for a hundred years. Before that, when the slaughterhouses were here, the animals were being put on trains live from Chicago. Saying [these shops are] going back in time is actually not true at all. We've created something totally new, us, the Meat Hook, and Marlow & Daughters.[16] I believe it is necessary to have the local component, because the entire industry culture of this mainstream commodity is so far from what people expect it to be. It's gone so off the deep end in terms of its practices that we need that accountability by having the local component. While maybe some of the things we make here and the butchering itself is an old school craft, that we are bringing in whole animals, which nobody has done for fifty years really, the fact that we are combining that traditional skill set with local sourcing is a totally new construct."

As Jake also implies, two other elements of this philosophy include using the whole animal, rather than just selling the most popular cuts, and transparency, or showing as much of the process as possible by breaking down whole animals and primal cuts in the shop in front of customers using traditional techniques. Ted, a counter worker in his mid-twenties, explains the importance of these elements: "It's to get [customers] in here and see the whole animal. Because the supermarket treats [meat] like any product. It separates you from the animal, on the Styrofoam tray, in the plastic. They treat it like Goldfish, or chips. The best way to respect the animal is to not kill it. But if you're going to, the best way to respect it is to use all of it."

On the strength of this philosophy, people at craft butcher shops lay claim to selling "good" meat. A constellation of factors beyond mere gustatory taste determines meat's quality. Jake raises some of these distinctions: "You can go to the supermarket or Lobel's and buy Prime meat and it will be delicious, but it's all feedlot beef.* It's inhumanely treated—hormones, antibiotics. I think if

---

* Lobel's is a New York City–based butcher shop that has been in operation for many decades. Located on the wealthy Upper East Side, it represents the high-end, high-priced shops that survived the rise of supermarkets.

people realized how far from what their agricultural ideal these farms are—I wouldn't even really call them farms—they wouldn't want this product. If they saw the way these animals were slaughtered and the volume that the industry is doing, they wouldn't want to buy it. The fact that they're selling this product at this ideal, this premium, Prime-grade beef, I think there's a problem there. For me, most of the problem is about humane treatment. You can find high quality, but you can't find high quality, generally, that is humanely treated."

Quality meat means it tastes good when you eat it. But it also means the animal was raised and slaughtered humanely and butchered properly.[17] These elements—a locally and humanely raised and slaughtered animal, carefully butchered with artisanal techniques—come together in the meat at craft butcher shops, distinguishing it from meat in other shops. Citing his mentor from Italy, Guy, a former butcher at Dickson's, explains: "Dario has his four pillars of righteousness that an animal needs: a good life, a good death—a respectable death—a good butcher, and a good cook to complete the circle.[18] In my view, as someone who really loves animals, I'm able to really elevate this animal that died who was going to be made for food. It was born with a destination and instead of it just being a steak or a chop, part of it going to this house and part of it going to that house, like, you make it into a real exceptional experience. That animal got to be something really special that maybe some of the other animals didn't get to be."

The butcher is but one link in the chain. They can control the work they do—namely, how they handle the meat and, in doing so, respect the animal.

"There are so many things on the spectrum that contribute to meat quality, right?" says Jeff, a former butcher at Dickson's. "It's really just a matter of, I think, what you're looking for, what's important to you [as a consumer]. If marbling is important to you, like fat content, then you could just buy a piece of meat from the Midwest, you know, boxed beef, and it's going to be consistent each time, USDA Prime, and it's going to be great. But, a bad butcher could screw up that USDA Prime cut, right? You could have a great farmer and a great product and the butcher could screw it up."

Food companies use ambiguous terms like "local," "artisanal," and "sustainable" to claim quality. They regularly use these terms to contrast what they do with other practices in their industry (such as Ted's comment about the shop's philosophy distinguishing it from supermarkets), but they are all highly debatable. There are several contested definitions in the craft butcher community. In the case of New York City, "local" usually means from upstate, and not from the Midwest, where most meat comes from (usually from feedlots). The policy at Dickson's is that the entire supply chain—from farmer to slaughterhouse to shop—does not exceed 400 miles. To provide transparency, the shop hangs small placards on the display case with the names of their farmers, the meat they get from them, and how far they are from the shop. Customers can read how Wrighteous Organics is 187 miles away and supplies the shop with beef and Sir William Angus is 235 miles away and supplies it with pork and lamb.

But for workers at other shops who also consider their meat to be "local," the supply chain is longer. The actual distance is arbitrary. Being upstate also allows workers at these shops to visit their farmers, which is both educational and enhances accountability. Tom, the owner and head butcher at the Meat Hook, emphasizes how important personal relationships are in the meat industry and for his business: "This is going to make me sound like a control freak, and I'm not really a control freak, but I like having complete knowledge of and control of the entire thing from beginning to almost end. Because it's the exact opposite of how we all grew up when it came to food. We close the shop for three or four days a year and we rent a big church van and put everybody who works for us, all of our interns and some of our favorite customers, and we drive up to go to one of our farms and we spend a couple of nights there. While we're there I teach everybody how to choose beef on the hoof, to know what to look for. If it's a diverse herd you can see one that looks really awesome and one that looks really shitty. It's like, 'OK, this looks awesome because it's square across the back and it's blocky and it has this much brisket fat and it's got a fat blob on the end of the tail.' Basically we have them slaughter in order of how finished they are. We want the ones that are not quite there to have the extra four or five weeks to get finished before they go off to the slaughterhouse. So we'll be like, 'OK, number 1, then number 68, then number 33, then number 67.' That's the kind of relationship we have with our farmers, and that's really important to us. We don't buy according to price or buzzword. We buy according to quality and who we're dealing with. We want to have a personal relationship with those farmers."

Without close proximity, these relationships and therefore meat quality would be infeasible. However, one place, Heritage Meat Shop, does not believe in only sourcing local meat, because they feel "local" does not necessarily mean "quality." As Dan, the manager, explains: "One of the things I talk to the customers a lot about is we are not local. We do have a local line and we bring that into the shop because that's what a lot of New Yorkers really like. But, the guys raising all of the rare breeds, who are raising them in large enough quantities, and doing it the right way are out in Kansas, Missouri, the middle of the country. [Our] stance on local, we're like, our stuff is better than most of the local stuff. So [if] you just want to focus on is it close to you, you're kind of doing your customers a disservice."

The people at Heritage acknowledge the power of "local" as a buzzword, a form of marketing. But location for this shop is significant insofar as the farmer raises a unique breed properly. "Good" meat comes from those farms, regardless of location. For them, distance is not and should not be a factor for quality.

Another occasional point of disagreement in the craft butcher community concerns grass-fed beef. Cows on feedlots eat all-grain diets (usually cheap corn), because it gets them fatter quicker, while grass-fed cows graze around the pasture all day, lowering their heads to eat grass, and working different muscles from cows who stand around in pens. Grain-fed cows can go to market sooner than grass-fed cows, and they're bigger. Selling and eating "grass-fed beef" has become both an ethical choice delimiting a "right" practice as well as a marketing buzzword in the food world. Not selling grass-fed-only beef puts a shop at risk of straying from the anti-feedlot element of the meat philosophy. Dickson's mostly sells "grass-fed, grain-finished" beef, or cows whose farmer lets them graze and eat grass until their final weeks of life, when he feeds them organic grains from the farm. (They also sell beef that is grass-fed only, which they source from a different farmer.) The people at Dickson's defend the grain-finished practice, citing the greater consistency in meat it yields and the humane way in which the small-scale farmer carries it out, unlike on feedlots. Jocelyn, the former head butcher at Dickson's, says: "I was at Lindy and Grundy, that was all grass-fed, grass-finished.[19] There was no corn at all, no anything. Then when I got to Dickson's, I was on my high horse, something like [spoken in a snotty voice] 'I'm sorry, I've only ever cut grass-finished' and this or that. But the way Martin [the farmer] does it, he finishes it on corn, bro, and I'm like, for lack of a better word, like I'm the same way. It's fine, it's not terrible. If you think about, people think cows are only supposed to eat grass, and that's like saying humans should only eat kale. I want a fucking French fry. They want a French fry, too. That will make them more delicious in the long run."

People in other shops, however, make a point of only selling purely grass-fed beef, for both the ethical practice it promotes and taste. As Sara, from the Meat Hook, explains: "Most of the time people are assuming grass-fed is better. Yes and no. A lot of people think it's better for you. We think so, it's better for the animals, and so on. It does taste different than grain-fed beef. Really good grain-fed beef is delicious. It's not a bad thing. We don't try to soapbox anything or make [customers] feel bad for their food choices. We just try to offer them what they might want. I would say grain-finished beef is a little more buttery. It's something that people are more used to in terms of flavor. Grass-finished beef can taste a little more iron rich, a little more . . . I don't want to say livery, but there is a difference. The meat is darker, there is more myoglobin, there is more blood being pumped to those muscles because they're moving around a lot more. It's a little mustier. I would say grain-finished beef is sort of that quintessential clean beef flavor that most people think of and conjure for themselves."

A final debate in the craft butcher community deals with breaking down animals on the butcher table or while hanging. The issue revolves around which practice is more "handmade," or more "artisanal." Cutting on a table is the more traditional way to cut meat. Hanging is a more recent practice, and faster. It's more common today in slaughterhouses and meatpacking plants, not retail outlets of any variety or style (which usually do not get whole animals to hang anyway). Guy trained by cutting on the table, but had to learn hanging while working at Dickson's. "They cut on the rail, I cut on the table," he says. "They use the hooks, use gravity. I like to seam cut. My way is a lot slower. *A lot* slower. I like to think my way is a little more precise and delicate." The goal of breaking the animals down into primal cuts is obviously the same whether they are lying on a table or hanging from the ceiling. But some craft butchers think cutting on the table provides greater intimacy between them and the animal. For Guy, cutting on the table puts him in touch with the butchery tradition: "It's hard sometimes to connect, but the work of cutting up an animal has relatively remained unchanged for let's say 5,000 or 6,000 years, maybe 10,000 years of using meat for food. When I worked at Dickson's, I asked Jake if I could come in an hour early. Because I had shit to do late in the day, can I come in early and just leave a little earlier? But really I would come in, no one was there, I would turn on like Verdi or classical and I would just slowly cut the case, and that was my time capsule. That was my Jules Verne time machine."

When the economic realities of the busy workday meet the traditional culture of slow cutting on the table, the former wins. Cutting on a table is not practical (or sustainable from a business standpoint) for shops that need to sell a certain volume of meat, because butchers simply cannot cut as much. Hanging is more efficient.

Other craft butchers think hanging requires more skill, because of the factors of gravity and the animal constantly getting pushed away from their body. And, because butchers who cut by hanging generally cut more meat, it gives them greater opportunities to use and hone their skills. Aldo trained by learning hanging in Mexico. When he moved to New York, he got a job at a shop in Brooklyn that used the table.

"It was table-style, like old school. I learned so many things cutting over there. It was not that great, but I was learning from these guys—the American way, all the cuts, all that."

"Why wasn't it that great?"

"It's good when you're first learning, because [the shop wasn't] that busy. They only have like one cow a week, maybe four pigs. The butchers there come into work, do some cutting, then walk around, then talk to customers. If you want to really get good, you work here [at Dickson's]."

Repetition is key to learning butchery, and while Aldo's former shop taught him more about table cutting and American cuts, it did not help him hone his knife skills. Besides, these butchers say, most hanging butchery is still done on the table. Butchers at Dickson's only use the rail to break down large sections of the animals, quartered cows and halved pigs and lambs. They plop these cuts down on the table after separating them from the larger carcass, and then cut them more finely. Good butchers "should" know both techniques.

Despite disagreements over its specifics, however, people in the craft butcher community agree on and work within the basic premises of a greater meat philosophy, and denounce the feedlot and industrial slaughter model of meat production, which is the status quo for much of the United States. Cultural omnivorousness in meat is a consequence of practicing this philosophy. These shops sell products that are traditionally both highbrow (filet mignon, bone-in rib eye) and lowbrow (Sloppy Joe's, hot dogs). The highbrow products are additionally distinct from those at other shops and supermarkets because of their advertised provenance and production methods, which follow from the philosophy of transparency. Meanwhile, these shops repackage products with lowbrow cultural origins as authentic and exclusive items. They sell, for instance, cuts of meat that are popular in Latin American cuisines, such as the palomilla and platanillo, and require different cooking techniques, next to more familiar American New York strip steaks and the consecrated French filet mignons. Sold in the same shop, cuts like rib eye steaks and high-end beef jerky are among the products that new upscale butcher shops present to customers as high quality and "good meat" because of the provenance of the animals and of the unique work practices that go into their creation.

The World of the Whole-Animal Butcher Shop

Coming from an entrepreneurial family, Jake always knew he wanted to own his own business. After graduating from Cornell University in 2002 and working for about six years in sales at American Express, he scratched the itch: "I had kind of been looking for the business I wanted to start. I didn't know what it was. I was really passionate about food, I worked in kitchens a little bit in college. I figured, you know, food would be a great option to start a business because I really like the topic. I was hunting around for what that business would be. At the same time, as a consumer, I was doing a lot of research and learning about meat. One day I woke up and I said, 'I'm a voracious carnivore and I know nothing about how it goes from how it's raised and how it gets to my table.' As I started doing all this research I became kind of horrified of how it did. The more I learned the less appealing I found it and also the more I looked for better options. They just didn't exist. It was either poor quality, but well-raised, or high quality and badly raised, or badly raised and bad quality. There were very few people doing it well. One day I said to myself, 'If you can figure out how to do this right, there must be a business there.'"

Jake quit his corporate job and worked on farms, at the Double L slaughterhouse, and at a small retail shop in Minneapolis. From these endeavors he learned about the industry and where he wanted to be within it. Jake started his business in 2008, buying products from farmers whose practices he respected and selling them at farmers' markets in the city. With a nationally scaled food chain model and too much competition from the Midwest, farmers in upstate New York had mostly stopped raising animals for slaughter. The rise of the city's foodie culture and consumers who desired "local" and humane products revived the practice. Jake became a retailer. While adhering to certain principles, his was a small-scale operation, still hidden from the public, and missing a personal touch (Double L's butchers broke down, vacuum-sealed, and froze the cuts, which Jake then sold). It was a start. "I kind of knew from the beginning that farmers' markets were not where I wanted to be, that the best place would be a retail shop like this one. We can do the most breadth of products and I can communicate the most with the customers to get my message out there on what I was trying to do, and get a premium as well."

He opened his shop in the Chelsea Market in 2009.[20] He got a good deal on a good space in a burgeoning foodie hotbed and a wealthy area with residents, professionals, and tourists—an enviable blend of food customers. In addition to the continuous flow of people strolling through the market's concourse, the space was raw with high ceilings leading to a loading dock in the back. It allowed Jake to create the system he wanted.

Craft butcher shops have a fluid division of labor that is not necessarily apparent at first glance. The greater the volume of meat the shop sells, the clearer the roles. To customers who walk into Dickson's, the place is like a hive, with workers zipping around carrying trays of meat, talking to customers, grilling hot dogs, coming in and out of doors, and operating large machines. Given its size and the amount of meat it sells, the shop has its own division of labor, which is based on task, reinforced spatially, and has an ethnic component. There are three sections with different sets of activities.

The first, which customers encounter when entering through the glass door from the market's concourse, is the "front of the house," or the counter area. The large, approximately 15-foot-long, enclosed refrigerated meat display case divides the room down the middle. Along with a gestalt of raw and cooked meat smells, customers immediately see the case on their left stretching out like a path in front of them. Along the wall on the right are barstools and a counter for people to sit and eat, and shelves with some condiments and other packaged goods (for example, potato chips, hot sauces, cooking oils) for sale. Some animal, meat, and charcuterie reference books also sit on the top shelves. They're not for sale, but customers may peruse them, as employees often do.

Counter workers work behind the large display case. This area features a pricing scale, butcher paper, cutting boards, some knives, a large rotisserie oven, and a refrigerator for sandwiches, bottled water, and sodas. The shop keeps some rotisserie chickens under heat lamps and a small electric grill for hot dogs in the front window facing the concourse, enticing passersby. The cash registers rest on a small table in between the large display case and a smaller, open one for prepackaged fresh products (for example, pork rillettes, chicken pates, eggs).

The second section is the cutting area, which is where the butchers and interns work. A large wooden butcher table on wheels separates it from the front of the house, but the section is fully visible to customers. Butchers stand and work behind this table, facing toward the front. Three bright lights hang from above, giving the effect that they and the meat are on display, even performing on stage (and providing the butchers with adequate light). Near the lights is a steel rail from which the animals hang. Customers lucky enough to be in the shop on a breaking day can watch the whole process, if they wish. But most of them (until around 5:30, when the butchers stop cutting) still get to watch the butchers prepare retail cuts for the display case or fill their own order, and can talk with them and ask questions if they like. This intentional design removes the common barrier between the front and back stages of meat production: the butchers perform the backstage dirty work of breaking down animals and preparing meat in the center of the shop.[21] There are also two smaller butcher tables along either wall, two large meat grinder machines, a vacuum-sealing machine, and an array of tools (for example, knives, a burger patty press, a rubber mallet) and supplies (for example, plastic bins, plastic bags).

Some people who choose to work at craft butcher shops as counter workers, butchers, or interns already have the shop's meat philosophy and meat knowledge (that is, cooking techniques) before working there. They know a lot about meat, and have a strong interest in and passion for food. They choose the shop and the shop chooses them because their philosophies match. Others already have an appreciation for food and a sense of food quality, but not necessarily the shops' meat philosophy or a substantial amount of meat knowledge. They learn both as they work there. Andy, for instance, gained an appreciation for food ethics and food systems in college, when he temporarily became a vegan. He worked on two small farms when he graduated, in Hawaii and Maryland, the latter through World Wide Opportunities on Organic Farms (WWOOF), a program that coordinates volunteers who want to work on small farms. "By the time I got out of school I knew that I wanted to do something either through the lens of sustainability or through the lens of food," he remembers. After a job on another farm fell through, Andy moved to New York City, sleeping on friends' couches, without a clear idea of what he wanted to do. He knew about Dickson's through his food circles, and became an intern. Working at the shop taught him the specifics of meat retail and meat knowledge. Without another job, Andy interned three days a week, instead of the customary two. He came in on both main breaking days, and eventually, after he gained some experience, spent the third day doing some basic cutting. An avid home cook, Andy made a mission of trying everything in the case. He was eager, and parlayed his internship into a full-time paid job as a counter worker. The knowledge he got from the cutting area came in handy: "In general, they prefer to hire people that have some meat knowledge and they prefer to hire people that either had meat knowledge that they learned at Dickson's or their own meat knowledge. And that's kind of helpful if you're working the counter because the way that we cut, the cooking recommendations that we have, that is a big part of what the counter is, is telling people how to cook. It's better to have a blank slate than it is to come from grocery store cutting, where it is completely different and you are cutting everything very thin and you're just handing the meat over the counter."

The butchers at Dickson's differ from each other in their training, which is based on their social backgrounds and attitudes toward the job. Two of the five butchers are from Puebla, Mexico. (They're actually from the same neighborhood in Puebla, but they met at Dickson's.) JM, with fifteen years of experience, is the head butcher, and Aldo, with seven years of experience, is second-in-command. They both primarily learned by working in meatpacking plants and large, high-volume stores in Mexico, such as Walmart, Soriano, and Bodega Aurrera (which Walmart owns), where breaking down whole animals is still common. (They also both worked at some smaller supermarkets and shops in New York City.) Since JM and Aldo worked with a lot of meat and sometimes with whole animals all day long at these places, they can work at a high level with great speed. They prefer such action. JM recalls when he switched jobs to work as a manager at a smaller supermarket. "It was fucking boring," he says. "Before, I was working with animals. I broke animals for eight years. But there, the meat came in boxes." This experience, however, taught JM how to properly fill and maintain a display case, which helped him when he came to Dickson's.

Like most immigrants, they both moved to New York City to earn more money. Aldo had lived in New York City and Dallas with his family when he was younger. He returned to Mexico on his own, where he began learning butchery again (he had dabbled with it earlier in his life), and then decided to move back to New York City. Unlike the front of the house workers and the other butchers and interns, these butchers are more concerned with the quality, craft, and volume of the work, rather than the shop's meat philosophy. Aldo, who speaks English very well because of the time he spent in the United States in his youth, sometimes works in the front of the house, if needed. JM, who knows some English, but is not comfortable speaking it, stays in the cutting area and only talks to customers if they ask him a question, such as about what he is cutting. While Jake and the managers prefer flexible employees, such as butchers who can cut well as well as take the initiative to interact with customers, they recognize the importance of having fast workers to reach their volume. Skilled butchery has declined in the United States, but Mexico provides craft butcher shops with much-needed talent.[22]

The other three butchers are in their thirties and well-educated: Giancarlo, from Colorado, who changed careers after a few years of managing a medical center; Brian, from Michigan, who started his own sausage company after working in marketing; and Lena, from the New York City area, who changed careers after working for eight years in marketing. Along with loving meat and food and being drawn to the craft of butchery, these three butchers also cite the shop's philosophy as an important aspect of their work. They didn't just want to become butchers; they wanted to become craft butchers, at a shop like Dickson's. Giancarlo first learned butchery from a certificate program in upstate New York. Brian taught himself how to cut pigs from making sausages and putting on underground dinners. And Lena first learned from working at a couple of smaller craft butcher shops in New York City. All three, however, really honed their skills at Dickson's by working with a higher volume of meat than they were used to and under the guidance of JM and Aldo, whom they cite as great mentors (especially JM). Given their backgrounds, they have less cutting experience and are slower than the Mexicans, but, as native English speakers with their meat philosophy and knowledge, they regularly work in the front of the house as counter workers, interact with customers, and teach educational classes the shop offers.[23]

Given their training, JM and Aldo care about speed more than the other butchers. For the others, quality, nuance, and contributing to the greater principles of craft butchery trump quantity and quickness.

"I'll never be as fast as JM," says Giancarlo. "As far as cutting the meat and the whole animal, he has been doing it for sixteen years. I've been doing it for two, not even, but I've come along quite a bit. I don't want to be that good. I mean, I would. I would want to be that good, but I don't have the time to do that as far as my aspirations to do something in the future of my own. I just don't, it's not conducive for me to know how to do everything JM does."

Craft butchers want to be good at the craft. But the craft to them includes creating a relationship between people and meat, discussing meat with others, working with meat in different ways (such as for entertainment and education), and constantly learning (and wanting to learn) more about the animal and its cuts. JM and Aldo understand their work differently.

"Actually, right now, for me, the way that I think I am a butcher, I can't learn anymore," says Aldo. "Well, I learn little things, but the thing is, I don't know, it is fun because what I do over there [at Dickson's] is real easy for me now compared with over there in Mexico. This, for me, is a game. Seriously, this is a game. I mean, it's my job and it's serious, but I know what I know already. What else can I do? What else can I learn about this? For me, maybe it's more about [learning] customer service, more about how to tell them how to do it, how to cook it, blah, blah, blah."

While Aldo sees butchery as cutting, which he has already mastered because of how fast he can work, with customer service and interaction as separate, the other butchers conceptualize craft butchery as more of a package of cutting, interacting, and learning, in the name of a meat philosophy.

The third section is the "back of the house," or the kitchen. This area is where two chefs and two assistants do "value-added" work by preparing such items as the fresh lunches (for example, cold cuts and pulled pork sandwiches), chickens for the rotisserie, charcuterie (that is, prepared meats, like bacon and guanciale, a type of salami), stocks, and sausages. The kitchen is also where the porters clean dirty items. A swinging door divides the kitchen from the cutting area, and just inside it are tall storage shelves and the large walk-in refrigerator. The head and sous chefs are both American, one white, the other of Chinese descent, respectively. The assistants are Hispanic (Guatemalan, Mexican, and Cuban), and the porters vary in race and ethnicity.[24]

In concert, these three sections help Dickson's adhere to its meat philosophy while selling a high volume of meat, specifically when compared to other new upscale butcher shops.[25] A basic but significant issue whole-animal butcher shops face is selling the whole animal. Supermarkets and most butcher shops, who usually buy their meat wholesale from large suppliers, do not have this problem. As Jake explains: "For me, my economics are totally different. I have to sell the entire animal. So, charging a lot for one [cut], I mean, I get every [cut]. If I raise the price and people don't buy it, then I'm stuck with it. It's not like I can say I've got a market for five cases of New York strip, so I'm gonna buy five cases of New York strip. I have to buy by the whole steer and the whole pig."

In a country where most people grow up buying meat from supermarkets or basic butcher shops, and thereby expect a shop to carry their favorite cuts, places like Dickson's present customers with a shopping challenge.

When entering the shop and seeing the large display case, with its unusual cuts and their bizarre names (Tiberio, platanillo, sierra), customers regularly stare with looks of wonder, confusion, and fear (sometimes all three). They also may not see the cuts they know. As Charlie, a counter worker, explains, "There are two hanger steaks per cow, you know what I mean? We're not going to all of a sudden have thirty hanger steaks available. It's just not going to happen." If they run out of a cut, they run out. The job then falls on knowledgeable counter workers like him to decipher the mysteries of the case, and explain how cuts are similar or dissimilar and how they may be prepared.[26] Without them and their knowledge, the rare cuts the shop must sell enough of to stay in business will likely go unsold.

Functional Aesthetics

While counter workers communicate the shop's meat philosophy through words, butchers do so through actions. The goal of their work is "functional aesthetics," to prepare meat—for the display case and for special orders—in a manner that combines a clean, natural, and pleasing presentation, an optimal gustatory taste, and an ease of preparation for the customer, in addition to the instrumental goal of food as nutrition.[27] Through certain skills, which concern aesthetical and technical decisions, they must endow meat with these qualities. They take meat whose specialness is based on the shop's philosophy and aesthetical goals (form) and enhance its cookability and gustatory taste (function). In this sense, craft butchers intertwine cultural and material production through their work.[28]

Like sculptors, butchers start with a large slab of raw material and use learned techniques and sensory considerations (that is, the look, taste, and mouth feel of meat) to gradually cut and trim it down into finer, more distinct pieces. Butchers often mention what a cut "should" look like, or how the work "should" be done to make it look that way. Different shops and butchers vary on these points, and how a shop wants a cut to look influences butchers' work.[29] Through years of practice, butchers learn to embody these required skills for breaking down an animal to prepare meat in a way that will make it look presentable and be easy for customers to prepare.[30] The exact technique they use may vary, depending on how they have embodied it, but it must result in a specific product, according to how either the shop or the customer wants it to be. Guy says that he was taught to use his knife, "Without fear and without fury," or, with confidence and careful precision, otherwise he risks ruining the meat. Confidence is the result of embodied practice, which comes through focus and repetition.

The goal of functional aesthetics is to use specific techniques to give meat the qualities that will reflect its "good-ness," despite the fact that it may actually look and taste differently from time to time because the raw material is natural. They especially concentrate on functional aesthetics for the display case. These meanings emerge when butchers provide instruction to each other.

One day Giancarlo works on deboning and tying a leg of lamb. Dickson's debones this cut because doing so makes it cook evenly when roasted, which is a common way to prepare it. He starts by scraping around one of the bones and separating the cut, trying to get as much meat off of it as possible. Aldo is working next to him and giving advice.

"Do I take the bone out this side?" asks Giancarlo.

"Yeah, always that side," replies Aldo.

After removing the bones he lays the cut flat, skin-side down, and removes excess fat while leaving some on. Giancarlo then rolls the leg up and uses twine to hold it together. Leg of lamb is a combination of muscle, fat, sinew, and other connective tissue, which means it is rather floppy when removed from the bone. Tying the leg and keeping it in a roll makes it highly presentable and also helps it cook evenly by making sure its contents are compact and stable. The goal is to tightly tie the twine in several places on the leg, starting with one in the middle, then one on either end, and then filling the spaces in between. Giancarlo goes slowly, taking his time and being meticulous.

"Just do it fast," says Aldo. "Don't fight with it."

"How do you make it tight?" Giancarlo asks.

Aldo then shows him the two knots—one that tightens the twine around the meat, and one that holds the first one in place—and where to put his hands on the leg. "That's how I tie it. You want to make it tight, but not too tight. You don't want to press the meat."*

After he finishes I ask Giancarlo about his performance. "I never worked with lamb before. And tying meat that's rolled up like this is hard. It keeps squishing when you tie it. It's like trying to tie a water balloon."

---

* By "press" the meat, Aldo means not wanting to tie it so tightly that the twine slices into it.

FIGURE 9. Giancarlo tying a pork loin. Photo by the author.

The leg of lamb at Dickson's is special because of its provenance (for example, raised humanely by a local independent farmer). But Aldo teaches Giancarlo how to debone and tie it in a manner that will endow the meat with the ease of preparation, at the same time as it makes it look presentable for customers. But the technical practices that craft butchers use take on an added importance because of the perishable nature of meat. A key example is how they make hamburger patties.

I walk into the shop on a Thursday morning and Giancarlo says he has to talk to me after I get changed into work clothes. After doing so, I go back to the cutting area.

"Your burgers suck. They wanted me to tell you that we had to throw out your burgers and ground beef that you did last week after a few days. They got too brown. You probably had them out too long and put your hands on them too much. So they got old too fast."

I apologize. I thought I had gotten the hang of making burgers and ground beef. I knew that beef loses its red color when it gets warm, and I tried to make sure I did not have the meat in my hands for long and only took the trim out of the walk-in when I was ready to grind it and make the patties.

"Don't worry about it," says Giancarlo, "it's not a big deal. Just make sure they're not out very long. And don't handle them too much. It's really fine."

Like the other meat in the display case, the butchers at Dickson's want to make sure the burgers are perfect, like red hockey pucks. Meat that begins to lose its redness and turn brown is still edible, but the shop does not keep it on display because they feel customers will not want to buy it. It must convey quality. The butchers use several steps to ensure the burgers are presented nicely and appetizingly. First, they put down several flat rectangular pads (which they call "diapers") that absorb the juices that may run down on the tray. Since the display case shelves are on a downward angle, presenting the meat directly at customers, juices cannot collect at the bottom end, pooling and possibly dripping. They then cover these pads up with two sheets of butcher paper, cut crosswise. Making the meat for burgers consists of grinding beef trim once, and then grinding it again more coarsely after mixing in large chopped chunks of bacon ends (the recipe is 80 percent lean beef and 20 percent fatty bacon). It is important to mix it up well so that the fattier bacon is evenly distributed among the leaner beef. They then weigh out half-pound balls using a kitchen scale and use a press to make perfectly shaped patties. The patties are placed on the tray in four rows of three, three levels of patties, with individual paper squares separating the levels.

As Giancarlo explained, it is important to accomplish these tasks quickly, because the meat should not be unrefrigerated for long. I also do not want to handle the balls of meat for too long with my hands, because their warmth will only speed up the "browning" process. So I try to work as quickly as possible. Aldo stops what he is doing, comes over to me, and notices something wrong with the burger patties I am making.

"No, no, no. You've gotta pack it tight. See these spaces? It's gonna break apart when you cook it. So press it hard, like a circle [he makes a gesture with his hands that looks like he's holding a baseball] in your hands, then press it."

I do as he says, packing it tight in my hands.

"I don't want to hold it too long."

"Right, right. That's why you gotta do it hard and thorough, but quickly. You gotta pack it quickly."

I quickly pack the clump of meat in between my cupped hands as hard as I can without it oozing out. He nods in approval. I then put the ball in place and pull down on the pressing machine.

"You have to press it more."

I try again.

"More, more," he says as he sees that I am not pressing down enough.

I finish and show him the patty.

"That looks delicious! Give me three!"

In the grand scheme of whole-animal butchery, making burger patties does not require significant skill. Unskilled interns regularly make burgers at Dickson's. They're important because they are a popular product and made out of otherwise unusable meat (that is, trim). But like all meat sold at the shop, from the highbrow (leg of lamb) to the lowbrow (beef jerky), the burgers have to maintain a specific look (reddish in color, evenly distributed fat) and structural integrity (packed and pressed tightly without spaces, for ease of preparation) that combine with the meat's unique provenance (reflective of the shop's meat philosophy) to make a product with a certain gustatory taste (which may vary). These are the lessons in consistency that butchers practice and try to impart.

As these episodes show, most of the conversations between butchers focus on the practicalities of their work, not the special meanings behind the meat, such as the virtues of eating locally or the authentic or exotic nature of the products they sell. When busy or performing routine tasks, they can just "be butchers" and go on autopilot, confident in their embodied knowledge.[31] Overall they focus on how to efficiently intertwine form and function, and work comfortably with faith in the superiority of the meat they use. A trained eye could discern meat's provenance (for example, marbling level as an indicator of a cow having been grass-fed only or grain-fed only), but otherwise the specialness of its origins is hidden in the meat, and butchers aim for consistent appearances.

Some businesses in the meat industry use elements of the business model of craft butcher shops. But workers at these upscale shops who promote such a philosophy are the latter's key distinguishing feature. Most importantly, these workers play key roles in putting this philosophy into practice. Butchers in other settings, such as slaughterhouses, use many of the same skills as craft butchers. Craft butchers are different because in addition to having a meat philosophy, the context of the shop—with its whole animals, rare cuts, butchery on display, and location in a place high in cultural and "culinary" capital—elevates the craft of butchery to that of "craft butchery."[32]

PART II

While each of the chapters in part I focused on one occupation, the four chapters in part II all provide a cross-occupational analysis based on a common theme. My aim is to show how workers from across these different occupational communities interpret various aspects of their industries, jobs, and everyday work lives through their words and behaviors, and explain why these meanings are important for understanding work today. I examine all four occupations in each chapter except chapter 7, which focuses on serving consumers and omits craft distillers, who do not engage in service.

I organize part II to discuss who gets these unique jobs and how they get them, what they do in them, and how they keep and excel in them. The chapters cover four unique themes. First, I show the paths workers take to pursuing these typically low-status jobs as careers without experiencing them as downward social mobility. The following two chapters examine the cultural repertoires these workers enact—namely, the role their sense of craft plays in their work practices and how they have come to interpret some aspects of these practices as creative, and the set of service work practices they engage in to teach their omnivorous tastes to consumers. Finally, I analyze how they become socialized into performing these cultural repertoires in their occupational communities with confidence—and how and why some people are not able to do so. While my theoretical goal in these chapters is to synthesize the behavioral explanations for these disparate empirical cases, I also point out examples of divergence and variation.

HOW MIDDLE-CLASS KIDS *WANT* WORKING-CLASS JOBS

5

The New York City Bar and Wine Show takes place every June at the Jacob Javits Convention Center, on the Far West Side of Manhattan. A trade event for bars, restaurants, and nightclubs, the Bar and Wine Show has exhibitors who promote products like lighting, sound, and security systems; absinthe fountains; plastic trays with special holders for shots; and, of course, wine and liquor. Booze brands hire women models to wear skimpy clothing and pass out free samples (in plastic trays with special holders for shots) in front of their booths. A party bus company parks its product in the back; the pounding bass can be felt from a hundred feet away. Flair bartenders compete.

Members of New York City's cocktail community have been working at the event over the past few years. They lead seminars, make cocktails for brands, and, quite simply, promote themselves. The United States Bartenders' Guild (USBG) has its own booth and small space for demonstrations. At the 2010 show, Maxwell, a young up-and-coming bartender at Jack the Horse Tavern and a consultant, stands behind a makeshift bar and prepares a drink, while Jonathan, the USBG's president and the president of his own consulting group The Cocktail Guru, stands to the side and narrates the steps and ingredients. He makes sure to name the products of their sponsors (Tuthilltown's Four Grain Bourbon, in this case). Convention visitors—industry folks and consumers alike—sit in rows of folding chairs. If they wait long enough, they can sample the cocktail Maxwell's making.

I stand in the back and watch. Through the stream of visitors to my right I see Hal walking toward me, wearing a shirt, tie, vest, and jeans, and carrying his brown leather bartender utility bag, designed by famed bartender

Figure 10. Jonathan and Maxwell giving a cocktail demonstration at the Bar and Wine Show, with Hal looking on. Photo by the author.

Jim Meehan.[1] Hal tells me he just finished taking the USBG's Advanced Bartender exam, on classic and modern cocktails and spirits, as part of its Master Accreditation Program. He feels confident in his performance.

Hal has come a long way since I first met him, the previous September, at a bartender competition sponsored by Barenjager Honey Liqueur. He has been progressing deeper and deeper into the craft cocktail world. Originally from Long Island, Hal started working for a finance company in their technology department after graduating from college. In 2005 Hal took a date to the Flatiron Lounge. "I don't know who I met, but I fell in love with cocktails," he says about the experience. "I grew up drinking Mudslides, Long Island Iced Teas, and shitty beer." The drinks he had that night were unlike anything he had ever tasted before.

Afterward, Hal started looking up other cocktail bars on the Internet and visiting them. He also gradually built a home bar, increased his cocktail knowledge, and honed his drink-making skills. He started to personally know bartenders around the city. After learning so much about bars, cocktails, and the New York scene, Hal began regularly recommending places for his friends to check out and drinks they should try. They encouraged him to publicize his reviews. In early 2009 he started a blog about his visits and home experiments. All of a sudden, liquor companies began to contact him and send him their products to review. Then they started asking him to create new cocktails using their products. Going out, mingling and networking with bartenders and his fellow bloggers, and writing about his adventures became his passion, but his tech job paid the bills.

"I'm working on a gin series," Hal told me the December after I met him, at a holiday event. "A bunch of [gin brands] sent me their products so I could write about them. Right now I'm researching them at Greg Boehm's and tasting them.[2] I'll write it all up soon. I'd like to do this to the point where I can quit my day job, but I can't do that yet."

In early 2010 Hal signed up for the one-day BAR ("Beverage Alcohol Resource") Smarts Program, which also has an exam with a tasting component. I saw Hal at an event the night before the program. Back then, he was unconfident. "A few of us had a study session last night. I'm nervous about the recipes because you have to get the proportions correct. I came at cocktails as a geek tasting at bars. I know them based on flavor, not based on classic recipes or making them." Instead of using a shortcut by learning cocktail categories, which tend to have similar proportions of ingredients, as most bartenders and other participants in the program were doing, Hal crammed by memorizing dozens of recipes. He still passed the exam.

The following spring I talked with Hal outside a service entrance to the main branch of the New York Public Library, the site of the annual Manhattan Cocktail Classic's inaugural gala, kicking off this industry event. We were both working at the gala—essentially a huge party with dozens of sponsored booths with bartenders mixing batched ingredients, food by celebrity chefs, and DJs blasting club music, all taking place in one of the city's most serene indoor settings. In the few months before the gala, Hal started working with Jonathan's consulting group, The Cocktail Guru, at various events, and he made drinks with him that night. He told me he got accepted into the BAR's five-day program, a far more intensive program run by BAR's master bartenders. He would also participate in the bartender apprentice program at the upcoming Tales of the Cocktail. I congratulated him, and reminded him that the apprentice program is hell. Apprentices equip the seminars with the ingredients to make the featured cocktails, which relate to the seminar topic and contain an ingredient of whichever brand sponsors it. They run around the event all day, squeeze juice, prep garnishes, and batch drinks. They get sticky and tired, like working back-to-back shifts behind the bar.

"I know," he said. "They've told me. I don't care, I need to learn how to bartend faster. Although, I wonder what doing the BAR would do for me. I mean, what does it actually mean for me getting a job?"

It's an open question Hal asks himself. I think about his progress as we stand next to each other at the Bar and Wine Show. After having just taken yet another certification that tells people he knows his spirits and cocktail recipes and how to make them, preparing for a fourth one, and gearing up for a week of scrambling around the Hotel Monteleone and French Quarter with buckets of batched cocktails and ice, Hal is closer than ever to reaching his goal. In a little over a year he went from being a cocktail enthusiast, to getting the attention of corporate brands with his blog, to gaining entrée and acclimating to the culture of the cocktail world through its accreditation programs, to working events, all for the purpose of one day building up to working as a bartender.

"I love this shit," he says while gazing around the convention center at nothing and no one in particular.

"What do you love about it?"

"Everything."

I nod my head. A few minutes later, he takes the stage and demos cocktails.

For young urbanites with hip tastes, these workplaces exude cool. To them, visiting the hidden bar for craft cocktails and unique small-batch spirits, the lodge-like masculine barbershop for a classic-looking haircut and an old-fashioned shave, and the local butcher for a rare cut of locally raised meat are fundamental to life in the city. People with certain sensibilities toward what they buy and do for leisure, with a certain level of awareness and desire for quality in how goods get made and tasks get done, and with a certain amount of money to spend on them seek out these new urban luxuries among the city's many other options. They represent fun, cool, and urbane alternatives to the more popular sports bars and loud nightclubs, branded booze, cheap and quick haircuts, and shrink-wrapped meat on Styrofoam trays. Surely working at these places must also be cool.

"Cool" jobs hold a unique position in the discussion over what is a "good" or a "bad" job in the new economy.[3] "Cool" jobs, even "bad" ones, possess an irresistible aura that can either overcome or mask their negative conditions.[4] Certain industries tend to have more of them than others. The cultural industries, for instance, feature star musicians, artists, and fashion designers who give their enterprises a glow of specialness. But even workers in cultural industries such as music, art, and fashion who are not among the popular frontline producers, who work bureaucratic office jobs in the background, still recognize the "institutional charisma"—or the compelling, structurally embedded glamour—in the work they do.[5] Despite the boring work for low (or no) pay and few (if any) benefits, they still feel special by being involved in the collective effort of making culture.[6] The industries of the jobs in this book—nightlife, alcohol, grooming and style, and food—are some of the hippest and most popular in today's cities, playing key roles in composing their cultural zeitgeist.[7] Nightspots, style, and fine dining have represented glamorous city life for a long time. Only recently, however, have the manual laborers in these industries shared some of the spotlight with the city's celebrities and elites, and become unique elites of their own.[8]

Consumers regularly tell these workers their jobs must be cool because they get to be creative and have fun. They see with their own eyes how these workers get to make and provide special but practical items and services for people. They see the enjoyment they have in their jobs. And they read how people in lifestyle and social media portray them as rock stars in their fields, using such terms as "startenders," "bar chefs," "mixologists," "master distillers," and "hipster" barbers and butchers. In the elevation of these manual labor jobs to a new elite status, the coolness factor plays a key role. People, then, *must* pursue them as careers because they seem cool to do.

The term "hipster" permeates media coverage and popular thinking on these occupations. Or, most importantly, the contemporary hipster's chief trait does: irony.[9] As the thinking goes, hipsters treat everything as a big joke. For instance, while usually well-educated and middle-class, hipsters identify with symbols of working-class culture, like cheap beer and trucker hats, to both show off "coolness" and play intragroup status games. The term is usually used pejoratively: the subcultural figure of the hipster acts insincerely, and is inauthentic.[10] Given this understanding, for some the thought of a college-educated person deciding to take a traditionally working-class job, dress old-timey, and play the part of a manual laborer is the epitome of hipster culture.

Or perhaps nostalgia contributes to the coolness of these workers and workplaces. The themes and motifs of these workplaces and brands, as well as the work practices and the appearances of some of the workers, all evoke feelings of a lost, better, and sorely missed Americana.[11] Speakeasies and classic hotel bars, rum-running during Prohibition, wooden hunting lodges with classic barber chairs, and slabs of meat sitting on a table. Hand-squeezing juices, pot stills, straight razors, breaking down whole animals. Vests and arm garters, chain mail and scabbards. Looking at each of these aspects through a lens of nostalgia takes them out of their historical time periods and holds them up as superior to their contemporary versions.[12] Store-bought steak on the shrink-wrapped Styrofoam tray is simply not as good as the steak the knowledgeable butcher just freshly cut from the hanging side of beef, as they did in the old days, for instance. These new elite workers are the ones bringing this lost world back.

But people rarely pursue these jobs as careers simply because they thought it would be cool to do. And while the romantic past plays a role in the motifs and themes of their workplaces, and sometimes in the cultures behind the work they do, even fewer people pursue these jobs for the purpose of reviving a lost culture. Most often the coolness and hipness of the work, the job's image, and the historical references do not factor into their initial choice to pursue it. Nor do they consider the imagery the essence or crux of the work they do, while the hipster's trait of irony has no role in their choices or place in either their work lives or professional identities.

The common social mechanisms behind why people pursue jobs in the fields and industries they do—social status and prestige, family influence, educational sorting processes—also do not neatly apply to them.[13] Some scholars have argued that middle-class youth get "bad" jobs, such as in retail, because of the relationship between identity and consumption, or because they identify with the brand of the store and get to spend time with their friends and "cool" co-workers.[14] These explanations do not apply to the workers in this book. How, then, do these workers come to pursue these jobs as careers, and how do they not experience them as downward social mobility?

These workers get cool jobs, but not because they're cool or they want to be cool. For them, getting one of these jobs is the result of a search for meaning in work, to get recognized (by both consumers and people in their occupational community) for what they do, and for an occupation to anchor their lives and provide them with purpose.[15] It is also a signal of their own privileged freedom to choose the career they wish, and a result of their ability to see and tap into the cultural streams of today's city. These specific occupations are far more than lifestyle jobs, and are not experienced by these workers as "bad."[16] The cultural repertoires these occupations require their workers to perform (the technical skills based on a sense of craft and the ability to understand and communicate a set of specialized knowledge) accomplish both goals of providing meaning and allowing workers to not experience them as downward social mobility. When these workers decide to pursue their job as a career, they understand it to be like a calling, or a vocation.[17]

There are several paths they take to reach this point. Just as many chefs "stumble into" their jobs, in some cases these workers discover it after a period of drift among one to several jobs, without a clear idea of what career to pursue.[18] For drifters, a number of factors, such as having mentors and becoming enmeshed in their community, and discovering the philosophies that undergird these occupations, guide them to the job. Some other workers switch careers, leaving a stable job to enter them. Finally, a select few of these workers do in fact admire the cool cultures or were exposed to the elite versions of these occupations at a young age, which distinguishes them from both drifters and career changers, while for some workers jobs in these workplaces are merely a temporary stop on a much longer career path. These types of paths are not mutually exclusive; workers often follow multiple paths to reach their career goal. Once they find their calling, these workers then work to create some kind of career, the likes of which these industries have not seen before.

The Drifter

On a slow Monday night Joaquin and I chat as I sit at the bar at Death & Co., nursing a Fancy Free (bourbon, maraschino liqueur, orange and Angostura bitters). Two men in their late twenties enter, pause to soak in their new surroundings, and slowly sit down at the bar. As Joaquin greets them and hands them menus, one says, "I hear there's some mixology here."

Joaquin smirks and nods, his eyes looking downward. He hears comments like this one often, and replies with a version of his stock response. "We're bartenders. This whole mixology thing is a horrible name. They should have come up with a name for people that don't know what they're doing and use 'bartender' for those that do. There's nobility in being called a bartender; there's honor there. We don't have to be called bar chefs."

The paths to a career in these jobs are rarely straight. The most common path is hardly a path at all, but more of a drift into the job from a variety of starting points, and with varying amounts and forms of guidance. Drifters hold a unique position in the new economy. They are typically college graduates, but working in the knowledge economy's lower levels, such as in an entry-level job, or they're outside it entirely and struggling to find work. Joaquin's path to calling himself a bartender, not the sexier "mixologist" or "bar chef," started when he was in college.

"I was the uber regular at my neighborhood bar in Boston, a little college neighborhood bar called the White Horse. Kind of college-y, Irish-y, neighborhood-y. And I had a standing job offer from them for a long time because I spent so much time there. So one day I took them up on it, they started me at the door for about a year, a little over a year, got bumped up to barback, barbacked for a long time, and then started bartending.*

"I had the incredible luck of having a lot of incredible bartenders at that place. Guys that may not have been good cocktail bartenders, but guys that were fast, guys that were efficient, guys that really understood the dynamic between regulars and the bar, and the customers, that knew how to take care of you. They knew how to make you feel welcome and were just *really* wonderful bartenders in that respect. Their sense of hospitality was just incredible. Ultimately, I felt like the places that I was working at were jobs, but they weren't careers."

Of the four occupations, cocktail bartenders and barbers are most likely to have worked in their industry in a more typical workplace—such as at neighborhood bars and barbershops, hair salons, and places that profited from volume—and in a more typical role. Many cocktail bartenders started out by bartending in college, or at nightspots or for catering companies upon moving to New York City to support hopeful singing, music, or acting careers. They worked behind the bar and didn't give much thought to the quality or origins of what they were serving. Joaquin pulled pints, poured shots, and opened bottles at his Irish-y, dive-y bar in Boston. At the time the lack of cocktail knowledge and skill of the White Horse's bartenders never occurred to him. But Joaquin does not dismiss his experience there. From his co-workers he learned the most important aspect of being a bartender—namely, the hospitality. He learned the universal tasks of bartenders: serve people and tend the

* A barback is like a busboy in bars.

bar. The cool knowledge and culture of making exquisite cocktails come later in one's path and are less important, as cocktail bartenders assert.

Like many young people Joaquin came to New York City after college with a vague idea of what he would do for work. It was early 2005 and he was 27 years old. At the very least he figured he could always bartend. After some difficulty he eventually landed a job at a tiny Italian restaurant in TriBeCa while he looked for office jobs.

"I thought, alright, I can do that and then in the meanwhile I'll see if there is anything else that I can pursue that might be more respectable or might make the family happier. So I was trying to apply for like grant writer positions for nonprofits. I was trying to, you know, use that English degree for something. But [I lacked] relevant experience. You spend eight hours a day writing cover letters and sending out resumes and not hearing anything back."

Dejected by his lack of progress, Joaquin hopped from bar to bar and restaurant to restaurant, and discovered pleasure in hospitality. Once a denizen of Irish bars and dives, he started going to the nicer places in the city he heard about through service staff circles and the media. He read in *Food & Wine* magazine about the opening of Pegu Club, a cocktail bar in SoHo owned by famed bartender Audrey Saunders, where he had an epiphany of sorts.

"So I remember going to Pegu for the first time and just getting a Manhattan, you know, with all of the pomp and circumstance that attends table service at Pegu. You get it down, you've got the little thing with the bottles and the droppers.* I just remember going in there going, 'Whoa, I don't think I've ever had a Manhattan like this before.' I remember thinking, 'OK, there is a lot I have left to learn,' and thinking, 'OK, I don't even know what this Rittenhouse [Rye] is, I should go find out.' And I realized I could buy a bottle of Rittenhouse for $12 and I had just been charged $14 for that cocktail. But it was such a good cocktail I remember not feeling like I had gotten ripped off. It was just so good. I was like, 'Wow, I couldn't have made that with this.' I never would have looked at this unassuming $12 bottle of booze and thought I could do something so delicious with it and just being so humbled by this. I was like, 'Wow, I have a lot left to do here.' I really just kept trying to work toward that in my own way. That first trip to Pegu was definitely one of those eye-opening experiences."

---

* Pegu Club is known for providing customers with a small condiment tray of bitters and juices in small bottles so they can adjust the flavors of their drinks themselves.

Over the next two years Joaquin gained a lot of bartending and service experience in the city and educated himself more on spirits and cocktails. He ran the bar program at a short-lived South American restaurant, where he used fresh juices, egg whites, and pisco. But bartenders prepare drinks that reflect the culture of their bars, and Joaquin realized he would only be able to pursue bartending as a career if he worked in a place that wanted to make craft cocktails. After eight years in the service industry he craved the cultural knowledge and skill to partner with the sense of hospitality that he had learned at the White Horse and had been inadvertently cultivating since then. He applied for a job at a new high-profile cocktail bar he saw advertised on Craigslist. He got hired for the opening staff at Death & Co. based on his personality. The knowledge and skills came later.

"It wasn't until I landed at Death & Co., and even within a year or two of being at Death & Co., that things really started to pick up a lot of steam. That was when my family first started realizing, 'OK, this is maybe not the dead end we had been assuming. Maybe you're not wasting your time.' At that point I could really talk to them much more intelligently about what I was learning, who I was meeting, why this was important, all of those things."

Like many of the workers with prior experience in their industry, Joaquin distinguishes between the jobs he had then and the career he has now. The former did not quite have all the elements he was looking for in the latter. I ask him: "Do you think you would have been as satisfied bartending if you were at a place that focused more just on the service, let's say, and didn't concern itself so much with the quality of the drinks that were being served? Would it have felt the same? Would it have felt like, 'This is my career now?'"

"I don't think it would have. I think what I loved so much about what Death & Co. showed me had less to do with the fact that it's so important what's in the drink as much as it is my job to understand what everything behind me [on the backbar] is. It is my job to have an answer for why I'm doing everything. I think it had less to do with the fact that we're making sure we count how many drops of this [bitters] we are putting in this [cocktail]. But as much as we are like, well, you know, 'I don't have the whiskey brand that you just asked for, but I know what that whiskey brand is, I know what its mash bill is, and I know which of the forty-seven American whiskeys I have behind me has a similar mash bill, and I can talk to you about why you should want this one instead and why I'm offering this to you instead of that.' And I think it had less to do with geeking out [and making the] perfect drink, and had more to do with, this is a place that said you have to know what all of this stuff is because that is your job. I think that is what I liked about it. I liked the fact that there was that intellectual part of it that you had to understand what those things were."

Joaquin moved to New York City with an English degree, a knack for service, and some bartending experience. While drifting from service job to service job to pay the bills and not having luck in the grant-writing field, he fortuitously found a world that could satisfy his search for meaningful work. Obviously not everyone with his background decides to forego searching for more traditional "good" jobs to pursue a career in beverage service. But his background in bartending and his enjoyment of service certainly guided him toward it. Like other workers who drifted into pursuing these jobs as a career, he discovered a passion within himself for bartending, provided it combined service with skill and knowledge (that is, cultural repertoires).

Learning Environments

Scholars have used the concept of "communities of practice" to refer to those informal communities in which people learn.[19] Communities of practice signify an ongoing learning process in which members of a group exchange ideas and learn from one another on conscious and unconscious levels. People learn simply by interacting with each other. Each of these workplaces represents communities of practice by design. Rather than only retail, service, and manufacturing businesses, they foster meaningful interactions between employees, which serve as learning exchanges.

Sometimes learning takes place formally, between a mentor and a novice. In most cases, mentors are senior workers with more experience. Once a newcomer realizes what they want to do and put themselves in a position to do it, a one-on-one mentoring relationship can seal the deal.

Jason is a 34-year-old barber whose body is nearly completely covered in tattoos. He regularly chats with his clients about ink-work, and other barbers often point to his slick undercut hairstyle when making suggestions for them. Jason worked in construction for many years in Massachusetts, before moving to New York City to live with his girlfriend in 2007.

"I was in construction and just wasn't feeling it anymore. Especially in New York, it's a little depressing. I grew up in the country in Massachusetts, and it's kind of what everybody does out there, doing construction. I had a car, and I could store my tools. Here is like a different ballgame. It's like a rush job, you hardly have time to do anything. And I had to lug my tools on my back.

"So I did that for three years here. And this past year I've been doing the barbering. It's kind of like the same thing, you know? A lot of shit-talking, it's got that kind of tattoo shop kind of vibe to it, too. Dudes come in to hang out, and obviously I like that. There's no way I'm a tattooer—I can't draw. I like the whole gentlemen's club kind of thing. I don't know, I was just like walking by a barber school, and I was like, 'That's what I'll do.'"

But Jason did not want to go to barber school. He wanted to learn how to cut hair in the comfortable setting of the barbershop. Few barbershops will take the time to train strangers who are complete novices. A friend of his told Jason about Freemans and he heard they were hiring.

"I feel like I lucked out working for these guys. I didn't work anywhere else, I didn't even go to barber school.[20] They taught me how to cut hair. I just walked in here one day and I saw they were hiring, and it was actually for the front, selling clothes. And then I was talking with Van [the head barber], like, 'Do you guys do apprenticeships, or hire guys to sweep the floor?' He was like, 'Not right now, but eventually. Just make yourself known around here.' So I was like so annoyed. I was coming here all the time, and one day they offered me a job."

"You were coming here just to hang out?" I ask.

"[Mm-hmm.] Asking questions, watching, sort of like an apprenticeship, but not really, not really on the books. I walked in one day and Van was like, 'You want a job?' I was like, 'Of course!'"

Wanting to train people to cut hair "right," Freemans often has apprentices. After hanging out and showing he was both serious about learning and easy to get along with socially, Jason became one at the shop. He got paid to work the front desk as a receptionist. The receptionist's job is to greet clients, manage the day's schedule, sell products, handle payments, and answer the phone. They also sweep up hair from the floor, refold aprons, run errands for the barbers, and make sure the barber stations have what they need, like hot towels and razor blades. These tasks occupied most of Jason's time during the day. But in the mornings and evenings, when the shop was quiet, he would give free haircuts to friends and people he found on the Internet. He learned from watching and chatting with everyone in the shop, but Van became his mentor. "You just go for it. I couldn't comb hair into my fingers. But now, it's like I could do it with my eyes closed. But I literally could not comb hair into my fingers, it was like so embarrassing. Van would just kind of take over and then once I figured out how to do shit, he would just touch everything up at the end, like show me what I'm doing wrong, show me what I'm doing right."

Jason had the right connection to hear about Freemans (a friend), the right look to get hired as a receptionist (that is, tattoos, clothing style), and the right attitude to become an apprentice barber.[21] He worked hard to learn the craft of barbering. He came in on his days off, came in early and stayed late, and eventually started doing half-price cuts when a full-time barber was out or at lunch. After five-and-a-half months as an apprentice, Freemans offered him a chair. The masculine, homosocial work environment and "gentlemen's club" vibe of the barbershop drew Jason, who was already used to working with his hands, to the idea of barbering. He then found the right cultural environment for his personal style and a mentor to help him learn the skills.

In addition to one-on-one mentors, like Van was to Jason, colleagues in the workplace collectively guide and socialize these workers into the knowledge and skills of the job. For instance, bartenders regularly ask colleagues about a drink they're making, distillers ask others about how they achieved a certain flavor profile in a batch, and barbers and butchers constantly glance at each other's work while they're working, in search of small differences that could yield big rewards. Newcomers learn from being surrounded by more seasoned practitioners and being embedded in the regular activities of the place.

Based on cocktail-making skill and knowledge, Joaquin was not the best candidate for the Death & Co. job. The other bartenders hired had backgrounds at places like Pegu Club and Flatiron Lounge, two well-known cocktail bars. But he knew he would acquire the skill and knowledge he needed for his career pursuit from working alongside them.

"My training had been such that the guest always mattered so much, so I just basically shut the fuck up and listened to my betters, as it were. Shut the fuck up and listened to Phil and Brian [his more experienced co-workers]. And I learned. 'Why are you reaching for that vermouth? What's the difference between that one and that one? OK, let's taste them. I've never heard of that classic, what is that? OK, let me write that down.' I was a sponge for the first year. It took me forever to even put a drink on the menu. I was terrified to give a recipe to Phil. I knew I was a good bartender, but I didn't have the background that these guys had. I hadn't been trained by Julie [Reiner] or Audrey [Saunders]. I didn't know Sasha [Petraske].[22] I didn't know these people.

So I shut the fuck up. Shut up and work. Be glad you're working here, try not to fuck up, smile, be gracious, and be nice. Don't lose any regulars that these guys have brought over from their tenure at any of the other bars. Even if you can't answer the question in the same way, then just write down whatever it is you don't know and study the hell out of it. So that was pretty much the first year or two at Death & Co."

For these workers who drift into the job, the manual labor is glamorous in itself, but only when it combines cultural taste and technical skills, which they learn through practice within a community.

Philosophical Guidance

Other workers have strong feelings for the career path they would like before entering these jobs, but have not worked in these industries. Craft distillers and whole-animal butchers in particular are far less likely to have such experience, which can introduce the path to them earlier in their lives, than bartenders and barbers. Some workers begin on a path to these occupations from having already adopted the philosophy that underpins the work. These particular occupations were but one of several possible job options for putting the philosophy into practice.

Originally from northwest Missouri, Joel joined the U.S. Army for a brief time before attending college. Afterward he became a brewer's apprentice in Kansas City. Around this time he became critical of the modern American system of food production and distribution, such as agribusinesses and supermarkets. Joel's true passion is sustainability and designing sustainable systems. He worked on small farms in California and New York for six years. He shuttled between the latter and apartments in Williamsburg, Brooklyn, where he hung out with artists and other creative people. Joel moved upstate with his romantic partner, where he worked on a farm and at a brewpub. Even though he did not have any experience distilling, when he heard about a job opening at Tuthilltown, he decided to take it because of how it could advance his interests. Naturally garrulous, Joel loves explaining the link between craft distilling and small-scale, local agriculture. One morning during a short break, he holds up a bottle of Tuthilltown's Corn Whiskey.

"This is like almost the idealization of moonshine. You're going to see a lot more of this. This is actually exploding. When I started here and they had this product I was like, 'That's cute but . . . OK. You're not going to sell anybody moonshine.' I was dead wrong. It is exploding. It's really exploding right now. The best bartenders in America are just in love with it. All of a sudden everybody is like 'We're over-sold and we need way more,' so I've put up eight batches. Eight batches of it! We're just going to start cranking it out because they love it, so great. It's really neat. It's a very credible thing and a very cool thing for the market to have. It's one more point of education [for consumers] and again one more thing that points back to the farmer. With this you really taste, you smell it. That smells like corn. I mean, it smells like popcorn, buttered popcorn."

"That really comes through," I say.

"That's really just one more thing that's going to help direct everything that way, to more holistic and sound practices; more genetic diversity [in agriculture] and all those things. It's just going to benefit the farmers directly through us. We're making alcohol, [so] we're going to benefit no matter what. We could make it out of sugar, the lowest available cost to us, and make garbage just like most of the people do, and make profit."

From Joel's perspective, Tuthilltown and other craft distilleries contribute to and help sustain a local economy by buying products they need to distill directly from nearby farmers. Authentic production at a craft distillery, which includes using local products, puts distillers in a direct relationship with farmers. The relationship means distilleries usually get ingredients that are more unique compared to those from large distributors, while farmers reap a financial benefit.

"Farmers are always going to be beholden [to the market]. The farmer is only going to make profit above what he would normally expect—and sometimes not even that—if the market at that point has its price point set higher than what he expected. [But] if he is selling directly to us at the same cost that we're buying it, he's cutting out the middleman.

"It's the exact same idea as a CSA.* Farmers are getting the money up-front. They've got the funding that they need. They're not taking a loan out and they're not waiting for the market to dictate how much it's worth. In eight months that's a horrible lag of time. There's a lot of empathy for the idea of farmers. [But] the fact is that nobody does anything to help them because they're not buying directly from them. And I feel like the only action that can

---

* CSA stands for "community-supported agriculture." CSAs are programs in which consumers purchase shares from local farmers. Shares entitle them to a certain amount of products like boxes of fruits and vegetables, usually on a weekly basis, while farmers make direct sales to consumers.

really be taken is on the localized level. Like me buying from my local farmers. That's the only thing that's going to matter."

The potential to become a part of and enhance such a system drew Joel to distilling from a background in agriculture. He learned how to distill and refined his palate for spirits over time. Of all the possible outlets for putting his passion for sustainability into practice, he chose distilling. Without this philosophy, it is uncertain, but probably unlikely, he would have become a craft distiller. But distilling is secondary—a mere conduit to achieve a greater purpose. By craft distilling, Joel can challenge the mainstream food system.

Of the four occupations, whole-animal butchers and butcher shop workers are most likely to come to the job in possession of a strong philosophy toward their industry—namely, food. Along with changing the public discourse around food, questioning how it gets made, and turning it into a fixture of popular culture, the foodie movement has inspired people to become part of the industry, as both professionals and amateurs. People come to work at butcher shops—as butchers, counter workers, cooks, and interns—because they already possess a strong affinity for some aspect of the food world. In some cases, meat was not central to their food beliefs or preferences. For some, their concern revolved around sustainable food communities, and the philosophy of new artisanal butcher shops fit the mold.[23] Food and meat in particular at some point became central enough to lead them to pursue a career in the industry, but only in its upper echelons.

"Can you cut jerky without cutting your finger?" Giancarlo asks me one day at the shop. The previous week I had sliced a solid piece off the tip of my right pinkie while learning how to cut bottom round. I ignored a basic rule of butchery (or of knife-work in general): always know where your other hand is.

"I'm a bit nervous," I say, "but I want to try again. That's the only way I'll get better at it."

"Right. Go get a bottom round."

I take out the only bottom round left in the walk-in and bring it back to the cutting room. I am careful to only remove fat from the cut and not any meat. After a few minutes I have a solid pile of fat on the table. Giancarlo walks over to inspect.

"Is this pile trim or trash?"

"Um, both? I haven't separated them yet."

"There's too much meat you're cutting off with the fat. You don't want to waste that meat. Do you know how much grain and grass a cow has to eat to gain one pound?"

I shrug, sensing the rhetorical nature of his question.

"A lot. We want to waste as little as possible. Make sure we only cut fat."

Giancarlo is originally from Pueblo, Colorado, and went to school at UC Boulder, where he eventually got a degree in economics. "It took me a little while to finish. I was a few credits shy because of some courses I forgot to take, and I was sort of tired of school." He got a job managing a medical center in Denver, which he also eventually grew tired of. The push from working a job that provided no meaning for him and the pull of a love for and interest in food and meat led him to make a change.

"When I was younger I always loved making food, and I always loved things that involved food. And the meat portion was always my favorite. I just wanted to know where my food came from. I was curious. When you go to the grocery store and you see all of this stuff in the Styrofoam or you end up watching YouTube videos or documentaries about animals and you see they put those little chips in cow's ears that constantly feed them hormones and stuff like that. It makes you wonder, you know? You don't want to eat that kind of meat. And those animals, they just hang out in their own feces."

His curiosity about food and meat led Giancarlo to quit working at the medical center and get a job at a charcuterie shop. With his interest piqued, he then went extreme: he got a job on the kill floor at a small slaughterhouse.[24] "I didn't eat meat for a month," he says about the experience. While it proved highly informative, Giancarlo didn't want to work at a slaughterhouse for very long. But being there got him interested in butchery. After saving up some money, he moved east to attend a career training and certificate program called "Meat Processing and Food Safety" at SUNY Cobleskill in upstate New York.[25] Along with enhancing his knife skills, the program taught Giancarlo about food safety, from meat temperature to killing bacteria. After finishing he moved down to New York City in summer 2012, where his girlfriend was starting NYU's Food Studies PhD program. He contacted local butcher shops that promoted the meat ethics he espoused and would teach him how to practice butchery. "I wanted to work at a place like a traditional, old-school butcher. Bring in the whole animal, cut it up." Jake offered him a position as a "butcher assistant." As he explains after the fact, Giancarlo wanted to see if he could grow into the job by gradually learning other areas of the industry. He reflects on his path: "I wanted to kind of work my way through. I feel like people in this industry, the service industry, the people that are very successful and end up opening tons of restaurants or tons of whatever, end up starting as the dishwasher."

"Working their way up."

"Yeah, then they're doing prep and they're cutting vegetables. Then they're the prep cook. Then they're on the line, helping them. Then they're a sous chef, then they're executive sous chef, then front of house, manager."

"Right. From the ground up."

"Yeah. And that way you know everything, all the facets. That's kind of what I wanted to do. I wanted to go backward. So I went from making sausage, like dry cured sausage to the slaughterhouse. That's how I wanted to know if I was going to do anything [in butchery]."

Pursuing a job to satisfy such preexisting philosophies as sustainable agriculture and ethical food resembles a focused drift. They guide people without a specific career in mind to pursue these jobs, which they can then turn into a career. But the philosophy guides them in a specific direction. Giancarlo's "dishwasher to owner" model mirrors the legendary "mail room to CEO" business story. It is not completely without precedent in the food world.[26] But among workers in each of these occupations, the story is highly romantic, since it is extremely rare. The vast majority do not start on the bottom rung of their workplace or industry and work their way up, while the support staff of these workplaces—the barbacks at cocktail bars and porters at butcher shops—are usually from minority groups, do not get promoted and enter these new elite jobs, and certainly do not go on to open their own places. Even though he did not start right away as a butcher, Giancarlo started working in the industry at a special charcuterie store, not at the lowest level, and his first job as a butcher was at Dickson's, an elite whole-animal shop, not at a more common supermarket or meatpacking plant. The philosophy that guides these workers to eventually pursue these jobs, such as the philosophy of ethical meat, specifically leads them to pursue their elite versions. The "bottom rung" for aspirants is not as a barback or even as a bartender at a neighborhood bar, a distillery hand, a barber at a high-volume barbershop, or a porter or butcher at a meatpacking facility. Starting low for these workers is still fairly high in status and prestige.

In each example of drifting into the job—gradual self-realization through practice and guidance by mentors and a supportive community, and guidance by philosophy—workers honed the cultural repertoires that characterize these occupations as they went along. Their early personal and work experiences before entering and while within the industry shaped their approach to their current work. Except in a few cases, they all had at least some college experience to fall back on and no major responsibilities, such as homes or families to take care of. But the unplanned path of drifting into pursuing these low-status occupations as a career is not the only one people take.

Career Changers

Youngstown is a small city in northeastern Ohio, in the heart of the Mahoning Valley, also known as "Steel Valley." It boomed during the height of the steel industry, and its population reached a peak of 170,000 in 1930. Destroyed by the painful decline of manufacturing, Youngstown today symbolizes the collapse of the industrial economy in the Midwestern United States: excessive levels of abandoned property, unemployment, poverty, and crime. Today its population is only 65,000, and shrinking. If they can, young people leave the depressed city for greener pastures.

"I come from a very blue collar area," says Rob in the back of the Blind Barber's cocktail bar before an appointment with a client. He regularly shares his roots with clients. Rob's grandfathers were a mechanic and a railroad worker back in Youngstown's heyday, and his father is a barber. The way he describes it, his father's life sounds like the blue-collar working man's idyll: he makes decent money and has a decent home, goes on a vacation every year, buys a new car every five to ten years, and in general lives modestly. He charges $7 for haircuts to local policemen, firemen, and workers at car, aluminum can, and steel factories (the ones still operating). The styles are mostly the same. Old ladies in the neighborhood bring him pies and trays of cookies around the holidays. Rob's father first taught him to cut hair, and he went to a barber school after high school. But he understood that getting out of Youngstown meant going to a four-year college.

"All of my friends and peers were going to college. I almost felt like that was what I should do. I had the opportunity to go and I moved to Columbus [to attend Ohio State University]. It was a struggle. Especially when you grow up in such a blue-collar area to where you have a lot of people, whether it be your parents or grandparents, working pretty long and hard hours to maybe give you a little bit more. It is almost like the idea of going to college was something which seemed out of reach and then you finally get there. I would go back to my dad's shop and work over winter break, you know, stuff like that. I always loved it, but even my father was like, 'You don't want to be on your feet all day.'"

Along with helping his father during breaks, Rob occasionally worked as a barber while in school to help pay his rent, and cut his friends' hair to keep up his skills. He got a student job in the IT department, where he worked in online learning. He got a full-time job there before graduating, and then moved to New York City and took a similar position at Polytechnic School of Engineering at New York University (NYU-Poly) in Downtown Brooklyn.

"That transition was just horrible for me. I worked in the office and a lot of faculty were very resistant to technology. Those who taught online really did not do a whole lot but put slides up. I did not meet barely any faculty or students. Everything was conducted over e-mail. It was very passive aggressive as well. You felt as if you were not making that true bond. It comes back to the idea of, if I work in a cubicle, and I operate via e-mail, and I might maybe leave voice messages—there are all these really underlying pieces that exist in a university atmosphere or business culture to where we are never working on anything together. We are working on all of these separate parts and all of these different pieces to it that never really join. I think when you look at some of the tangible pieces of more blue-collar work, even in culture, in terms of—if I were to walk in, and this is no disrespect to you . . ."

Realizing he is about to say something about people who work in academia I may find offensive, I wave my hand to brush aside any controversy. He continues.

"But if I were to walk in and deal with a faculty member regarding an issue, it is a much different tone and different presence that you need to have, as opposed to if I deal with a maintenance individual and just say, 'You know what, we need a lamp changed in an LCD projector that needs to project in this class. This is a job that needs done. It is straight to the point, let's do it,' as opposed to going through a bureaucratic set of fifteen e-mails to accomplish one basic task. That to me is also something that was just very difficult to handle after a while.

"I guess for me it was like, can I really try and strive to make six figures, sit behind a desk, and feel removed, or do I do something where I may make less, but feel more fulfilled and more connected to what I do? I am not saying that there were not certain people that I worked with [in academia] that were great. [But] I think about how guys feel if they work on a line in a GM plant or a Ford plant and they build a car. They say, 'You know, we kicked out forty

Cobalts a day,' and they feel like every piece of them kind of goes in to building this tangible thing you can touch and feel. You build such camaraderie. I just had this idea of blue-collar work and looked at really what it meant and really what it meant to me. I think that was the biggest transition for me, was the idea that I can build something, I can build more of camaraderie with not only the people that I serve, but the people in which I work with.

"As much as I felt fortunate about having a 9 to 5 and having really secure benefits and vacation time, maybe checking my Blackberry or my iPhone for my e-mail—I felt like I was accomplishing things, but I could not touch, see, or feel them really. It felt as if I felt really empty at the end of the day. I received a set paycheck, which is great in a way, it is great to have a salary. [But] there would be days where I would walk into work in maybe a tie and a flat front khaki or something and feel if I got on the train to go home I was not myself. I did not want anyone to see me until I could be me, you know? It also feels good to create something or to provide an honest service at a fairly decent or honest rate and receive compensation for it as opposed to just receiving a set salary no matter what I did."

The values Rob learned from his blue-collar, working-class background conflicted with what he felt he "should" do to earn a living in today's economy. He went to college, became specialized in the information technology sector of higher education, moved to New York City, got a "good" job in his field, and acquired a suitable wardrobe. He was on a career path. He had support from friends and family. And Rob admits to having enjoyed some of the perks of full-time office work: the high salary, the regular paycheck, the health benefits, and the vacations (in short, the stability and security). But it wasn't for him.

He is not alone among "second careerists," or people who were already working a full-time job, which paid them a regular salary, included benefits, and entailed working in a specific environment and with a distinct set of skills (that is, a "good" job), but then voluntarily decided to transition out of it and into one of these occupations.[27] Recall Hal, from the opening vignette. Hal is a career changer who discovered and fell in love with cocktail culture while in his late twenties, and then gradually worked his way into the industry with the goal of being able to quit his day job, which he eventually did. He became a bartender, consultant for brands, and brand ambassador for a couple of whiskey companies. In Rob's case, he had been a barber before—as a job, not a career—and decided to go back. Rob felt ambivalent about having an office job (recall Giancarlo's quote in the preface about not wanting to "sit in a box"). Many career changers say they enjoyed the security of full-time employment in an office setting, but did not feel fulfilled in their work. They did not like working in a cubicle, being separated from other people, and having their work existing in the ether of digital technology.

Rob, and others with family connections to the industry (most especially barbers), is unique because his blue-collar background influenced his expectations for work. But he craved the tangibility of certain types of work, not especially the blue-collar setting, such as what exists in a place like Youngstown. He chose a cool shop in the East Village, not a local shop in a working-class neighborhood. For a college graduate with hip urban tastes, a place like the Blind Barber would meet Rob's work needs from both a cultural and technical standpoint. Not every one of these workers learned the values of manual labor from growing up: having to work on your feet, use your hands, make something tangible, and serve other people. Still, for people in a knowledge-based career who switch to manual labor, the lure of using their bodies as well as their minds to interact with the material world proves strong.

Strivers and Culture Seekers

Joaquin, Joel, Giancarlo, Rob, and Hal are all in their thirties, and when they were in college in the 1990s and early 2000s the rarefied cultures in their respective industries were not nearly as widespread as they became just five to ten years later. With cultural currents setting them in motion through interpersonal networks and traditional and social media, and the number of positions rising as the niches expanded, some of these workers developed a passion for the culture at a young age and pursued the job vigorously.

Nicole is originally from Syracuse and went downstate to attend Manhattan College, where she majored in chemical engineering and graduated in 2006. As a teaching assistant for an "Introduction to Engineering" course in her junior and senior years, Nicole helped her professor show the class how to make beer. Fascinated by the process, she thought of how she could turn it into a career.

"And then it occurred to me that there was just one other step to take that to whiskey. Distillation is really the core of engineering, that the understanding of distillation is not much different from all the other engineers.

It made sense for me, it was like a natural progression. I'd never contemplated moving to Kentucky so I was kind of like, 'Oh, wouldn't that be cool, but it's not really going to happen for me so I need to go somewhere else.' I contemplated the idea of going to work for Budweiser. I actually interviewed with them."

After graduating Nicole got a job at an environmental services firm, which allowed her to stay in New York City. At the time, in 2006, not a single distillery was open in the city. Over the next few years Nicole read as much about distilling as she could, spoke with the people at the American Distilling Institute (ADI) about distilling and potential job openings, and heard about a few distillery projects in the five boroughs, where she wanted to stay. She heard about the New York Distilling Company when it was in its infancy, experimenting with recipes in some distilleries upstate while they built their own space, and contacted the owner.

"I was like really impressed by what they were doing. They had a lot of financial backing. It's a job. It's a potential career choice. So I e-mailed [an owner] and he was very polite and said, 'We are not going to be doing anything for quite a while, get back to me.' I was disappointed but hopeful. So I put it off."

Shortly thereafter she heard about Kings County Distillery, which had recently opened in Bushwick.

"They were doing a moonshine tasting and I showed up and introduced myself: 'I'm your newest employee. Nice to meet you. I will be standing next to this table until you agree to meet with me.' I hung out there for a little while. They agreed. I went a couple of days later and I was like, 'I will work for free. I just want to be part of this. I want to learn about this.' Everybody realized that and that was that. I was just so excited at the idea that there was someone doing that here. I didn't have to sacrifice my whole life in New York in order to do the thing I really wanted to do in life."

A tiny operation, Kings County would give Nicole the opportunity to learn distilling by working directly on every step of the process. She always wanted to experience its hands-on nature.

"The other thing that kept me from going off and moving to Kentucky was my [interview] experience with Budweiser. Everything that intrigued me about brewing you don't really get when you work for a large-scale producer. They already had years of tradition and master brewers. They know what they're doing. They know their formula. If you go there you're going to be in charge of making sure the fermenter is always 76 degrees or whatever . . .

they're not playing around. It was less understanding. It was less creativity of artistry. It's more classic engineering."

As the business grew Nicole was able to eventually quit her day job and become Kings County's "master blender" and parlay her expertise to become a consultant for other craft distilleries and the president of the New York State Distillers Guild. Nicole is an example of someone whose passion for the job emerged early in her life while in college. Once the small batch distilling seeds got planted in her head, they guided her pursuits. For other workers, a passion for the culture of the job itself, including the romance surrounding its history, led them to it.

"I will tell you—and you cannot repeat this until your book comes out, and at that point, I'll be well-established. No, no—I'm serious. It's my dirty, dirty secret."

Jeremy and I are sitting and sharing cocktails at Death & Co. in the early evening. I first met him at Raines Law Room, where he was the opening head bartender. Now he is the brand ambassador for Russian Standard vodka. Jeremy usually wears tight dress clothes for his slight frame, a fedora, and brightly colored socks. He also sports a Clark Gable mustache and small black plugs in slightly stretched earlobes. I have a Daisy Buchanan, an original at Death & Co., with chamomile-infused rye whiskey, dry vermouth, Aperol, and Yellow Chartreuse, while Jeremy sips a rye Old Fashioned. I had asked him how he got into bartending, when he swore me to secrecy.

"I won't tell anybody about this," I promise.

"I told you the story about my interest in Americana. My father was a missionary. And I would travel with him to a lot of other countries in Southeast Asia, and to Africa. And I would come back to the U.S., and the older I got, the more void of culture I suspected America to be. This was unacceptable to me. And so I began to investigate American culture. When I was in graduate school, I got in a very heated debate with my classmates. I was taking a class on—it was a craft course, and we were studying grief—the issue of grief within international poetics, and this all led to a very intense emotional debate about American grief. And I said, 'Americans don't know how to grieve. We just don't. And we don't'—and then I made this statement— 'We don't have a culture.' And immediately one of my own friends said, 'What about baseball?' You know, 'What about Cracker Jacks? What about . . . ?' And it was just, you know, all kinds of pop culture. And I said, 'I don't buy it. These

things are superficial conflicts, ways of trying to stimulate culture.' Our culture, from its inception, from the very beginning, was in turmoil, and was
never—it never had a solidarity. And it's the same reason today why we enlist
something like globalization to come to our aid; why we would refer to that as
a tool, rather than a consequence.

"Now don't get me wrong, I'm not a racist—I mean, my wife's Russian-
Armenian. It's nothing to do with nationalism. But secretly at night, when I
lay in bed, and I want to have little fantasies, my fantasy is about an America
that had its own nationality and its own culture a good five hundred years
before it became populated with any other nationality. That said, the cocktail
exists because of other nationalities coming into America, and our exposure
to them. So my investigation into American culture was an investigation into
how we used other cultures, and what value they've had to us."

Jeremy began reading and studying about classic American characters,
such as those in the works of Herbert Asbury.* He came to love gamblers,
jazz musicians, gunfighters, and bartenders, and realized bartending was the
only role he could take on, in a healthy way (he plays the banjo, but only rec-
reationally, and finds the jazz musician scene too competitive). In bartending
he saw a possible career.

"All this to say what my dirty secret is: I've only been a real bartender since
January of 2008 [less than two years ago]. Before that, I was purely a text-
book, at-home bartender. So my introduction into this industry is very much
like Doc Holliday's introduction into gunfighting. He became a gunfighter.
He was not a gunfighter. But he wanted to be, and he practiced shooting a
barn, you know, behind his dental practice, which was failing, and became
a gunfighter. He even started rumors about himself. And that's largely how I
became a bartender.

"[But t]here's this debate that comes up in a lot of articles online, and it's
the debate between mixology and bartending. And I agree with one particular stance, and that's this: a bartender is someone standing behind a bar. A lot
of people see mixology as the superior title. I don't. Mixology, anybody can

---

* In addition to such well-known works as *Gangs of New York* (1928) and *The French Quarter*
(1936), early twentieth-century journalist and writer Herbert Asbury also wrote about the
famed bartender Jerry Thomas in H. L. Mencken's magazine, *The American Mercury*. He also
edited the 1928 edition of Thomas's *The Bar-Tender's Guide: How to Mix Drinks or, The Bon
Vivant's Companion*. The character Thomas fit perfectly in the grainy, underground nineteenth-
century worlds that Asbury specialized in.

practice it. You can practice mixology. What he does [he points to Joaquin behind the bar] only he can do. He's a bartender. He's tending to this bar. *That* is so many things beyond mixology. Mixology is just drinks. That is 40 percent of what he does. He makes sure this atmosphere is comfortable. He makes sure everybody has the water, that their drinks are to taste. Mixology is just the art of making the drink. Showmanship, right?"

Jeremy got a master's degree in poetry from Mills College, and had been working in marketing at an architecture firm in New York City. He wrote poetry in his spare time, researched cocktail history, and started amassing a massive home bar of more than three hundred bottles, including seventeen different bitters, some of which were his own recipes. "I have the best bar in Queens, and I will put money on that," he says. When he grew sick and tired of his job, he scoured the Internet, typing his fantasy term "mixology" into Craigslist. An ad for bartending positions at a new bar, Raines Law Room, came up.

"They were having a walk-in interview the next day. I played hooky from work, I went in and I didn't have any experience, so I bluffed some. I took a photograph of my home bar, I go in, I show him the picture, and I say, 'Look, when I come into work, you can bet your ass that whatever drinks I'm making, I've been making on my own time and with my own money. I can vouch for this shit because I make it myself.' So, that was my pitch to them. Michael, he's from Milk and Honey, was the consultant on the job. So he was there with the owners of the place, and I appealed to him. I said, 'This is what I want to do.' He recommended me for head bartender when they left. They hired me. I set up their menu for the year, and that's still the menu now."

Without bartending experience, and without having to work his way up, Jeremy still landed a head bartending position at a place with a strong pedigree. He did not drift into bartending, possess a sensibility toward service or a philosophy toward quality, or have a personal connection to the job or industry. He had an unfulfilling job, like many of these workers, but his interest in Americana and the folk figure of the bartender drove him to consider bartending as a career. Jeremy's "dirty, dirty secret" is also significant. He carefully lays out the common notion among cocktail bartenders of the difference between bartending (tending the bar) and mixology (making drinks). Jeremy certainly knew his mixology from making drinks at home. While he successfully affected himself to be a bartender, he knew his lack of experience made him a target in the cocktail world, as it does for inexperienced people in the other three occupations. As these occupations transformed into "cool" jobs, they became more attractive for young people out of college who had never worked in the industry before. Jeremy is genuine in his appreciation of the romance of the job. He did not decide to become a bartender to play a role and revive an old practice. He developed a sincere interest in the job from learning about its classical culture in American history and decided to try it out for himself.[28]

Short Stops on Longer Paths

Not every worker at these workplaces is in one of these "cool" jobs and pursues it as a career. Each workplace needs people to fill support roles, which are often less sexy and rewarding than the activities of the main jobs. These roles include barbacks and servers (who are almost always women) at cocktail bars, tasting room and gift shop workers at craft distilleries, receptionists at barbershops, and counter workers and porters at butcher shops. Bartenders will wash glassware and barbers will sweep up hair, when needed. Usually, though, these dirtier tasks fall to specific workers.

For some support workers, like barbacks and porters who wash dishes at cocktail bars and butcher shops, it is just a job, usually done backstage, and the workplace does not attempt to train them anyway to make them think otherwise or move up to a higher-status position. These workplaces follow an ethnic and racial division of labor in the roles of their support staff. Workers who deal with customers and clients, such as the barbershops' receptionists, the waitresses at cocktail bars, and counter workers at butcher shops, are from similar backgrounds as the new elite workers and the consumers they serve: mainly white, usually college-educated, culturally savvy, and fit the business's style—they "look good and sound right," as previous research on aesthetic labor shows.[29] The people who fill backstage roles, who have limited if any interactions with customers and clients, are mainly ethnic and racial minorities without advanced degrees or outward interest in the cultural repertoires of the work. When a workplace trains someone from a support role to be one of these new elite manual workers, they almost always come from similar backgrounds and possess a similar aesthetic as its existing ones (such as Jason, who started as a receptionist at Freemans).

Some support staff do more than just fit the aesthetic of the workplace. Owners expect them to be familiar with and even passionate about the cultural repertoires of the main jobs as these new elite workers are, because the support workers are often the ones interacting with consumers. They must be extensions of these workers, carriers of these repertoires, and representatives of these businesses. Some may learn the job and move up in the workplace, as Jason did when he first worked at the Freemans desk. But even if they do not, these workplaces offer more than just a retail or service job. They provide learning and networking opportunities for them to use when they leave.

In his late twenties, Charlie grew up in Greenwich Village and can trace his family on his father's side in New York City as far back as the mid-nineteenth century, all in Manhattan. He went to college at the Fashion Institute of Technology and got an office job in design at an advertising firm after graduating. "I worked in that for a while. I got tired of the office, so I started doing freelance design work from home. [But then] I didn't like working alone all the time. [So] I chose to do the blue-collar thing."

Charlie initially worked in sales and repairs for a short time at the Apple store in SoHo, and then his friend told him about a job as a line cook at a new restaurant being opened by 3rd Ward, an artist collective that ran an events space and affordable studio for artists to work in East Williamsburg, Brooklyn.[30] At the time Charlie was a home cooking hobbyist. Since he had nothing else to do, and since he had an artistic background and hung out with artists, he decided to try it out. From there he became very interested in food and cooking. On the strength of a barbecue dinner party he threw with his roommate at their loft, which attracted more than two hundred people, he started an underground dinner group called the Brooklynauts. With his partner he soon began hosting events and catering parties and fundraisers around the city. He also attended the French Culinary Institute, to improve his food knowledge and cooking skills.

After the 3rd Ward restaurant closed, Charlie cooked in a few other kitchens before having trouble finding employment for two months, in 2011. He then saw an ad on Good Food Jobs, an online forum for restaurant and food retail work, for a counter worker at Dickson's. He had considered butcher shop work before.

"It was funny, I was walking through Chelsea Market with a friend a week before [seeing the ad]—she was curating a little gallery around here for a few days—and I said, 'Oh, that [Dickson's] would be a cool place to work.' Because I'm really good friends with the Brooklyn Kitchen and the Meat Hook guys, [but] I didn't want to work in a place where I kind of have a friendship relationship with them.[31]

"I was humble [on the Dickson's interview]. I didn't know anything about butchery, so I went in there and I was like, 'I want to learn.' Obviously, it worked out. But I knew, for me, it was temporary. I knew I was going to start my own thing at some point. I knew it wasn't the right time. And Jake, from day one, knew that. He said, 'I don't expect anybody to stay here. You have different things going on and that's why we hired you. Everyone here is a multifaceted person.'"

Charlie and Dickson's were a good fit for one another. Dickson's wanted someone passionate and knowledgeable about food, and Charlie wanted to work in the high-end food world. His experience working at the Apple store, another high-end retail shop, helped him deal with customers shopping for expensive items. Dickson's understood Charlie needed to learn more about butchery, and that he would eventually leave after learning a lot.

"[At first] I was able to speak to the customers about the kitchen end of the meat very easily. 'I want a cut, I want to make a stew.' I knew what they needed. I could cut a steak, but I looked at a cow and it was like, 'Uhhh . . . .' I had a basic idea, but certainly not enough to label the subprimals, you know, just like that [snaps fingers]. But it's like anything else, you learn quickly when you have to. And working in restaurants helped because there was a certain urgency in the restaurant."

During lulls at the counter, Charlie would regularly walk over to the cutting section to observe the butchers and ask them questions about what they were cutting and doing. He would also often go back to the kitchen to chat with the chef and his staff about recipes. Then, after a little over a year of working at the shop, Charlie moved on after the busy holiday season to work on his own restaurant project. As his story shows, many of these workplaces serve as both places of employment and learning experiences for someone with other ambitions in the industry. For them support work is often more than just a retail or service job. It can be a deliberate stop on their longer career path.

Some support workers try to move up into one of these jobs but realize it is not for them. They fit the workplace and job in every way except in terms of desire. Simon started working as a receptionist at Freemans in the fall of 2011. Originally from Bermuda, he went to college in Canada before moving to New York City to become a fiction and screenwriter. Tall, thin, and lanky, Simon's casual fashion sense fits the shop. He normally wears tight V-neck t-shirts or loose button-downs with pants rolled up at the cuff and a pair of classic Converse sneakers. Simon also fits in socially. He regularly banters with and teases the barbers during the day. Working in retail at a shop like Freemans allows Simon to earn some money while he builds his writing career, and puts him in a hip downtown environment that suits his personality and style.

One day after soaking towels in water and eucalyptus oil and putting them in the oven, Simon stands behind Miles as he explains cowlicks to his client. "Cowlicks don't really exist. You're just making the hair do something it doesn't want to do," says Miles. Simon has a curious look on his face as Miles talks about the whorl and part. Noticing, Van asks him, "Are you finally interested in learning how to cut?"

"I'm just curious," says Simon, who had been working at the shop for several months at this point.

"We're gonna get you a baby doll to practice on," Van teases.

Over the next few months, Simon learns how to cut hair a bit. Doing so was never his intention when he first started at Freemans. He simply wanted a flexible job in a cool environment. Near the end of the shift as barbers are doing their final cuts, he stands by Ruben, Van, and Miles as they instruct him.

"Man, I was doing a beard trim the other day and I was so nervous. It's easy to do on myself, because I know how much pressure, and I know my own hair and beard. But I don't know how much [pressure] to put on someone's face. I was using like two hands and felt like I was shaking. It took a real long time."

"Are you doing it because, 'Why not, if you're here anyway?'" I ask.

"Exactly. I'm in here every day, I might as well learn. I'd regret it if I worked here and didn't do it."

A month later I ask Simon how the cutting is coming.

"I haven't been doing much. I mean, a little bit. I just don't have the passion for it like these guys."

For Simon working at Freemans is different from working as a receptionist elsewhere, such as at a more typical barbershop. He fits in very well culturally and socially with the group and with clients, and his sense of style and interest in fraternizing match the shop's philosophy. But his passion is in writing, not cutting hair. Working at Freemans, where meticulous haircuts and precise techniques are central to the service, every day made him curious about learning the craft. But for workers like Simon these workplaces will remain simply a cool place where they once worked.

A customer at a table at Death & Co. orders a Martini through the waitress, who brings it to Alex, tonight's bartender.

"Did he say how he wanted it?" he asks her.

She shakes her head. Alex nods to himself and starts making it. He takes out the bottles of Plymouth gin and Dolin dry vermouth, measures out two ounces of the former and one of the latter and pours them into a mixing glass, puts in the ice, and stirs it with his free hand behind his back for over a minute, glancing down at it past the end of his nose. When he finishes he strains out the drink, peels and adds a twist, and places the coupe on the waitress's tray. Since Martinis can be made in a variety of ways (with gin or vodka, with varying ratios of spirit to vermouth, shaken or stirred, up or on the rocks, with an olive or with a twist—or with a pickled onion, to make a related drink, a Gibson), I ask Alex if they make Martinis the same way every time.

"Yes, we always make it the same way when it goes out on the floor. You have to stand behind the version of the drinks that you [the bar] make, because they are the best. But an order at the bar always leads to a conversation, because there are so many ways to make a Martini and everyone has their own preference. We can't do that at the tables, unless they specify with the waitress."

One Thursday in the early afternoon I assist Liam as he distills. First we have to transfer the mash to the still upstairs. I take the cloth top off one of the fermenters and give it a stir with large plastic paddle. It bubbles a little.

"It's probably still fermenting, which explains that CO_2," says Liam. "But it's been in there for a week, so it's just about done."

He measures the brix, or the suspended solids in the liquid, which is a test for sugar levels, and then we hook up a pump to the tank that runs upstairs to the still. We transfer two hundred gallons into it, which will distill down to thirty to thirty-five gallons of spirit. Liam and the distillers transfer fermented mash into the first still twice per day, once in the morning and then again around now (mid-day). After a first run, the spirit goes through a second, rectifying run in the other still. We're making Corn Whiskey today, and this morning's first run is going through its second distillation. It slowly drains into a thirty-gallon stainless steel drum. Liam then does what he calls an "intermediate cut." Or he wants to see if he likes it after a gallon or so. If he does, then it goes back in the drum. If not, he'll start the tails. He takes two small glass snifters and fills them with a bit of the draining liquid. He hands one to me, and we smell and sip.

"It's a strong alcohol taste," I remark.

"I agree. That [taste] should be prominent. It also tastes like wet clothes. We'll cut the tails fairly soon, which is the difference between U.S. whiskeys and scotches, because scotches are aged longer, so they cut deeper into the tails. The tails can be rough, but aging smoothes them out. Since U.S. whiskeys are generally not aged as long, we cut the tails sooner, and then run them along with the heads through the still again."

A bit later Liam says, "See, the liquid coming out now is cloudier and milkier instead of clear as it was before. The cloudiness is caused by fatty acids and oils and is very rich. It lets you know that you are at the end of it."

"You guys probably don't like it when people show you photos," a client says to Miles after sitting in his chair.

Barbers get this question often. For some reason clients think barbers don't like referring to pictures, perhaps thinking they're unhelpful or a form of cheating. Not true. Barbers love seeing photos. "Pictures are the best explanation," says Ruben, since clients often cannot clearly articulate what they want. Photos of themselves are the best, because a barber can see how short and what style they want. But sometimes clients show photos of models and celebrities from magazines. These visual aids are also helpful, but come with a warning.

"Pictures work so much," says Miles. "The only time pictures don't work [is when] they want to look like that person. I've had people come in, sit down, and show me a picture and say, 'I want this.' I'm like, 'You see this photograph of this guy sitting on a beach with a beautiful woman in a nice beach chair with a drink? That's what you want. You don't want that haircut.' It's not that the haircut is bad, but I can just look at you and say that you do not want that haircut."

In these cases, barbers size up their client, put their thumb over the man's face to separate the two and better visualize how the style might work, and make an honest assessment. In this case, Miles's client has a glossy page from a magazine with a picture of a fashion model. Luckily, the style can work on this client.

"OK, your hair right now is a bit too short from having been buzzed. You could totally do the side part, but your hair is still a little short to do it. But I could cut it so that by your next haircut you could do it."

At ten in the morning, just as the butcher shop opens for business, I walk in from getting coffee and see Aldo standing by the books, casually flipping through *Whole Beast Butchery*, which he grabbed from the shelf.[1]

"You ever refer to a book for your work?" I ask.

"I used to sometimes, when I started working. They were helpful, good for learning. There was one old one I used, a simple one, I think we have it."

He can't find it in the mini-library, and he can't remember the name. Aldo keeps flipping through the book, pointing out what he thinks is wrong or what he could do better. He opens to a photo of a Frenched rack of lamb, and points to the meat still on the ends of the bones.*

"You see that? Now, look."

He brings me over to the display.

"Those are beef [bone-in rib chops], but you can see how clean it is. We do it good."

Making "the best" version of a classic as the house recipe. Judging when a spirit is ready. Visualizing style and its compatibility. And using proper technique to make "good" racks of ribs. Workers in all kinds of occupations have an "occupational aesthetic," or an idea of right and wrong in how their job should be done, what the products and services should look like, and what the results should be.[2] It's what makes every worker in any occupation an artist, at some level. The workers in each of these occupations are no different. Their sense of right and wrong is deeply rooted in the cultural repertoires of their niche jobs. A sense of craft and craftsmanship is central to the cultural repertoires these workers enact. This sense is a conscious focus on the technical aspects of their work, bundled with the cultural knowledge they learn and

---

* Frenching a rack of lamb means removing the meat, fat, and tissue from the ends of the bones, giving them a clean appearance.

communicate. As enacted in their techniques, it also holds a central place in the social world of their workplaces. They perform their craft publicly, for the purposes of transparency and to spark conversation.[3] But they also all believe in doing their work well for its own sake, such as when they stress over details no consumer would ever notice.[4]

What does this sense of craft look like and how do they enact it? These workers all identify aspects of their work that are beyond their control, or where they must respect nature and follow specific procedures (science), and aspects that demand their input (art). Learning the limits of each—when, where, and how science and nature end and art and creativity begin—is fundamental to a successful, confident performance.

Respecting Nature

On delivery day in the early afternoon, JM enters the cutting area from having lunch in the back to break down more cows. Giancarlo and Brian had already brought two more sides out from the walk-in to hang. JM picks up his knife and runs it along the sharpening steel. As he turns around his eyes widen when he sees one of the carcasses before him.

"Oh, look at that," he says. "That's Prime."

"How can you tell?" I ask.

"Look at the fat."

Later on in the day I observe Lena breaking down a cow shoulder on the table.

"It's old," she says without looking up from her work.

"You mean it was in the walk-in for a while?" I ask.

"No, the cow was old."

"You can tell?"

"Yeah. The meat is stuck on the bone."

Experienced butchers can answer a lot of questions about an animal from looking at it hanging in front of them, split into large sections. What did it mostly eat when it was alive? Was it active or more docile? Was it panicked when it was slaughtered? The insides give answers. Since grass-fed cows are less fatty than grain-fed ones, it's rare to get Prime-grade cuts from them, since meat grades are largely based on fat content (or marbling). The best level whole-animal butcher shops usually hope for is Choice-grade cuts, one notch below Prime. JM was surprised because he doesn't see such a fatty grass-fed cow very often. He certainly used to in previous butcher jobs.

At some point in their work lives, some aspect of the process is out of these workers' hands. Nature produces both consistencies and inconsistencies. Butchers are able to learn how to break down animals because they are all the same in their anatomy (that is, muscle groups), but they also vary as organic products. They must work on efficient and consistent butchering to make the cuts they sell as uniform as possible. But consistency in the final product is an elusive goal. More importantly, butchers at craft shops attribute its elusiveness to their meats' provenance (grass-fed, or grass-fed, grain-finished), and thereby to their meat philosophy. In other words, their occupational aesthetic incorporates their sense of "good" meat into their idea of "good" butchery technique.

"I think the trick with the local small farm kind of model is that there is so much variation in the meat," explains Jeff. "Some weeks the meat comes in and it's beautifully marbled, and some weeks it comes in and it's a bit floppy. But that doesn't necessarily need to matter if what you care about is that it's local and it's sustainable and it comes from a small family farm. There is a certain allowance you leave for the variation there. There wasn't that, like, consistency that they get from supermarkets or something. When I first started as an intern I was actually surprised that more customers didn't come in complaining that there was such variation in 'quality.'"

Since the shop sells artisanal, not mass, products, which is how quality meat "should" be made, customers "should" therefore accept degrees of variation in appearance and gustatory quality. But the situation presents a paradox: butchers aim for preparing products that are consistent in the quality of their presentation and taste, while recognizing that they work with natural products that will often vary. Animals that are pasture-raised on small farms (as opposed to feedlots, where their growth and eating habits can be more efficiently monitored and controlled) will occasionally be different in appearance and taste. Workers at whole-animal butcher shops think that many meat consumers equate Prime with quality, because it is what they have been taught to think by the mainstream meat industry. To them a lack of customer complaints about the variation in the meat is a testament to the shop's ethos and ability to successfully educate the public.

As this example shows, the science and nature aspect of their work presents these workers with a constant tension as manual laborers working for a business: while they will always be beholden to degrees of inconsistency, which is one of the foundations of their businesses, being wildly inconsistent puts their businesses at risk, since modern consumers have come to expect great consistency in the products they buy. Butchers can't control what nature does to animals. They can only choose their farmers wisely (and their animals, if they want to visit the farms themselves) and focus on their butchery techniques. "On the fresh meat side I would say 80 percent [of quality is] farmer's quality and 20 percent [is the] butcher's ability to cut it," says Jake. "Not that you can't destroy good meat by being a bad butcher, but I think what makes the product special is mostly the quality and how it's raised."

This paradox, tension, and deference to something beyond their control exist for each of these occupations, in different ways. Like other bartenders, cocktail bartenders use a lot of alcoholic products that companies make in large quantities. They avoid some of the big-name brands, such as Grey Goose, Bacardi, Jose Cuervo, and Bombay. But cocktail bartenders can reasonably expect most of their spirits and liqueurs to be consistent in their taste. Like the meat industry, the spirits industry has techniques for ensuring a consistent flavor in their products. An example is blending, or combining multiple batches of a spirit—from barrels or other containers—before bottling. Like when making a soup, blending together multiple ingredients can smooth out any imperfections. Many larger spirits companies employ "master blenders" along with "master distillers," because their consistent flavor comes as much from the right blending combination as from the distillation. As a result, cocktail bartenders feel the pressure to not ruin what is already "naturally" good.

"We have a lot of respect for what goes into these bottles," says Joaquin. "When we meet master distillers, it is an *amazingly* humbling moment to meet the guys that actually do this. It's great! They have incredible palates and a great skill set, and all we can do is tell them, 'We're trying to not get in the way of what your work is. We're not trying to mask your life's work with a bunch of unnecessary liquors. We're trying to round out those flavors that are already existing in the bottle. We're trying to bring them out, we're trying to showcase them well,' and the way you do that is by choosing the spirits for your cocktails wisely and then executing them precisely every time. Pretty much every time I get, 'Wow, you're so good!' [from a customer, I say] 'You know, when you're mixing with these mixers that were juiced that day, when you're pouring these spirits, I don't need that much credit for doing this. They're doing all the heavy lifting for me. I'm only providing texture and temperature. These guys are giving you all the flavor.' That's the beauty of it."

In this sense the distiller becomes nature, and nature is perfect as is. Cocktail bartenders cannot control, however, how a small batch of a spirit is going to taste from one bottle to the next, or the quality of the citrus they use (they can only squeeze it right before mixing it). Smaller craft distillers often sell products on the market fully aware that batches vary, because they have been experimenting (different recipes, different barrels, no blending) or still haven't settled on their recipe. For the cocktails they use craft spirits in, cocktail bartenders can only sample the bottle beforehand, follow recipes, and adjust their modifiers as needed to achieve the flavor they want. These products represent the inconsistency beyond their control in their work lives.

Craft distillers credit farmers for their work. They're the ones who grow the products they need to distill. As with cow, pig, and sheep farmers, their farmers also deal with organic products. And craft distillers also tend to source their base ingredients from small farms, which increases the chance of inconsistent products. Furthermore, even with consistent ingredients, the distilling process in itself yields question marks.

"You're working with a natural product, so there are so many variables," says Nicole. "How the growing season was for the corn and how long it was stored. Each barley is different. Then the barrels—each tree is different. You can't really control the temperature in the distillery. There are just so many variables that even if you try to regulate and regiment everything you're always going to have those amazing barrels and then the shitty barrels. Everybody has that."

For upscale men's barbers (and for all barbers), the science factor in their work is human anatomy. People's hair (straight, curly, wavy, oily, thin, receding), heads (large, small, narrow, wide, bumpy), and faces (round, oblong, big ears, small foreheads) are what they are. Barbers have no choice about who their clients are or what nature gave them. Hair tells them what they can and cannot do to it. Experienced barbers learn how to listen, follow, and respect what hair wants; there is no sense fighting it. The difficulty in dealing with science for barbers is when social and cultural factors intervene—namely, when clients ask them to go against nature, to defy what their hair genetically wants to do (for example, go in a certain direction due to their whorl) or be (for example, straight, thin). People's biological differences always factor into their work, for better or worse, and barbers often discuss them openly.

On a Wednesday evening a suited Asian man sits in Van's chair for an after-work shave. Husky with a large neck, the man doesn't have a thick beard or a pronounced jawline. From the start it is clear he doesn't want to chat. After answering Van's questions ("Have you ever had a straight razor shave before?" "Do you go against the grain?"), he immediately closes his eyes and relaxes. Van starts the process and tries to take his time. As he works he shows Miles the new shaving cream that he's using, holding it up for him to see.

"The shit?" asks Miles.

"Awesome, and you only need a dime."*

Before I know it the shave is over and the man has thanked and tipped Van and left.

"That was easy," I say.

"Super easy," says Van. "Big fat guy. And he had a mix of hair. He was Filipino, or something. Japanese guys are the hardest to shave, because their hair is so thick and straight. Straight hair is like a circle, curly/wavy hair is like an oval. You pull out as much straight hair as you shave. How long did that take me? Ten minutes?"

Van's client was a barber's dream. Regardless of his actual ethnicity, his hair was a mix of straight and curly, and his beard wasn't thick. Certain ethnic and racial groups have tendencies in their genotype, which shape patterns (and stereotypes) about their appearance. In showing preferences for people of certain appearances, barbers can come off as prejudiced. But they are really commenting on what people's genes have determined they look like. And his body type—specifically his rounded jawline—meant no edges. He had little visual separation on the skin between his face and neck, which meant a smooth, continuous surface for Van to shave (like having a long cheek). Slightly curved surfaces are much easier for shaving. These factors combined to make this shave quick and easy, no matter how much pomp and circumstance Van added.

Using the Senses, Harnessing Time

Given the role of nature, an important aspect of these workers' work is learning to control and harness it, specifically where and when in the process and how to do so. They place a strong emphasis on training their bodies' senses to

---

* Here Van refers to the amount you need to use per shave, a dollop about the size of a dime.

know when and how, and on their potential to use their senses and abilities to manipulate time. Time for these workers is both a constraint and a luxury. It structures the work they do.[5] Each occupation has moments when workers feel pressure to work quickly. It could be during a shift, such as when the post-work crowd walks into a cocktail bar, a time of the week, such as Fridays and Saturdays at barbershops, or a time of the year, such as during the holidays at butcher shops.[6] But owners of these businesses deliberately design their method of operation to give their workers more time to do what they need to do to make a quality product and provide a quality service. The aim is not slowness per se, although they do their jobs more slowly than other versions of these occupations in the sense that it takes them longer to accomplish their main objective (make a drink, make a spirit, cut hair, cut meat). The goal is to do their jobs "right."

Each occupation requires workers to have well-honed senses. Cocktail bartending demands the use of all five of them. Taste is perhaps the most obvious. Like chefs, cocktail bartenders aim to sharpen their palates to identify the flavor profiles in ingredients, for the sake of discovering combinations for new drinks and for explaining what's in a cocktail and why it tastes as it does to customers. Tasting is what they mainly focus on in their educational programs. And of course, smell is integral to taste. Cocktail bartenders develop their palates and taste memories over time. They hone their senses of smell and taste by constantly sampling products.

"We're always tasting and refining palates," says John of PDT (Please Don't Tell). "One of the things that you'll see bartenders do specifically is that whenever we're working behind the bar we'll take a bottle and smell it, just so we're registering the smell of a liquor, which helps us when we're pairing something. It's like, 'Hey, I remember smelling something that would go good with this. It was this crème de violette. This would go really good with this drink I'm making now.' So we're trying to register smells and tastes somehow. There's a lot to remember. We have fifty-six, sixty bottles behind the bar, each one very distinct from each other, especially when you get down to like gins and scotches and whiskeys. There are differences between them, like [Old] Overholt's a more grassy rye, so knowing off the top of your head all these differences and how they match really helps with the drink design. So we're always tasting and mixing."

Less obvious in their work is the role of hearing, touch, and sight (beyond the obvious ability to see what they are doing). The sound (and sight) of a bartender vigorously shaking a cocktail in tins is a main attraction in cocktail bars. When the sound fills the air, customers regularly stop their conversations and look up at the expressive, and somewhat violent, display behind the bar. While bartenders adopt their own shaking style (some change theirs over time due to injuries and soreness in their elbows and shoulders), the aesthetic has a function. They are mixing the ingredients well, breaking down the ice to add water (a key ingredient) and tiny ice crystals for the cocktail, and getting it cold. They know when a cocktail is "done"—diluted and cold—in the shaker by both listening for the large ice breaking up into smaller pieces (the sound changes from heavy thuds to light rattles) and feeling the metal get colder and colder, sometimes turning frosty, in their hands. (Unless they're making a drink with egg whites, cream, or a thick syrup, each of which requires harder shaking for longer durations, they know a cocktail will be well-mixed at the end of a standard shake.) Brian, who is known for having a hard and theatrical shake, explains his shaking: "When I think about my shake that's when I screw up. That's when I knock the shaker over or the jigger hits the side of the glass. It's an internal mechanism. You can shake it too much, even with the block ice, and you can dilute it. You have that internal clock. I used to count how many times I shake, but now that I've done it so much it's a sound, like I just know when the drink's done. There's also like a dance, [and] sometimes I can tell when my shake's off. Like when I'm shaking too short I haven't done it enough but my arms are kind of tired and they're tightening up, and I just stop early."

And once they've shaken or stirred a drink or already poured it out into a glass, cocktail bartenders regularly taste it (with a plastic straw) as a form of quality control. In this way they can tell if they made it right, that is, well-balanced: measured, mixed, and diluted correctly, and cold. Sight, meanwhile, sometimes plays an important role in a new cocktail's aesthetics. While sometimes it can't be helped because of the ingredients they use, cocktail bartenders want their drinks to look beautiful. They sometimes combine ingredients to make vivid colors, with garnishes that provide attractive accents and contrasts.

Cocktail bartenders think about time in terms of how long a drink takes to make and what happens to it once it's poured. They must be strategic in their drink-making process to ensure the right coldness and dilution in every cocktail they make, every time they make it. With practice, they can control both and ensure the cocktail will taste as they want it to.

Karla, one of Milk and Honey's servers, places a ticket with the names of five drinks on it on the side of the bar. Mickey picks it up, looks at it for a second, and places it back on the bar with the top under the rubber pad. The order calls for four shaken drinks and one stirred drink. He places four of the smaller halves of the shaking tins and a mixing glass on the pad, in a row. Mickey starts with the stirred one, a Greenpoint (a Manhattan variation that Mickey created), measuring and adding its ingredients (in order: Angostura and orange bitters, sweet vermouth, Yellow Chartreuse, and rye). He cracks some ice chunks with his bar spoon, adds them to the glass, and stirs for about five seconds, abruptly leaving the spoon upright in the glass. Mickey quickly glances down to the ticket on his left. Three of the four shaken drinks require muddled fruit, so Mickey then grabs and puts some strawberries in one of the tins, blackberries in another, and raspberries in a third. He muddles each in turn, quickly and forcefully. Next come the ingredients for each one, such as lime juice, lemon juice, and simple syrup. He consults the ticket after adding each ingredient; he has lined up the drinks on the bar in a specific order (top-to-bottom on the list means left-to-right on the bar) and doesn't want to miss anything. He stirs the Greenpoint for another five seconds. He then adds the spirits to the tins: bourbon, gin, gin, and bourbon. He quickly tastes the Greenpoint with a straw, gives a little nod, places a julep strainer in the glass and pours the drink out into a chilled coupe from the freezer, letting it sit on the bar. He then adds ice chunks to the first two tins, shakes them vigorously, one in each hand. He does the same to the other two. Karla, meanwhile, has taken out the cocktail glasses Mickey needs—two rocks glasses and two Collins glasses, each with the appropriate type of ice—and prepares the garnishes. Mickey grabs some Hawthorne strainers (one for each drink), and pours out each one. He then adds a little soda water to the tall drinks. They both add the garnishes, place them all on a serving tray, and Karla brings them to the table.

Each order presents its own challenge for cocktail bartenders to ensure quality and consistency. From first seeing the order, Mickey knows to start with the stirred drink first. Not only will it take longer to dilute and get cold than the shaken drinks, it will also be served up, without ice, so it won't dilute any further as a customer drinks it (it will just get warm). He knows he has to let it sit for a bit (or, if it were the only order, stir it for longer). The other four drinks are all similar in their preparation, which means Mickey must work quickly on them and build them simultaneously.

As with cocktail bartenders, taste and smell are the most important senses for craft distillers. They taste at multiple steps in the distilling process, such as while proofing, when a spirit is aging (to determine if it is "ready"), and during distillation runs when cutting the heads, hearts, and tails. Large distilleries often use computers to make these cuts automatically, such as by measuring the temperature in the still, and ensure consistency. But craft distilleries do so manually, by simply having someone decide when to do it. Workers have their own way of gauging when to make cuts, such as by seeing how much volume has been distilled and the color of the distillate coming off the still, and, primarily, by tasting. Craft distillers taste constantly, their own products and other brands. I ask Liam to explain how he determines when to make the cuts: "You can taste that foul, almost fuel-type thing, nail polish remover [in the heads], and then also like the texture of it, kind of dry and chalky. You're getting to that spot of the cut and you taste increment by increment, very small, you'll notice that it's a pretty sharp like chalky sour, then sweet. Sweet and chalky, then [the chalky] disappears and it's sweet and you know that's your product. The tails cuts sort of taste like a damp, wet rag, or again you get some methanol at the end, it comes back so you can kind of taste that. It depends on what you're [distilling] too. If it's white [corn] whiskey and it's not going into a barrel, it's going to go right to the bottles, you have to be a little more conservative about those flavors. Whereas if you're going to put it in a barrel for six months to a year to two years to six years you really have a lot more leeway with it. Different alcohols are oxidized [differently] as time goes on."

While subjective to certain degrees, tasting and smelling is how craft distillers maintain consistency and quality control. The people at Kings County Distillery keep a bottle of their moonshine on the shelf with "Gold Standard" written on a piece of masking tape. After numerous experiments and comparisons, it's what they decided their white whiskey should taste like. They use it to compare what comes off their still. Finally, because they are the manufacturers of the four occupations, craft distillers have the longest timeline from the start of their work to the finished product. As mentioned, their chief means of manipulating time is aging in small barrels.

Upscale men's barbers and whole-animal butchers both rely primarily on sight and touch, most especially the relationship between the two. Both jobs require advanced hand-eye coordination to do the work well and avoid injuries (they are, after all, both working with blades). They train themselves to learn how to use their tools confidently, and to get a "feel" for the raw materials they use (hair and meat). Sometimes subtle changes to these elements can have consequences.

The barbers at Freemans get their scissors sharpened every two or three months, depending on the brand they use. They all use a California-based company called BW Boyd. They send them their tools to be sharpened, and

Figure 11. A spirit coming off the still at Tuthilltown. Photo by the author.

the company returns them a week later. It's more than double the price of the local company they used to use, but the barbers swear by its quality and don't mind the cost and wait time. The company provides them with "loaner" tools to use while sharpening theirs.

One day while cutting someone's hair Van lets out a loud "Dammit!"

"What happened?" asks Miles.

"Nothing, I just cut myself."

He stops and goes to wash the cut on a finger on his left hand and put on a Band-Aid. He apologizes to his client for the delay and gets back to work. A few minutes later he says, "Oh, fuck, I'm so sorry."

"What now?" asks Miles.

"I cut his ear a bit."

"You serious? What's wrong with you today?"

"It's these loaners. I'm not used to the sharpness and the longer handle."

Van, embarrassed, apologizes profusely to his client, who says not to worry about it and that he didn't even feel it. The cut is very small and stops bleeding after a minute.

Over time the scissors, clippers, and razors become extensions of the barber's arm. Eyes, hands, and tools coordinate to cut hair and achieve style. When one is off, such as a different pair of scissors, sometimes the process gets compromised.

Barbers deal with time in the long term and short term. Long term they build relationships with clients and learn about their hair and their lives. Over time—perhaps a couple of months, perhaps a couple of years—barbers figure out what style will work for their clients, while the clients come to trust the barbers with their hair. Also, some styles require multiple visits to achieve, which means a single haircut is part of a long-term plan, a step in a series. In the short term, the haircut itself is a process. Because of the amount of time they allot for a haircut, upscale men's barbers can use techniques that barbers at other shops do not (and sometimes cannot) use. These latter barbers have to work quickly and are not aiming for a unique style. I photographed Miles working on haircuts from a variety of angles and distances, and then met with him afterward for an interview to discuss his technique.[7] In the first few photos Miles is spraying and combing.

"I'm just trying to knock out anything that is in there. If there is any product in his hair I'm trying to get through it, that way when I grab it, it doesn't feel gross in my hands, and you know, break up the product well enough so the comb never really uncomfortably pulls on the hair when I'm trying to grab it. It helps break down the product. I know specifically that he puts a lot of real hard product in his hair."

Miles already has a feel for his client's hair from experience. But after the consultation barbers always start by either running their fingers through their clients' hair or combing it over and over, to get a feel for it (its direction, its texture, and so on). Like having an "eye" for style, this "feel" for hair only develops over time.

"Now I'm starting to cut his hair," says Miles about the next photo.

"OK. You start in the front, then, right?"

"I personally do. The thing is, it's funny, I cut hair completely backward compared to everybody else. I taught myself and it just kind of makes more

FIGURE 12. Miles working on the back. Photo by the author.

sense to me. I think it also has a lot doing with me being left-handed. With shorter guy's hair, you know, they usually tell you to start on the back and the sides. I like to start directly on the top. It seems to move a lot quicker for me."

"Can you visualize it better or something?"

"Well, I only have to do things once, whereas when I cut from the back and the sides I end up doing the back and the sides first and then the top and then I have to blend the corners of the head, where it's kind of like stepping back down to the bottom anyway. So I don't even go to the bottom, you know what I mean? I just do it all in one step."

The photos proceed to show Miles starting to cut his client's hair in the front, and working his way to the back on the center of the head. His style is unusual, as he—and his fellow barbers—point out. But for these barbers, wherever they start is merely a placeholder for the rest of the haircut.

"The front, when you do that first line where I'm doing right there, is just a guideline for the rest of the back. That's not what the end product is going to be in the front."

By the time he gets to the back he's cutting the hair shorter and shorter the farther down he gets to the base of the neck, since the client wanted his hair cut shorter on the sides and back. He then goes back to the main part of the head. He starts with the center strip to use as a guide for length, and then works on the sides.

"So, at this point, are you thinking about any of this right now or are you kind of like . . ."

"I've been doing it so long it's just kind of like muscle memory. The majority of the time I'm thinking in my head, like, the groceries I've got to buy, you know? It's just all kind of muscle memory."

In addition to training himself to feel and see his way through the process, Miles is also working on a regular client who requests the same basic haircut every time, so he knows exactly what to do. Miles proceeds to blend the sides to the center of the back of the head, and then he starts doing scissors over comb. I then show a picture of him snipping around the ear.

"Now I'm just cleaning the edges, making sure it's neat. That's kind of what people see when they're getting a haircut.

"What of this stuff would you not be doing if you were at a different kind of shop?"

"I would not be doing any of this."

I laugh.

"Yeah. If I was in kind of like those more neighborhood shops, like an old Russian shop or something like that, none of this happens at all. They charge maybe $12 a haircut, whereas I charge $40. So they don't make as much money as me. Well, actually they do, but they do double the haircuts I do. But the reason why they can do double is because this guy [the client] would have stepped in, they would have asked him what he wanted, he would explain it, they would have said, 'No problem.' They would have taken a number four [clipper guard] straight up the side of his head, shaved all around the ears, the back of the neck, cut the top with scissors, just one pass through, and kicked him in the ass and said, 'Alright, that's $12.' Because they don't have that time, you know."

The rest of the haircut consists of more detailing.

"This is me just cleaning around the edges, giving him a nice shape to it."

I show Miles a series of photos of him working with a feather razor, or a serrated straight razor, over the comb.

"All I'm doing [now] is just going through it all to make sure it all looks uneven. Because I know I cut it perfectly. So, actually, perfect-looking haircuts look strange, so you want it to look slightly messed up, because that's what gives it texture and character."

"What does that do, the razor?

"What that does is it essentially takes out volume and adds texture simultaneously. So, because it's like a straight razor it's not cutting everything perfectly. You're getting strings of hair that are kind of like left behind. The general length of it is left alone, but you take out that weight and mass from the bottom of it; that way when you let it go the hair kind of separates and extends, looks a lot more feathered, gives it way more texture."

Technically, Miles and the other barbers give perfect haircuts. The extra time they have allows them to work on those details that build a unique style for their clients. They use it to their advantage.

Butchers are very similar to barbers in that learning to be precise with their tools, for quality work and safety, is of utmost importance. They aspire to cut efficiently, but not recklessly. As with barbers, doing so requires hand-eye coordination and exact body position, as well as a feel for the animal.

Brian has been working at the shop for a couple of months. Originally from Michigan, he moved back to Detroit after attending college in Oregon and living in Portland for a few years. He started a sausage-making business with a friend, and he became very familiar with pork and breaking down pigs. But he is only just learning beef, and today Giancarlo is showing him how to break down the cow shoulder.

"This is the elbow," he says to Brian while pointing at his own elbow. "You go around the bone and separate the meat. This is shoulder tender, the brisket, the clod, and the platanillo. *See* the cuts coming off."

Brian nods along and slowly follows the seams with his knife.

Getting a feel for the animal for butchers in part means learning where the seams are for the different cuts they're after. Butchers can often remove, or "seam out," sections of animals, especially cows, in a variety of ways. The seams can represent different muscles entirely or different sections of the same primal cut. Shops and head butchers determine what the retail cuts will be, and butchers are interested in the decisions other shops and butchers make.

One night I assisted Sara, a butcher from the Meat Hook, during a demonstration she was doing for a small group of consumers. Sara broke down a whole side of a cow for them, explaining the process as she went along. The next week I tell the butchers at Dickson's about the demonstration and the different cuts that they do.

"I would love to see how they do it," says Giancarlo.

"They have some different cuts from us."

"Like what?"

"The Denver steak."

"Well," he says, "the Denver is the boneless chuck short rib."

"Theirs was larger. And the Delmonico, off the shoulder, which I think is our feather steaks."

"Hmm," says Giancarlo, "JM, where's the Delmonico?"

"It's usually between the rib eye and the chuck."

"Then [their Delmonico] sounds like old-style country ribs."

JM thinks for a second, and then nods in agreement.

"Well," adds Brian, "their Delmonico sounds like our feather and sierra cuts. It seems they keep those groups together."

"They also seem to cut into our palomilla," says Giancarlo. "It certainly sounds like they combine several muscle groups into single large cuts, like the Delmonico and the Denver."

"And they call our flatiron a blade steak," I say. "They use the name 'flat-iron' for another cut."

"Which one?"

"I don't know."

"Well, that's weird."

New butchers—to the shop or the occupation—must learn to see what the retail cuts in the display case look like on the animal. Once they do, they must learn to properly remove them.

Later in the day Giancarlo starts working on the tri-tip, a section from the hindquarter that includes the tri-tip, top sirloin, sirloin fillet, and culotte cuts. It's a tricky section to remove because the butcher is both pushing the carcass away from the body with the knife while pulling it toward the body with the hook, and it's very heavy. As he works on removing it from the carcass, JM notices his knife work.

"You're killing the cow again, you fucking asshole."

Giancarlo gets it off and plops it down on the table.

"Argh!" utters JM.

Dave, the chef, has been vacuum sealing some bags and watching with a curious look on his face.

"Show me what's wrong," he asks JM.

JM brings him over to the hanging carcass.

"You see, the line should be here to get the flank [points to the hanging carcass]. But it's OK, I don't want a lot of flank."

Giancarlo then starts taking off more of the suet that is still on the animal in the tri-tip area. JM shakes his head as he watches him slice it off.

"What's wrong with that?" I ask JM.

"It should have come off before. Because then you're pulling. Now you have to break it apart."

In other words, Giancarlo missed his opportunity to remove the suet efficiently when he was removing the tri-tip with his hook. Now he must slice it off piece-by-piece, which is time-consuming. He also cut too much into the flank cut when he removed the tri-tip, because his seam was off. He didn't visualize it as well as he should have. As a result, they'll have a small flank to sell. These are both skills butchers learn over time, through practice.

Along with visualizing the cuts and finding the seams, butchers also learn to cut along the bone. The goal is to separate the meat and leave the bone as white as possible, so that they use as much meat as they can and preserve the integrity of the cut. To do so butchers must learn to control their knives as if they were sharp fingers on their hands.

"Want to do some knife work?" Giancarlo asks me on a slow Friday morning.

He brings a pork rib loin out of the walk-in and puts it down on the pork table.

"You're going to debone it to make a pork loin roast."

He removes the tenderloin from the cut himself and puts it to the side.

"First [putting the cut meat-side-down], you trace around what's left of the ribs with this boning knife. You've gotta be very careful to cut as little of the meat as possible. Don't cut the loin. Keep the tracing along the bone. And don't cut your finger."

"I only did that once."

"And don't cut the loin," he repeats. "Next, you cut underneath the rib bones to separate them from the loin. You have to slice next to each rib bone, make a line [alongside it], and then slice between it and the loin. Then you just pull it [the rib bone] up, first with the knife and then with your fingers, so that they break at the base bone."

A pork rib loin looks like a fleshy mini-piano. To make a roast out of it butchers have to remove the bones. The goal is to see the bones' indentations in the cut once they're removed. I start by tracing along the ribs at the edge of the cut, trying to separate it from the meat. Given the cut's appearance, the task involves moving the knife in a wave-like motion, up and down at rounded angles. It requires delicate movements.

"Come on, doctor," says Giancarlo, as I am clearly leaving some meat on the bone.

I finally finish tracing along the bones, and then start slicing a line between each rib. Giancarlo demonstrates how to pull the first one. I leave some meat on my first attempt, but not much (although more than on his). I improve as I go along. With the ribs broken off, I can now trace along the base bone to completely remove it from the cut. I show my work to Giancarlo.

"OK, not bad. Clean it up [remove excess fat and any silvery skin], roll it up, tie it up, but not too tight. Run the cross twine, but not so that it will squish it lengthwise. And make sure the tie is not on the nice meat side."

When I finish I show it to Giancarlo and JM. They approve. I put it in the case, in the space next to the other one, and vacuum seal the tenderloin.

As with the other occupations, the shop's busyness influences how fast butchers work. Having worked in high-volume places, the Mexican butchers, JM and Aldo, often talk about breaking down animals quickly, and regularly tease the other butchers for being slower than them (while secretly recognizing they're still new to it). But speed for the butchers is relative. Given how much meat Dickson's sells, the butchers do have to work quickly on delivery days, quicker than butchers at shops with less volume. They try to spread the animal-breaking out over a few days, to both cut down on the workload on delivery days, and to have whole animals to break down over the week. Butchers therefore try to control time to make their lives easier, and to expose more customers to the process. They also do not go as fast as they can because of safety concerns.

"Have you ever been to Adam's shop?" asks Noah, one of the interns, to JM as he works on kalbi cuts on the table.

Adam used to be the head butcher at Dickson's, until he left to start his own consulting company and open his own shop, which is located in a section of a restaurant on the Lower East Side, in a street-facing window.

"No," JM says. "He got injured."

"I heard. Do you know how long he can't work for?"

"I think a few months. He couldn't move these fingers," says JM, holding up and showing the three end fingers on his left hand. "He cut his tendon [in his arm]."

"He goes too fast," says Aldo. "You can't do it like that. If I got cut like that and I couldn't use my hand, I'd quit. No more."

"He goes too fast?" I ask. "Is he careless?"

"Yeah," says Aldo.

"So you don't have to get cut, you can avoid it?"

"You'll get little nicks [he shows me by quickly moving his knife near his fingers and hand, pretending he's cutting something for real]. But then you pull away and stop [when you feel that you've nicked yourself or given yourself a little cut]. If you go too fast [he then shows a quick move and brings the knife edge close to the inside of his wrist], what are you doing? Like, I cut my leg because I was standing too close [to the table] [he stands where he was standing on that day]. Now you see I stand back when I debone."

"So, you want to go fast, but not too fast?" I ask.

"Yeah, exactly," he says.

Last year Aldo punctured his thigh with his knife while he was deboning pork shoulders. He didn't think anything of it at first, but then he felt something warm going down his leg, and he saw that he was bleeding pretty badly. He had to go to the hospital and take time off from work. Aldo realized he was being careless by not positioning himself correctly. He has adjusted this aspect of his cutting, so that now if he misses or slips with his knife he won't cut himself. He can work efficiently now, without worrying about puncturing his leg.

I later ask JM about Adam and going fast.

"He was being filmed by his partner when he cut himself," he says.

"It's on film?"

"Yeah, I saw it. But he [his partner] pulled away after he cut himself."

Adam likes to sometimes film himself cutting so that he can see how fast he is going and how he can shave time off his work.

"He always cares about faster, faster, faster," says JM. "In a factory, you go fast, but you have protections, you have metal on your arms, your chest. When I worked in Mexico in a factory, we had armor on our whole body. But if you don't, you can't go that fast."

Being Creative: Templates and Improvisation

One year at Tales of the Cocktail I attend a panel called "How to Bang Out Drinks Like a Maniac," run by Philip Duff and Dushan Zaric, both longtime bartenders and cocktail bar owners. They designed the panel as a counter to the panels and overall discussion in the industry that elevates bartenders to the level of artists. Drinks must be of a high quality, they contend, but cocktail bartenders must also be honest about themselves. Their business-oriented talk and slideshow focus on achieving efficiency without sacrificing quality. Halfway through, Philip chides bartenders who spend too much time tasting and refining a cocktail, trying to achieve some level of personal perfection, before they serve it.

"We are not tortured artists. I'm going to drag up another guy from the past who said it better, I think, than anyone before or since."

He then changes the slide to a quote from Patrick Gavin Duffy, a cocktail bartender from the golden age:

> Bartending is an old and honorable trade. It is not a profession and I have
> no sympathy with those who try to make it anything but what it was.
> The idea of calling a bartender a professor or a mixologist is nonsense.[8]

"It is an old, and honorable trade, no more, no less," continues Philip. "Like making hats, or being a plumber. You can see Patrick getting a little dig at somebody there, someone calling a bartender a professor or a mixologist. But he's right: it's a trade. Like a carpenter measures twice and cuts once, and then he gets on with his life."

None of these workers refer to themselves as artists. Most self-identify with their job's basic label ("I'm a bartender"), not its superlatives ("mixologist"), and say it's their career, profession, or occupation, not their calling. Still, they all readily recognize the art and craft behind their work, and strive to do their jobs well regardless of whether anyone will recognize it. As part of their cultural repertoires, this sense of craft and craftsmanship and the creative potential of their jobs is central to the meaning they derive from their work and to their desire to pursue their jobs as careers. They all focus on the "art of" what they do rather than call themselves artists.

The art of doing each of these jobs means learning how to follow, bend, and sometimes break a set of rules that their occupational community follows and enforces. Each occupation requires its workers to work with a set of templates. When they first start working, these workers train themselves to learn the templates of their jobs. Learning means knowing the technical skills in both their minds (what to do) and bodies (how to do it). The former entails mentally grasping and memorizing the bases of their actions, while the latter refers to developing a "second nature," or when they can easily enact the technical aspect of the cultural repertoire. Once they learn the template, mind and body, they can then manipulate it. They can improvise. These workers, then, are not dissimilar to jazz musicians, who work to learn patterns common to many songs, and once they do are able to play songs they've never played before and even add new elements to them.[9]

When making cocktails with existing recipes or when creating new ones, cocktail bartenders aim to achieve balance. When they succeed, no single ingredient overwhelms the others, or an ingredient has been manipulated (tempered or enhanced) to create a new flavor.* The drink is not too boozy, sweet, bitter, or diluted. Several templates exist for making balanced cocktails.

"To get balance," says Toby, "there's the triptych, which is strong [boozy], sweet, and tart, and you want all three. If a drink has too much of any one of those things it's not going to be balanced. And so if you have two ounces of booze, three-quarters of an ounce of fresh-squeezed lime juice or lemon juice, and three-quarters of an ounce of simple syrup so it's one to one, you're going to have a perfectly balanced drink. It just works that way. If you have a Daiquiri, a Gimlet, those all have that template. And so once you start jiggling that triptych—say you're going to make a Margarita—you know that Cointreau isn't as sweet as simple syrup, so you know you have to bump that up or bump the other one down. And so it's all about these little, tiny movements, of the mixture of it. And once you get that in your head and you just know it, then you can make up drinks."

"You can substitute," I say.

"Exactly. And just by little, tiny bits—one-sixteenths of an ounce sometimes—[of something] that you [add or subtract] or you add a splash of this or a splash of that, but you're still in that template. And you've created a style. I could look at some recipes and almost tell you who came up with the recipes because I know everybody has their own little quirks and their own little things they like. Like, the other night I was at Death & Co. and somebody

---

* I'm referring in this latter point to cocktails without many ingredients, specifically the Old Fashioned, which is just a spirit (traditionally whiskey), bitters, a sweetener, and water (that is, from ice). The spirit obviously dominates in this cocktail. The goal of the sweetener and bitters is to round out and/or enhance the flavors of the spirit. Given the number of spirit categories, varieties, and brands and the number of types of sweeteners, and bitters, the possible combinations for an Old Fashioned are practically endless. An Old Fashioned is "bad" when the spirit is too forward (that is, when its flavor hasn't been altered to create something new), or too masked (that is, oversweetened, diluted, or off because of too much bitters).

said something about a drink with Licor 43 in it.* Brian goes, 'That's Toby's, isn't it?' Because I love Licor 43. I just think it makes such a great flavor, and I use it a lot. It's one of my go-to flavors. I like Peychaud's bitters better than Angostura bitters, so a lot of my drinks that would normally have Angostura would have Peychaud's in it. So somebody would pick that up."

Phil refers to this process for cocktail bartenders as "Mr. Potato Head" bartending: "I think the reason why we're good bartenders is that we've studied the classics, we know how to make classic drinks, and then most modern drinks are just an elaboration of a classic. You learn how to make classic drinks and what you do is you take them apart and you put them back together. It's like templates: you learn those classic templates and you take the templates apart and you can take this out, put that in, if you put that in then something else is going to work there. The two most important things when you're making drinks is taste and balance. Arguably balance might be more important, [but] it's like a two-sided sword, because you can't have a pleasant taste without good balance, and balance is probably the most important thing."

Today's cocktail bartenders have many recipes memorized, but knowing templates, or understanding the conventions behind why certain drinks "work," is far more important. Improvising for them refers to swapping and adding ingredients and adjusting ratios. Creativity stems from improvising within templates and developing a unique style.

"Everything is a reference to something else," says Joaquin. "Everything. Everything is basically a riff on a handful of some classics. Everything you make. There's nothing new under the sun. Where people get creative is with what you're using as your ingredients, but for the most part you have the same basic formulas. The real art of it is fine-tuning it into something that's really special and stands on its own and can count as its own creation, its own cocktail, regardless of what the inspiration for it was. When I made the Latin Quarter I knew I was making a Ron Zacapa Sazerac with a dash of chocolate bitters added to it. That's exactly what I was making. I knew that. But it works on a different level than a Sazerac where it's not the same drink. It's not as spicy. But does it work as a cocktail? Absolutely. Did I reinvent the wheel? Hell no. But I made a good drink. There's only so original you can get."

---

* Licor 43 is a citrusy Spanish liqueur with forty-three ingredients of fruits, herbs, and spices in it.

Like cocktail bartenders, craft distillers work with ingredients and recipes. But balance is more subjective for them. Craft distillers aim to adjust ingredients and recipes to achieve a flavor they're after. If cocktail bartending, as Tom described it in chapter 1, is more like baking (without precise measurements the bread won't rise), craft distilling is more like cooking. There are recipes (for example, mash bills, or the proportions of grains, and the ratios of botanicals for gin), which are templates that craft distillers create themselves, and there are many precedents and conventions in distilling, but there are too many factors involved in the craft distilling process to ensure precise replication.

"I think the thing that makes it sort of artful as opposed to straight science-y is the pure engineering approach doesn't work for whiskey," says Nicole. "There is such an art to just getting the fuel for the process. What makes a good whiskey? Getting the feel over what your process should look like. You can use a recipe but you really have to know how it is supposed to feel. Kind of artful."

With its chemical processes and complex machinery, craft distillers blend art and science the most of these four occupations, and emphasize both as integral to their work. The workday at craft distilleries is an interplay of sensing and measuring, tasting and operating. Creativity comes out of creating recipes, constructing a process, and making decisions based on tasting.

"I think that science is a foundation," Bill says. "The art and the tasting is crucial. When it comes down it, who cares what's going on with the alpha amylase as long as the whiskey tastes good? But the flipside of that is that having a really good foundation and knowing what's going on will allow you to really make creative decisions that make sense. When everything's going right, then it's perfect. Tasting, you're like, 'All right, this tastes good.' But, if something goes wrong, your sense of things and your gut instinct doesn't help you as much. Having that understanding underneath, behind the curtains, that allows you to troubleshoot, and it allows you to gain efficiencies. This is a business, and so the art and the craft of it allows you to have a very good product. Once you have a very good product and you've been selling it, all of a sudden you need to get that efficiency up because you're a business. If that understanding allows you to boost production in certain ways, if all of a sudden you can, because of your knowledge about sugar to starch conversions, you're getting an extra 2 percent on your fermentation, that's a really meaningful jump. For those reasons the scientific understanding is really important, especially if you're going to start putting it at a meaningful volume. You have to know what's going on."

Multiple factors can impact the final product, such as the quality of the ingredients being distilled, the fermentation process (for example, open- versus closed-top fermenters, outside temperature), the make-up of the barrels in which the product is aging, and, as Bill states, distillers' tasting abilities. Creativity for craft distillers stems from the decisions they can control during various stages in the distilling process, even if they lead to uncontrollable outcomes. Like cocktail bartenders, they experiment with ingredients and recipes, sometimes following existing templates. These include choosing different varietals of base products (corn, rye, barley, wheat) or botanicals (juniper, cardamom pods, fennel seeds) in different combinations and ratios. They decide on fermentation technique, the type of still they will use, the number of times they will distill their products, and when to make the cuts. And they choose the proof level, the water they use (to cook the mash and adjust the alcohol percentage), the size and type (that is, char level) of barrels to use, how long to age the spirit, and whether and how to blend the barrels. Each choice represents a different way for a distiller to create a unique product, but most also add an amount of uncertainty into its quality.

Unlike cocktail bartenders and craft distillers, barbers and butchers are not working with ingredients and recipes. Adding material items is not part of their work process. (Exceptions are when barbers use pomades at the end of a haircut to preserve a style's shape, and when butchers tie cuts of meat.) Improvising on their templates is not about substituting or making adjustments to ingredients. They base their templates on what they know about and their experience with the material products they work with, specifically people's hair and heads and whole animals. Over time they build their knowledge of these templates, and hone their abilities to work with them and improvise.

Like with Miles, I also photographed Ruben as he worked on haircuts. One time he was very busy with clients afterward and we weren't able to look at and chat about them until a week later. Knowing he had personally done scores of haircuts and seen even more since then, I jokingly ask him if he remembers this one as we sit down to look at the pictures on my laptop outside the shop.

"Of course I do," he replies, while looking at the first photo.

"You do?" I ask, surprised.

"Yeah yeah. I mean, it's a typical haircut."

Like the recipes of cocktail bartenders and craft distillers, barbers have templates for the styles they create, which are based on the work process, the client's physical makeup, and what the client wants. The first photo I took of Ruben during this haircut simply showed him using his clippers on a section of his client's hair above the right ear that he was lifting with his comb. Based on what it showed, the fact that it was the first in a series, and what he saw was the client's hairstyle at the start (as viewed from behind), Ruben, an experienced barber, "remembered" it and could then explain the rest. In other words, he could mentally put himself in a position he has been in countless times before.

"The first thing you do is you try to figure out where the part is," Ruben says about this type of haircut. "The part usually is very simple. You look at the cowlick, and then from the cowlick that's the direction [the hair goes in]. You narrow down where the part is. Once you've figured that out, you obviously find out what they want, and what I did on this guy's hair, it was a three-and-a-half [clipper guard] on the side, you kind of draw an invisible line over here [on the side of the head], and you always have to keep the line below the cowlick area, because once you raise this up it becomes frizzy, so you're trying to avoid that as much as possible. So you do a nice gradual line all around. It starts by where the temple is, and it finishes on the other side by where the [other] temple is."

Here Ruben follows the work process by finding the part and learning the direction the hair goes in. Hair directionality is natural and immutable for everyone. Where it goes and what happens to it in its course (for example, length, texture, bald spots) varies from head to head. The photo doesn't show it, but before finding the part Ruben had to figure out the stylistic direction. Barbers have to "find out what [clients] want" or help them figure out what they want or what "works" for them. With this information they can choose and follow a style template (or simply follow the one the client tells them to do). Implementing the style template varies by client, then, because people's hair, heads, and faces are different, and, crucially, people have different ideas of what they want. These factors sometimes conflict, such as when a client with a certain hair type has an incompatible request.[10] Ruben sees from the first photo that he's doing a "typical haircut": short on the sides and back, longer on the top. The guard size he starts with (three-and-a-half) tells him more about the style he is working to achieve, because the guard determines the length of the hair.

The general style at Freemans is for more "natural" looks, which includes gradual fades rather than sharp lines. For a typical haircut, Ruben knows to start the guideline (literally a line he will eventually blend into the rest of the hair) by the temple with the largest guard size, and then use smaller and smaller guards to fade the hair down the back of the head and into the neck, disappearing into the skin like a song fading out. Since he started with a three-and-a-half, Ruben immediately has an idea of the style template he's following. A three-and-a-half won't create a stark contrast between the hair on the top of the head and the hair on the sides and back. A one guard all around, for instance, would, which is a much different style (known as an undercut). This client clearly didn't want this more striking style. He wanted a typical haircut.

Creativity for barbers comes from several related sources: regularly working with people who have their own unique combination of hair, head, and face as well as their own sense of style; getting to improvise within style templates based on these differences and by using an array of techniques; and developing their own style.

"Each client is different," says Eric of the Blind Barber, "so you can't give the same haircut for every person. You have to change up per client and that is where the creativity comes in. And everyone's hair is different, it grows in different ways, different patterns. [You're] working with what they have. And you know, some people are a little bit more out there and let you go in different directions and are more trusting and do not want a simple haircut, they want something a little bit more stylish or a little bit more avant-garde. Then you really get into being creative."

Working within a community of practice, barbers often learn new techniques to use from each other.

"I learned a comb and a razor from Van when I first started here," says Joey. "Everyone picked that up. Because no one was doing that. Van started doing that. Like, messy, a little bit. Now everyone [at the shop] does it. [And] Ruben started parting the hair with [a straight razor]. He's been doing hair for so long, [and he's like] 'This is an easier way to part the line now.' Now I see Jason is doing that."

Barbers first learn the basic and more specialized techniques of cutting hair, in which they eventually become confident. As they do, they gradually develop their own style for how to improvise within the style templates. Personal style is an added level of creativity for barbers. Bret, who handles hiring at Freemans' shop in the West Village, explains this idea by comparing different barbers: "[Some new barbers] who come [to work] here have a little more limited training and want to grasp some of the more advanced, creative techniques. Some of the guys all learn how to cut really short hair—typical barbering. I wear long hair. They couldn't cut my hair. I mean, they could do it, but they wouldn't be practiced or have fun doing it, because they don't know where to start and where to end. Just practicing and doing a few simple techniques and tightening up the skills that they do have, just make sure it's nice and crisp. I interviewed someone Monday, someone came in and did a few haircuts. The haircut overall was good, the shape of it and the design of it. But you got into the details, the finishing points of it—the neckline and all that—that's what sets you apart. The haircut should be technically good, but every part of the haircut should be really good. Some people can do really, really clean around the ears, nice square neckline, but the interior of the haircut is a mess. But it looks sharp from the outside to the common eye. So that's where you want it to look really clean. That's the idea to have it really clean but have the shape that grows out and looks really good."

Barbers at Freemans can spot someone on the street who got his hair cut at their shop, because they share the technical aspects of what they do (for example, natural fades) in common. Regular clients may even be able to tell, also. But the barbers can also often tell which barber cut someone's hair, because of the style details on top of the technical details. The former are standard, but the latter sometimes take time to emerge, such as when a barber is learning about a client and his hair and building trust over multiple haircuts. Examples of these details include the use of a straight razor to enhance or create a part (Ruben) or the feather razor to create the look of messiness (Miles). Finer details are less about following style templates and more about making personal decisions.

"I was at a restaurant the other day," says Anthony, "and I'm always looking at people's hair, and this guy came in and I could tell it was a good haircut. Like, technically, it was very good. But I could see where the barber made decisions that I wouldn't make. That's fine, because that's his style. I would do it differently."

A country's meat culture and the choices of the shop often shape the templates butchers follow. The anatomy is obviously the same around the world. ("It's a cow," says Aldo, "it's not going to have like a fifth leg or two heads— 'This head is not for eating, this head is for eating.'") But different cultures prefer different parts of animals, which influences how slaughterhouse work-ers and butchers break them down (for example, keep more pork belly on the ribs or have more of it for bacon; leave more meat on the shoulder or more for the ribs). Butcher shops around the world have different primal cuts, sub-primal cuts, and retail cuts, parts they throw away, and parts they use (and different uses for the parts they use). An American butcher would have to get oriented in the Italian, Spanish, or Mexican style, and vice versa.

"I'm always trying to learn about the different muscles and cuts," says Giancarlo. "I learned one the other day [from JM] on the top round that I did not know."

"What was it?" I ask.

"Well, [we] always get the Spanish names. It's called the piñón and it hon-estly looks like a piñón nut, a pine nut."

"Oh, alright."

"It's one of the tender muscles on the top round. I would always just cut it off and put it in the bin [for trim], but if you dress it and make it nice it's a good tender little roasting piece of meat."

The animal itself, then, presents butchers with one basic template (cows, pigs, and lambs are different from each other), but culture (of a country or region) and the preferences of a shop present them others; hence the interest the butchers at Dickson's had with how the people at the Meat Hook break down a cow shoulder. The creativity, or the art of butchery, comes in how clean one cuts the meat (which includes seaming it out and trimming and presenting it). Jeff explains: "The wrong knife pass, you know, too much saw-ing motion, taking off too much fat. The meat could quite literally look butch-ered, which it shouldn't. I've definitely been to some butcher shops and some other farmers' market stands and the meat looks like it's just mangled and butchered, literally, just horrible. You could have a subpar piece of meat with regard to quality and a good butcher can spruce it up to a certain degree."

Creativity also comes from what one can discover on the animal. Once they learn these templates, butchers can then sometimes figure out how to seam out new retail cuts from primals and subprimals.

"Where does the flatiron come from again?" I ask Lena one day at the shop's All Good Things location in TriBeCa.[11] With so many unusual cuts to learn, I often asked a question like this one to a butcher during a lull.

"It comes off the top blade where it connects with the ribs and rib eyes," she says. "You want to see a cut that doesn't have a name and that no one sells?"

Lena leads me into the walk-in and takes down a dry aging rib section, from which the butchers will saw the popular and pricey retail cuts of rib eyes and strips. She turns it lengthwise, to show where it was removed from the shoulder section (the other end would have been removed from the loin section).

"So here is the end of the palomilla [points to the bottom part] and flatiron [top part, just beneath the fat cap]. You could easily see where these cuts end on the rib section. We cut it off for grind. But this is the best meat. You could eat it raw it's so good. But it's only a half-pound steak, and there are only two of them on every cow."

"Why not cut more into the shoulder blade?"

"Because everyone cuts at the fifth bone. That's the American style. There's more money in the rib section. I'd like to name it. It's really hard coming up with a name. I have to look at the Latin names for it."

Americans love ribs and bacon, which explains why American slaughterhouses and butchers break down cows and pigs as they do. But by thinking about how to break down a cow differently, Lena discovered a cut she would like to sell, if she had the chance. Since she works at Dickson's, she cuts meat the Dickson's way, and can only make suggestions to the head butcher and owner. In finding hidden cuts, butchers learn to separate meat from the animal in a new way, with a different flavor profile and cooking procedure. Their creativity comes from learning how to manipulate the templates they have learned to use.

7 | SERVICE TEACHING

A woman in her late thirties walks into Dickson's late on a Thursday afternoon and steps right up to the counter without looking in the display case, staring toward but not at Charlie and Ted, the two counter workers. Charlie asks her if he can help.

"Yes," she says. "I'd like a pork loin, please."

Charlie slides the windowed door over and removes a platter of pork products. He holds the loin up for her.

"I only want half of that."

"Do you want me to weigh it, or do you just want half of what you see? This is probably about five pounds."

"Um, you can cut it in half and I'll buy both halves. I'll keep it in the freezer for another day."

As Charlie turns and places the loin on the counter to cut it in half and wrap it up, she walks down and checks out the other meats in the display.

"What is a red cockerel?" she asks.

"It's our chicken. It's a heritage breed. It's very tall, so the leg and thigh meat, there's a lot of that. Smaller breast and wings, so a lot of dark meat. A lot of flavor, so it's great for soups and roasts."

The woman nods her head with widened eyes, pays for her pork loin, and leaves. A young man then walks in, but with his head down and eyes fixed on the display. He paces slowly, maintaining his stare. Ted says to him, "Let me know if there's anything I can help you with." The man briefly glances up at him and mutters affirmatively, and then after a minute of more staring exits without saying a word. Another customer, a young south Asian man, enters and slowly walks up to Ted.

"Um, lamb shanks?" he asks, in a tone of uncertainty.

Ted takes a lamb tray with four shanks on it out of the display and asks him how many and which ones he would like. He picks out two and asks, "Is that fat?"

FIGURE 13. Ted serving a customer. Photo by the author.

"No, this is the bone, and that's the gristle around it. It won't change the flavor when you cook it."

"Can you cut it?"

"I can't. Our [band]saw is turned off for the day. I can trim it around here," says Ted, pointing to the area on the shank with his finger.

"No . . . that's . . . OK," he says.

"You sure?"

"Yeah, I can do it."

"It's really not a problem."

"OK," he says while laughing, and sounding relieved.

All bartenders, barbers, and butchers face a dilemma when someone first walks into their businesses.[1] They don't know exactly what consumers want out of their experience, but they need to find out to do their jobs. Some retail workers, like cashiers, play a passive role in a consumer's shopping experience. And often these workers have a script, which their employer (such as a large corporation) mandates they follow.[2] But bartenders, barbers, and butcher shop workers in general are far more interactive. They all come face-to-face with customers and clients, and the interaction influences what the consumer gets and how the experience goes.

The new elite service workers face an additional dilemma. Context counts. Given their reputations in the media and their price points, their consumers expect more from them than from workers at similar types of businesses. For example, bartenders at a neighborhood bar need not worry too much about their customers' actual order. They serve what their bar stocks—bottled and draft beer, a limited wine list, basic spirits' brands—and customers generally don't have any questions about what they'll be drinking or need the options explained to them. Their customers don't expect advanced knowledge of their drink, and bartenders aren't expected to be well-versed in mixology.[3] Instead bartenders need to focus on their customers' other needs, like if their water glass is empty or they want to talk.[4] Most barbers and butchers are similar. Some barbershops have a formal or informal list of cuts they do, which simplifies the consultation. Butchers can only prepare and sell what their shop decides to stock, which rarely requires advanced butchery techniques.

But people who go to cocktail bars, upscale men's barbershops, and whole-animal butcher shops often want more out of their experience than the commonplace. With omnivorous tastes, they want a unique product and service. They want to learn more about what they're consuming, the service being provided, and the work being done. They want an experience they haven't had before. The additional dilemma for new elite service workers vis-à-vis consumers, then, is the need to accommodate them and meet these expectations. The owners of these businesses do their best to create a certain experience, such as through décor and ambiance, and they give their employees the conditions they need—tools, ingredients, support staff, time—to make products and provide services that reflect omnivorous tastes. A lot of research has been conducted on omnivorous consumption, focusing either on the meanings and attitudes of consumers themselves or on the images and discourses in the media.[5] But a key place where omnivorous taste get created and spread—where wants get fulfilled, unknowns clarified, stories told, and tastes taught—is the point of sale, in the interaction itself between service worker and consumer.

Like the tasks that go into making the products and providing the services, these interactions are performances based on cultural scripts the workers follow and enforce. Most importantly, along with doing their basic jobs—serve a drink, give a haircut, sell meat—they also strive to teach their customers and clients about their own taste, give them confidence to know what they like, and, ultimately, bring them into the taste community upon which their businesses and occupational communities stand. I refer to the set of practices they use to accomplish this goal as "service teaching," or education through service. Service work at these unique businesses is more than just providing something for consumers. It is how omnivorous tastes get inculcated, and forms a key foundation for the professional identities of these new elite service workers.

Consumer Types

Workers in each of these workplaces break their customers and clients into different types. They do so based on a multitude of information. Interactions reinforce some of the interpretations these workers have of their customers and clients, which influences the service they perform and products they make. The types are not mutually exclusive, and workers can reclassify a consumer based on how an exchange proceeds. Exchanges such as the three at Dickson's in the opening vignette are typical and have strong similarities with those in the other two workplaces.

Experienced

Some consumers are like the first customer—they walk into the shop, know what they want, and order confidently. This woman knew she wanted pork loin, a fairly simple product. Counter workers will respond to these straightforward orders with follow-up questions like how much of the product they want (the whole cut or half, in this case). Cocktail bartenders and barbers get similar customers who know what they want.

The first time I met Joaquin was early on a Sunday evening, when Death & Co. was fairly empty. I had been there only twice before. He greets me and hands me a menu while placing a black cocktail napkin on the bar. I briefly check out what they have, but already know what I want.

"Can I have a Negroni please, up?"

"Sure. How would you like it," asks Joaquin, "more gin-heavy or more of an even mix?"

"Yeah, more gin-heavy."

"OK."

He turns and gets to work. Cocktail bartenders laud the classic Negroni for its simplicity. The standard recipe is "1-1-1," or equal parts gin, Campari, and sweet vermouth (an ounce of each).[6] Joaquin has made it many times before.

By ordering a classic cocktail straightforwardly, I signaled to Joaquin that I was possibly experienced with cocktails. But these new elite service workers require more information even from consumers who know what they want. It could mean just the weight or size of a pork loin (or which half of the loin, if one half has more fat content than the other), or the preparation of a basic cocktail. The Negroni falls in a specific drink category (gin-based, stirred, and bitter). But customers need not know much about cocktails or their own tastes to know the Negroni and order it. Joaquin still needed more information to make the "right" version of the drink for me (the standard recipe, or more gin-heavy). As Alex, another cocktail bartender, explains, "An order at the bar always leads to a conversation, because there are so many ways to make a [drink] and it's often the case that everyone has a different interpretation and preference." For barbers, this interaction happens during the consultation and sometimes continues throughout the cut.

Thorin looks tired. It's near the end of the day on a Friday, when the shop is typically busy with people wanting haircuts for the weekend. After finishing with one client, he takes one of the hot eucalyptus towels, unfolds and twirls it to cool it down a bit, and wipes his face. After doing so he looks more alert, and then really perks up when he sees his next client is a regular.

"What's going on, man?" he says while slapping his hand and drawing him into a hug.

They make brief chitchat as Thorin leads his client into the chair and puts the apron on him.

"All right, what are we doing?" he asks.

"Shave the sides, close cropped, and keep it long on top," the client replies.

Thorin nods and gets to work. They ask each other how the summer is going and if they have any travel plans. Knowing he has a family, Thorin asks after them. After shaving the sides, Thorin sprays his hair with water and begins combing it. The client wants it long on top, but Thorin will still cut off a bit. He cuts one side, but then stops.

"Sorry," he says, interrupting what his client was saying about a renovation project he may have done on his home. "I just wanted to see if that's enough to take off the top."

"Yeah, that's perfect."

When a client asks for close-cropped shaved sides, barbers usually need to find out how short. Thorin's client knows what he wants and is a regular, so he knows what "close-cropped" means for him. Still, he asks him if he got the right length on top. Barbers regularly use a status check (or a series of status checks) during the cut, such as by asking "How's that side?" or "How's the length?" before continuing. While experienced consumers, such as regulars, who know what they want may seem easy, for these new elite workers they still require attention. In fact, since they are confident in their own tastes and very familiar with the offerings and services at these businesses, regulars often challenge these workers to stay on their toes, or to keep coming up with new products and styles for them to try. Even experienced consumers can be taught.

Curious

A second type is the "curious" consumer, or someone for whom the unusual products, services, and techniques spark their curiosity, which provides these workers with the opportunity to teach them something new. They show a desire to be lured into the taste community. The first customer at Dickson's, who asked about the red cockerel, signaled she was possibly curious as well as experienced (they often go together) because of her question. A fresh red cockerel certainly looks like a chicken, which it is. Dickson's purposely labels it "Red Cockerel" because it knows some customers will be unsure. Curious ones ask, which gives workers the opportunity to explain.

Display cases are almost always front and center at butcher shops, but cocktail bar owners decide how to present their products. Joaquin says, "[Our ingredients] are all out there on display, they're supposed to provoke a dialogue: 'Oh, God! Look at those strawberries! What's made with that?' 'Well, that depends. Would you like that in a rum drink? Would you like it with tequila? Great, here you go.' Start muddling away at the strawberries. It's a way of triggering conversation."

Before I can take a sip of my Negroni, Joaquin cuts a small disc-shaped peel from an orange and grabs a quick-strike match from a clear glass candleholder on the bar. Lighting the match, he carefully brings the flame to the rind-side of the peel and goes around it in a circular motion. Using his thumb and forefinger he then quickly squeezes the peel in the direction of the match, which creates a little burst of flame.

After groaning, he says, "That didn't have the desired effect."

"What is that supposed to do?" I ask.

"Well, it's functional flair. When you set the twist on fire it caramelizes the oils in the peel and you get a nice smoky taste in the drink. It's supposed to create a larger flame than that and look cool, but this is a dead spot in the bar with the fans going. There're a few dead spots where the candles go out."

In this case, I'm the curious customer. Functional flair at cocktail bars, like lighting a peel, shaking two shakers at once, and stirring four drinks at once, accomplishes a taste goal and looks cool.[7] It's meant to be eye-catching and start a conversation. Similarly, curious clients often ask barbers about unusual techniques, products, or tools they use during a haircut.

A man in his mid-thirties sits in Miles's chair for a basic haircut. A bit more than halfway through, after shaving the sides and cutting the top with scissors, Miles picks up his thinning razor, which looks like a straight razor except for the serrated edge of the blade.* The client doesn't notice the difference. A straight razor on the top of the head is unusual.

"So, what does that do, the straight razor?" asks the client, with interest, not concern, in his voice.

"It's a thinning razor," says Miles. "I'm using it to thin out your hair. I'm just taking out some of the volume and keeping the length so the rest separates and expands. You can only do it with slightly wavy hair and you can do that with pin straight hair. It's kind of generally [for] white guys."

The products and services these three businesses sell and tools these workers use, then, have both their own form (or aesthetic) and function as objects that spark curiosity and draw people to want to learn more. These workers enjoy experienced and curious consumers who know what they want and want to learn. They are existing or potential members of their taste community (or "in the know") and allow these workers to draw from their wealth of cultural knowledge and use their communication and technical skills and interact during the exchange more deeply.

Lost

A final type is the "lost" consumer, someone who is outside of the taste community. A lost consumer is closed off, in the dark, and in need of guidance toward the light of quality taste and style. How a customer is seen as lost varies by occupation. An example is the second customer at Dickson's in the opening vignette, who just stared at the display and left without saying anything. Whole-animal butcher shop workers interpret their silence as a sign that they are overwhelmed by the shop's excessive and foreign choices. "People are creatures of habit, and are intimidated by cooking," says Ted as we stand

* The thinning razor is what Miles uses in the photo series I analyzed in chapter 6.

behind the counter during a lull. "You've walked into the shop before. It's like fifteen feet of meat [in the display case], of which they've never heard of, unless they're in the restaurant industry." Because of their past experiences shopping for and cooking meat from supermarkets, butcher shop workers feel lost customers are afraid of what they don't know. They don't know what they want and like (and don't know what to do with it once they get it), and/or don't know that what they think they like is not "good." Cocktail bartenders think similarly. They see their customers' behavior as habitual and uninformed, which they feel explains why they order well-known brands and drinks.

"Marketing and habit," says Phil. "Those are the two things that keep people drinking really bad things. Like the most popular booze, be it Patron, be it Bombay Sapphire, be it Grey Goose, be it Jose Cuervo, they're the worst examples of the booze; they're the lowest quality and they're expensive. That's a battle we have out for us. When people ask for Patron I say, 'Fortunately for you, we don't have Patron here. You don't have to drink that tequila today.'"

Like customers in bars, clients in barbershops always say something about what they want. But sometimes they are effectively silent, such as when they ask barbers for "whatever you want to do" with their hair, essentially deferring to the expert. To barbers, clients with this approach show a lack of understanding about how the barbershop works, a lack of knowledge of their own hair, and perhaps a lack of personal style, and they are perhaps insecure about their appearance. "I tell them [clients who defer to me] I'm going to shave their head, because that's easiest for me," says Van. "I can make more money if all I did was shave heads and not do haircuts. When I say that they look surprised. Then they start talking." Cocktail bartenders and butcher shop workers sometimes also get such deference from customers, usually in the form of a question: "What's your favorite drink/favorite cut of meat?" They all dislike this question and respond with some version of "It doesn't matter. Let's find your favorite drink/favorite cut of meat."

Opening Windows

As in the case of the first customer at Dickson's, who asked about the red cockerel, the interaction with the third, who unconfidently ordered lamb shanks and then seemed nervous about the bone and gristle on them, potentially provides counter workers with an opportunity to engage with and educate the customer about the meat. While not curious about what he was buying (he seemed to have never heard of lamb shanks before), the third customer still asked Ted a question and gave him a chance to say something about the meat and cooking. These new elite workers are all looking for such chances. They are looking for cracks in the windows of a consumer's tastes, which they try to open further. Curious consumers, who are open to learning, and lost consumers, who do not know what they want or do not know how to express it (or to do so confidently), offer such cracked windows, while experienced ones often offer them the chance to use advanced knowledge and skills. A goal for these workers is to spread knowledge of their taste culture, educate people about their own taste (even in subtle ways), and bring them into their own taste community, all through the order/consultation and subsequent interactions and work performances.

Like omnivorous consumers, these producers of omnivorous tastes promote a democratic understanding of taste. They have confidence in their products and services and in their abilities to find a way to get people to realize they like them, if given the chance.

"Opening peoples' eyes to things, that's like one of our jobs," says Phil. "That's like what the most important part of our jobs is. The thing is you have the vodka drinker coming in, they say, 'I hate gin.' You don't hate gin; you just don't know that you like gin. You've never had gin in the right way. So we open people's eyes to things they don't like. When people tell you they don't like something, it's very exciting because it's a challenge to you to make them realize that they really do like it."

If being lost means being in the dark, these workers understand their job to be opening windows to let light in. And as Phil implies, many believe the light is already inside consumers, just waiting to be let out.

Since the people at Dickson's understand that many customers will neither share the same tastes as they do upon first entering, nor possess the same knowledge about meat, they want to share their meat knowledge with them, for both cultural as well as economic reasons.

"In the beginning, it was tough," says Jake. "We had to train our customers to buy in a different way, but at this point they've kind of learned and it's very smooth. We've found a balancing act with both prices and quantities and training customer behavior, that we sell the case in a pretty flat manner so we're not left with any one thing all the time."

"How do you mean, 'train them'?" I ask.

"The customers? Education. You know, teaching them about the cuts. When you run out of one, knowing how to describe the other to make that cross sell: 'This you cook in the same way. These are where it's different.' That is one reason I need really confident front-of-the-house guys. We get a much more conversational person, somebody who doesn't see it as just a job; it's something that they're actually excited about."

People who shop in supermarkets are used to thinking their favorite cuts won't sell out, like their favorite cereal. Jake realized how important it was to tell customers about the shop's principles early on. Doing so fulfills the cultural imperative of sharing their ideas behind "good" meat, as well as the economic imperative of having to sell the whole animal, lest the business goes broke. Shop owners and workers assume the average customer needs help understanding their meat philosophy. They assume they need to be "trained."

A young man in his early twenties comes into the shop. He walks up to Sarah, who right now is alone behind the counter. In her mid-twenties, Sarah has been working at Dickson's for a little over a year, after graduating from college and moving to New York City.

"I'm making a steak tartare," the customer says.

"OK, do you want us to cut it for you?"

"No, but can you pick for me your freshest cut of filet mignon?"

Sarah pauses briefly, looks down into the display, and says, "Would you like to try top sirloin?"

"Oh, is it a better flavor?" he asks.

She nods. "Yeah, it's more flavorful, and good for a steak tartare."

"OK. Could you cut a new one?" he asks her as she takes it out of the display.

"This one is pretty fresh, [the butchers] just cut it."

"You wouldn't be just trying to make me feel better?"

"No, no, they just cut it."

I ask Sarah about this interaction later on in the day. "I noticed you steered that customer away from the filet mignon for the steak tartare."

"I could tell he didn't want to spend the money, so I wanted him to know that he would still be getting something good. And I try to get people away from the tenderloin. I mean, filet mignon's not that great. It's tender, but when you cut it that many times, like with a tartare, it doesn't matter how tender it is."

"People have an idea in their heads of what they want and of what's good?" I reply.

She nods. "They're scared. They can't cook. They either make the same thing the same way or someone gave them a recipe and they don't want to do anything different because they're afraid they're going to screw it up. I try to give them confidence."

Counter workers, whose philosophy asserts that the shop's meat is superior to retail outlets, who possess considerable knowledge of meat and its preparation, and who act with confidence in these beliefs and in their knowledge, aim to convey both the meat's form and function to customers. They feel they can "read" customers well when it comes to their desires, needs, and tastes. A customer's order serves as a starting point. Lamb shanks, as the third customer asked for earlier, are a very specific cut of meat that cannot be substituted for something else. Hence Ted merely told him about the physical presentation of the cuts and how the gristle won't factor into the flavor during cooking, but still offered to trim it since he seemed to be bothered by it.

Sarah's customer, however, presented her with an opportunity to expand his tastes. She "read" that he ordered filet mignon out of habit, or because he thinks it's a high-quality cut of meat, or perhaps out of a degree of fear of trying something different, and that he did not really want to spend the money on such an expensive cut. If he had said, "I'd like filet mignon, please," Sarah might have simply asked how many pieces and sold it to him, as Charlie did with the pork loin order. But he specifically said he was making steak tartare from it on his own, which told Sarah, who knows what tartare "should" be made from, that he knows something about meat, but not a lot. He offered a cracked window, which Sarah opened. By showing lost customers that they can have a better cut of meat, counter workers feel they provide them with the "confidence" to be not just better consumers, but better cooks. By using their own confidence in their knowledge and ability to interact with customers, they aim to "train" customers. While not using this term, cocktail bartenders and barbers also aim to educate their customers and clients about their taste community.

A young man walks into Milk and Honey on a Wednesday night and takes a seat next to me at the small, four-seat bar. Tonight's bartender is Mickey, who is originally from Belfast, Northern Ireland. Mickey got serious about cocktails and bartending in college, and he decided to move to New York City when he heard about Milk and Honey so he could work there. He greets his customer and asks him what he would like.

"I'm waiting for my friend, but I'll order anyway. I'll have a vodka Gibson."

"I'm sorry, but I don't have vodka, or pickled onions. Are there any other flavors you like?"

"Um, something minty?"

"Sure. Maybe with another light spirit, like gin?"

"Hmm, I never really get gin."

"I'll make something with gin but that doesn't have a strong gin taste."

"OK, yeah."

As Mickey starts making the drink, the man's friend arrives and sits down. They chat a bit, and Mickey takes the friend's order.

"Good evening, sir. Have you been here before?"

He shakes his head.

"OK, well we have a verbal menu. So what I'm going to need from you are hints or clues, flavors or spirits that you like, or that you don't like, so that I know to steer clear of certain things."

"Well, I normally drink vodka, but he [his friend] says you don't have it."

"Right. How do you usually drink vodka?"

"Just vodka tonics."

"OK, so the effervescence. Do you like raspberries?"

"Yeah. But not sweet."

"What I have in mind has sweetness to it, but isn't sweet."

"Sure, sounds good."

Mickey makes both drinks and presents them to the men.

"For you, sir, I have an East Side Rickey, that's gin, soda water, fresh lime juice, and mint. And for you a Raspberry Fix, that's muddled raspberries, gin, lemon juice, and some simple syrup. Enjoy guys."

Cocktail bartenders use several tactics, in the form of questions, to find the right drinks for customers. On this night Mickey begins with the standard introductory question at Milk and Honey: have you been here before? (Mickey asks this question to the second man, but not the first.) If they have, then they may have an idea of what they like and want. A negative answer tells him that these customers may not be familiar with craft cocktails or the bar, which means he may have to dig a little deeper to find the right drink for them. Through the order he gradually gathers information on what the customers like.[8]

Mickey uses several common sets of inquiries. He asks what spirits or flavors they like, in search of "hints or clues." Cocktail bartenders learn a lot about a customer's tastes from the spirit or flavors they name. Gin, for instance, is a light spirit, like some rums and tequilas, as opposed to most whiskeys and aged rums, which are dark spirits. Because of the effect of aging, dark spirits tend to have bolder, more complex flavors than light spirits. Cocktail bartenders stay within these general spirit categories when conceiving a drink. They don't want to give a customer who is unfamiliar with craft cocktails or spirits a strong, complex flavor. Doing so might scare them off from the taste world.

"I always say acquired taste is a just reward for an effort put forth," says Phil. "Think about scotch. It's such an intense, really big flavor, you have to like work your way into drinking it. But once you get your way into drinking it, it's like an amazing, amazing, it's probably, arguably one of the most complex spirits. Just from different Highland scotches to Islays, which are really peaty. It's an amazing spirit. But you can't just decide that you're going to drink Laphroaig one day.* If it's the first time you drink it straight, you're going to be like, 'Ugh, this shit's terrible.' Well, it's not actually terrible, you just made a bad decision to try Laphroaig first rather than trying to drink a strong gin drink, then bourbon, then work your way up to scotch."

In other words, in the democratic spirit, taste takes times to develop, but it can be developed through effort. Cocktail bartenders don't want to quash that effort from the jump.

Mickey's first customer orders a vodka Gibson, while the second normally drinks vodka tonics. Vodka is the lightest of light spirits, since it's flavorless, colorless, and odorless. Gin is a potentially easy substitute for vodka drinkers, since it is also (mostly) colorless and can be mildly flavored. I ask Mickey about this order and how he came to choose these drinks later in the night, after the men had left.

"A vodka Gibson is a strong vodka drink," he says. "When he said he liked mint, I knew the East Side would work. He wasn't sure about gin, but it's not a strong gin flavor, and he already drinks Gibsons [which are strong]. The other liked effervescence and fruit, so I made another light gin drink."

Mickey uses both drinks as "gateways" to open a customer's "window" of curiosity, match them with a product that suits their tastes, and inform them of mixology.[9] Liking strong vodka drinks and the flavor of mint and fizzy vodka drinks and the flavor of fruit and citrus made Mickey's job easy.

---

* Islay is an island off the coast of Scotland known for its peaty/smoky scotches, which are very strong in flavor. Of the nine distilleries on the island, Laphroaig's whisky is probably the strongest.

Finally, he deals with the issue of "sweetness," by explaining to his customer how the drink he's making won't be sweet, but will still have a sweetness to it. According to the basic principles of mixology, a successful cocktail must be balanced. Here Mickey does not mean a sweetened drink, but a drink with sweet elements, or "notes" in it, such as a type of spirit or liqueur. While cocktail bartenders regularly use a variety of modifiers to round out flavors, such as sweetening agents, sometimes a drink is categorized as sour or bitter rather than sweet, depending on the ingredients and their ratios in the recipe. By knowing if a customer prefers sweet over sour, cocktail bartenders can home in on a particular drink family.

These lines of inquiry are how cocktail bartenders "read" a customer. Each question narrows the field of possibilities for what drink to make. If a customer likes vodka, they avoid dark spirits. If a customer likes fruity drinks, they make something shaken. For cocktail bartenders, the customer's order is more than just passively receiving information. They see it as an exchange from which they learn how to provide customers with a unique tasting experience while informing them of mixology. And the order is most important for those lost customers. As Joaquin says, "I'll ask people to tell me what they want and they'll probably say five things, and maybe the third or fourth one's actually the one that they mean, they just haven't really thought about it."

Whole-animal butcher shop workers often use very similar tactics. Sarah's customer earlier knew what he wanted, but often a worker will ask customers what meat they normally eat, how they normally cook it, and what they want to do with it for the evening ("what's on tonight's menu?"). As with cocktail bar customers, their responses inform butcher shop workers of their taste (that is, if they're experienced, curious, or lost) and narrow the options of what cut would be the right cut for them. For instance, if they're just cooking for themselves and don't want to fuss, workers will suggest a pan-searing cut. Throughout the order they gauge a customer's tastes and cooking skills, and suggest meat on these bases.

Finally, barbers also have their own ways of reading and educating clients. But more so than cocktail bartenders and butcher shop workers who deal with people's taste in and knowledge of meat and drinks, barbers must deal with more sensitive matters concerning men's perceptions of their looks and their own body. They also have to actually touch their clients. These facts add extra challenges to the consultation.

One afternoon a young man named Damian sits in Van's chair. Damian's hair is dark brown, a little unkempt around the ears, and not very carefully

FIGURE 14. Van consulting with a client. Photo by Chantal Martineau.

styled. After introducing himself, sitting Damian down, and getting the apron to put on him, Van asks his regular first question.

"So what are we doing?"

"I want it short on the sides," replies Damian.

"How long ago did you get it cut?" By now Van has put the apron on and is casually running his hands through Damian's hair from behind, talking to him by looking through the mirror.

"About a month. It grows really fast."

"So take it back a month?"

"Yeah, especially the sides. It's too puffy."

"It's puffy because you shampoo it," says Van. "I just touched your hair once and I can feel you wash it at least a few times a week."

A little surprised, Damian nods in agreement as Van continues.

"Hair grows the same speed for everyone. It grows fastest in the back, then here [points to Damian's sides], then here [holds top of Damian's head]. The blood comes up the back and then along the sides. You have a lot of hair, but it's not really that thick. Do you use any products?"

Damian puts on an unsettled face, as if he is not sure what he means by products or is offended by the question, and responds, "No, I like things easy."

"Well, don't shampoo, how easy is that! Try cutting it in half."

Damian seems very receptive to what Van is telling him. Van, who has sprayed Damian's hair with water and is now combing it, continues.

"The reason your hair is the way it is is because of shampoo. It moves really well. You have great movement in your hair. What kind of shampoo do you use?"

"I don't know . . . it's in a green bottle."

"Well, if you want to shampoo sometimes, I recommend a moisturizing shampoo."

Like sure-spoken orders of pork loins and Negronis, many haircuts are simple. A client clearly explains what he wants, the barber understands, asks some basic questions (for example, what size clipper guard to use), and gets to work (or he is a regular, in which case the barber already knows what he wants and what to do). But some are tricky. Barbers face two interrelated obstacles, based on the different types of clients they encounter, which potentially get in the way of accomplishing their goal of giving them a "good" haircut—one their clients will like and an experience they will enjoy—and teaching them a sense of style.

To barbers, many clients are both insecure about their appearance (which may or may not translate into a lack of confidence in other areas of their lives) and uncertain about what they want their hair to look like, or at least how to convey what they want it to look like (similar to cocktail bartenders and whole-animal butcher shop workers thinking customers don't know what they want and/or how to express it). Like cocktail bartenders and whole-animal butcher shop workers, barbers also claim they can "read" if clients are insecure about their appearance and uncertain about how to clearly express what they want. One day I ask Thorin if he can tell whether a client is insecure.

"Oh my god! Oh yes. It's just unbelievable. Unbelievable insecurities, yeah. Next time you're in, watch. I have one client like that. It's brutal; you can't cut his hair. He literally is looking like this the whole time [tilts his head down], away from me the whole time. I'm like, 'Hold your head up.' I always have to talk to him like a child. Like, I do that with little kids that come in, little six-year-olds. 'Now, can you look in the mirror and just look at yourself? Be nice and straight and still.' Like, I want to say that to this 35-year-old guy who is married and has got a kid on the way. I'm like, 'Dude, it's okay.' And I know that's [being insecure], it's just weird. So strange."

By considering some clients as insecure about their appearance, despite not knowing them personally, barbers put themselves in a caring role of helping them to improve how they feel about how they look.[10] As professionals, confident in both their technical and social skills, they feel they can use their expertise to understand and provide what their clients need in a manner that will not intimidate or insult them.[11] Barbers also think clients usually have an idea of what they want their hair to look like, but often lack the ability to communicate it to them clearly. Bret explains the importance of asking clients questions: "Somebody will come in and say, 'I want short on the sides,' 'A side part,' whatever it is. But it's trying to get to the point where, 'Do you want short?' or 'Would you like really short? Would you like a clean look, more of a clean look?' I think it ends up being the questions I ask them, because they really don't know. They know what they want but they don't really know what they want. Trying to make it to the point, 'Would you like it short? How short will you go? Do you want clipper short, sheen short, or scissors nice and neat?' It's difficult to decide how you get to it since it's knowing what to ask and interpreting. It's the way they come in and how they look."

By "interpreting," Bret refers to both understanding what clients tell barbers about what they want, as well as "reading" their clients' lives and personalities, through both direct and indirect means.

"We get a lot of clients who come," says Miles, "they'll sit down the first time, and you kind of size them up—who is this guy?—as much as you can. A guy told me he was a lawyer and he moved here from Kentucky. He's probably a very simple, nonchalant, easygoing guy. He doesn't want anything extreme, he doesn't want to stand out. He just kind of wants a basic, clean, classic haircut."

"A classic kind of lawyer, corporate kind of look or whatever," I add.

"Exactly. Sometimes he might say, 'Oh, I want something a little more edgy.' 'Edgy' to him is putting product in his hair, you know what I mean?"

"It's not like a faux hawk or anything like that."

"Yeah, exactly. Then you'll have like the kid who comes in who is like a fashion student or like a photographer and he doesn't really have a job or he works freelance and that allows him to kind of do whatever he wants. He sits down, and you know, his shorts are shorter than ever and they were obviously jeans at one point and he has a million and one tattoos and he's real cool and edgy, you know? Those dudes, you know you'll be a little more loose with your scissors and leave some sections super long, some parts really short, and he's going to be OK with that because he's looking for that extreme look. Just sizing people up, really."

Even if they have a regular who gets the same haircut every time he comes in, barbers still ask what they want (for regulars, a simple "Same thing?"

suffices). After the general "So what are we doing?" question, Van, in the previous example, asks Damian how long ago he got it cut. For clients whom they read are uncertain of what they want, this question is very common because the answer tells the barber how much hair to take off (or what "short" means). Hair grows about a half an inch a month, on average, so for Van "taking it back a month" would probably satisfy his client (if he liked his last haircut). Van also touches Damian early. Like other barbers who use this strategy, he does so to set the client at ease, to begin the touching while asking questions when the client may not even notice (and by the time he does, the haircut has already begun).

In this case, Damian presents Van with a clear problem during the consultation: he thinks the sides of his hair are too puffy. Barbers stress being honest with their clients and are quick to point out their hair issues to them directly, such as a bad part and places where they are losing hair, or when they make impossible requests. For instance, as mentioned earlier, barbers love when clients show them pictures of themselves, so they can see exactly what they want. But sometimes clients show barbers pictures of other people, like celebrities. I ask Michael how he handles these situations: "I mean, they can't get offended if you tell them honest things. If their hair isn't that texture, you can't do it. We don't alter genes. You can chemically relax hair or straighten it, but you can't change the nature of your hair. Compromise [with them], and do what you can logically do."

Confident in their professionalism, barbers feel clients should accept that what they tell them about their hair is correct, while also listening to the advice they may have to give, if they want to "look good." But along with being honest in the previous example, Van also compliments Damian by telling him he has a lot of hair and that it has great movement. Barbers want clients to know their hair's strengths and weaknesses, and how to accentuate or work with the former and minimize or avoid the latter. Most importantly, Van assures Damian that following his advice will make his life "easier." Improving their clients' lives, such as by making them look good while also simplifying how to achieve a stylish look, is an important part of the job for barbers. They want to provide their clients with styles they can easily replicate on their own on a daily basis. As Miles has said to clients at the conclusion of haircuts, "You can part it, but I cut it so you won't have to."

Along with telling clients about their hair, barbers also show them how they can care for it, when possible.

Mark has a client in his chair with a big, bushy beard, which he says he wants trimmed.

"OK. What do you want me to do?"

"I don't know. I like the length. I just want it to look a little less . . . feral."

"OK. I see it's much thicker here [points toward the jawline]. But we'll see, in two weeks this will grow in [shows by the cheeks]. But I can use scissors on little bits and parts. I'll just do some stuff here [at the jawline] and we'll see."

He agrees to Mark's suggestion. Mark puts the headrest on the chair, reclines it back, and gets to work.

"What's the best way to maintain a beard?" asks the client as Mark starts.

"It depends," Mark replies. "If you want it clean and sharp, then machine [he holds up his clippers]. If you want it to look more natural, then scissors. But it's trial and error. If you like the length you have now, then use scissors, like I'm doing. Here, [tilts the chair up a bit] you'll watch what I do."

Mark proceeds to trim his client's beard, indicating when he is cutting areas on his face that are especially thick with hair, and highlighting how he is "shaping" it. Most clients getting a shave or beard trim do so infrequently and for relaxation. Some clients, like Mark's, grow a beard without knowing how to care for it. He asks for advice, offering Mark a clear window to open and enter. For barbers, the trim and any other service are potential teaching moments, when they can show clients the difference between "clean and sharp" and "natural" and teach them about how to care for the hair on their own bodies.

With these examples in mind, we can ask a simple question: are these workers right in their interpretations of these consumers and their tastes? Sometimes they probably are, and sometimes they probably aren't, but the answers are unimportant. These workers act as if they are correct about how their customers and clients behave, think, and taste, act confidently to influence them, and shape their consumption experiences.

Creating Regulars

I walk into Death & Co. on a Wednesday evening, as they are opening. Phil greets me and takes my order. After a few minutes Avery Glasser, a co-founder of Bittermens, a nascent company that makes small batches of bitters, comes in, greets Phil and hands him a small medicine bottle full of homemade grapefruit bitters. He thanks him and they talk for a bit before Avery goes downstairs to talk to Dave, the owner. He asks Phil to save him three seats at the bar, which Phil agrees to do. After a few minutes, a couple in their thirties come in and sit at the bar.

"What can I get for you?" Phil asks the man.

"Well, I think I want something different. I want a drink that reminds me of the wavy horizon line, where the sky meets the earth, like you see when you're driving in a desert."

Phil doesn't react in any specific way. He just looks up in thought for a second, and then asks the woman what she would like. She orders the Buffalo Soldier, a bourbon drink on the menu.

After working on them, Phil puts both cocktails down on the napkins in front of the couple.

"Buffalo Soldier, and for you, something I've been working on."

Indeed, the drink is cloudy, and the refracted candlelight from the bar gives it a certain wavy quality. In interpreting the order, Phil aims to capture the visual description.

This order surprises me. Cocktail bartenders typically don't like it when customers make obscure requests, like a drink that reminds them of a feeling or, in this case, something visual. Several other bartenders had told me about hating such orders, so I expected Phil to say something like, "I'm not making that. Let me know when you're ready to really order." But I later learned from Phil that the customer was a regular. Being a regular customer of a business always comes with certain perks.[12] These businesses are no different, except the extra personal attention revolves around their unique products and services. And the relationship also goes both ways between workers and regulars. While Phil wouldn't normally fill such an unusual order, he does for regular customers, who in turn provide feedback on new drinks.[13]

They feel creating regulars—a goal of these workers—is a matter of gaining people's trust as they teach them, shape their tastes, and bring them into the taste community. Cocktail bartenders gain the trust of their customers by making them the right drink, initially and consistently. The start can be a gateway drink. As Theo explains: "If they haven't been [to a cocktail bar], there are drinks that they are not used to. There are definitely certain things that you know that people are going to love. Start with like a Gold Rush.* After that first drink you can do something with a little more [complexity].

* A Gold Rush is a simple, refreshing bourbon-based cocktail with lemon juice and honey syrup.

'You want something bourbon again?' You put out a Paper Plane, which is amaro, bourbon, and lemon [juice].* That's moving up. It's just so interesting watching the progression of how people who have never been somewhere like this will experience [it]."

"Moving up" to these workers is a sign that their service teaching is working. Cocktail bartenders intend the orders to build throughout a night and over multiple nights, from drink to drink, until a customer acquires a new understanding of and a new vocabulary to discuss taste, and hopefully comes back to the bar. Bartenders start with drinks in certain families, and then branch off from them to a higher level of complexity based on an ingredient. The key is trust. As Toby says: "The more educated drinkers you could have at your bar, the better. Try to get the customer exactly what they want, and if they order something that you don't necessarily think is a great drink, make it for them, but then you try to, on their next time, once you have a little bit of trust, push it. *Then you have them.* I think I can speak for all the bartenders I've ever worked with, when somebody's interested in what you're doing and wants to learn, that's awesome. That's the greatest customer to have, is you get to show them the way, especially somebody who is so set in their ways" (emphasis added).

The timeline for gaining trust and creating regulars varies by occupation. People often have more than one drink in a night. Sometimes they have three or more. So bartenders have a few cracks at teaching them and shaping their tastes before they may never see them again. They pride themselves on turning vodka drinkers into whiskey drinkers by the end of the night. But most people don't get haircuts every week. Some go once a month, every two months, or longer. When a new client gets a haircut, a barber has no idea if he'll return for another. For this reason, barbers usually give fairly basic haircuts to first-time clients. But crafting a hairstyle for a client takes many visits.

"It's great to nail a haircut on the first haircut," explains Miles, "but it's also really cool when they come in and say, 'Yo, I loved the haircut you gave me last time, but there are just a few adjustments I'd like to do.' Like, that's perfect, because now at least we have something that we can base off of what you want. 'This is what you wanted, this is what you told me, this is what I

---

* Amaro is a type of herbal Italian liqueur and is usually bitter and syrupy. The Paper Plane also has Aperol in it, an Italian aperitif that is also bitter. Sammy, a bartender at Milk and Honey, invented it.

did, but you really meant you wanted. . . .' Kind of like critique some things. It's like a working process. By the third haircut absolutely I'm going to give you exactly what you want."

Barbers follow their instincts when reading a first-time client (for example, does he seem adventurous? What kind of job does he have?) and try to stay close to what he requests. They do so to build trust with the client, who will hopefully like the haircut, return, and perhaps become a regular. Many barbers echo what Miles says about third haircuts. He doesn't mean the first one isn't good in a technical or stylistic sense. But since the goal is to create a style that works for the client and perhaps to push the client out of his normal style, they need time to both learn what he wants and, since everyone's head shape, face, and hair are slightly different, really learn what his hair can and can't "do." At the same time the client needs to come to trust the barber to understand and give him what he wants. The more experienced and confident the barber is, the sooner he or she will offer advice on different and more experimental styles for clients.

One day Ruben finishes cutting his regular client Matt's hair, for the third time. They have a pretty good rapport when he's in the chair. Matt has a basic weight line-style haircut, long on top, a bit shorter on the sides, naturally parted on the left side of the head. Ruben goes all scissors except on the sideburns and neck.

"Thanks, Ruben," Matt says, as he hands him his tip.

"No problem, bro. Next time, maybe we'll do something [slight pause] different."

"Oh yeah, like what?" asks Matt.

Ruben looks at his hair and thinks for a second.

"Maybe something in the back, because the way you have it, it could only be long or how you have it. Do you have one cowlick or two? It could be the part."

"I think I only have one, over here," he says while pointing.

"Next time we'll wet it, break it, and comb it over and see if you have another part."

Matt agrees and leaves. About six weeks later, he returns, but asks for the same haircut. The next time goes differently.

"I'm bored," says Ruben as he puts the apron on Matt. "I'm bored with your hair."

"We can try something different," Matt says.

Ruben then combs his hair repeatedly, switching between looking at it through the mirror and down in front of him.

"You ever try switching someone's part?" he asks Joey, who's working next to him.

"Yeah. Why, he's got a deceptive part?"

"I think."

Ruben then shifts all of Matt's hair over to the other side, so he can get some ideas. He combs and inspects and then says, mostly to himself, "No, this is the problem right here. That's why you do it this way."

The haircut begins and they start talking about music. After a few minutes, Ruben starts using the clippers on the sides, which he hadn't done this early in the haircut before.

"What is that, a three [guard] you're using?" Matt asks.

"Four. I'll use a three on the very, very bottom. The reason I'm doing it is because I don't want that [pointing to the side of the new part] to be a problem. With a four it's easier to avoid a problem."

The haircut and banter continue. When Ruben finishes he takes the handheld mirror to show Matt the back and sides from different angles. Since he used clippers, it's a lot shorter on the sides now, and the part is now on the other side of his head. By using clippers to switch the part, avoid a problem area, and create more of a fade, Ruben completely changed Matt's hairstyle, not radically so, but noticeably.

"Nice," says Matt.

"I did it *super* short on the bottom."

"I noticed that."

"I was afraid of that, but as long as you keep this [the new part], it'll work. Check it out, see how nice and round it is, from the profile? As long as your top is long enough, you could have it somewhat shorter. And this is without product."

Matt gets up to pay while Ruben cleans up. He shakes his head as Matt comes back with his tip.

"Switch the part. I can't believe it took me so long to figure that out."

"Yeah, you suck. I can't believe it took you so long," says Matt, sarcastically.

"Oh yeah, well, it took me a year to figure it out, but you've had your hair your whole life. So who sucks now?"

They both laugh.

By the third haircut, Ruben figured Matt for a regular, and he had figured out Matt's hair. With over a decade of experience cutting hair, Ruben is confident in what he can do and where he can take a relationship with a client. This state of affairs is good for both of them. Ruben can now give Matt exactly what he wants. He also assumes Matt trusts him to give him what he wants consistently, to be honest with him, and to push him beyond his current style (if he is in fact curious and wants to be pushed—not all regular clients, or any regular customers of the other businesses, do), without leading him astray from who he is stylistically. Matt confirms Ruben's assumption by letting him push him, and Ruben confirms Matt's choice to trust him by giving him a hairstyle he likes. Ruben gets to use his technical skills and sense of style, and Matt gets a new hairstyle (and sense of style) and learns how to re-create it. It takes nearly a year of haircuts, but it happens.

The timeline for gaining trust and creating regulars for butchers falls somewhere in between cocktail bartenders and barbers. Customers must take the meat home and cook it before judging its quality, if it was easy to prepare, and if what the butcher told them about it (how it tastes, how it cooks) was true. They may not return the next day (some do), or even within a week (some do), to buy another cut, but if they liked it they probably won't wait four to six weeks like people often do between haircuts. Butchers use very similar techniques and language for the process of creating regulars as cocktail bartenders and butchers. The shop Dickson's opened for a brief time in TriBeCa, in the market All Good Things, presents a good example. Given its small size and low volume, usually only one employee worked at the All Good Things location. I joined Lena there one Thursday.

"When I started working down here, Jeff and Dana told me that I would only sell tenderloin, because that's all that anyone buys," says Lena while she trims some brownish spots from a tenderloin to redden it up. "They warned me not to expect to sell skirts or anything like that. Now, I'm selling skirts, feathers, and even marrow bones, although people mostly buy them for their dogs."

"How were you able to break people out of buying the same thing?" I ask.

"You've just got to talk to people. If they trust you, you could get them to try new things. 'Another customer of mine gets this. . . .' Something to bring them in."

Three successive customers come in throughout the day who show how butcher shop workers try to create regulars, and how they interact with them once they have them.

A middle-aged woman walks up to the counter and orders two rib eyes and a rack of pork. There were two racks in the case, right next to each other, with the bones facing one another like parentheses.

"I have two. Do you want the shoulder side, or the loin side?" she asks.

"Ummm," utters the customer, unsure.

"The shoulder side is fattier, and the loin side is a bit leaner."

"I'll take the loin."

A woman with a child in a stroller then comes up to the stand and stares into the case.

"Do you have any questions?" asks Lena.

"I'm trying to remember what I got here last time. What's the one you sear on all four sides? Is that the culotte?"

"No, that's the zabuton. But the culotte is a very nice alternative to the strip steak."

"Is it fattier?"

"Well, the zabuton has more fat marbling, and the culotte has a fat cap. That's really the only difference in terms of fat content. The culotte steak is the cap of the top sirloin, with a similar texture as the strip, which is in the loin section of the cow. But the texture is not that accordion style like the zabuton or the boneless chuck short rib over here [she points in the display]. It's denser. It's usually left on the top sirloin at the supermarket. But then the texture changes so much in the cut, and the culotte tastes very different from the top sirloin, even though it comes off it."

Nodding along, the woman says "I'll take two [culottes]."

Mel, a middle-aged man of Chinese descent, and one of Lena's regulars, comes up to the stand.

"How was the pancetta?" she asks after greeting him.

"Delicious."

"How did you make it?"

"In pasta."

They then chat for a bit about food, particularly some of the grosser products. They talk about bung, or pig rectum, and intestines, and the different ways that Chinese prepare them compared to Latinos (as a half-Chinese and half-Cuban, Lena has experienced both).

"I'm not into that kind of stuff," says Mel.

"I like some of it, and the ones that I don't like I'm grossed out by because of their flavor, not because of what they are."

The conversation drifts to different dim sum items that they like and dislike, until another customer arrives to pick up an order. They resume when Lena finishes.

"What's the difference between the lamb shoulder chop and the arm chop? Are they lean?" asks Mel, who had been glancing in the case in the meantime.

"The shoulder chop is fattier, so it has more flavor. I prefer more flavor," she says.

"Me too. I'll take three of the shoulder chops."

These three customers are at different stages of being "brought in." By asking the first question, Lena teaches the first customer a bit about the different types of pork ribs, which she seems to have not known about. Ribs are ribs, she probably figures. She gives information about a topic the customer never would have thought to ask. With luck, this extra knowledge brought this customer in. The second customer has been to the shop before, Lena later tells me, and has already tried rare cuts like the zabuton, which Lena introduced her to. Lena gives her a more detailed explanation of the differences between the zabuton and the culotte than to most customers, and how they compare to more common cuts like the strip steak. The woman clearly took Lena's last advice about searing the zabuton on all four sides, but forgetting the name lets her really go into depth. Mel, the final customer, has been brought in.[14] He knows his meat and how to prepare it, and he is curious about unusual cuts. He comes to the shop at least once a week, and he and Lena have a casual relationship based on their love of food and sharing an ethnic heritage. Lena doesn't give him as much information on the difference between the lamb shoulder chop and the arm chop as she did for the zabuton and culotte. It isn't necessary for a regular.

Creating regulars is rewarding for these workers. But the best and most frequent rewards are the "emotional tips," or comments about the product and service they receive.[15] They serve as intrinsic rewards and validation for the work they do, and can come from anyone they serve whether they're regulars or there for the first time. Workers from all three workplaces speak in very similar ways about the feeling they get from giving consumers what they want. I asked these workers what they like the most about doing their job. Their responses revolve around customer and client reactions from having combined specialized service and cultural knowledge in their interaction. Jason, a cocktail bartender, says, "There's that moment of serendipity when people first taste the drink that you have made for them, and their eyes light up. They go [gasps], 'Whoa! *That* is a good drink.' Everything else is just the pursuit of that moment." I ask Jeff what he likes about being a butcher: "The part I like the most is helping a customer and then cutting something custom for them. Like, they come to me and they're not really sure what they want, but they know how they want to cook, they know how they want to eat, or they know how many people they're serving, and they know what they want it to look like. Then I'm like, 'Oh, well, what's going to be perfect for what you want to do is this and I'll cut it for you this way.' Start to finish it's like a custom job, which is pretty cool. That's different than just selling meat out of the case that I've already cut. If we have an exchange where it's like, 'I'm not really sure what I want, but I want to slow cook, it's going to be for this many people, maybe beef, maybe pork.' That's the exciting part. I'm thinking about what do I have in the walk-in? What could really wow this person's guests? What's the perfect size for the pot this person has? Just really tailoring exactly what they want for how they want to cook or how they want to eat, all of those dimensions."

Finally, I ask Bret what he likes most about being a barber: "It's probably making people feel good about themselves. Most of the time people walk out and they do feel good. They want to look their best. That's kind of [why I] started [barbering]—I knew I could make my friends feel better than they already did. It's about making someone feel better about themselves, so the old adage was 'looking good, feeling good.' You do feel good. You walk out, buy a new jacket, a new shirt, and you feel good about yourself. Your hair, no matter what you're wearing, your hair is always on you. You could have the highest fashion or jeans and a t-shirt—if your hair looks good, that's a change. And *understanding* that they feel good about it. They feel good about it because they do look good and they *understand* that they look good. Dissecting some haircuts and getting them to where they would look the best or feel the best about it."

In other words, it is not just the quality of the product or service that makes consumers feel good. The knowledge behind why it is of high quality, which these workers teach to their consumers, also contributes to the feeling.

Handling Challenges

As these examples show, while interactions with customers and clients seem personal, with the exchanges meant to deliver a more tailored service and/ or product, these workers still follow a script. It isn't, however, a corporate-driven set of rules for behavior. It is rather a cultural script of their own occupational community's and business's making based on the philosophies of their taste community. Cocktail bartenders have a lot of recipes committed to memory. But when customers tell them what they like, bartenders rely on proven drinks (that is, drinks many people with similar tastes enjoy) and established templates to make a cocktail for them. Barbers refer to specific aspects of their clients' hair and head during consultations and when giving advice. But many haircuts require the same procedure, and most hairstyles require the same set of steps to achieve. And butchers have dozens of cuts on display. But when customers say what they want to cook for the evening and/or how they want to prepare it, the options shrink immediately. Situations sometimes constrain their ability to follow this script, such as especially busy periods and consumers who assuredly want a specific item (that is, experienced consumers).[16] But for the most part, they are able to regularly use it to teach while serving. Given their confidence and status as knowledgeable experts, these workers expect an easy exchange with consumers, especially those who are unsure of their own tastes or of what they want. In other words, they expect them to play their part in the performance of interactive service. They grow frustrated when consumers go off script, challenge their expertise, and don't follow what they say. These acts are challenges to their self-identities as knowledgeable workers.

A woman walks into Dickson's and asks Charlie, "Do you have cooked chickens?"

"Yes, they're rotisserie."

"Are they organic?"

"No, they're all-natural, hormone-free, from local farms. But they're not organic."

The woman shows a concerned and puzzled look on her face. "What does that mean then?"

"There's the long answer and the short answer. The short answer is that small farmers started doing things organically, and they had their own rules for what was organic. Then the government said, 'That's great, let's do that,' and they took the rules of the farmers times a thousand. Many small farmers don't bother paying for the designation. The long answer I've gone to school for."

"Oh. Are they good?"

"Very good."

The woman still looks concerned. She takes a step away from the counter, looks down at the meat in the display, and then after a few moments walks slowly out of the shop. Charlie looks at me and shakes his head. I ask if people ask him the "organic" question often. It was early in my internship, so it was the first time I had heard it.

"Every day," he says. "Some people leave without hearing what we're about."

"The word 'organic' is that powerful?"

"Yeah, if they hear we don't have [organic products], they leave. They just don't get it. Some people are receptive, if they're into cooking. Some you know are not, and they're just going to roast the shit out of it [the meat they bought]. Those people are hopeless."[17]

People at Dickson's hold critical opinions of the larger meat industry and of potentially misleading labels in the food world like "organic." Whole-animal butcher shops source their meat from small farmers who cannot afford the expensive USDA "organic" label. For workers at these shops, a label means nothing. Knowing the farmers and how they raise their animals means everything. But their approach in interacting with all customers is to inform, not criticize, regardless of how they really feel about their tastes. In this manner they resemble professional musicians, also cultural experts who know what's good, and who dislike the tastes and requests of their audience members, but still play the same popular songs for them.[18] Butcher shop workers expect people to be receptive to what the shop is all about when told. Customers who do not "get it," or do not follow their role in the interaction appropriately, are "hopeless," or will continue following bad food habits, thinking wrong thoughts about meat, and having "bad" tastes.

Like butcher shop customers, the cocktail bar customers who do not "get it" do not follow the script of ordering. They also try to "out-cocktail" the cocktail bartenders. For instance, I didn't learn that Phil's customer, the one who ordered a drink that would remind him of the horizon line in a desert, was a regular until after that night. It was an off-script order, which is why at first I was surprised Phil didn't chide him for such a silly request. Later on that night I went to Milk and Honey and talked to Mickey about it. After telling him the story of what I had just seen, he rolled his eyes and shook his head. "That's so fucking annoying, man. Just tell me sweet or sour. I also don't like it when customers ask me for a cocktail like how it was made in 1916 or something."

With verbal menus or when customers ask for something off the menu (known variously as "bartender's choice," or "coin toss"), bartenders can seem like they have hundreds of recipes committed to memory. A customer gives a hint or two—"I like bourbon," "I don't like bitter flavors"—and voilà, the bartender has a drink. And given the hype and fanfare around them, cocktail bartenders give the impression that they know every cocktail there is. While they know a lot of drinks from memory from having made them repeatedly, used them as starting points for variations, and read about them, bartenders are not above using shortcuts and aids. They keep a few basic drinks in rotation, usually gateway drinks they feel most people will enjoy, they will refer to books or notes or even a spreadsheet they keep on their phone, and they'll ask whoever else is behind the bar with them and even text bartender friends if they can't remember a drink or recipe or need advice. But some customers challenge them as so-called experts who know everything, and bartenders dislike customers who try to stump them. John, a bartender who works at PDT, recalls a customer he had: "Between myself and the other bartenders, we have a pretty wide knowledge of obscure cocktails, but they'll come in, and I know conceptually of the name. Like somebody came in and wanted a Japanese cocktail. I knew it was Carpano [Antica Vermouth] and rye, but I couldn't remember the proportions. And then the guy got upset. I said, 'Look, I have the Savoy [Cocktail] Book here, let me look it up.' He said, 'No! You shouldn't have to look it up. You should know this off the top of your head.' I said, 'You know, I'm sorry. I have a pretty good drink knowledge, but I can't remember the exact proportions. I know what ingredients are in it, I could make it how I think it should taste, but I'd rather make you a drink as it's called for. So I'll look it up in a second.' And the guy got upset."

With so much information about drinks available on the Internet, it is easy for a customer to ask for an obscure drink few people know. Doing so goes against the cultural script behind the order and undermines the authority of the bartender. Making the right drinks correctly, as John tried to do for his customer, is more important to bartenders than knowing them all by heart.

Barbers can teach their clients a lot, about their hairstyle during a cut and how to re-create it on their own and just generally improve their appearance. They meet resistance from them in two ways. Since men's perceptions of themselves and how they want to look come into play at barbershops, barbers often get strange requests from clients, or requests that barbers feel won't look good on them. They try to steer them away from their idea and toward a better one. Biology often comes into play, even the physical traits that form the basis of race. As Michael said earlier, "We don't alter genes."

"There's things I could do and there's things I couldn't do," says Thorin. "I think I'm pretty good at being able to relay that, but some people don't want to hear it. Some people *do not want to hear it.* I'll give you a specific example. I have an Asian guy who comes in. He shows me a picture of Ryan Gosling every single time he comes into the shop. I'm like, 'My man, that's going to be really tough because he's got thin white guy hair, like *thin*, Caucasian hair. You have fishing line.' Like, he has literal fishing line coming out of his head, which is totally fine. He's got thick, beautiful, black hair. It will never bald, it will never do anything, it will be jet black until the day he's 110 years old. But he's never going to have that head of [white person's] hair. Never. And he tries every time. I'm like, 'Alright, I'll give it a shot,' you know? But it's impossible, it's impossible."

"How do you do that, then?" I ask. "How do you get beyond that and try to show them, like . . . ?"

"I try to make him happy with what I'm doing. Technically I should just convince him to do something else, that it's just not going to work, but he doesn't want to hear it. He's in law school, he feels pretty entitled, I'm sure. He probably thinks he's very smart, and I'm not going to take that away from him. He probably is very smart, but he's wrong about a lot of things, which he'll learn as he gets older. He's probably 23 to 24 years old and just doesn't know. I try to meet him in the middle, you know? I try to do what I can with the way he wants it and then I try to style his hair the way he thinks it would look good given the style that he likes, you know? Truth be told, I think he looks insane; he looks crazy. It's like you [me] coming in and being like, 'I want a curly, black Afro, and I want jet black hair, and I want it to be nappy and curly.' I would say to you, 'No. No, I just can't do it. Now, maybe if you go to some salon and they chemically treat and dye your hair and perm you' and all that shit. One, I don't have time, I don't ever want to learn that shit, and it would look terrible on you."[19]

If a client's in a barber's chair for the first time, the cut will be basic and the unsolicited advice limited. Greater honesty emerges with greater trust. But barbers usually speak up even with a new client when the request is more or less impossible to fill. They feel something prevents clients who don't listen from accepting the advice they give. For Thorin's client he thinks it's some combination of feeling entitled and being young. Usually clients are very receptive to the knowledge and stylistic advice barbers give them during the consultation and cut. But sometimes barbers perceive resistance from clients to their advice, which both compromises their status as experts over what clients "should" do with their hair and reinforces their understanding of clients as insecure and uncertain.

One early afternoon a tall, thin man named Chris sits in Van's chair.

"So what are we doing?" he asks.

"I'm looking for a clean look. Cut the sides and back closely, and thin out the hair on top. It's too clumpy."

Van looks at him through the mirror while standing behind the chair and putting on the apron. After running his fingers through the top of Chris's hair, he immediately asks, "Do you use shampoo every day?"

"Yes," says Chris.

"That's why it's clumping up. That's not your hair. Your hair is coarse and curly, and it's like a Brillo pad on top since you shampoo it every day. What I'm going to say to you, if I said the opposite, I'd make $10. But it's about making your life easier, which is what I'm going to do."

Van then provides Chris with a history of shampoo and shampooing, and explaining that since he has curly/wavy hair with a cuticle layer that comes up like fish scales he should avoid using shampoo because it removes its natural oils. He also describes hair as "alive or dead," or alive when it is left on its own, and dead when it gets too much shampoo. He ends with a question.

"Do you have dandruff?"

"Yeah."

Van moves Chris's hair from the crown of his head.

"Your head is bright red from the chemical burn from the ammonium, the alcohol, the ether, the lye, the sulfates. So in about three days when you stop shampooing, which I highly recommend you do . . ."[20]

"Stop *altogether*?" asks an incredulous Chris.

"Stop *altogether*! You never have to shampoo for the rest of your life. But in three days your head's going to itch like crazy. And in about four days, you're going to have flakes. Light flakes, not that kind of chunky, where with your fingernail you could take a chunk of head out. You're going to have a little bit of flaking, for the most part. You're going to have a little bit of scabbing because your head is so damaged from it. You've probably been using the dandruff shampoo, right?"

"Head and Shoulders."

"Right. You use Head and Shoulders because you have dandruff, which is dry skin. All Head and Shoulders is shampoo times two. Instead of taking off what normal shampoo takes off, it takes off twice as much and *really* dries your scalp out. That's why your head gets so red, because you're using twice the amount of shampoo. But in a month, your hair is going to be perfect. You're never going to have to wash it again. You can go twice as long between haircuts. You don't have to worry about thinning it out—you have thick hair, which is great, but it's going to sit down, it's going to look perfect, and it's going to feel great and moisturized. It's going to feel like hair, as opposed to the Brillo. Now, you can wash your hair once a week, if you feel like it. But with your hair I don't recommend it."

"Why?"

"Because your cuticle layer is so exposed, it's so opened up, that it's still going to damage your hair pretty good, and it's going to create a problem for you. If you want to wash it, this is all you need [holds up his comb in the mirror]. This and water."

"What about, like, styling products?"

"All are, for the most part, 90 percent plastic, so that [your hair] looks the way it did before you started processing it in the beginning. But most hair products that they're making are water soluble, so you don't have to worry about it too much."

"Plastic?"

"Plastic. Now, I know I sound fucking crazy saying all this shit, and I'd say 10 to 20 percent of people think I am. But I'm not wrong, is what I'm not."

The whole time Chris stares at Van in the mirror, with looks that range from pensiveness to disbelief. A few minutes of silence go by while Van cuts his hair.

"I've never heard this," says Chris, shaking his head.

"No, well, why would you?" says Van. "I used to be in product development with Chesebrough-Pond's, helping them develop products: colors, shampoos, conditioners, everything. And Chesebrough-Pond's owns like everything. They don't only own hair products; they own half the stuff you eat, half the clothes you buy.* So the biggest contributors to our magazines, our television shows, our movies are these conglomerate companies and some of the biggest-selling products they own are completely made up. It's a billion, billion, billion dollar business, shampoos and hair products, all that stuff. And every magazine, that's the biggest contributor. So why would they tell you? And they want your barber to tell you, like myself, because all I could do is lose money. It's contradictive to making money, but at least my soul feels better. I think you'll be very happy."

* Chesebrough-Pond's makes such products as Vaseline, Pond's body creams, Q-Tips, and Ragu spaghetti sauce. Unilever, the giant multinational consumer goods corporation, bought it in 1987.

After several minutes Chris asks, "How long does the itching last?"

"About a month."

"I'm *very* skeptical."

"What's the skeptical part?"

"I don't know. I've never heard this, ever."

"Believe me, it's not something I'm telling *you*," says Van. "It's something we say all day, every day, and it's why we have the clientele we have. It's because we're here to help, not sell you products. A lot of places are just set up to sell products, because they could make more money selling products than cutting hair. Because it's free money—cutting hair we actually have to work for—and we're telling you not to buy the products."

Once the haircut is over, Chris says he will consider giving up shampooing.

"You gotta commit; it's not a one-week thing."

"I'll try."

Minutes later, Van has a client named Nate in his chair. He goes through a similar conversation about avoiding shampoo to improve how his hair looks, but he avoids some of the details he gave Chris.

"How are you doing, Richard?" he asks me after the consultation.

"I'm doing well. How'd it go with that last guy?"

"You see how frustrated that guy made me, when I gave that whole speech? I wanted to stab him in the ear when he was like, 'I'm skeptical [in a whiny voice].' "

"Yeah, he was skeptical," I say.

"You've gotta be fucking kidding me. After all that shit! That's why I try not to, like even you saw me start to tell him [Nate] about shampoo, and I was like I can't do that again and have him be like, 'I don't believe you.' What do you mean you don't believe me? I'm trying to *not* sell you shampoo. *Not!* I'm trying to *not* make you give me money!"

"I guess he's so used to being told he has to buy something."

"He's what I hate about this fucking, well, the human race. Like, fine, you see it on TV, it must be real. You have a *professional* tell you, he's fucking crazy. I gave him *all* of it, and you know why I did that? Because I knew he wasn't going to believe me. But I still had to be like, 'No, I'm going to change this guy's mind.' 'I'm skeptical.' Yeah. He's an asshole."

As the barbers try to do, Van wants to make Chris's life easier. Given his cutting experience and background working on developing hair products, Van often shares his knowledge of shampoo with clients when they have a problem with their hair as a result of washing it. He aims to show them how they could simultaneously have more stylish hair while reducing the need to work on it. The advice fits with the shop's ethos of masculinity: men need not compromise their manhood by overgrooming themselves, which counters the emotional labor that's happening in the shop. As confident professionals who feel they know what works with hair, what does not, and how clients should take care of it to achieve the look they desire, barbers generally react to disbelief in or rejection of their advice with a shrug. In this case, Van does not; he pushes against it. But not obviously succeeding does not deter barbers from working on their clients in the same manner in the future, as Van does right away with Nate (albeit with less detail). Their confidence remains unshaken. Instead, not succeeding can lead barbers to reclassify a client who does not believe their advice is sound. The client goes from being "lost" to, in this case, becoming "an asshole." (Charlie similarly reclassified his customer who didn't listen to his explanation of the term "organic" as "hopeless.")

Unlike many service workers, frustration, exasperation, and any negative feelings for these new elite workers stems not from having to manage their own emotions or those of their customers and clients, or from the "bad" conditions of their jobs. It comes from having their authority and expertise questioned and challenged, and their advice ignored. For these workers, buying products like humane meat and craft cocktails and having services done like a well-styled haircut in these unique workplaces is as much a performance for consumers as it is for them in selling, giving, and making them. They must be "skilled consumers" as much as these workers must be skilled at their cultural repertoires. Sometimes these workers succeed in teaching and training customers and clients how to act and think while in their taste world, and sometimes they do not. Their indomitable confidence in the "good-" and "right-ness" of the products they sell, services they provide, and knowledge they bestow keep them teaching through service.

"Your ears are off, I can't do a straight line," jokes Jason to his client, nervously.

For the last half hour—the minimum amount of time Freemans allocates for normal haircuts—Jason has been trying to give his client, who happens to also be his roommate, a skin fade, or a tight cut that fades into the skin as it goes down the neck. After trimming the top and front of his head, Jason began by buzzing a line around the back, by the top of the ears, but it was clearly not straight. He then tried again near that line, but was also off by a bit. His roommate now has two crooked lines in the back of his head.

"You're fucking it up," says Miles, whose chair is diagonally opposite from Jason's in the shop.

As he works on his own client, Miles has been glancing at Jason through his mirror and occasionally turning his head directly at him. Barbers rarely comment on each other's work while they are with clients. When they do, that means a friend of the barber's is in the chair and they intend their comments to be instructional. Miles uses the shop's parlance to offer help, and Jason, embarrassed by his performance, takes it in.

"Tap! Tap the machine."

"I can't tap. Miles, you've got to show me how to do this."

"Turn the machine around."

Jason then turns the clippers around and starts using it in the other direction, which seems to work better.

"Go with the line," advises Miles, while still cutting his own client's hair.

"Up from the line?"

"How do you fade?" Miles says in a "you've gotta be kidding me" manner, cocking his head for emphasis.

"I'm not as good as you," says Jason, half-seriously.

Miles then leaves his client and goes over to Jason. Jason hands him the clippers and Miles shows him how to tap and follow the line. Left-handed, with subtle, quick motions that produce high-pitched buzzes and zaps, Miles opens his stance so Jason can see.

"Just do this all around."

Van, who has been watching from the cash register, holds up his wrist and taps on an invisible watch with his finger.

"I got another hour!" says Jason to Van's sarcastic "time is money" gesture.

Miles finishes with his client and comes over by me. He starts explaining to me that the fade starts too high, when Jason notices us.

"What? You talking about me?"

"Nah, well, yeah. I'm explaining to him what you're doing."

"Don't tell him, tell me! He's writing a book, I'm learning."

Miles and I go closer and he provides Jason with detailed instruction. Jason asks him many questions and frequently expresses being nervous that too many people are watching.

When he finally finishes, he sighs and says, "All right, guys, I'm going back to painting walls."

The next day, Miles and I are chatting over coffee next door at the restaurant with the espresso bar. I bring up Jason's haircut.

"Why was he having trouble with that? I mean, it seemed like he was . . ."

"Jason is brand new. Like, he is fresh out of the box. I think he has been cutting hair a total of six months."

"Oh, wow."

"Which is not a long time. Six months, professionally, on the floor, having to deal with the customer back to back to back to back. Before that he was an intern.[1] He spent the whole day running the shop and then at night he would do a haircut, maybe two. It's like working out. Someone tells you, you know, do twenty-five pushups, you can do it. Doing three sets of twenty-five pushups is where it gets difficult."

"Sure, yeah, yeah."

"And that's kind of like what he goes through right now, you know? So, he may come in and he's just trying to hang [in] with the rest of us. He comes in and he works and once in a while he'll just slip up. It's weird. I remember that feeling, like, when you first start you don't want to mess up, especially if you're someone like me. Jason is a great barber, I think he's going to be a great barber because he takes his craft super seriously. He really, genuinely wants to be good at it. He doesn't just do it for the money. But when you start noticing that you're kind of losing your grasp on a haircut you get this anxiety feeling, which just causes you to fuck up even more, you know?"

"Kind of like when it rains it pours, it just kind of . . ."

"Exactly. And I don't know if you noticed, as I stepped in, he was literally saying, 'I just want to go home right now.'"

"Yeah, yeah."

"He wasn't lying."

"He was ready to quit, he was like, 'That's it, I'm going back to painting.'"

"Exactly."

"I felt bad," I say. "You know, I wanted to see what was going on, but I think I got him a little more nervous by watching him."

"It was more me, you know? The other thing is, the haircut he was doing is a skin fade."

"Right."

"Those are probably the hardest haircuts to do. I probably applied the pressure on him a little bit because I told you I used to cut in 'hood shops. All we could do was skin fades, you know what I mean? Just skin fades, skin take-ups, and everything perfectly straight. So I have the most practice with that. I actually find that stuff easy at this point because I've been doing it for so long. Whereas, long hair might be where I'm not as good because I just haven't been doing that, whereas, Van has been working in a salon all of his life. So, Jay is Van's apprentice and Van is showing his strong points. Jay is now real good with long hair, but he really wants to be good at short hair. He wants to be good at everything, you know? But Van is very like, 'Long hair is where the art is, don't worry about the short hair, the short hair stuff is easy,' so he never really got to practice. Jason likes doing short haircuts and when he screws it up, especially with his friend . . . luckily it was his friend."

"Right, luckily it was his friend. Yeah, that guy was cool with it."

"Yeah, yeah, uh-huh. He just got a little panic attack. But sometimes you take it on the chin and you just kind of keep going, you know? Skin fades are very difficult."

Four days later I bring up this haircut to Jason while he is between clients. I still feel the need to apologize. I did not mean to cause him further anxiety by standing close. After a beat, he remembers the incident.

"Oh no, it's, when it's like my friends and shit like that, I freak out. Plus, I live with him, so I gotta stare at it, and that's all I've been doing for the past week, is like staring at his head. Actually, it looks all right, I think I just brought it up a little too high. No, it wasn't you. Miles gets to me too, though, because he'll stare at me and I'm like trying to look at what he's looking at.

You know, I'm newer at this, so I don't see everything. It happens when I do [my roommate's] hair."

"You do it a lot?"

"With his, yeah, because he wants like a really, super-tight fade, and I want it to be perfect. I beat myself up."

Each of these occupations requires more than having to simply "look good and sound right."[2] Once these workers get a job and decide to pursue it as a career, they learn to perform the cultural repertoires of the occupation as the people in their workplace and occupational community define them. These repertoires are protected by a code, which consists of a set of behaviors and behavioral expectations regarding their conduct during tasks and interactions, the stock of knowledge they should possess of their work and the larger industry, and the approach to the job they should take to put on a successful performance in their jobs.[3] Demonstrating technical skill represents just one aspect of these repertoires. They can only hone technical skill through practice. Jason, for instance, acknowledges Miles's point about experience. He knows he can cut, but he knows he is new, and that his skills wobble under certain conditions, like when a friend is in the chair, he works on a technically challenging style, or more experienced barbers watch him work. With effort and help, which Miles will give him because he demonstrates he is serious about the craft and does not just "do it for the money," Jason knows he will enhance his skills for the skin fade haircut in time.

But this example presents another dimension to performance besides technical skill. Both Jason and Miles acknowledge the rise of anxiety in situations when skills waver. Jason gets nervous, tense, and unconfident during the haircut. Eventually, he forgets a basic technique of fading up from the line. Barbers say it takes several years before they are confident behind the chair. "I'm doing hair eleven, twelve years," says Joey. "After the fourth year, it got to become my second nature. You get that confidence boost on you. You're comfortable with yourself enough. The end product's going to come out good." At that point they can do many haircuts in a row throughout the course of the day without fear or anxiety. But before this point it is common for barbers to have lapses. It is no surprise, then, that Jason would struggle a bit with his technique and feel nervous after cutting hair for only six months.

Doing the job for workers in each of these occupations includes displaying confidence while performing tasks. Confident behavior serves as the ideal representation of the various elements in the cultural repertoires: the combination of technical, social, and communication skills, cultural knowledge that marks their specialized profession and industry, and a work ethic that guides their approach to the job. The code guides their practices and interactions in the workplace, and displaying confidence characterizes a successful skilled performance.[4] In some cases people already possess elements of these repertoires before they first start working in the job, but rarely all of them.[5] As with Jason and Miles, teaching moments serve as opportunities to round it out and inspire confidence.

Teaching the Repertoires

Philadelphia is only ninety miles south of New York City, a perfect distance for cocktail culture to spread easily. In 2009 Mike, a Philly bar owner, hired Dave, one of Death & Co.'s owners, and Alex as consultants on a cocktail bar that he wanted to open in his city's Rittenhouse Square neighborhood called The Franklin Mortgage & Investment Co. Inspired by Death & Co., Mike wanted a similar aesthetic and concept: dark and jazzy with exquisite cocktails based on the classics from the golden age.[6] Dave handled the design, while Alex handled the drinks and trained the new staff.

I arrive at Death & Co. at 11 a.m. for the first training session for The Franklin's newly hired bartenders. I leave behind the morning air and sun, enter the bar, and face all its normal features: candlelight, sweet aromas, jazz music, and Alex and Joaquin in uniform behind the bar. They want to replicate the work environment for the new hires as much as possible. Each of the four bartenders Alex hired has some bartending experience, but only one has cocktail bartending experience. Alex hands me the thick service manual that he created and that every employee received and was supposed to have read for today's session. According to the introduction, The Franklin will focus on classic, pre-Prohibition cocktails and be the "best" bar in the world. It also promotes a common refrain of contemporary mixology: bartending was once a well-respected trade, and part of their goal is to reestablish this status.

The new bartenders arrive shortly after I do. Joaquin and Alex make quick introductions, and then Alex says, "This is how we start in the morning, with a drink." They both vigorously shake already prepared tins. The bartenders watch awestruck. One pauses mid-sip of coffee. They then pour the drink—a

Corpse Reviver, a classic cocktail meant to be consumed quickly as a hang-over cure—out into small glasses for everyone to sample. We all drink, and some, including me, pucker at the mix of strong alcohol and coffee flavors in our mouths. A small din of chatter about the drink quickly emerges and fades, as Joaquin starts the session.

"The most important thing when people walk out of here is they always understand that every bottle that is back here—every bottle that is in our row, all of the cheater bottles—is there for a very specific reason. There is not a single bottle back here that we do not believe in and we do not know. It takes time to do that. You've got to taste a lot, read a lot, you've got to drink a lot, and it's really a lot of fun.

"When we reach for a given bottle for a given recipe, it's for a reason. When we're testing our house drinks, when I say we put forty new drinks on [the menu], that means we tasted around eighty or ninety, and those are the ones that made the cut. Out of those eight or ninety, each of those probably went through about five to six incarnations before settling on maybe, again, a for-mula and testing it with a variety of different brands of a different spirit, to see which one works. So this stuff gets tested *a lot*.

"And when a brand ambassador shows up here, 'Oh, whoa, that Whirling Tiger sounds delicious. Could you make that for me with Maker's Mark?' We just very politely tell him, 'No, we chose Buffalo Trace for a reason for that drink, and we're sticking to it.' That's one of the hallmarks of what we do here is that level of consistency. What's coming out needs to come out the same on a Tuesday at 7 as it would on a Saturday at 11. It doesn't matter who's back there, it doesn't matter what's going on—every time the drinks go out they have to look and taste and smell exactly the same. And that's really what we try to do and we do it by jiggering, we do it by tasting, and we do it by being consistent in our technique and in our methods."

Alex then takes over.

"This really all has to go toward diligence before we open, and really spend-ing a lot of time caring about exactly what you're doing. This little metal piece [holds up smaller shaker], and this one here [the larger one], are going to be your best friend. They're going to be everything to you because that is your vessel to get to that consistency. In consistency, what he's talking about is Saturday night is just as important as if having an empty bar with one person. The same quality of service and same consistency of product, always. And that's really one of the biggest things we're here to help you do, because we can teach you recipes, we can teach you about classic cocktails, we can teach you about spirits, but really when all that theory comes into practice, it's a whole different game, and when you're working on a busy Saturday night and you're slammed, you want to be able to have those tools to be able to handle it correctly. And that's hopefully what we're here to help you do.

"So, basic foundations of what we do. Quality, and what is quality? Starting from the base up, start with fresh juices. Always fresh juices. Taste your juice every day. And I know tasting fresh lemon and lime juice is not the greatest thing in the world, but you can develop a way of tasting and be diligent about that, again, this word 'diligent,' and 'consistency,' all the time. So you start with the foundation, fresh juices, good syrups, quality syrups, and quality sugars—not boiling them—and then building up from there with spirits, liqueurs. And quality doesn't mean expensive. For example, this bottle of bourbon, Elijah Craig's 12-year [is] $18, $17, not ridiculous. Excellent, excellent bourbon. You don't need to use something expensive, but really, everything has its own flavor. So it's that foundation of understanding, what he said, of using things for a very specific reason."

Both philosophy, the cultural knowledge behind the specialized work these workers do, and practice, the actual technical skills they perform, permeate the lessons Joaquin and Alex teach to newcomers. Here they impart the principles of mixology (for example, fresh juices and syrups, specific ingredients) and an approach to doing the job (for example, tasting everything regularly), while they allude to the technical skill involved (for example, use of specific tools). The end goal is consistency, which entails practicing these repertoires to the point of embodiment (or "second nature," as Joey put it).[7] Later in the session, Alex discusses other cocktail bartender practices—chiefly performing different types of service by using social and communication skills.

"When a customer walks up to a bar, there are conscious details that they notice. They notice these things [points at cheater bottles on the bar], they notice bitters, they notice what you're wearing. This is what I wear at work all the time, except I'm wearing Vans [today], and I don't [normally] wear Vans back here. Those are conscious details that you need to pay attention to. But there are unconscious details that I find really, really vital to any service [business]. These are the details that make some of the best restaurants the best in the world. When somebody walks up to your bar and you see them and you make eye contact, even if you're busy, you say hi.

"Unconscious things like this: if I approach a bar, do I notice that all the speed pourers are pointed to the left? Do I notice that these guys right here [cheater bottles] are pointed in the other direction? Do I notice that actively?

Probably not, unless I'm someone like me, who really does pay attention to those things. No, but really, what does that set the context for? That says, 'Something is organized here. Something is right here. Something is put together here.' When you set down a drink for a customer at a table or wherever, you don't go like this with a cold glass and set it down [demonstrates putting a drink in front of someone hastily]. You pick up the glass, you hold it as far down as possible, and you give it to them. These little unconscious details: you're setting napkins down at a table, the napkins point in the same direction. It's just consistency and it really gives the customer the experience that is special and really important. They might not notice it, but they're going to leave feeling something was right there, something was on there."

Joaquin picks up the topic.

"They'll feel oddly pampered, they don't know why. It's that strange sense of minimal luxury.[8] It's not like you're eating at a four-star restaurant, you have a phalanx of servers that are all putting the plates down at the same time. We're not that fussy; we're making drinks. You don't have to go to those extremes. But you want there to be approaching that level of care and detail. You want to put a fresh napkin down for every drink, because the other one's been weeping moisture down onto it. There's little attention to detail like that and that's really why we stress it so much. That's what makes places run nine, ten years later."

"And it's also," adds Alex, "continuing on with that, as far as preparation of drinks and giving drinks to customers, gender equality and all that and everything, a lady gets a drink first. That's *always* the case. I don't care if you build your drinks and you make sure your drinks come out at the same time, you hand the drink to the woman first. I don't care if it's old and archaic. Don't give a damn. That's the way it is. You don't want to make a big thing out of it, you know, 'For the lady, I have this.' It's just the way it is, you just put it down. They don't even notice that, it just happens, it's consistent, it's always that case. Old world things, that's what we're doing here. This is old world things. Sure, we live in a modern day, and those rules don't really apply in my daily life and they're kind of silly. But when it comes to service, I think there's an importance."

"We're wearing arm garters," says Joaquin. "It's old school."

The session goes on for four hours and covers more technical topics— shaking and stirring techniques, the importance of measurements, how to properly cut garnishes, obtaining citrus essence—none of which the new bartenders will master right away. But by introducing these philosophies, practices, and approaches, Alex and Joaquin aim to inculcate the cultural repertoires of cocktail bartending. Through sustained practice, the newcomers will hopefully learn how to work confidently: make quality drinks, create new drinks based on a wide-ranging taste profile, serve customers, and tend the bar consistently.

But consistency for these workers refers to the outcome, not necessarily the process. In terms of technical skill and approach to the work, personal style plays an important role. These workers teach newcomers the importance of being consistent while they also get them to cultivate a sense of personal style. Sometimes, they strive for consistent inconsistency, or practices that all but ensure different outcomes. Personal style plays a role in technique, and practice ensures variation in the outcome.[9]

On a slow Monday at Freemans, Amanda complains that they do not want her to do shaves at the other shop, where she usually works. Amanda originally went to beauty school, received her cosmetology license, and worked in salons. So she does not have as much experience shaving men as barbers who worked in barbershops.

"I practiced on Jason the other day, but I cut his chin and felt bad."

"She cut me," says Jason. "Look at my chin."

"You look like shit!" says Van.

"I know, all busted up here."

"He wanted me to cut him," Amanda jokes.

"If I look at a razor, though, I fucking break up," says Jason, trying to be supportive.

"You can practice on me when I'm done," says Miles, as he works on his client.

After a few minutes, Sean, a friend of Amanda's, comes in with a beard a few days old. Van suggests that she practice on him for free, and he agrees. Van supervises as Amanda puts on a few layers of towels, folding them over each other.

"You're making it too complicated," he says.

"I feel like there's not enough towels. I always get cream on the shirt."

"If you do, you do. It's shaving cream. Basically it's 80 percent water."

"I know, but I still don't want to get shaving cream on it."

"It won't even stain the shirt. Same as when you cut somebody, just leave that as well. By the time you're done with the shave, it's all going to be taken care of on its own. He won't even notice it."

Amanda then picks up the water bottle and sprays his face.

"That spraying water's completely unnecessary," says Miles, who watches from his chair.

"What, on his face?" asks Van. "You don't like to do that?"

"Yeah. Because I figure if oil is a lubricant in itself, and the shaving cream's made out of like 70 percent water . . ."

"I like a little bit of water. I don't use rose water, because it has alcohol to it, and I feel like it's going to cut the product a bit."

". . . and then the towel has tons of water on it, then the foam's water."

"But Miles, do you use coconut oil?"

"Nah."

"You don't like it?"

"It just smells edible."

"Yeah, yeah, it does."

"Ruben told me to get it really, really, really, really, really wet," says Amanda, in reference to a man's face.

"No, you don't have to get it really, really wet," says Van.

"Ugghhh!" screams Amanda at the mix of information she has gotten.

"Take what you like from everybody. As long as you get the order the same, the products could change or vary how much you like it. Me, Ruben, and Joey use coconut oil. This is also a pre- and aftershave. It's an amazing aftershave. You mix it up in your hands good and it turns liquid right away. And it's just a great, it's super slippery, so it's just good for the razor over the skin, and it keeps the skin super moisturized."

"Yeah, remember the time that I shaved you and Ruben put the coconut oil over your whole head?" says Amanda to Miles.

"Ruben uses a lot of product."

Amanda then starts applying the coconut oil on Sean's face.

"I like to use both hands, just to really rub it in," says Van.

"OK."

"Part of the reason why they're [clients] here is, because they can shave their own face, so it's kind of important to do the extra things. The more informed I keep them on the process, the better it comes out every single time. At the beginning, like if he were my client right now, and I was getting him ready, I'd be like, 'How often do you shave? Are you sensitive going against the grain?' If they're like, 'I don't know,' or 'I think so,' or they have red hair, I say, 'Well, we'll see. We'll go with the grain, we'll see how you feel. Let me know if you have any irritation.'* They're never going to let you know. That's

* People with red hair often have sensitive skin.

something a guy will never do is tell you 'my face hurts.' It's just not going to fucking happen. But, you see that it's irritated enough, you know not to go against the grain. Just say, 'You know, I notice you're a little sensitive to this, so we're going to stick with the grain, we'll get you as close as I can.' Make it so that both of you are involved in it, and then whether you get them super close or not, the more information you give them, the more you're like, 'You're a little sensitive here, so I'm not going to get as close here blah blah blah blah blah,' the happier they are with everything you're doing."

Amanda then gets a hot, eucalyptus-soaked towel out of the heater and puts it on Sean's face. She gets the shaving cream ready to trap in the heat from the towel. After applying the shaving cream, the time has come for Amanda to use the straight razor. Van advises how to hold it.

"So the way most people do it, three [fingers] in front, one in back."

"Like this?"

"Yeah. It's your choice, it's whatever you feel comfortable with."

She finds her grip and makes a pass.

"Good, but it could be a lot shorter and quicker [shows her], like that. The slower you go, the more the blade's gotta work through that hair and take it up, so it's gonna pull. So those quicker snaps like that, it's gonna go chop, chop, chop, right to the root of it, go right through that hair."

Amanda makes the adjustment.

"Good. Notice the change of direction in his hair," says Van, pointing to a section of Sean's face, "so follow that direction. You want to do that thirty degrees, but it turns out that the flatter these blades are, the smoother the shave's going to go. So you're going to keep that, not flat flat, but pretty flat, like fifteen degrees."

"You're doing a great job," says Jason to Amanda, sarcastically, as he walks by.

"A good trick for this is actually pull [his face] that way," continues Van. "And you see, I'm pushing hard. That doesn't hurt, does it Sean?"

Sean shakes his head.

"No, the face really doesn't have many parts that's going to hurt. So you pull it nice and hard, even see right up there, and then you just go up in this direction and you kind of come in around."

"Like that?"

"Yeah, that's fine. As long as you get that stretch [on the face]."

Amanda makes another pass on Sean's face.

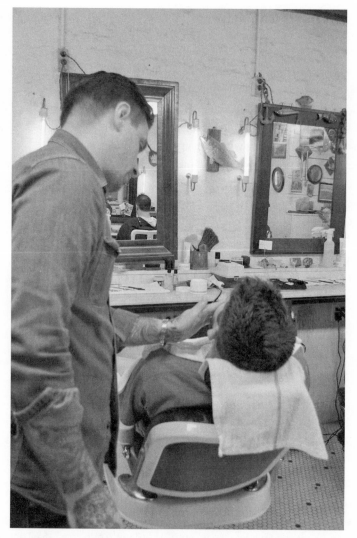

FIGURE 15. Jason preparing to shave a client. Photo by Chantal Martineau.

"That's not good. Did you see how his skin went with the razor?"

"It wasn't tight enough?"

"Yeah, so that's when you would have to pull on it. Have you shaved back-hand yet?"

"A little."

"This is where backhand is kind of key. As long as your blade is flat, at first your hand's going to feel a little funny doing it, but you keep doing it, keep doing it, keep doing it, it gets more and more confidence in it. You just lay this down nice and flat, pull it there, and you've got that perfect angle."

Similar to Jason and his difficulties with the skin fade, Amanda has some problems with shaving. But she has been cutting hair for longer than Jason, and does not lack confidence overall as a barber. Her issues are with the Freemans shaving process and with using a straight razor, and Van uses the opportunity to emphasize the importance of little details to the brand of the shop, such as keeping the client involved in the process and of finding her own personal style (as long as she adheres to details). He specifies that her hand, not her, will get "more and more confidence in *it*" as she practices.[10] Already familiar with the service aspect of the shop and skilled in cutting hair, Amanda needed only to learn how to apply these elements of the job to shaving with a straight razor.

I wondered if being a woman had anything to do with Amanda's issues with shaving. As Van is someone who has trained many barbers, and who designed the shaving program at Freemans, I ask him after his lesson if it is harder to teach women to shave. "No. The only difference is that they don't have a frame of reference." These differences between teaching men and women became clear when I observed barbers train other men how to shave with the straight razor. They instructed differently, such as by making fewer references to the areas on the face that are more sensitive, since men are more likely to know them. Like with cutting hair, men barbers also say that they are not likely to be better at shaving clients than women barbers. After all, while most men shave themselves, they're not used to shaving others, and usually not used to using a straight razor. The key is learning the basic techniques and developing a personal style to provide a unique service.[11]

These examples demonstrate how the people in these occupational communities and communities of practice inculcate the cultural repertoires of their jobs to newcomers and members. These "teachers" all stress confidence and practice, until the repertoires become second nature. Some, however, do not reach this point.

Incomplete Performances

Successfully performing these repertoires means a worker has achieved a degree of technical, social, and communication skill, obtained a degree of cultural knowledge, and adopted an approach to the job that can include their own personal style. But not everyone learns how to perform them properly, or with confidence. Some people do not *get* it. For various reasons, and with varying consequences, they do not master certain elements of the repertoire, or do not fit within the culture of the workplace. They may feel confident in their performance, but co-workers and members of the occupational community, who are alert to any violations of the code, do not agree.

Tuthilltown recently hired Aaron through the internship program of the American Distilling Institute (ADI), a trade and advocacy group for artisan distillers. Interns receive a $3,000 stipend to work at one of the companies that participates in the program. Aaron lives in Bushwick, a gentrifying neighborhood in Brooklyn. He commutes to Gardiner Monday mornings, returns on Friday evenings, and camps out on Tuthilltown's property during the week. Aaron had not heard of Tuthilltown before he saw their name on the ADI internship program list. "I wondered what distilleries are around New York City, and I found this one. Pretty much every other distillery in the New York area is vodka and grappa."

Originally from Indiana, after college Aaron spent some time with friends in North Carolina, near Asheville and the Smoky Mountains. Some of them got into moonshine—making and drinking it—from the mountain culture. "It was poor, really poor, and it's a way to make money. So I started looking into it. I did a bunch of reading and was like 'I could do this.' I also have this obsession with wanting to get good at something that pertains to all five senses." When he moved to New York a couple of years ago, Aaron became a hobbyist. He bought a tiny pot still and two fifty-five gallon barrels, which he used as fermenters. "I had a few fuckups in the beginning, but my first stuff actually didn't taste too bad."

Aaron then spent a lot of time learning fermentation and distillation, to the point where he was able to start experimenting. He came to Tuthilltown full of ideas and enthusiasm, but did not know how a distillery actually ran. One day, three weeks into his internship, Aaron and I take a break at the picnic table in the field to chat. He rolls a cigarette on a windy day and shares some of his plans and ideas.

"At this point, I'd just want to produce my product here and whatever products that I want to, because these people are so awesome and I'm getting along with them so well. Especially me and Joel, because he's such a visionary, he's really trying to revolutionize many things in the distillery industry, and I just love his enthusiasm. And I feel like I share the same amount of enthusiasm and passion and all-around vision and all that kind of stuff. So it probably makes sense to take whatever startup costs that I would have to get and pretty much throw it into this place. And to have [it] mutually beneficial, like, I get to do my thing, but then they also make more money because I'm doing it with them.

"What these guys are doing, which is something I thought I thought of on my own, and then when I found out they were doing it, I got really excited. I started getting into ratios as to surface area of wood per volume of liquid. The idea was that for the longest time people were only using the fifty-plus gallon barrels, for whatever reason. And then they started doing the Baby Bourbon in the smaller barrels. But one area that I feel is very unexplored is the use of different types of woods. I mean, every American whiskey, and even rum, is American white oak strictly. People are starting to experiment in terms of ingredients, like blue corn instead of regular corn, so they're doing blue corn bourbon. And they actually kind of ripped off this place and call it 'Baby Blue.'"[12]

He rattles off a few other ideas—like returning alcohol to some of its medicinal roots and redistilling already aged products—and asserts the kinship he feels with Joel and his affinity for the idea of a farm distillery. We usually worked in different sections of the distillery, so I did not watch or work with Aaron much. His knowledge and enthusiasm rang true, and I initially took his plans and relationship with the distillery at face value.

A couple of weeks after Aaron's internship ends, I spend the day helping Liam with proofing, or bringing the distillate down to the desired proof, the Single Malt out of the barrel and the Four Grain bourbon off the still. We want to get the Single Malt down to about 46 percent from about 57 percent, and the Four Grain down to about 57 percent for barreling. The key is finding out how much water to add to do so (a delicate step, since once added, water cannot be removed). It is a complicated process that requires careful attention, some basic math skills, and constant documentation. After some calculations I figure out about how much water to add (it's always approximate, since Tuthilltown has very inexact measuring techniques). I run into trouble with barreling, losing track of which drum I was transferring the distillate from and which I was transferring it to. We now have to swap a tube for a valve, which means some of the spirit will spill on the floor.

"Goddammit!" I yell.

"It's all right," says Joel, who has been supervising. "You have to fuck up to learn how to do it right."

Sensing that I am upset about having made such a dumb mistake, Joel tells me a story of a time when he first started working there.

"I forgot to secure the hose to the fill door as it was being filled up, and the hose fell out of the fill door. The tube was spouting distillate everywhere. And my first instinct was to go for the hose, when I should have been going to turn it off. But the hose was going wildly, and I ended up getting distillate in my eyeballs. It was shooting up my eyelids and knocking my hat down and pushing it into my face and I couldn't see."

Liam adds his own embarrassing tale.

"Yeah, when I started here last summer, I was also filling the still when I saw the hose come out and spray everywhere. And I also went for the hose when I should've just turned off the pump. The hose bounced everywhere in an almost cartoon-like manner and ended up nailing me."

I feel better about my mistake after hearing these stories. Even they have made mistakes when learning, and theirs were worse. But these mistakes demonstrate the carefulness of the distillation process. Despite Joel's teasing, they were not upset with me. At the end of the day, Liam expresses his gratitude.

"Thanks for all the work today. You're a much bigger help than the last intern, and he was here for eight weeks."

"You mean Aaron?" I ask.

He looks up from the barrel he is filling, stares with his eyebrows raised, and nods his head.

"What was wrong with him?"

"He knew what he was talking about and he had good ideas, but terrible work ethic. He wouldn't do half the stuff that you did today, and it has to be done every day. He just went at his own pace. That's just my opinion. But then my opinion happens to have some weight around here."

"Even though I make more mistakes?"

"Mistakes will happen. You learn from them. I still make mistakes. It's how you go about making mistakes and what you do with them."

Aaron never came back to work or to make his products at Tuthilltown, as he had hoped. Like some craft distillers, he became interested in distilling through friends, already had a desire to make products that appealed to the senses, and was wary of the mainstream alcohol industry. He falls under the small group of hobbyists who had distilling experience prior to working at a distillery, and he knew about ADI and the artisan distilling industry. Since it is such a small operation, the workers at Tuthilltown even expressed relief that Aaron was a good guy who they got along with as a person. And Aaron clearly possessed the cultural knowledge, technical skills, and creativity required to distill spirits. But knowledge and ideas were not enough. He never adopted the work ethic of the workplace, which often requires careful, if boring, math, and manual labor. He never learned to work independently or efficiently. As much as promoting sustainable agriculture and providing alternatives to mass-produced brands, this work ethic is central to understanding the work of a craft distillery. While the cultural knowledge and technical skills are the "cool" aspects of these occupations, each requires an array of mundane, manual labor-oriented tasks.

It is not just newcomers who have difficulty performing the cultural repertoires. Often people with experience in the job falter in their performance. In these cases co-workers and community members sanction them.

One day I chat with Ruben at the front desk as he waits for his next client to arrive. An ethnic Russian and Bukharan Jew originally from Uzbekistan, Ruben moved to the United States when he was 10 years old. His family eventually settled in Brooklyn, where his father opened a barbershop. Ruben learned how to cut hair from his father when he was 16 ("My dad kind of made me do it," he says), and did not initially want to become a barber ("I wasn't really feeling it—I thought I was going to be someone else"). But he cut hair in college to pay the bills, enjoyed having money, realized how much he enjoyed cutting hair, and decided to devote himself to barbering. After working in a series of Russian, neighborhood, and chop shops throughout the city and growing frustrated at having to cut corners and not having time to give detailed haircuts and hone his craft, Ruben found Freemans through a client who "cheated" on him and went there one day while Ruben was away. When he sees Mark go to lunch, he calls Coco over.

"The board was red [full] all day the other day, but his [Mark's] final count was [$]740, and mine was [$]650," he says to her.

To him, this means that Mark was going too fast.

Coco nods and replies, "Sometimes I get his clients, and I see where he has gone too fast."

"Look," says Ruben, "I can go fast too, faster than anyone, and clients can go to a $12 place for the same thing, but that's not what it's about here."

Later in the day, I see Ruben talk to Mark, while Mark nods his head understandingly. This incident was not the first time I heard a barber comment about another's habit of going too fast. Most of the experienced barbers have worked at places that are based on volume, which demands speed. They know how to cut corners and cheat their way through a haircut in under ten minutes.

But Freemans uses time in a manner that adds value to the haircut and the haircut experience. Doing so is what they are "about." Perhaps reacting to a busy day, Mark strayed from the element of the repertoire that puts the idea of slowness as a way to achieve quality service and style into practice. As an experienced barber, it was not difficult for Mark to correct the problem. In some cases, however, the issues with performing the repertoires are more difficult to overcome than being aware of timing or honing the technical qualities of the job. They tie into the less mutable aspects of the performance.

Ruben feels like having a salad today, so I join him at Whole Foods for lunch. He has a lot to get off his chest. People at work have been bothering him, specifically the owner. Ruben and the others do not feel the owner understands how a barbershop is supposed to run, since he isn't a barber, which affects their work. Meanwhile, four barbers quit at the other shop in the last month, leaving the company in need.

"They [the company] are now realizing how hard it is to find barbers. I could easily find ten Russians who will work twelve-hour days, but that's not what they want. They want to stand out, and one way in which they stand out is by not hiring $12 barbers. They want to hire barbers who aren't boring, who love life."

"But you've found people for them," I say.

"I found replacements. I picked them because they are people who can follow authority and look stylish. I found one who's starting soon. But the new guy I recommended doesn't dress the way he should for this clientele."

The barber in the image of the classic barbershop in New York City is often Italian. But today many barbers in barbershops are far more likely to be Russian. Ruben knows many of them from his background and days working at shops around the city. He then changes the subject to cars, and we go back to the shop. A week later, I walk into the shop just to say hello, since I was in the neighborhood. I notice a new person working in Ruben's chair, and ask Miles who he is.

"That's Nicky. He's Ruben's boy."

I hang around for a bit and notice Nicky keeps to himself and doesn't say a word to anyone (he speaks English fluently). He lets his clients sit down, puts on the apron, and glances at them through the mirror with a wordless "what do you want?" look. He smiles when they tip him, but he says very little.

The next week I meet Ruben and Miles at the restaurant down the alley during their break. They're chatting about recent photo shoots they've done. Miles goes back to work, and I ask Ruben about Nicky.

"Was it the guy who looked like he didn't fit in?" he asks.

"Yeah. He was quiet, didn't say much."

"That's him," says Ruben, nodding. "He's Andre's cousin. He was filling in for me. I hired him and some other people at the other shop because they're thin and they got the Brooklyn shop opening."

Andre is Ruben's friend from childhood. They grew up and worked in Russian barbershops together. He has been working at the West Village shop for a few years, on Ruben's recommendation.

"What do you think of them when you see them work?" I ask Ruben.

"I told them [management] they [the barbers] need work [training], but they hired them full-time anyway. They're not ready for this place. I have to point out all the stupid mistakes they make."

"You mean with the haircuts?"

"Yeah, but more than that. Nicky's only worked at 'hood shops. He knows how to cut hair, but it's these ten-minute haircuts. But he also doesn't know how to handle Manhattan people, you know what I'm saying?"

At first glance the criteria Ruben uses to hire replacements appear to exemplify aesthetic labor. The shop wants people who "look stylish." But Ruben makes several additional points when he mentions "mistakes" and "Manhattan people." He certainly means barbers have to dress and present themselves in the shop in a certain way. Attached to a men's clothing store and in the middle of a trendy downtown neighborhood, the shop is fashionable, and the barbers dress in a certain style, usually with button-down collared shirts and nice pants, some of which cost more than a hundred dollars per item. They have to "look good and sound right," but doing so goes beyond mere aesthetics. They also have to engage with their clients, ask them questions, build a rapport with them, and listen to and consult on what they want to have done. They have to be receptive to their clients' sense of style, and know what style would work well for them. The elements of the cultural repertoires at Freemans that are essential for a successful performance—possession of cultural knowledge (for example, men's fashion, popular restaurants and cuisines, films) and an ability to openly banter—may elude people not familiar with or comfortable in a downtown cultural scene. In terms of technical skill, they have to take their time with the cuts and attend to small details, which they may not be able to do from having only done ten-minute haircuts. They have to make the cut into more of a special experience than a functional service. From growing up in immigrant communities and from having worked in 'hood shops they may not have these abilities for a neighborhood like the

Lower East Side. They therefore cannot perform the upscale barbershop's cultural repertoires properly, and certainly not confidently.

Our conversation about Nicky continues during the short walk back to the shop. Miles hears us talking and brings up an incident that occurred the previous week, when Nicky couldn't pick out New Jersey on a map. Ruben joined in the teasing, but says he apologized to Nicky that night. Miles also brings up the time Andre thought that rain came from space. Ruben shakes his head and says that this incident embarrassed him as well.

Later in the day I join Ruben outside while he has a cigarette after he finishes with his client.

"I think I understand why you feel embarrassed when that happens with Nicky and Andre," I begin. "I figure it's because you feel that other people will think the same way about you."

"You're right, but I can't believe that some people don't have that basic level of intelligence, like knowing where Jersey is on a map, even though he's driven there hundreds of times."

Ruben then explains how Andre often puts his foot in his mouth when talking to clients, such as by discussing inappropriate topics or using foul language.

"How has he lasted at the West Village shop then?" I ask.

"I've backed him since he started. I've known him since we were kids. But Andre just doesn't get it. When he first started Andre didn't dress right, he didn't act right, so I had to explain to him what the place is about. Now he has his clients and he knows when to keep his mouth shut, usually."

Ruben is comfortably fluent in two social worlds. He still has friends and family in the oft-provincial Russian communities of Brooklyn and Queens from his youth. He learned to cut hair in his father's Russian 'hood shop. He used to "bang out" haircuts at Astor, a large, well-known downtown barbershop where speed and a cutthroat attitude, not quality and convivial banter, is the game. But Ruben was drawn to the cultural scenes of downtown Manhattan. He wanted to dissociate from his familiar environment and take his haircutting craft to a higher level. He learned how to dress and act properly for the setting, and he gained the cultural knowledge that matched his work interests. Being culturally bilingual, he could translate to people in these two worlds, could recognize when they "need work," and could see their "mistakes." But without a personal connection and some coaching, like the Russian barbers have with Ruben, it is unlikely that anyone from the city's immigrant communities would gain access to new upscale barbershops. In cases when they do not have a translator or someone to support them, the consequences can be greater than ridicule among co-workers.

After a week off in August, I walk into Dickson's and get dressed.

"Did you see the schedule?" asks Giancarlo.

I take a look at it, but do not notice anything strange.

"You see a name missing?"

"Where's Aldo?" I ask after another glance.

"He got fired last Wednesday."

"What happened?"

"He came in, and Jake said he couldn't afford him anymore. Aldo said, 'That's OK, just pay me less.' But Jake let him go. He took it well, and he thinks he already found another job. Jake's closing the TriBeCa location, and All Good Things is hiring Aldo to work their own new meat counter."[13]

Aldo was the second most experienced butcher at the shop, after JM. He has been a butcher for seven years, and he trained in Mexican supermarkets and processing plants where speed counted. He has far more experience than Giancarlo, Brian, and Lena. And the holiday season is approaching, which is the busiest time of year in the shop. I find it very surprising that Aldo lost his job. Later in the day, I ask Giancarlo why he thinks Aldo was fired.

"Dana and Dave [the manager and chef] didn't like his attitude, and they had enough of it," he speculates while shrugging.

"Well, with TriBeCa closing it would seem Jake would have to cut some staff."

"Yeah, but your number two [butcher]?"

During the day I reflect on the past two months at the shop. Earlier in the summer Jake closed the meat counter he ran at Foragers, a nearby grocery store that specializes in local food products. With one less outlet, he had to make room for extra staff at Chelsea and TriBeCa. To make sure the newer butchers got some work cutting meat, he rotated who worked behind the counter. Since Aldo speaks English well, better than JM, he took a regular weekly shift in the front of the house, serving customers. But while he could speak with customers, I noticed how Aldo often did not communicate the meat philosophy that the shop promotes.

One day in July, a customer comes in and asks for filet mignon.

"How many pieces?"

"Three."

"How thick?"

Aldo takes the tenderloin out of the case and holds it in one hand.

"Here?" he asks while indicating a place on the tenderloin with his knife.

The customer points to a spot on the tenderloin, and Aldo turns around to cut it. Giancarlo, who is also behind the counter, filling the display case, teases Aldo.

"'You want tenderloin? How many pieces? Here?'" Then he mocks wrapping it up and throwing it at the customer.

"Ohhh, master butcher John Carlos," says Aldo in retaliation. "'Mommy, mommy! I wanta be a butcher and work at Dickson's!'" he says to Giancarlo in the high-pitched, childlike voice he often uses to tease him.

Giancarlo stares at him and walks back to the cutting room.

Jake wanted whole-animal butchery in his shop from the outset. Despite the increasing interest in rare animal cuts in New York City's expanding foodie scene, not many people actually knew how to break down a whole animal. The skill has faded from the butchery trade, especially in New York City. Jake hired JM and Aldo because they had the requisite skills. They could work much faster than they do and often slow down to teach the less experienced butchers and interns, to demonstrate for customers, and because they simply do not have to go too fast in a shop with relatively low volume compared to processing plants. Jake needed talent, and two young men from Mexico, where butchers are more likely to know about whole-animal butchery, provided it. Like Russian barbers in an expanding men's grooming industry, JM and Aldo found themselves with marketable skills in an expanding food industry. The growth of these industries created a talent gap, which forced owners to sometimes hire people who did not necessarily fit the image they had of an ideal worker.

But as at each of these workplaces, being an employee at Dickson's requires more than technical skill. Workers must learn the social and communication skills required for interacting with customers, the cultural knowledge of meat and cooking to guide their orders, and the meat philosophy that undergirds the shop's very existence. And food industry jobs, including ones that require manual labor like butchers, now attract people like Giancarlo, Brian, and Lena, who, unlike JM and Aldo, had other employment opportunities but chose butchery. The same expanding industry that welcomed people like JM and Aldo has grown to the point where their inclusion becomes precarious.

My internship ended shortly after Aldo was fired. I brought it up in interviews with employees in the following months, asking them what they thought about it. I sat with one of the managers at a bar near the shop and asked about Aldo.

"I think that what it really comes down to is we had a couple of people on the chopping block, basically. At some point we realized that the future of the cutting room was off. It had just gone awry. There are many explanations as to why and we can think about that and analyze that all we want, but really what we decided was how can we make the biggest change in the cutting room? A lot of it came down to who is most willing to step up and help customers. We are downsizing as a company, so we need people who can work up front and are happy to work up front. I spent a lot of time with [Aldo] in TriBeCa. He's a great guy, he's such a talented cutter, I mean *really* talented. He's very fast, he's very strong, he's extremely knowledgeable. It was a very hard decision to make and it was almost somebody else for a very long while. In kind of laying all the cards out it was like, well, what makes the most sense for what we're trying to achieve long term? A lot of it had to do with where people seemed to be ideologically and in their versatility and how can we make the greatest cultural change to the cutting room. We need people who take initiative to look at the order book, organize the order shelf, things that directly affect the whole of the shop. In a small food business, every single person has to be willing to do every single job, in my opinion."

The idea of "versatility" or "flexibility" came up with each employee I spoke to, as did the concept of "ideology" or philosophy. They want their employees to be versatile, or to be able to perform the cultural repertoires properly. I heard workers from each industry express the same sentiment to me under different circumstances. The workers who succeed in their workplaces and industries do not just want to focus on the technical skill involved in their jobs, despite its status as their industry's sexiest and coolest attribute. They embrace and want to show off all aspects of the job, and they expect others to want the same for themselves.

In terms of philosophy, Jake told me on the first day I met him and set up my internship that JM and Aldo were great butchers, but did not necessarily hold the same ethics of the shop, or at least the principles behind Dickson's were not the reason they worked there. I came to see what he meant as I watched them work and compared them to the others. JM and Aldo love the craft of butchery. They enjoy the skill involved and take pride in their work. But they are not especially interested in whether the animals are grown locally, raised in pastures, and slaughtered as humanely as possible. They do not know much about the latest food trends or restaurants, and, even though they do have a lot of meat and cooking knowledge based on their supermarket experience and familiarity with Mexican cuisine, do not communicate it to customers. They do not put the philosophical aspect of the cultural repertoires into practice.

The week after I learn of Aldo's firing, JM and I go to the bar downstairs after work. I ask JM if he was surprised that Aldo got fired so suddenly. His eyes widen as he nods his head and says that he was.

"Especially with the holidays," he says. "I have Brian and Giancarlo, but Brian is slow. Aldo is fast, and a good butcher. Brian talks but doesn't know the job yet. When you learn the job, then I'll hear what you think. Maybe one day, but not now."

He stops and thinks for a minute, then says that with TriBeCa closing, he guesses it had to happen that someone had to go. He just didn't think it would be Aldo. "But Aldo will be OK. He's a good butcher. There are jobs."

Along with being sad for Aldo when he got fired, I was also sad for JM. JM and Aldo are both from the city of Puebla, and they spoke a street Spanish with each other at work (sometimes to hide what they were saying in case a customer understood Spanish). Since he speaks better English, Aldo often translated for JM. And since JM had more experience than Aldo, JM took him under his wing and taught him even more than he already knew.

JM then mentions how the other day he saw an ad on Good Food Jobs, the classifieds website, for a head butcher and cutting room manager at Dickson's—which is JM's job. He says that he recently met with Dave and Jake and asked for a raise, which he has not gotten in two years. When they said they could not do it, he said OK, but that he then wanted more hours. I ask JM why he thinks they are trying to replace him. He shrugs and ignores the question.

"They would have to find someone as good as me."

"Will they be able to find someone as good as you?"

"There are butchers as good as me. Like Adam, he's very good. Very good butcher.[14] But to hire a gringo to be the head butcher, he [Jake] will have to pay more."

"How do you feel about that?"

"It's not right."

He then takes a sip of beer, shrugs again, and puts a positive spin on the situation.

"No me importa. It's just a job. There are other jobs."

He mentions a place in Brooklyn that he knows is hiring, but he says they just do beef, and it sounds like a processing/meatpacking place rather than a boutique butcher shop.

"There are other jobs."

JM is aware of his talent and skills as a butcher. He is also aware of his status as a Mexican immigrant in the food world. People like JM are typically in the backstage areas of New York City's food scene: prepping food, doing dishes, or silently clearing tables. But at Dickson's, with an open cutting area and the expectation of butcher-customer interaction, JM is on the front stage, and therefore has more responsibility than simply standing in place and cutting meat. Aldo didn't interact with customers much. JM interacts with them less. In replacing him, JM assumes a "gringo" butcher would demand and receive a higher salary than he gets (although JM earns more than Giancarlo, Brian, and Lena). By putting him in charge, he feels Dickson's gets a highly skilled butcher for a good price. But after Aldo was fired, even though he's a better butcher than the others, and after seeing the ad, JM feels his job is in danger. While upset about a situation he feels is unfair, to him Dickson's is still "just a job"—something he's good at and can earn money from—not a calling. If it comes down to it, he'll simply move on.

Performing these jobs well is more than just having some knowledge, having experience within the industry, or even knowing the technical skills. Members of the occupational community, especially people in power like managers and owners, are adept at recognizing weak or incomplete performances. Consequences range from warnings to firings, but one can see how the requirement of having to enact these enforced repertoires—in concert, and with confidence—can also restrict people from entering and being considered for these jobs in the first place. Exclusivity in these new elite jobs of omnivorous cultural taste-making comes down to one's performance, under watchful, well-trained eyes.

More than five years after it opened, Joaquin was the last of the original bartenders to leave Death & Co. Even some bartenders who had started after him had left for other opportunities in the industry. Since the bar opened, in early 2007, cocktail culture had expanded tremendously in the nightlife industry of New York and cities around the country, as well as in the liquor industry. Craft cocktail bars proliferated; bars, restaurants, and hotels started cocktail programs; and liquor companies created custom cocktails for their products—all based on the principles of mixology. Cocktail lists have become as common in nightspots as wine lists. Joaquin's co-workers moved on to higher bartending positions at other cocktail bars, become consultants for new bar and restaurant projects and for liquor companies, and/or opened their own places based on their own ideas. As a prominent member of the occupational community (he was voted Bartender of the Year at Tales of the Cocktail in 2012), he certainly got his share of offers over the years, but kept choosing to stay put.

"I definitely had that mentality going in of, 'You've just got to prove so much. You've got a long way to go before you can really consider yourself to be anywhere near where these guys [his former co-workers] are at,' but [moving up] was always the goal. I really wanted that to be the case. Being in that environment was such a great opportunity. That is why it took me so long to leave. I had numerous opportunities where people had offered me to run programs: 'You have control over this,' and 'You can do that.' I kind of never bought it. So many of those I am really glad I didn't take because I saw what happened with those spaces later and I heard about who took the jobs and what they had to deal with there. I was like, 'Man I'm so glad I didn't leave Death & Co.' That's why it took five and a half years for me to finally leave the warm, dark embrace."

Joaquin kept working, and kept learning. He did some work for brands and events, which shaped his understanding of the industry. The right situation eventually appeared.

"As those opportunities came up and you're like, 'Oh, I'm good at doing this stuff with brands,' 'I'm good at doing event work,' or 'I don't like doing this kind of event work,' I was able to see how many more facets to the booze business there were and even how those things were changing. But after a while, five and a half years at a place, especially a place like that, you're kind of ready to spread your wings and do something of your own. Ultimately, what Death & Co. does is it trains you to run your own program. That's what that bar program is built to do. It gives you such a great education in terms of drinks and how to create menus and how to do all of this stuff. Also, it was such a high-profile bar that it then opened up doors in terms of media opportunities, abilities to do event work, consulting opportunities. That's actually how I hooked up with these boys at Alchemy [Consulting]."

Two veteran New York City bartenders, Toby Maloney and Jason Cott, run Alchemy Consulting. They have opened cocktail bars in Chicago, Minneapolis, and Nashville, the first of their kind in those cities. Joaquin finally decided to leave Death & Co. and join a group with a strong pedigree, with the goal of becoming an equity partner in a bar—to finally own his own place—which he accomplished in 2013, when Pouring Ribbons opened in the East Village, a ten-minute walk from Death & Co.

"We found a space we liked. I knew I wanted a more open and egalitarian bar. I wanted a bigger bar, which I have certainly done here. We wanted it to be a place where grownups came to drink, but you could still have fun at. We didn't want it to be pretentious or elitist."

"Open and egalitarian" signifies a conscious shift in the cocktail world. The first generation of craft cocktail bars resembled cathedrals, holy business tributes to cocktails with policies like no standing and reservations. Sasha, Milk and Honey's owner, famously engaged in social engineering, such as by setting a maximum of five people per party (ensuring only two conversations could ensue at once), having his staff go "Shhh!" when the din got too loud, and hanging a list of "Rules of this Bar" in the bathrooms:

1. No name-dropping, no star-f**king.
2. No hooting, hollering, shouting, or any other loud behavior.
3. No fighting, play fighting, or talking about fighting.
4. Gentlemen will remove their hats. Hat hooks are provided.

5. Gentlemen will not introduce themselves to ladies. Ladies, feel free to start a conversation, or ask the bartender for an introduction. Once you speak to a man, he is free to speak to you. If a man you don't know speaks to you, please lift your chin slightly and ignore him.

6. Do not linger outside the front door.

7. Do not bring anyone here unless you would leave that person alone in your home. You are responsible for the behavior of your guests.

8. Exit the bar briskly and silently. People are trying to sleep upstairs. Please make all travel plans and say all farewells before exiting this bar.

In short, these bars were clearly designed to be different.

Cocktail bartenders and owners say these early efforts were necessary to introduce classic cocktail culture—genteel and sophisticated, although often including low-status products—and taste to a mainstream drinking audience. These bars and workers, they say, succeeded. More people now know more about classic cocktails than before, and when these more educated consumers go to cocktail bars, they know how to order (correctly) and make more challenging drink requests. As the knowledge has spread, cocktail culture has grown beyond the cathedrals. While many new cocktail bars still adhere to the discrete speakeasy style, many have also opened as more conventional bars, without the pomp and circumstance.

An example is Attaboy, which Mickey and Sammy, Milk and Honey's bartenders, opened in the same space, in 2013, when Sasha moved his bar to a larger space uptown. After many years of bartending there and at Little Branch (Sasha's other cocktail bar), and flying around the world giving talks, workshops, and consulting, they decided it was their time to become owners. But they didn't want to replicate Milk and Honey. They wanted to place craft cocktails in more of a neighborhood bar setting.

"It [the change] definitely had to happen," says Mickey. "The way we do things, it's like a stripped-down kind of version [of Milk and Honey]. We get to wear jeans and a Henley now. We don't wear suspenders and the shirts. And the music is livelier. We're playing like the Talking Heads and Fleetwood Mac and stuff. And we're serving shots and beers, which is awesome. Everyone is like, 'Man, it's so nice to come to a bar like this,' where you can get an Old Fashioned well-made, a Negroni well-made, a Penicillin, a Dark and Stormy, a Tom Collins, you name it. But you can also get a can of Coors and a shot of whiskey, too, on the side. I still think there is a time and place for that small, quiet, dark, intimate, cocktail bar, though. But I think the way we have done our bar was the right approach for us. We're getting guys that are on their way home, just like coming in, having a Negroni and then heading home, which is really, really nice. Which is what you kind of want for a neighborhood bar. It's more just going into like your regular bar, if that makes sense."

At the same time, as cocktail culture has expanded cocktail bars have also become more specialized within the symbolic boundaries of mixology. For instance, Phil, Death & Co.'s head bartender, left there to open Mayahuel, which focuses on cocktails with agave spirits (tequila and mezcal). Other cocktail bars have opened based on tiki drinks, American spirits, and punch, while some have been adopting contemporary technology (for example, "molecular mixology," such as using liquid nitrogen to freeze glassware), experimenting (for example, aging cocktails in barrels), and deliberately reviving very old practices (for example, serving ice-less cocktails, to recall prerefrigeration days). The reemerged knowledge and practices of classic cocktails, then, have trickled down into more traditional bar settings, with varying degrees of adherence to mixology's principles (for example, not every bar with a cocktail list has an ice program), while also plunging deeper into the culture. In both cases, the opportunities for bartending have only grown.

The rise of these new elite jobs as niche occupational communities in their industries has occurred because of shifts in people's understanding of taste and consumption, new sociospatial dynamics in cities due to gentrification, and larger economic shifts that have redefined "good" jobs in the "new economy." A lot of research has been conducted recently on how workers are adapting to life in this new economy of precarious work conditions and individualized risk. Some workers have thrived as risk-takers and have adopted the mindset of being their own entrepreneur, sellers of their own human capital.[1] Some are reorganizing their traditional occupational communities to better help members deal with these changes, such as musicians who have reconstituted their networks and relationships to survive in a shifting music industry.[2] And some have struggled to adapt, stagnating in their careers, experiencing unemployment, and internalizing their struggles as personal failures, rather than as outcomes of structural conditions in the economy.[3]

In this book I have shown an alternative path for how workers are dealing with conditions of the precarious new economy. They are entering common occupations in everyday workplaces that people don't normally think of as knowledge-based or culturally relevant, and transforming them into high-end, quality jobs that fuse mental and manual labor and that people with other work opportunities see as viable career options. These workers experience manual labor as meaningful and even fun through the enactment of a set of cultural repertoires that allow for physical, bodily labor, challenging mental problem-solving, cultural understanding, and interpersonal communication. The jobs require the confident performance of each of these work practices in concert, not independently of the others. Along with vaunted jobs like those in the information technology, high-end service, culture, and media industries, these workers show how the expanding knowledge-based economy also includes previously low-status, dirty jobs in the beverage service, alcohol production, grooming, and food retail industries.

In entering these occupational niches these workers engage in activities that take them out of the traditional roles these workers play, and away from the brick-and-mortar businesses where they typically work. Once they get a job and achieve success in their workplaces they must work on building a career out of it, or advance in status within the industry in a way that does not abandon the meaningful work they perform. Doing so entails forging paths that are often uncharacteristic of traditional workers of these jobs. As Joaquin's story shows, cocktail bartenders do more than bartend. They work as hired guns for events on behalf of brands, and become brand ambassadors, traveling around the country and the world to promote their product. They lead educational programs, and write books and for magazines and blogs. They also consult for brands and for other bars, restaurants, and hotels (some have been hired to create cocktails for airlines, resorts, and casinos). And networks within the extended cocktail world introduce them to potential business partners to open their own places. Working in high-profile cocktail bars exposes them to these opportunities.

Workers in the other three occupations also follow this path. Craft distillers also become consultants and brand ambassadors (for their own brands and, sometimes, for others), and get involved in their trade associations (the American Distilling Institute [ADI] and the Distilled Spirits Council of the United States [DISCUS]). Working at upscale men's barbershops exposes barbers to the fashion and film worlds, which has given them many opportunities to work for photo shoots and on film sets (positions usually held by stylists). And whole-animal butchers have also opened their own shops, consulted, written books, taught, and gone on to work for restaurant groups on their meat program. Two butchers at Dickson's, for instance, left to work for Mario Batali (Guy) and April Bloomfield (Jocelyn). And workers in all four of these occupations have media presences, in traditional print and digital.

In other words, in making a career out of working in these niche occupational communities workers have shown the ability to be nimble and flexible. They stretch their occupational identities across multiple roles, essentially becoming "multis," or workers with hyphenated titles. Not content to confine themselves to their workplaces—stuck behind the bar, at the still, behind the chair, and behind the counter—they branch out and become ambassadors of their craft and its cultural knowledge. In doing so these workers are both turning away from the strictly knowledge-based work of the new economy while embracing many of its ideals: work should be fulfilling, vocational, flexible, and something that allows them to tap into their creative potential.

But as performed, these occupations are not as inclusive as they could and should be. As the profiles of these workers and the analyses in this book show, only people from certain social backgrounds and paths of life and with certain cultural dispositions and social abilities get and keep these jobs; their social and cultural capital play significant roles. Workers who lack these forms of capital and who struggle to put on a complete, confident performance of these cultural repertoires experience precariousness or are denied entry. And formal opportunity structures for people in more common versions of these jobs to move into them, and thereby benefit from their status and networks, do not exist. While workers have shown that meaningful, high-status, and knowledge-based manual labor is a possible career path, as constituted they remain an elite occupational niche. Perhaps they will one day adopt a systematic program to allow other workers from more diverse backgrounds to also tap into their creative potential through craft- and knowledge-based work.

Toward the end of my craft distilling internship, in summer 2010, William Grant & Sons, a Scottish distilling and spirits company, bought Tuthilltown's Hudson Whiskey line of products (these include the Baby Bourbon, Manhattan Rye, Single Malt Whiskey, New York Corn Whiskey, and Four Grain Bourbon). William Grant & Sons began in 1887 in Speyside, a region in Scotland. They became famous for making Glenfiddich, one of the most famous single malt scotch whisky brands in the world. Independent and still family owned, William Grant & Sons acquired other spirits brands over the years. According to Ralph, Tuthilltown's co-owner, the company appreciated the handmade, craft nature of their business: "[They were] watching us for two years before they even picked up the phone and called us and they came to us and said, 'We like what you're doing, we like that you're innovating and doing something different and we want to be a part of it.' Charlie Gordon, who's the major shareholder in that family-held company, flew over here and came up here and had lunch with us sitting in the distillery with the rest of us on barrels and he was saying, his exact quote was, 'Innovation never comes from the inside, it always comes from guys like you.' Their company started with William Grant and his sons building their distillery from scratch by hand. Just the way we did."

William Grant & Sons only bought the brand, not the distillery. Tuthilltown remains independent. It is essentially under contract to make the Hudson Whiskey line it created. It has become a contractor, while William Grant & Sons handles marketing and distribution. Large companies with more mainstream products buying smaller ones outright or their brands are common directions in which the craft spirits industry is heading. In the years since the purchase, as the Hudson brand has grown with support from a large company, Tuthilltown has had to gradually increase production, which has raised the question of authenticity.

"That's been an ongoing question," says Gable, Ralph's son. "How do we scale up? How do we increase efficiency without compromising the authenticity? The discussions of not hand-dipping the wax anymore, or not numbering the bottles. Just little things like that. At what point does it not become hand-bottled? If we stop hand-writing on the bottle, is that it? If we keep hand-writing will we stop hand-dipping? At what point? If we're not hand-rolling the labels on, but they're getting spun on? That is always a balance. It's always been a balancing act."

Today Tuthilltown is in many ways unrecognizable from when I worked there. Once only ten employees, including the owners, now there are sixty (only five are distillers and four are bottlers; most work in the offices, such as in HR and graphic design). Once only two buildings, now there are eleven. The granary with the rickhouse is now the store, tasting room, visitor center, and storage space. Three new, large warehouse-like buildings located elsewhere on the property serve as rickhouses. They are phasing out the ten-gallon barrels, which are the smallest ones they use (they also used three-gallon barrels in the early days), and now mostly use twenty-five and sixty-gallon barrels to keep up with production demands.

Cooking and fermentation still occur in the other granary, but the process has changed to accommodate the volume. They have a new cook tank that can hold nine hundred gallons of water, and a silo that holds twenty-four tons of grain (they never had one before), which they use for the Baby Bourbon and the Manhattan Rye. Otherwise, they still open up grain bags by hand to go into the mill. The two hundred-gallon plastic fermenters are gone. In their place are eight three-thousand-gallon giant stainless steel fermenters with cooling systems for controlling the temperature of the fermenting mash. Basically, in the plastic fermenters without temperature control, production would falter in the heat of the summer and the cold of the winter, because the yeast would either burn up and die or hibernate, respectively. Along with being considerably larger, the stainless steel tanks allow them to increase the amount of alcohol they get from each batch.

They no longer distill upstairs from the fermentation room, and they do not use the old two-hundred and one-hundred-fifty gallon pot stills that I remember. In their place are four larger pot stills: a three-hundred-thirty gallon still, a six-hundred-fifty gallon still, an eight-hundred-fifty gallon still, and a "Franken-still": they welded the rectifying column from the old one-hundred-fifty gallon still onto a beer brewing tank, and welded copper inside the tank, resulting in a five-hundred-eighty gallon still. Without having to worry about innovating on the Hudson whiskeys, and with a steady cash flow, Tuthilltown was able to come up with new products on its own. It now makes a gin and two liqueurs (a cacao and a cassis), and has revamped its vodkas. They use the older, smaller stills for some of these low-volume products. They reserve the larger ones for the Hudson whiskeys, which account for about 96 percent of their total output. Today Tuthilltown produces 100,000 proof gallons a year, which is more than double what they made three years ago.

The barrel blending and bottling operation now has its own building, where much of the process has become automated with an assembly line. But workers still dip the bottles in wax—in a pot on a hot plate—and number the bottles by hand. They ship twenty-five hundred bottles a day. And it found two new revenue sources on the property: solar panels, which power the entire operation and feed the meter, and a full-service restaurant. In short, while it still operates on a budget and repurposes some materials, support from William Grant & Sons and their own success have allowed it to make numerous upgrades for the sake of efficiency. But many core steps remain done "by hand," such as dumping grains to be milled, basing cuts and barrel blending on individual taste, and some aspects of bottling.

Once he stabilized the production of the Hudson lines after the William Grant purchase, and after the Prohibition Distillery owners started making

Bootlegger Vodka in their own facility, Joel focused on research and development. He created the recipes for Tuthilltown's gin, cassis, and cacao, as well as other products that haven't yet reached the market. But he felt Brian, the co-owner, was marginalizing him from making key production decisions. Then, after an explosion in the distillery in late 2012 caused serious damage (but no injuries, luckily), Joel felt even further removed from the discussions of the new safety mechanisms they were going to put in place. After some disputes, Joel decided to leave in early 2015 to start Quinta Essentia Alchemy, a craft spirits consulting group, providing a full range of services for people looking to distill at a small scale or to improve their business. He saw it as his chance to continue with his mission of creating sustainable, local economies by fostering relationships between people with ideas for a distillery and farmers.

"[You start with a] $2 million investment with VC [venture capital] or investors, and you find the project manager, you find the hobbyist distiller who wants to be pro, you sort of assemble a team, and find the location—[that's] the traditional way of [starting a distillery], which is very capital intensive, and starts off with a deficit of expertise. [I want to do] something that's much more holistic and small-scale. For instance, a farm, who is looking for ways to diversify their revenue stream.

"One of the last things I did [at Tuthilltown] was build a tiny distillery, a 12 by 12 shed. It was about $3,000 total, all in, and we produced fantastic products from it that sold. Actually the first two weekends of retail sales paid our salaries. It showed me something. Building this 12 by 12 shed and doing something in a very intimate and direct hands-on way. I'm not looking to make the next Hudson whiskey. I'm looking to make the next thing that people drive 20 to 30 miles to the distillery store for where it's exclusively available.

"[My goal is] the expansion of the concept of what a distillery can and should be, against the concept that it has to be capital-intensive, that it has to be competitive or even in a New York City market. I don't care the least bit about being competitive in New York City. That was the core from the beginning of Hudson's success. It doesn't matter if we're in every restaurant and bar; it matters if we're in the right ones. If we're in the ones where people are going to go and spend $70 on pre-dinner cocktails and then go ask where they can buy that thing. We know that the market is there, and now it's more mature. Building that tiny distillery there demonstrated something to me, that it wasn't the burden or the scope that it was perceived to be. You didn't have to compete in the same markets, and that it was much more accessible."

While most of his inquiries are from young people who are interested in craft distilling as a local and sustainable enterprise, most of his billable clients have thus far been in the more traditional mold: capital-backed entrepreneurs, including people who have already been successful in finance and want to move into a new venture (like the Prohibition Distillery owners), and an existing successful brand owner looking to diversify his portfolio by creating a craft label. With his expertise and experience, Joel is well-suited to work on all aspects of a craft distillery business, from production and safety to compliance and distribution.

The case of Tuthilltown shows how co-optation has occurred in the spirits industry in general, and there are similarities among the other three occupations. Mainstream actors in their industries have noticed the innovative work practices of these workers, and have had a few responses. Large companies have created their own smaller brands with the "craft" label and artisanal imagery, such as Diageo, the world's largest spirits producer, and its Barterhouse Whiskey label, and the Jack Daniel's Single Barrel. And along with finding craft distilleries as contractors, some owners of new brands are also buying their products from industrial distilleries. A famous example is Midwest Grain Products (MGP), in Lawrenceburg, Indiana, which makes whiskey for some fifty small brands, some of which attempt to hide the fact that they don't distill anything at all behind their origin stories. And the work of cocktail bartenders, as we have seen, has also had an impact on the spirits and nightlife industries, such as when bars, restaurants, and hotels hire bartenders to create cocktail programs.

Upscale men's barbers and whole-animal butchers are both part of and contributors to major changes occurring in their industries. The work of barbers in upscale shops is part of the sales growth of men's grooming products, as their work helps spread knowledge about these products and how to use them. Whole-animal butchery emerged on the heels of the foodie movement, and shares some of its major principles in common, such as knowing the source of food and using "artisanal" techniques to produce it. As the meat philosophy of these shops has spread, high-end restaurants have begun using whole animals, while larger retailers that sell "organic" products, such as Whole Foods, have created their own meat counters with a more diverse set of offerings than typical supermarkets.

The big question in each of these industries, of course, becomes what and how much of the cultural repertoires get lost when co-optation occurs. As

Gable says earlier, authenticity in business is a balancing act. Does a cocktail lose its status as a craft product when it has been batched? Is whiskey less of a craft product when cuts are automated? Do haircuts decline in quality when barbers must work faster? And are butchers who break down animals on the rail less artisanal? These are all open questions being hashed out in these communities and in larger society.

In short, the omnivorous cultural production of these workers has become highly profitable in a culture in which consumers are interested in the origins of what they buy. Whether it's how their drinks get made, what's in them, how they can achieve a certain style in their hair, what certain products can do to their hair and make it look like, where their meat comes from, how it ends up on their plate looking as it does, and, in each case, who makes or does what they're paying for, people want to know. And they will pay a lot when these products are authentically craft-based, or at least have the appearance of being so.

The ownership group of the Freemans empire split into two in 2013. One group, led by Sam, the main barbershop owner, took control of the two barbershops, moved the one that served as my field site to the nearby neighborhood of SoHo, and opened a third in Williamsburg, Brooklyn, renaming them all Fellow Barber. The other group took the restaurants and clothing stores (consolidating them into one location), keeping the Freemans name, and opened a new store in Tokyo. Initially, the barbers at Freemans were going to work for Sam and simply move over to the new SoHo shop. Instead, three of them—Ruben, Miles, and Joey—joined the other ownership group as partners in a new barbershop, located in the space next door to the old shop in the back of the clothing store on Rivington (it's in the space where they used to get coffee—the restaurant closed). "We couldn't go over there," says Miles. "SoHo's not us." The situation was ideal for the three of them to become owners. They were experienced barbers who regularly talked about what they would want to do if they were in charge. The three of them knew each other and worked well together. And the Freemans ownership group owned the space next door. The time was right. They turned the old shop into a changing and fitting area for the clothing store.

There are a few differences between the old shop and the new one. It's a larger space, with seven chairs instead of five, which means the barbers are more spread out than they were, and they have hired more barbers, including two who started as apprentices. They also started taking appointments instead of just being a walk-in shop. The major difference is that now clients tend to book appointments with a specific barber and become their regulars. As a result, a barber may go the whole day only cutting people they know without seeing new clients.

All the barbers who I came to know stayed at Freemans, and some from the West Village shop came to work there instead of staying at Fellow Barber. Van, who was the old shop's head barber, the first one hired who helped set up the concept, is an exception. Halfway through my fieldwork he was fired from Freemans because of a dispute with the ownership over a business deal and a clash over how best to manage the shop. Sensing it coming, in the month leading up to getting fired he got in touch with Russell Manley, a barber/stylist and owner of Tommy Guns, a shop a few blocks east of Freemans on Ludlow Street.

"I knew of him and he knew of me. When he was opening [Tommy Guns] he used to get his hair cut at Freemans. Great guy. I worked in [his shop] for two days [after getting fired] to see how I liked it and he liked me. It was an obvious fit. It's a great fit. It's awesome to be concentrating on style again. Because over [at Freemans], as much as I got passionate about doing old school cuts and introducing it to New York—that weight line, I kind of reintroduced single handedly. I hadn't seen anybody doing it so I was like, 'I gotta do it, I want to see it.' It's just such a great look. So I started doing it and then you see everybody with it. So it's great to be in a shop where you start thinking, 'Alright, I want to do something different, I want to try a different cut, a different style,' and then start walking around the city and see people, start to see it pop up, the little things you've done to influence down here. It's awesome."

While he harbors some bitterness, getting fired for Van was a blessing, in a way. He had found himself stuck in a rut stylistically at Freemans, and working in a new environment, in a new community of practice, inspired him. In the week or so leading up to his firing, Van gave his regular clients his e-mail address, asking them to contact him the next time they needed a haircut to see where he would be working. Many followed him to Tommy Guns. After working there for a couple of years and having a second child with his wife, Van moved to the Boston area, where his wife is from and his in-laws live, and started cutting hair at an upscale barbershop in the city. He eventually opened up his own upscale men's barbershop in Boston in summer 2016.

Through these cultural repertoires, these workers provide the potential for bad jobs to be good, and not just to be experienced as good.[4] Today we are seeing a return to skilled manual labor in an age of knowledge- and high-technology-based jobs and skilled and unskilled service work. But as I've shown this return comes in very limited and restricted forms and for a very small segment of the workforce.

Young, well-educated workers are reinventing other manual labor jobs by using similar cultural repertoires. The food world alone features a number of them, such as chefs, who have reached a high level of stardom. Once a fairly lowly, dirty job, except at elite levels (such as in French restaurants), today chefs have become true multimedia celebrities, respected for their craft, and sometimes for making high-quality lowbrow street food, such as in the case of Eddie Huang. Others have charted new paths in the food world, such as by making careers out of owning food carts or specializing in a single dish or food item.

We also see examples of these transformed jobs in other industries. Craft brewing is the closest parallel to craft distilling. But light manufacturing based on a sense of craft and craftsmanship has become widespread in the United States. The website Etsy, for instance, has become a hotbed for a variety of small arts and crafts producers, who sell their handmade and vintage wares (clothes, furniture, pottery) directly to consumers, while a number of on-the-ground flea and craft markets have also sprung up around the country for the same purpose. We are also seeing elite versions of other service and retail jobs, such as baristas who are passionate about and knowledgeable in coffee.

But why have these particular jobs in these industries undergone these transformations and not others? Why are there no "cool" plumbers, electricians, or maintenance workers? Perhaps because they usually do their work in confined, private settings. A central aspect of these new elite manual labor jobs is that they are performed publicly, in front of a knowing audience. Doing so and being transparent in their work practices is an important part of the philosophical underpinnings of their jobs. And for them validation for a skilled performance is integral to achieving status through work. This opportunity is not available for every occupation. These philosophically guided performances happen in the context of places of urban postindustrial cultural production, where hip omnivorous tastes get created and sold. The skilled nature of the work cannot be separated from the setting.

After getting fired from Dickson's, in summer 2013, Aldo went to work at the new meat counter at All Good Things—ironically in the same space where

Dickson's had its satellite shop. The owner hired Aldo to run it. But after four months or so, he grew frustrated with the owner and no longer wanted to work for him. With "Dickson's" on his resume, Aldo had no trouble finding other work in the city. He went to work at Cannibal, a meat-heavy gastropub in Manhattan, for two months, and then moved to Heritage Meat Shop, a whole-animal shop in the Essex Street Market.[5] Wanting more hours and responsibility, after a few months there he moved to Citarella, a gourmet market with several locations in the city and metropolitan area. Aldo loved the company, but they wanted him to work at their warehouse in the Hamptons, far out on Long Island, where they break down the animals to be distributed to their stores. He didn't want to travel that far. When their plans of opening a second warehouse in the city fell through, Aldo got bored of just working in the retail shop, and was ready to quit after a month.

But then he found out that Dickson's was hiring again.[6] Since getting fired, Aldo had come to realize what he had been doing wrong in his time there. "Because I never listened to him [Jake]," he says when I asked him why he thought he got fired. "In the beginning I was not doing it. And I was working more the JM style, like not talking [to customers]." The upscale, whole-animal butcher shop is a dynamic environment, a community of practice, and a place for co-workers to learn from each other and customers to learn from the staff. Aldo hadn't been enacting the cultural repertoires of the shop. "[Jake] wanted me to be more like a team member, more of a leader, put it like that. I get it now. I'm more about talking, and saying what you're supposed to do, not to do. Like I said, a team member. When he told me he rehired me he said to me, 'I never did this before. You will do history at Dickson's because I never rehired someone that I let go.' I was like, 'OK, let's do history.'"

I spoke with Jake about Aldo's firing and rehiring two years after my internship ended.

"We had a dynamic that developed in the cutting room that could not go on: feeling like they were untouchable, too much horsing around, and inappropriate. I needed to break that cycle of that kind of trifecta of Giancarlo, Aldo, and JM. At the time I felt like I could not fire JM; I needed him. Aldo and Giancarlo posed a lot of problems at the time. It was actually a toss-up who was going to get fired, for a while. Aldo, unfortunately, immature, not good with customers at the time, didn't care, he tried to avoid working and talking to customers. JM could make the argument that he didn't speak English well enough, but Aldo speaks perfect English. And so Aldo got cut. Aldo's a good dude, I like Aldo, but he, unfortunately, was the one of the three that I decided was the best one to fire for the organization.

"When we were looking to hire again, Aldo applied, we sat down, and he told me all the right things. He said, 'I understand what I was doing was wrong. I understand the need to help customers and be part of a team.' He's like, 'I get it. I kind of learned my lesson.' He went and worked other places, and he did not enjoy it. He realized that he had a good thing here. We treat our employees well, we work hard, you get to work with good meat, and we can have fun, but it just can't get out of hand. I will say Aldo's awesome. He comes in, he bangs it out every day, he is pleasant to be around, he is very fast, and does good work. I'm very happy with Aldo. He is our highest-paid, by far, hourly employee within the store, and it's deserved. I'm sure he'll ask for a raise this year, and I'll give it to him. I want Aldo to stay as long as he can, because unlike JM, who could just bang it out, Aldo brings a lot less baggage, and he will gladly help customers if you ask. It might not be his favorite thing to do, but if we're busy, he'll come up [to the front], and he'll help customers. He understands the importance of it. JM, it got so bad in the end."

As Jake implies, Dickson's was hiring for a butcher again in part because they had fired JM a few months after my internship ended. I asked Jake to tell me about his decision.

"JM went off the rails. He always had gone up and down on his drinking, partying. He would be cleaned up for four months and liked going to the gym, and then he'd fall off the wagon again. He'd be showing up late and hungover as hell. It's too bad, because JM was a great teacher, a good guy. When we'd talk, have a few beers, he would tell me all the things he wanted to accomplish, but he had no discipline to actually accomplish them, to be the leader that he wanted to be. All the other guys followed his example. He was their leader.

"But the truth is the cutting room just needed a leader, and they didn't have one. In theory, JM wanted to do it all. It became untenable when he was starting to show up late so often. We were trying to crack down on that across the whole organization and become a more professional organization. Basically, he thought that he would never get fired, unfortunately. I told him, when had our first ever all-staff meeting, I texted him the day before, and I was like, 'JM, do not be late to this meeting. Do not be late, or there will be serious consequences.' He showed up 45 minutes late. He basically forced my hand to fire him."

Much of what Jake says resonated with me. JM certainly liked to go out, and occasionally came in late and hungover during my research. He would also sometimes talk about some ideas he had for the display case or for cuts, usually at the bar after work, but he wouldn't always bring his ideas to Jake, the manager, or the chef. He never helped or talked to customers, certainly in part because he wasn't comfortable speaking English. And while JM was a gifted teacher, the other butchers usually had to initiate a lesson by asking him questions or asking him to observe them working.

After firing JM, Jake hired Jocelyn, formerly of the whole-animal shop Lindy and Grundy, in Los Angeles, to be the head butcher. And when she left, after Aldo was rehired, Jake promoted Giancarlo to the head butcher position in 2015, where he remains today. Giancarlo was relatively new to butchery when my internship began. He was very knowledgeable and skilled, but not at the level of JM and Aldo. The two Mexican butchers gave him a rough time, at first, mainly through teasing. (The situation was quite a rarity in the New York City food world: immigrants from Mexico with power over a college-educated white man.) He felt he had to prove himself by taking their jibes (he dished them out, too) and working hard to improve, which he did. Giancarlo's successful path—from going to college, to managing a medical center, to becoming a novice butcher in New York City, to finally becoming the head butcher at an elite whole-animal shop—is the dream for many of the people in this book and younger aspirants in these industries. Many like him get to live it.

METHODOLOGICAL APPENDIX

In this appendix I will provide specific details on the research I conducted for this book, and discuss some of the issues I faced in the field and with participants. My goal is to show readers exactly what my analyses, narratives, and arguments are based on for them to judge the merits of each for themselves and replicate this project to the greatest extent possible. Like all social scientists, qualitative researchers have the burden of providing evidence for their data's accuracy and consistency. This full discussion of how I obtained these data satisfies the obligation.

Timeline, Choices, and Data Collection

I began working on this project on Tuesday, February 20, 2007, when I first walked into the cocktail bar Death & Co. I went there because of my dissertation research. The previous week I had attended a local community board meeting for downtown Manhattan's Lower East Side area at which a group of residents protested the liquor license for the bar.[1] On that night there happened to be two items on the same agenda from which my new project arose. One was Death & Co., and the other was Mighty Ocelot, a proposed café owned by Sasha Petraske, who also owned Milk and Honey, the first of the new craft cocktail bars in New York City.[2] Both places attracted considerable opposition from residents at the meeting. Whenever residents heavily contested an opened bar, I always went to it in the days or weeks afterward to check it out and speak with the owner. Mighty Ocelot hadn't opened yet, but people brought up Milk and Honey many times at the meeting and said it was the quietest bar in the neighborhood, if not in all of New York City. I wanted to check out both bars, and the following week I did, Death & Co. on Tuesday night, and Milk and Honey the next night.[3]

They were both unlike any bar experience I had ever had. Hidden doors and inconspicuous façades, unique sights, sounds, and smells, detailed service, and drinks I had never heard of before, let alone tasted. I was fascinated. Despite having a dissertation to finish, I kept going back to these bars, taking notes, and talking to people. I spoke to Dave, Death & Co.'s owner, and Sasha about both the neighborhood and their community board struggles, and about the world of craft cocktails. I learned about the growing community of cocktail bars, bartenders, and enthusiasts in New York City and other cities around the country and the world. I started interviewing them and attending events around the city, such as cocktail demonstrations and tastings, and bought and read the books they used. I knew I wouldn't be able to include everything about this community in my first book. So I began to think of it as a side project.

I attended my first Tales of the Cocktail festival in 2008, and returned the next two years. There I met people from around the world who were involved in craft cocktails in some way. Back in New York City I attended educational events, such as the BAR (Beverage Alcohol Resource) Program, and cocktail competitions sponsored by brands. Whenever I traveled, for business (that is, to attend an academic conference) or pleasure, I always looked up the city's craft cocktail bars and got in touch with their owners and bartenders to set up interviews. I never got to the point of developing a solid framework or argument for what I was observing and learning, except the idea of how a cultural movement emerges and takes shape, its points of cohesion and discord, and how important the storied past has become in many of today's cultural revivals. I mostly kept gathering data.

By 2009 I started to gravitate toward the liquor industry, specifically craft distilleries that were making new spirits. I was meeting people from these businesses at cocktail bars and cocktail/spirits-related events and learning about their products and their connection to the cocktail world, but I wanted to see the actual distilleries and the production process. One evening at a tasting event I met a young college student named Nick, who was working at the table for Tuthilltown Spirits. Nick's uncle, Ralph, was a co-founder of the company, and he worked there to earn some money. I knew Tuthilltown and its products—namely, its Hudson Whiskey line—from the cocktail bars. Cocktail bartenders respected what Tuthilltown was doing: handcrafted, farm distilling with local and sustainable products. I told Nick about my project (or as much as I knew about it at the time), and said I wanted to see how craft distilling worked. He nodded his head and said it would certainly be possible, since they've had part-time and temporary workers at the distillery before. Nick put me in touch with Joel, Tuthilltown's chief distiller, and after a phone conversation he accepted what I wanted to do and we worked out a schedule. Four times a month, usually on Thursdays and Fridays, I would put on my brown "Distilleryman" t-shirt, khaki workpants, and boots and ride the Trailways bus two hours up to New Paltz, the town near the distillery. Joel or Nick would pick me up. I became a craft distillery intern. Somewhat to my chagrin, several craft distilleries opened in New York City, much closer to my home, after I finished much of my internship at Tuthilltown. They spread in the wake of the Farm Distillery Act's passing, in 2007, which made opening a small distillery more economically feasible. I conducted more fieldwork at two of these—Kings County Distillery and New York Distilling Company. But if I had waited a year or two more, I could've avoided the four-hour round-trip commute.

It was during this internship that I slowly began changing the focus of my project. I became increasingly interested in the workers making the drinks and spirits and interacting with customers and visitors. I was drawn most strongly to their work, and how different it was from what we expect college graduates to pursue as a career. Wanting to study this phenomenon outside of the craft cocktail and spirits world, I used "theoretical sampling" to find other cases to examine.[4] In my personal life I had recently become aware of new men's barbershops that offered classes for men to learn how to shave with a straight razor. At one point fathers would have simply taught their sons how to shave with a straight razor, but disposable razors and cartridges had all but ended the practice. Today men interested in learning how to do so, out of utility or curiosity, often learn it from a professional. I had been shaving my face with a safety razor—the historical bridge between straight razors and disposables—for a little while at that point, so I had taken note of the classes. I saw a connection between these classes for learning a lost practice and the cocktail-making classes I had attended and studied, as well as between cocktail bars and new barbershops as revivals of classic institutions with traditional services. (I was also in need of a new barber.) On two occasions in the spring and early summer of 2011 I went Freemans Sporting Club, first on Horatio Street in the West Village and then on Rivington Street on the Lower East Side, got my hair cut, and spoke with the barber cutting my hair about his work. After the second visit I knew these shops and their barbers would be my new case. I then spoke with Van, the head barber at the Rivington Street shop; Sam, the owner; and a representative from the company's PR firm. They all approved my project, and I began conducting participant observation research at Freemans in July 2011.

I went to the shop approximately three times a week for several hours a day for a year.

During my fieldwork at Freemans I realized I didn't want barbers to be the only non-alcohol-related case. To find another one I thought about the larger industries in which these jobs were embedded: nightlife, alcohol manufacturing, and grooming, with strong ties to the fashion industry. Each was expanding and transforming in today's city. Quite simply, I asked myself what other industries were undergoing similar changes? It did not take me long to think about the food industry, both retail and production. I could easily have studied chefs, which is another traditionally low-status manual labor occupation undergoing a segmented transformation today with the rise of foodie culture. But I was more intrigued by other food retail businesses, especially new versions of classic community institutions. I discovered new butcher shops through the lifestyle media and had been visiting one (Fleischer's, in Brooklyn) to buy my meat.

After surveying the butchery scene, I contacted Jake, owner of Dickson's Farmstand Meats. We scheduled an interview in July 2012, and I told him about my project. Luckily, Dickson's also had an internship program, like Tuthilltown. I would go to Dickson's to work once or twice a week, mainly in the cutting area, for around eight hours a day for a year. I usually wore the same khaki work pants and boots I wore at Tuthilltown, with a shop-supplied white snap-button shirt, apron, and black-and-white Dickson's trucker hat.

I formally left the field on August 28, 2013, the last day of my internship at Dickson's, and six-and-a-half years after I first walked into Death & Co. and began my project. Over the following years I attended a few special events here and there, such as a party for the release of the New York Distilling Company's new "Rock & Rye" product and a social event Dickson's held for the whole-animal butcher community in New York City. And I kept in touch with the people as much as possible by casually going to their businesses. I'd pop into one of the bars, go buy meat, and regularly get my hair cut. I went as a consumer, but would inevitably learn something new while catching up with the people I knew. Most importantly, after leaving the field I conducted many follow-up interviews with them and interviewed some new people as I worked on presentations, publications, and this book.

Based on this overview of my project's evolution, it seems that of the four, I did the most work on the cocktail world, which is true. I spent the most time studying the cocktail scene and went to many cocktail-related events because when I started I thought the project would only be about the cocktail world and all the industries connected to it. So I went to events on topics like special glassware and craft spirits, because cocktail bartenders found them important. I wasn't sure of the project's new direction until my internship at Tuthilltown. I did not attend as many events external to the main field sites for the other jobs, particularly barbers and butchers, for two reasons. First, I wanted my focus to be on the workers and the workplaces, not related industries (such as companies for men's grooming products or restaurants). Second, and more importantly, there are far fewer barber- and butcher-related events than there are ones related to cocktails and spirits. Their occupational communities differ from those of cocktail bartenders and craft distillers in this regard. When I analyzed my notes on the cocktail bars and cocktail bartenders for this book, I made sure to focus on my time in the actual bars, but the other sites also inform my analysis.

For each phase of this project I typed up the short, handwritten notes I made in the field once returning home or the next morning. In the case of the distillery, I would type up my notes on the bus ride home. Once I felt comfortable in each setting, became familiar with its routines and rhythms, and began to see which activities were most pertinent, I also occasionally ran a digital audio recorder in my settings to accurately capture lengthy discussions and interactions. While most of the statements in quotation marks in this book are from transcriptions of these recordings and recorded interviews, some are from my notes. I keep them in quotes because I feel I was able to capture most statements accurately in my note-taking, perhaps not verbatim, but close to enough to document the meanings and intentions of the people speaking, whom I had come to know and which I had come to understand. I recognize how such understandings can be more difficult to achieve in studies when the researchers are very different from the people they study.[5]

I sometimes edited quotes for readability, such as by taking out extra words, and sometimes combined quotes from responses to different questions in an interview. While I identified multiple quotes and episodes from the field that represent my data points, I usually selected quotes and episodes for inclusion in the book that I felt "best" demonstrated the point—that is, they did so clearly and comprehensively, with vivid phrasing and/or through a memorable story. I also selected quotes from and episodes involving a smaller number of my participants than the total amount I studied. These are not necessarily the people who I came to know the best or observed the most. While this book's analysis is informed by the sum total of data I collected, I wanted to limit the number of people presented in the book for readability's sake. When writing I therefore decided to return often to the people who seemed to represent greater points and patterns most directly and clearly. But I could have easily provided different quotes from and episodes involving other people for each claim I make.

Roles and Relationships in the Field

Since the researcher's body is literally the data collection instrument in ethnographic fieldwork, and since everyone's body contains multiple socially constructed meanings and identities (for example, race, gender, age), which mediate how they interact with other people, it is important for researchers to reflect on how their social positions influenced their data collection. And by social position, I mean specifically where they were spatially vis-à-vis their participants and what they were doing while among them, and, more importantly, how who they are in terms of their social backgrounds and identities had an impact on the relationships they formed. In short, we need to know what role researchers played in the field among their participants and what kinds of relationships they had with their participants, how both influenced the data they collected and analyzed, how their social positions presented issues for communication and understanding, and how they tried to overcome these issues, when possible.

I played different roles in the field for each of the four jobs I studied. These roles influenced what I did and saw and how I understood what I was doing and seeing, which certainly had an impact on my analysis. The social order of the workplaces and how varied the work roles were for the job largely determined the roles I played. And in each site I tried to compensate for how the role limited my data collection.

To study cocktail bartenders, I simply became a regular of cocktail bars and of the cocktail scene. I was used to this role from my previous project. Bars are excellent places to conduct fieldwork. They're very social, and it's easy to blend in as a customer. And cocktail bars are great places to have and hear conversations, because they're quieter than other bar types. I went to the bars often, usually two nights a week for several hours a visit. I would often visit two bars per night. Along with Death & Co. and Milk and Honey, I also went to Little Branch (which Sasha also owned) and PDT. I always sat at the bar. I took notes in a small notebook underneath the bar and in the restroom. The "no standing" policy at these bars made it difficult to speak to many customers, except for the ones sitting right next to me. But it allowed me to focus on the bartenders, their work practices, and their interactions. I drank slowly, and the bartenders graciously allowed me to nurse my cocktails, even though I was taking up a seat. I asked them a lot of questions about what they were doing, drinks they were making or working on, other cocktail bars and bartenders, other aspects of the industry, and interactions they were having with customers. And sometimes they welcomed me to see the bar behind-the-scenes before they opened, to observe the preparation involved.[6] In short, my aim in becoming a regular was to be a fixture in these bars and the larger cocktail world.

I learned a lot about the cocktail bartender's work life, but I did not become a bartender myself. I considered trying it, and considered becoming a barback, to get the perspective from the other side of the bar, but did not pursue either seriously. (Since I had no bartending or service experience in my life at all, no cocktail bar would've hired me as a bartender. I would've been hired as a barback anyway.) I was writing my dissertation and teaching during the day while also trying to get a full-time, tenure-track job as an assistant professor. A job at a cocktail bar would have meant even later, tougher nights than I was already doing in my fieldwork. But not doing so meant I would miss out on learning the embodied knowledge of making craft cocktails by following the principles of mixology, and on interacting and engaging with customers as these bartenders did.

I tried to make up for this limitation in a number of ways. First, I bought cocktail-making tools and a lot of booze. I mined old and new cocktail books and websites for recipes and ideas. I experimented with flavor combinations and ingredients, and served drinks to friends, following the cultural scripts I heard cocktail bartenders use (that is, asking them their favorite ingredient). Basically, I made a bar and acted like a cocktail bartender at home. I gained some perspective on cocktail-making and customer interaction from doing so, but obviously nothing close to tending an actual bar. I also signed up to be a volunteer at the Astor Center, which offers many classes on a variety of food and beverage topics taught by experts: wine, spirits, and cheese tasting, microbrewing, and how to make cocktails. Mostly for entertainment, people pay to learn the basics of a topic (I regularly saw people on dates). Volunteers would help set up stations (such as bar tools and garnishes for cocktail classes), make sure no one ran out of anything during the class, assist the instructor (usually a cocktail bartender), and then help clean up. In a way, volunteering showed me a bit of what barbacking is, while I also learned how bartenders talk about and teach their work to the public. Finally, I was also a member of the New York chapter of the United States Bartenders' Guild (USBG), to which nonbartenders were welcome to apply. Along with participating in events like product tastings and field trips to nearby distilleries, companies also sometimes asked USBG members to help run events. For instance, I volunteered to essentially be a barback for the opening gala of the Manhattan Cocktail Classic, an event similar to Tales of the Cocktail.

My internship at Tuthilltown was very different from my fieldwork on cocktail bartenders.[7] Bars have very clearly defined roles: bartender, barback, customer, and, sometimes, a manager. When busy, a bartender will regularly perform tasks that barbacks normally do, but they mostly take orders and make cocktails all night long. Being a customer gave me access to each role, and to the action. Craft distilleries are very different workplaces from bars, and each one is different from another in terms of how it operates. Distilleries are manufacturing spaces for production, not consumption spaces for socializing. There are no "God spot"–like seats from which to witness all the action. It did not make sense to merely observe.

Since so much of the operation at Tuthilltown was done by hand, and since the staff wasn't very large, everybody did everything at some point. As the manager and chief distiller, Joel did bookkeeping and worked on projects most of the day, but he would often work on solving little production problems. With so many small and large tasks to complete, it was very easy for me to blend in there as a worker. Since I was part-time with no experience, I mostly performed some of the smaller tasks, such as bottling spirits, packaging bottles, and cleaning equipment. But there were sufficient breaks throughout the day to walk around to the different work areas, observe, ask questions, and take notes. I did not distill (that is, run the still), but got to taste the points when distillers would make the cuts, and got to ask them questions about their decisions and tastes. By the end of my internship I was proofing spirits and keeping records. In short, the internship at Tuthilltown was very hands-on and showed me the steps and hard physical labor in some harsh conditions (mainly very hot rooms) required to make craft spirits. In addition to sight, taste, smell, and hearing—the main senses I used at cocktail bars—I also got to feel what distilling work is like, and thereby understand some of their meanings about the process from a firsthand perspective.

My fieldwork in other craft distilleries—namely, Kings County Distillery and the New York Distilling Company—and at craft spirits–related events, was more traditional participant observation. In these places I joined tours they regularly give to curious consumers who want to see how small batches of spirits get made. Their owners welcomed my presence and gave me access. As with cocktail bartenders during classes, on these tours I heard how distillers explain their craft and products to the public. Similarly, craft spirits events, such as tastings and seminars, gave me the opportunity to hear how distillers and owners presented their products and ask them about their brand.

The roles at barbershops are even more clearly defined than they are at bars: you cut hair, or you have it cut (or sit and wait to have it cut). I never considered becoming a barber. First, the training is long and expensive. (A popular program in New York City, at the American Barber Institute, covers 660 hours of instruction and costs $5,060.) Second, it takes many years of constant cutting to truly feel comfortable as a barber. None of the shops I was interested in would've ever hired me until I had more experience.[8] I could have become a receptionist and answered phones, greeted clients, sold products, and swept up hair. But not only are receptionists busy at their own tasks, at the Freemans location on Rivington Street, my main field site, the front desk was in a separate room from the shop. So working as a receptionist there (which they had openings for during my fieldwork) would've been counterproductive to my goal of participant observation.

But barbershops are also like bars because they are very social places and the client's role is similar to a customer's: sit and have a service done for you. After explaining my project to the owner and head barber, they allowed me to simply sit in the shop, ask questions, and take notes. I always tried to sit in the seat closest to the barber chairs. Being a regular client at a barbershop is not the same as being a regular customer at a bar, since people don't get their hair cut every day (and new upscale shops aren't hangouts for men). But I became a regular presence in the shop for the barbers. In a sense I treated the barbershop the way the owners of these shops want them to be treated: as a place for men to hang out, even if they're not getting a haircut. I was the only person who used it that way, other than people who lived or worked nearby and would pop in to quickly say hello to their barber and then leave.

As with cocktail bartenders I used a few data collection strategies to make up for my lack of firsthand knowledge in cutting hair. First, I tried asking questions about what the barbers were doing while they were working. I sometimes did not have to ask them to explain the techniques they were using or circumstances they encountered with people's hair. They came to know what I was interested in, and would sometimes call me over to see what they were doing. Second, I used the "photo elicitation" method, or took pictures of barbers cutting someone's hair, and interviewed them while showing them the photos.[9] The aim was to get barbers to see their work from a different angle and discuss aspects of the haircut and their technique that they might take for granted and not realize while they were doing it. (For both strategies, the barbers always asked their clients for permission to let me observe what was happening with their haircut.) I used this technique with two barbers, Miles and Ruben, as I show in chapter 6. I did not use it with cocktail bartenders, because their techniques are easier to understand (for me, at least) and practice at home, and bars offer more opportunities to ask bartenders about the technical aspects of their work while they're doing it than barbershops do. Barbers are often talking with clients while working, and I did not want to disturb this important relationship with questions about their cutting techniques. I only did so, and they only invited me to observe, when the client clearly did not want to talk to them. While very social, cocktail bartenders are more likely to temporarily cease conversations with customers while making cocktails. But they answer questions when they are doing so if asked.

If my role in barbershops was similar to my role in cocktail bars, my role in butcher shops was similar to my role in craft distilleries: I became an intern. Like craft distilleries, whole-animal butcher shops are dynamic workplaces with a lot of tasks both large (butcher meat, serve customers) and small (grind meat, affix labels to bags) that need to be done. They are also not social places like bars and barbershops are, so once again it didn't make sense to find a convenient place to sit and observe (no such place existed). Interns at whole-animal shops perform many of the smaller tasks. Dickson's, my main field site, had a more formal internship program than Tuthilltown did. They regularly receive applications and conduct interviews with candidates. Interns are asked to work two days a week for three months. They mainly work in the cutting area with the butchers on a planned set of tasks. But there was ample opportunity for me go to the counter, which was clearly visible from the cutting area, and observe customer interaction (and even to interact with and serve customers myself during busy periods). Like at Tuthilltown, I kept a small notebook in my back pocket and took notes in the restroom, on the outside loading dock, and in the walk-in refrigerator during lulls. And as with my distillery internship, working at the butcher shop allowed me to use all of my senses to collect my data and understand the meanings these workers attached to the work they did while being embedded in the setting and working alongside them.

Overall I blended in very well socially to each field site and community. It wasn't very hard, given my identity and background and the identities and backgrounds of the people I studied. I am a young (mid-thirties), white, straight, middle-class, and well-educated man. Most of the people I studied for this book have very similar backgrounds. I was 26 years old when I started this project, and 32 when I left the field. Most of the people I studied were about my age, sometimes a little younger or older. I lived in Brooklyn during my research, sometimes near the people I studied, and had a lifestyle similar to theirs. In fact, given my social life and sense of taste and style, I would have gone out to the bars and restaurants, shopped at the butcher shops and liquor stores, visited craft distilleries, and gotten my hair cut at the barbershops even if I weren't conducting this research. My lifestyle in many ways matched those of these workers, who are quite diffuse and omnivorous in their own tastes. As I discussed in this book, there is a lot of crossover between these worlds in the sense that workers are very aware of the other businesses and cultures. Cocktail bartenders and craft distillers are the best example, since cocktail bartenders use craft spirits and craft distillers ask cocktail bartenders to make cocktails out of their products. But I also talked about cocktails, bars, and spirits with both barbers and butchers, and meat and men's fashion with bartenders and distillers. I ran into cocktail bartenders on a few occasions at barbershops. Some barbershops serve craft cocktails to clients during haircuts. And one barber used to bartend in a cocktail bar.

Given the different roles I played and my own background, my relationships with people from the field sites also varied somewhat. The cocktail bartenders treated me like a special regular customer. They occasionally bought me a drink (which really helped me out as a graduate student with a small income), and also gave me samples of new drinks they were working on to offer feedback. Since people from the cocktail world regularly visit each other's bars, and since the bartenders knew what I was doing there, they would also introduce me to other bartenders, owners, and other people of importance in the scene. Of the four jobs, cocktail bartenders go out to other cocktail bars (and other bars in general) and cocktail-related events the most. People in the other three jobs rarely do with any frequency, but they are very aware of other places and workers in their industry. I would sometimes accompany cocktail bartenders as they went out to other bars, which gave me more perspective on their lives away from work. I also often saw people from the distilling world at bars and events, which gave me similar insights. In fact, I learned a lot about the people in this book by hanging out with them away from their workplaces, where their roles and behaviors are more defined. After work at the distillery my co-workers and I would often sit by the picnic tables near the field, drink whiskey and beer, and chat. I often went to lunch or out for coffee with the barbers, and often went to a nearby bar after work with the butchers. These times were invaluable for my relationships with them and my data collection, because we got to see each other outside of the proper workplace. While out, they would sometimes speak differently about the job or their co-workers. For instance, Aldo and Giancarlo became friendlier toward each other at the bar after work compared to the constant teasing and name-calling they would do while working (especially Aldo toward Giancarlo). These were also times when workers would express to me some of their secrets, such as insecurities they have about their abilities or ideas about opening their own place.

I blended in differently with people at the barbershop. Since social life at the barbershop resembled more of a show of masculinity by the barbers for clients than a truly community-oriented experience, I tried to not interfere and simply maintain a presence as a waiting client. While I occasionally participated in the barbers' group banter by joining a discussion, which made me unusual for the setting since clients (which I likely appeared as to others) almost never talk until they are in the barber chair, I never initiated these exchanges and usually just sat there, laughed, and took notes. I joined in when I had something to say. In addition to other aspects of my background, I am also a native New Yorker, as many of the barbers I studied are (or from its outskirts), which gave us many similarities in terms of our biographies and knowledge of the city. Of the four jobs, I think the barbers liked having me around the most, because of my role more than my personality. When I would arrive in the shop they often told me about stories I missed, like an argument between two barbers, which they thought I might find interesting for my research. "You're not gonna believe what happened yesterday!" they would often say. The barbers enjoyed including me in their group banter, sometimes using me as an independent third party to resolve an argument they were having.

And socializing differed at the craft distillery and butcher shop because we were working alongside each other. As mentioned, Tuthilltown was rather spread out, with one large room for bottling, another for distilling, another for cooking and fermenting, another for aging and selling products, and a lot of outdoor space where a variety of work activities take place (cleaning, loading, transporting). A worker could be working alone in any one of those spaces, which sometimes limited conversation. But situations often brought workers close together, like when I was working with or near someone else, during lunch, breaks, or at the end of the day. At these times conversations drifted from the work we were doing to music to romantic relationships. Dickson's had separate work areas, but the shop is much smaller in size than the distillery, and the boundaries between the areas are highly porous. I never worked alone for more than a few minutes. When I was in the walk-in taking down the meat inventory, someone from the kitchen would come in to work on sausages. The cutting and counter areas are highly social places for workers, who regularly made jokes and talked shit to each other when customers weren't around. Since I was a worker working alongside them, I would also join in with the joking and light teasing. Teasing and getting teased were expected of anyone in the cutting area.

People in each of the field sites would regularly refer to my own job or to my project, and would specifically mention that I was studying them. At least one person in each field site called me "doctor." (Cocktail bartenders especially made a big deal of it because I got my PhD during my fieldwork at the bars.) On a few occasions the barbers talked about which Hollywood actors would portray them in a movie based on my book. They also sometimes teased me about really being a psychologist who was there to "mess with their heads." One of the butchers made the same comment, and I felt for a time that he was unsure of what my presence meant, since he kept asking me what I was doing there for the first month or so of my fieldwork. Over time, however, he said he figured it out and felt more comfortable talking to me. But I cannot recall a time when my educational background or occupation led people in the field to treat me differently.

Of all of my identities, being a man (and a straight, white, well-educated, middle-class man living in a hip neighborhood in a hip city, at that) most likely played the biggest role in influencing my relationships. Most of the people in this book fit this profile, and it was easy to see how their interactions with me mirrored those with each other. Along with our backgrounds, our humor and cultural references were also similar.

Interviews

In addition to my fieldwork, I conducted a total of 109 formal, semistructured, recorded interviews with people in these industries: 44 cocktail bartenders, cocktail bar owners, and other members of the craft cocktail community (for example, media members); 19 craft distillers and owners; 20 barbers and owners of upscale barbershops, as well as receptionists; and 26 whole-animal butcher shop owners, butchers, and workers. (The high number of cocktail bartenders reflects how this project began as a study on the craft cocktail community.) These interviews served to provide details on these workers' personal backgrounds, thoughts on their paths to these jobs and industries, and their attitudes toward their occupations, industries, and work practices. Each interview lasted at least an hour, and I conducted multiple interviews with several participants. I conducted all of them in person except for four, which I did over the phone or via Skype, and almost all were with people whose behavior I observed in their work setting, which allowed me to compare what people said with how they actually behaved. Student assistants, online services, and I transcribed each interview, and I coded them myself according to relevant themes and codes.

I addressed a number of themes and asked a number of questions in my interviews. I usually talked to people about their backgrounds and career paths while in the field, but the interviews gave me the chance to mine them in depth and record them for the greatest accuracy. We also often discussed their work in situ, but the interviews allowed me to take a step back and really ask questions about such topics as technique and customers based on my field notes. And since they were almost always conducted away from their businesses (or when they were closed), the interviews allowed me to ask participants about their workplaces, co-workers, and occupational communities without them being heard.

Analyzing the Data

I used a mixed qualitative analytical approach for my data. I wanted to show the unique characteristics of each individual case as well as provide explanations for the phenomena across these four cases. This approach is how I broke down this book into two parts, with part I focusing on each individual case and part II presenting my cross-occupational analysis. For the former goal I used a more guided grounded theory approach of devising themes and codes based on my data and highlighting variation in the data across the cases.[10] After learning the central role mixology played for cocktail bartenders and cocktail bars, for each occupation I used grounded theory to determine the philosophical underpinnings of the these businesses and of the work these workers do. For the latter goal I used analytic induction, or an iterative analytical process of revising explanations to fit new data.[11] As I accumulated new data, such as on how these workers understand their paths to their occupations, I continuously came up with ways to explain them. But as I encountered new data that did not fit these explanations, I simply revised them so that they would fit. This data analysis technique is how I came up with the different explanations for how people choose to start working these jobs and pursue them as careers. In that case I discovered multiple explanations for how they did so, and preserved that variation.

While a few self-described ethnographers in sociology emphasize using participants' real names in publications, there is very little scientific imperative to do so.[12] The ultimate decision is the researcher's, based in part on his or her relationships and agreements with participants. I use the real names of some of the people in this book. I base my decision on whether they said they wanted their names used, on how closely in contact I remained with them, and on whether I felt their comments and/or portrayal would cause them any harm. Most of the people whose real names I used in this book read the sections in which they appear, and approved of the argument, their portrayal, and the use of their real name, while offering some excellent feedback.

Limitations

No single book or study can encompass all of a social problem. They always have blind spots, or limitations. Researchers are who they are and make the choices they make based on a wide set of criteria (including who they are). A goal of the author and researcher is to acknowledge what those blind spots are and discuss how the project could have been different if they were addressed or if different choices were made (or if they were different researchers). These limitations can certainly serve as beginnings of future research projects on this and related subjects. Here I will discuss a few major ones in my project and in this book. (There are, obviously, many more than these limitations, both major and minor.)

The first one concerns social distance. As mentioned, I felt rather comfortable in these settings and with the people I studied, and I feel they were comfortable with my presence and inquiries. I attribute this comfort to the many characteristics we shared in common, and how they acted toward me when I was in the setting. But I always ask myself what I missed. What did I take for granted? What about my background blinded me to some key issues? While I felt I was still able to maintain a critical distance between myself and my participants despite the relative ease with which we got along, I have no doubt at all that a different researcher—of a different gender or a different race, or older—would have noticed behaviors and meanings I completely missed and would have a different interpretation of the words and actions than I had.

Second, while I spoke to dozens of them (and observed many thousands more) to get a suggestive picture of who they are, why they go to these businesses, and what they're all about, I did not systematically study consumers and do not include them in this book. Quite simply, I made the decision early on to focus my research on workers, and work-related topics form the basis of my framework. But consumers are obviously the other half of these businesses, and these workers don't exist without them. As I've pointed out, a lot of research has been conducted on omnivorous consumers, but not much of it has been qualitative. A study would surely benefit from exploring how consumers of these products and services interpret the interactions they have with these workers and how they make sense of their own taste.

Third, I also didn't systematically study other, more mainstream versions of these jobs and workplaces. (Bartenders are an exception, because I studied people who bartend at a local neighborhood bar for my first book. But I hardly bring that analysis to bear here.) I therefore cannot conduct an intra-industry analysis of how the meanings held by these new elite workers toward their jobs, consumers, and work practices compare to those of people who work in the more common versions of these occupations. As with consumers of these businesses, such a study would be fascinating and make a needed contribution to the work and occupations literature.

Finally, a common issue in qualitative research is "sampling on the dependent variable," or selecting cases on the basis of meeting certain criteria and then using those cases as evidence for the criteria. I chose to study people who are involved in these industries and occupational communities and have, for the most part, succeeded (that is, either built or laid the groundwork for a career in these jobs and/or industries). I mainly base my arguments about omnivorous cultural production on them, their backgrounds, and their work. I do not analyze many people who fail to enact these cultural repertoires and put on a good performance and thereby get excluded from these industries and communities, or people who simply choose to leave and work in another field, for whatever reason(s). While I do not feel neglecting people who are outside of these industries and communities detracts from the main argument, I certainly recognize that we would need more research on outsiders and people who fail in the enactments of these repertoires if we are to fully understand new forms of manual labor as alternatives to strict knowledge work in the new economy.

NOTES

Preface. The Daily Grind

1. Hughes (1958), 42.
2. Most names of people are real, and all place names are real. I discuss these decisions in the appendix.
3. See Ocejo 2014, 5, 133, 146–47, 161, 176–79.
4. I get the concept of a "taste community," or a group socially constructed around the preferences of its members for particular artifacts and cultures, from Ferguson's (1998; 2004) influential work on the origins of a national French cuisine.
5. They are like many of the artists Lloyd (2006) studied in Chicago, who identify as "artists" even though most of their income comes from service work.
6. I use Becker's (1996) notion of achieving "breadth" in qualitative research, or trying to find out at least some information on every topic that the research touches on, as a guiding principle in my work.
7. I discuss in detail the specific research methods I used to obtain the information in this book, and provide further methodological insights, in the appendix.
8. As I explain in the introduction, most of this book focuses on men.
9. In their classic formulation of "grounded theory," Glaser and Strauss (1967) refer to this technique as "theoretical sampling." I discuss my selection of field sites and interview participants in the appendix.
10. Scholars generally credit Braverman's (1974) work with setting off discussions and debates on the process of deskilling in work. I will discuss how each trade experienced deskilling, and how these new workers interpret this history, in the chapters of part I. But in general these reasons include some combination of shifts in their larger industries and in the greater economy, changes in the cultures of their workplaces and in the perceptions people have of these jobs in larger society, and technological advancements.
11. Van Maanen and Barley (1984) define an "occupational community" as "a group of people who consider themselves to be engaged in the same sort of work, whose identity is drawn from their work, who share with one another a set of values, norms, and perspectives that apply but extend beyond work related matters, and whose social relationships meld work and leisure" (287).

12. See Brown-Saracino (2010); Grazian (2006); and Lloyd (2006); as well as my previous book (Ocejo 2014).

13. Peterson (1992) first developed this concept in his research on people's musical tastes. I discuss it in much greater detail in the introduction.

14. See Kalleberg (2011).

15. Based on findings from two surveys by the National Opinion Research Council (one from 1947; the other from 1963), Sennett and Cobb (1972) cite the most desirable jobs in the United States in the middle of the twentieth century (221–25). Out of ninety occupations, bartender and barber rank in the bottom quarter. Distiller is not on the list (although "machine operator in a factory" is, and it also ranks toward the bottom), and neither, oddly, is butcher. In a more recent piece, Simpson et al. (2014) find that butchers today still assign great value to their work for the income it gives them to raise their children and support them through college so that they don't have to become butchers.

    Hughes (1958) developed the concept of "dirty work" to refer to jobs that deal with activities that are physically and/or morally degrading or repulsive (a garbage collector is an example of just the former, while an embalmer combines both). Since they perform a necessary function, society delegates these activities to certain jobs, which in effect stigmatizes them. Of the four jobs in this book, only butcher combines the two, because of the ethics surrounding the slaughter of animals. But all four are dirty jobs in a physical sense. See Ashforth and Kreiner (1999) and Dick (2005) for additional discussions of the term.

16. See Kalleberg (2011).

17. Swidler (1986) defines a cultural repertoire as a set of knowledge, skills, and symbols that provide the materials from which individuals and groups construct "strategies of action." Also see Lamont's (1992) comparative analysis of how successful American and French men are able to define value, and Faulkner and Becker's (2009) work on how jazz musicians rely on shared repertoires to perform together, even as strangers.

18. I continued conducting interviews and doing occasional fieldwork after this date. But I conducted the bulk of the research during this six-year period. See the appendix.

19. See Sennett's (2008) work on the relationship between "head" and "hand" in practice. And see Cornfield's (2015) work on how musicians reconstitute and resocialize their own occupational community in response to shifts in the music industry and the emergence of precarious work conditions in the new economy.

Introduction. A Stroll through the Market

1. I obtained much of this history from Christopher Gray's "From Oreos and Mallomars to Today's Chelsea Market," *New York Times*, March 7, 2005. Available at http://www.nytimes.com/2005/08/07/realestate/from-oreos-and-mallomars-to-todays-chelsea-market.html?_r=0 (accessed June 5, 2015).

2. Zukin's (1982) classic work traces the political economy of SoHo's transformation from a manufacturing district into an artists' colony, and eventually into an area for middle-class "loft living" lifestyles. In the decades after Zukin's work, SoHo would transform yet again into a wealthy area with among the highest real estate costs in the city and upscale clothing boutiques.

3. See Indergaard (2004) for a discussion of the rise of "Silicon Alley," New York City's answer to Palo Alto, and see Ross (2003) for an examination of the culture of workplaces in the new economy, based on research at two Silicon Alley companies.

4. See Halle and Tiso's (2014) work for an analysis of the gentrification of Chelsea and transformation of Manhattan's Far West Side.

5. These are the basic arguments Gans (1999) makes in his work.

6. I am very briefly summarizing Bourdieu's (1984) classic model of taste and power in the social structure in this paragraph.

7. Based on his research on musical tastes, Peterson (1992) coined the term "cultural omnivore" to describe those elites who were becoming more open to examples of lowbrow and midbrow culture (also see Peterson 1997; Peterson and Kern 1996; Peterson and Simkus 1992). Building from Peterson's work, scholars have applied the concept to analyze people's tastes in music and the fine arts in the United States (Atkinson 2011; DiMaggio and Mukhtar 2004) and other countries (Fisher and Preece 2003; Kanazawa 2001; Van Eijck 1999, 2001; Van Eijck and Bargeman 2004); in other cultural industries such as television (Rebers et al. 2006), comedy (Friedman 2012), and film (Rossel et al. 2006); and to such phenomena as youth cultures (Van Wel et al. 2008) and the role of advertising in the shift toward omnivorousness (Taylor 2009).

8. Khan (2010).

9. Scholars addressing these questions have mainly argued that despite the omnivore thesis's implication that elite tastes are becoming more democratized, and hence more accessible to a larger segment of the population, inequalities surrounding taste and taste as a powerful marker of distinction remain, albeit in altered forms. The arguments in these studies typically reinforce Bourdieu's (1984) ideas on the social reproduction of inequality through cultural consumption and the distinctions in taste (Holt 1997), and rely on qualitative approaches to do so.

Atkinson (2011) finds that although omnivorousness seems to characterize his sample of music fans, who all profess to have eclectic musical tastes, his interviews reveal their tastes to be consistent with key elements of Bourdieu's model, such as the development of a cultivated disposition toward classical music in early childhood among people with greater socioeconomic status. Scholars have also shown cultural omnivorousness to have personal consequences. By examining the life histories and tastes of comedy consumers, Friedman (2012) finds that only upwardly mobile people demonstrate omnivorousness, which leaves them culturally adrift, residing in both lowbrow and highbrow taste cultures without feeling completely comfortable in either. And see Lizardo and Skiles (2015), who argue for the compatibility of the cultural omnivore thesis with Bourdieu's theory of the stratification of taste.

10. See Ferguson's (1998; 2004) analysis of the formation of French cuisine, its role in the construction of French nationalism, and its position as a globally recognized elite cuisine; also see Kuh (2001) for a discussion of its downfall in the United States.

11. Lamont (1992).

12. I base this example of foodies exclusively on Johnston and Baumann's (2007; 2010) research.

13. See Khan (2010); Ocejo (2014a); and Rimmer (2012). From examining students at an exclusive prep school, Khan (2010) argues that new elites have shed the sense of entitlement that traditional elites took for granted because of their economic standing and today display "ease" in their privileged environment. Since democratization has made culture, taste, and knowledge more easily accessible to people from diverse social backgrounds, new elites maintain their high status by embodying ease in their everyday behaviors. Rather than merely "knowing" cultural phenomena, these teenaged members of the new elite learn how to think and act comfortably when confronted with all sorts of cultural material, and how to not act snobbish when discussing their own tastes. Despite being distant from necessity, they learn to act like they earned their achievements, just as, they contend, all people have the opportunity to do. Those who fail in their performances (that is, demonstrate traditional elitism or appear stressed in their efforts), do not "get it," or do not see the importance of confident doing over confident knowing. New elites learn to perform taste (and other behaviors) with ease in a world where access to taste has been expanded.

14. Khan (2010) shows this point among the students he studied (98–101).

15. Occasionally I spoke with workers who talked about the exclusivity of what they sold, especially in the craft butcher community. These people talked about the expense of meat and the limits of expanding humanely treated meat (that is, pasture-

raised, ethically slaughtered) in a manner that would reach a broad population and make a significant impact on the American food system of mass production more than workers in the other occupations talked about comparable issues in their own industries. However, workers at craft butcher shops have the same confidence in the quality of their products and their ability to shape their customers' tastes as workers in the other industries do, and they express these characteristics more often and clearly than their skepticism about the societal reach and impact of their work.

16. Often stemming from the work of such "Chicago School" scholars as Robert Park (1925) and Louis Wirth (1938), there have been many studies on neighborhood and community life in the industrial city for a variety of groups (Drake and Cayton 1945; Hannerz 1969; Kornblum 1972; Liebow 1967; Lynd and Lynd 1929; Suttles 1968; Whyte 1943). Herbert Gans's work on an Italian enclave in Boston, *The Urban Villagers* (1962), is the quintessential classic study on the "urban village" concept.

17. Members of the Chicago School developed an "invasion-succession" model of neighborhood change, in which new immigrant groups gradually replace more established groups (see Park 1952). Such influxes often led to conflicts between new and existing groups over jobs and the use of public space (see Kornblum 1972; Suttles 1968). And see Gans (1962) and Berman (1982) for analyses on the impact of urban renewal programs on ethnic groups in the city. And see Duneier (2016) for a discussion of the history of the "ghetto" as a place and idea.

18. The meat industry also moved to rural areas around the same time and for similar reasons, as I will discuss in chapter 4.

19. I discuss these processes in my previous book (Ocejo 2014). I also base many of the earlier points in this paragraph on Zukin (2010).

20. See the readings in Brown-Saracino's (2010) comprehensive edited volume on the various debates over gentrification, including the process's origins, the extent of residential displacement, and the reasons gentrifiers give for choosing to move into the neighborhoods that they do. And see Marcuse's (1985) discussion of "exclusionary displacement," or the phenomenon of a neighborhood gentrifying to the extent that future low-income groups are excluded from settling there, effectively "displacing" people before they even arrive by making a historically affordable area (or affordable in recent history, at least) exclusive.

Meanwhile, new immigrant groups from Latin America, the Caribbean, Asia, and Africa have been coming to American cities since the 1970s, forming their own urban villages (see Foner 2013). In some cases these neighborhoods have also become destinations for young cultural omnivores in search of unique cuisines. See Lin (1998; 2010) for discussions of how Chinatowns have become tourist destinations. See Hum (2014) for an examination of how people in the immigrant neighborhood of Sunset Park work to build and plan their own community amid impending gentrification and major urban developments.

21. I do not discuss craft distilleries here because as wholesale businesses they are not community institutions. Cocktail bars and specialty liquor stores (which are also among the new elite in retail and strive to be community institutions for cultural omnivores) in gentrifying neighborhoods, however, carry craft spirits for their local customers.

   On the other hand, craft distilleries regularly have tasting rooms, tours, and even bars attached to them. They open in spaces where they can meet their production demands as well as attract visitors, such as in gentrifying neighborhoods, as the other types of businesses do. I discuss these points in chapter 2.

22. For the most part, the cocktail bars and men's barbershops have become destinations, or businesses people from around the city seek out for their special products and services. Fewer people venture beyond their own neighborhoods to buy meat or spirits, so most butcher shops and liquor stores have mainly local clienteles (with some exceptions).

23. I get the concept of "taste communities" from Ferguson's (1998; 2004) work on French cuisine. They are very similar to "imagined communities" (Anderson 1991) of people who feel a sense of connection based on shared understandings of specific products. Unlike Ferguson's and Anderson's work, the taste communities I discuss in this book do not have nationalistic implications.

24. For an example of a study on work in traditionally elite spaces, see Sherman's (2007) research on service and service workers at luxury hotels.

25. For examples of research that explores this relationship, see Lloyd (2006); Ocejo (2014); Patch (2008); Zukin (2010); Zukin and Kosta (2004); and Zukin et al. (2009).

26. This number is according to the U.S. Bureau of Labor Statistics.

27. These are the people of whom C. Wright Mills (1951) and William H. Whyte (1956) are critical in their classic works.

28. I obtained some of the points in this paragraph from Moretti (2013).

29. Moretti calls these phenomena the "productivity paradox" (2013, 36–40).

30. I also obtained these numbers in July 2015 from the U.S. Bureau of Labor Statistics.

31. See Bensman and Lynch (1988); Buss and Redburn (1983); Dudley (1994); and Pappas (1989) for studies on the impact of deindustrialization on working-class urban communities.

32. Many scholars have created a variety of terms to describe today's economy and society. In his *The Information Age: Economy, Society and Culture* trilogy of books (1996; 1997; 1998), Manuel Castells describes contemporary society as depen-

dent on a highly networked "informational economy." Richard Florida (2002) focuses on the "creative class" of workers in the "creative economy." And Moretti (2013) pushes the term "innovation sector" in the "innovation economy." Each describes the rising importance of human capital in economic growth.

It is important to note that there are places in the United States where material-based industries, such as agriculture and manufacturing, still drive local economies. There are also places where basic services drive or significantly support local economies, such as places with large tourism and hospitality industries. But today these industries make up a smaller portion of the national gross domestic product than those information- and knowledge-based industries, and a much smaller one than they once did.

33. I get this point from Moretti (2013, 12).

34. Since they are a manufacturing business that creates a valuable product with their labor, as 30 percent of the workforce did at the peak of the industrial era, it would seem craft distillers are different from the other three service jobs in this regard. However, as I explain later in the introduction, light manufacturing of the "craft" variety is remarkably small in the United States in terms of employment and economic impact. They create niche products and depend on high-achieving people in the new economy as both consumers and investors.

35. In his historical work, Cherlin (2014) documents the rise and fall of the male breadwinner-based working-class family, and argues that while the decline of this arrangement should not necessarily be lamented, it has not been replaced by any other kind of stable family system for this segment of the population.

Cornfield (2015) refers to such scholarship as the "new sociology of work," which corresponds with the shift to the new economy: "The new sociology of work has emerged since the 1980s to analyze casual employment relations in all economic sectors, and especially in freelance occupational labor markets in personal and business services, arts, new media, communications, and the knowledge economy" (10). Also see Kalleberg (2011) and Smith (2001).

36. See Harvey's (2005) discussion of neoliberalism for more on these basic points.

37. See Ho's (2009) ethnography of Wall Street for an analysis of how financial firms emphasize maximizing shareholder value and short-term monetary gain at the expense of desecuritizing jobs through layoffs and outsourcing.

38. See Kalleberg (2011).

39. See Beck (1992, 2000); Cooper (2014); Neff (2012); Pugh (2015); Sennett (1998); and Sharone (2013) for discussions and analyses of the personal harms of precarious work in the new economy.

40. Ulrich Beck (1992) has famously talked about today's "risk society," in which our period of modernity in the West has created societies where people experience and internalize an assortment of risks (for example, environmental, political,

economic) privately. He refers to this phenomenon as the "individualization of risk" (2000). Also see Smith (2001).

41. See Hatton's (2011) history of how temporary workers carved out a permanent place for themselves in the American labor market.

42. Workers who want to break out of these constraints and achieve such autonomy are central components to Richard Florida's (2002) famous "creative class" thesis.

43. As Wilson and Keil (2008) point out, not all creativity in the new economy is created equal, or even recognized. They argue that the real "creative class" in today's cities is the poor, who must use their own ingenuity to survive: working multiple jobs while arranging child care, obtaining inexpensive food and running a household on a shoestring budget, and organizing an informal sharing economy (see Stack 1970; Venkatesh 2000). And collectively their actual work, typically in low-level service jobs, contributes significantly to today's economy. Such efforts do not get rewarded or compensated by leading companies, nor framed as "creative" in the media or popular culture.

44. Neff (2012) refers to such a path as "venture labor," while Lane (2011) discusses the concept of "career management," or how people come to see themselves as "companies of one," or their own CEOs and marketing departments, outside of a company's constraints. Both studies focus on workers in high-tech industries and look at how they experience precariousness in their own lives.

45. Labor economist Guy Standing (2011) uses the term "the precariat" to refer to the group of workers around the world who have a bundle of insecurities because of unstable conditions in the new economy and in the realm of work. With increasingly precarious economic conditions and a declining social safety net, he sees this group, which includes immigrants and well-educated people, as a social class in-the-making, with the potential to rise up and make change happen. The idea of the precariat, then, signifies an interesting counterconcept to Florida's (2002) more positive "creative class," or people connected to each other by their use of personal ingenuity in work.

46. These categories are from Kalleberg's work (2011), in which he provides an excellent statistical analysis of these criteria.

47. Hochschild (1982) first developed the concept of "emotional labor" in her work on flight attendants. Also see Leidner (1993).

48. Journalist Barbara Ehrenreich (2001) worked at these jobs for her book on the working poor, or people who work full-time at difficult jobs but who still struggle to make ends meet. Also see Newman (1999).

49. This fact is especially the case for whole-animal butcher shop workers and craft distillers, who earn a bit above minimum wage. Although the incomes for bar-

tenders and barbers are relatively high, they are based on tips, which fluctuate. However, if bartenders and barbers worked in establishments with higher volumes of customers, instead of craft cocktail bars or upscale barbershops, they might earn more money.

50. Ehrenreich (2001) and Rose (2004) have argued against these conceptions, claiming that even basic service work entails considerable mental power and creativity. (See Schwalbe's [2010] critique of these perspectives.) Crawford (2009) also argues for the significant mental capabilities required in repair work.

51. This justification is most common among bartenders. In his work on Wicker Park, in Chicago, Lloyd (2006) shows how well-educated artists who become bartenders justify their jobs as temporary stops on a more significant career path. I also studied artists and musicians who bartended to make ends meet as they worked on their "real" careers (2014). But some barbers in this book cut hair and some butchers cut meat to pay the bills when they were going to college, not expecting to continue with it after they were done.

52. Amy Wrzesniewski has conducted numerous studies, as a solo author (1999; 2002) and with colleagues (Rosso et al. 2010; Wrzesniewski and Dutton 2001; Wrzesniewski and Landman 2002), on how people search for meaning in work, particularly in challenging circumstances.

53. Cornfield's (2015) study analyzes the importance of recognition from colleagues for musicians' self-worth.

54. These statistics are based on information from 2015. I base only the gender breakdown of these occupations on my own sample.

55. This line of inquiry originates with Hughes (1958).

56. I get many points in this paragraph from Kimmel (2011).

57. Cherlin (2014); Faludi (1999); Mundy (2012); Rosin (2012).

58. See West and Zimmerman's (1987) work on "doing gender." I discuss this work in greater depth in chapter 3.

59. Heying and colleagues (2010) coin this term in their work on Portland's various artisanal businesses. Moretti (2013) refers to the artisan economy as "hipster manufacturing" (30–33) and cautions against the idea that these businesses represent a renaissance in American manufacturing. Their production is very small in scale, they provide relatively few jobs, and the products they sell are highly niche and usually expensive compared to mass-produced versions of them, and scaling them up would kill the specialness of their artisanal production. And see Jakob (2012) for information on the rise of craft workers.

Chapter 1. The Cocktail Renaissance

Portions of chapter 1 have been published in "At Your Service: The Meanings and Practices of Contemporary Bartenders," *European Journal of Cultural Studies* 15 (5): 642–48, 2012; and "'What'll It Be?': Service and the Limits of Creative Work among Cocktail Bartenders." *City, Culture, and Society* 1 (4): 179–84, 2010.

1. As Tales of the Cocktail grew in popularity and size, which coincides with cocktail culture's expansion, the festival spread to other nearby hotels. But the nerve center remains in the Monteleone.
2. Tanqueray began production in 1830.
3. He refers here to David Wondrich, who is also a founder and director of the BAR Educational Program. In his fifties with a PhD in English, Wondrich is mainly a drinks writer, historian, and home enthusiast who gained fame in the cocktail world through his cocktail writings, such as his columns on cocktails in *Esquire* and his researched books *Imbibe!* (2007), on the life and work of the famous nineteenth-century American bartender Jerry Thomas, and *Punch* (2010), on the history of the "flowing bowl." Although most of the contestants have more bartending experience than he does, he commands respect from people in the cocktail community, who vault him into the pantheon of living legends.
4. This vignette combines scenes and conversations from two of the three Tales festivals I attended, in 2008 and 2009 (I also attended in 2010). Most of the people featured in this telling attended both and attend Tales every year.
5. See Parsons (2011).
6. See Wondrich's (2010, 3–11) brief history of European spirits.
7. I derive much of the history in this paragraph from Wondrich's books (2007; 2010). Wondrich (2010) also forwards the argument that the English invented the cocktail because some English bars in the 1700s offered individual servings of punch.
8. It was in the *Farmer's Cabinet*, a newspaper from Amherst, New Hampshire. Brown and Miller (2009) document the first ever use of the word in print in the *Morning Post and Gazetteer in London, England* in 1798. Meanwhile, no one knows where the name "cocktail" comes from. See Regan (2003) for a synopsis of a few claims.
9. It was in *The Balance and Columbian Repository*, from the town of Hudson in New York, about 120 miles north of New York City.
10. The first edition featured only ten recipes for cocktails. The rest were for punches, sours, slings, cobblers, shrubs, toddies, flips, and other varieties of mixed drinks. Thomas's editors were afraid readers would not know what cocktails were, whereas

punches and toddies were already popular. Today most of the drinks in these categories are considered cocktails. Thomas distinguished cocktails because they contained bitters.

11. These examples come from Harry Johnson's *Bartenders' Manual, or: How to Mix Drinks in the Present Style*, originally published in 1882. Johnson was a contemporary and rival of sorts of Jerry Thomas. He also purchased one of Thomas's bars in New York City and opened his own. The title page describes Johnson as a "Publisher and Professional Bartender, and Instructor in the Art How to Attend a Bar." And as the pronoun "his" implies, Johnson assumed bartenders were making cocktails for men.

12. The rise of standards in making drinks through the proliferation and dissemination of texts that were codifying, authoritative, and definitive in some ways parallels the rise of a national French cuisine that Ferguson examines (1998; 2004). Like gastronomy, mixology resembles a cultural field (Bourdieu 1991), although cocktails have never been part of a mission of nationalism like French cuisine has.

13. I refer here to Thorstein Veblen's notion of "conspicuous consumption" in his *The Theory of the Leisure Class* (1899). In short, Veblen contended that in an industrial society people used material items to show their status.

14. Wondrich (2007, 23–25) refers to some in this group of classic cocktail consumers as the "sporting fraternity," or the gamblers, jockeys, boxers, managers, entertainers, and other "sports" who lived life in the fast lane, who were wealthy one week and broke the next, and who would have been among the clientele sipping cocktails at elite bars.

15. Wondrich (2007) documents that the term "mixologist" originated in 1856 and had spread widely by the 1870s (45).

16. The elite chefs Leschziner's (2015) examines also highlight the importance of balance in dishes.

17. As mentioned in the preface, I feature Dave and his bar several times in my previous book (Ocejo 2014, 5, 133, 146–47, 161, 176–79), mainly as a new bar owner in the East Village whose decision to open in the neighborhood sparked controversy among his neighbors.

18. As mentioned, Jerry Thomas wrote the first cocktail book. Charles Baker was a cocktail and culinary author in the first half of the twentieth century. A world traveler, he collected many exotic recipes. He would've fit perfectly in today's foodie culture. He probably did not make any drinks, as Brian claims in this quote. But he was writing about cocktails and mixology at a time when very few people were. I discuss this period of time in the coming pages.

19. Gary Regan is mainly a drinks writer who lives in the New York City metropolitan area and wrote an influential book, *The Joy of Mixology*, in 2003 (he also was one

of the first to produce a new brand of orange bitters, a fundamental ingredient in many cocktails). I met a few bartenders who cite his book as one of the first they read on cocktails, which both informed and inspired them to pursue it as a career.

20. I discuss the meanings behind creating "new" cocktails as part of a sense of craft in chapter 6. And Brian called the drink he made the 19th Century.

21. Audrey Saunders opened Pegu Club, a bar in SoHo, in 2005. Pegu is where many well-known New York City cocktail bartenders got their start. Audrey had previously trained under Dale DeGroff, and she is highly respected by people in the cocktail community, who consider her one of its founders.

22. Brian's title is inaccurate. In 1948, David Embury, an attorney and classic cocktail enthusiast, published *The Fine Art of Mixing Drinks*.

23. See Lerner (2007) and Okrent (2011) for in-depth studies on Prohibition. The former focuses specifically on Prohibition in New York City.

24. See Kreindler's (1999) family memoir of the 21 Club.

25. See Curtis (2006) and Regan (2003).

26. An example is Harry Craddock, who left the United States in 1920 to work at the American Bar in the Savoy Hotel in London and wrote the influential *Savoy Cocktail Book* in 1930.

27. See Blumenthal (2000) and Peretti (2007) for discussions of the early era of post-Prohibition nightclubs, also known as "Café Society."

28. See Harry Braverman's classic work *Labor and Monopoly Capital* (1974), which led to considerable debates over the deskilling process in occupations and industries.

29. As with Dave, the owner of Death & Co., I feature Sasha and Milk and Honey several times in my previous book (Ocejo 2014, 117–23, 134–36, 144–47), also because of his role as a new bar owner who sought to expand in the area.

30. See Bill Ryan, "'Smirnoff White Whiskey—No Smell, No Taste,'" *New York Times*, February 19, 1995. Also see Curtis (2006).

31. Today vodka is the most consumed spirit in the United States, accounting for approximately a third of all sales, and still relies heavily on marketing and branding. See Grimes (2001) for a discussion of vodka's role behind the bar.

32. I discuss the role interactive service plays for bartenders in inculcating their customers with a sense of taste in cocktails in chapter 7.

33. Cultural sociologist Pierre Bourdieu refers to the consecration of cultural items as necessary for achieving cultural legitimacy (1993). Cocktail bartenders generally do not consecrate vodka as a part of this legitimacy.

34. In my research I often discovered a distinction between the bar's policy and the attitudes of bartenders. If drinks are an important part of a bar's identity, and one takes a hard stance against vodka, bartenders must follow it. But when I spoke with bartenders outside of the bar or after they had left a particular bar, I learned

that some were just following the bar's policy in their responses. They in fact did not have such a strong anti-vodka stance, even if they admitted its shortcomings in cocktails. Most importantly, they enjoyed trying to push a vodka-drinking customer toward other spirits, which I discuss in chapter 7.

35. See DeGloma's (2014) work on the common elements in various forms of personal awakenings—specifically, the monumental shift from "darkness" to "lightness."

36. Again, see Sennett and Cobb's (1972) work.

37. We see elements of these relationships in several ethnographies of bars in urban neighborhoods, such as Brown (1983); LeMasters (1976); Lindquist (2003); and May (2001). In addition, several historians of American working-class saloon culture point out the authoritative and respected bartender, as well as the potential for political influence if he (they were almost always men) were also the owner. See Duis (1982) and Powers (2001). And in my previous book (2014), I show how bartenders at Milano's, a small neighborhood bar, were respected by regular customers, but did not attract attention outside of that world (also see Ocejo 2012).

38. Richard Lloyd's (2006) examination of artists in Wicker Park shows these points.

39. Frenette (2016); Menger (1999); and Oakley (2009) have all studied the importance of nonmonetary, intrinsic rewards as motivators for culture workers. I also discuss this concept more in chapter 7.

40. Several, however, use similar monikers as part of their own personal brand, for promotional and consulting purposes. They understand the power these names have outside of the cocktail community.

41. I discuss this distinction in greater depth in chapter 6.

42. I examine the points in this paragraph in an earlier article (Ocejo 2010).

43. After my fieldwork ended they added the bar's name in a cursive font in the ground at the doorstep, which is still not very visible to passersby.

44. The growth and consequences of "destination culture" through an examination of nightlife scenes is the focus of my previous book (Ocejo 2014).

45. Death & Co. has a short menu of small plates. Craft cocktail bars in general do not offer much food and follow the small plates style when they do.

46. I examine this point in greater depth in chapter 7.

47. I attended two of the days in the five-day program in 2009. The program costs $3,950, although liquor companies pay for some participants to take it. These leaders include Dale DeGroff, Doug Frost, Steve Olson, Paul Pacult, Andy Seymour, and David Wondrich. I provide a bit more detail on these programs in chapter 5.

48. This and other programs serve a similar role as the certifications wealth managers take, as Harrington shows (2016, 55–56).

Chapter 2. Distilling Authenticity

1. There is considerable debate in the craft distilling world over titles, especially that of "master distiller." Since no standards in the distilling world or legal criteria exist for determining who is a "master," the title has different meanings behind and criteria for the label that often vary by distillery. (By contrast, "master barber" is a legal designation, backed by standards and licensure, which one must achieve. However, these standards vary by state and not every state has it, so once again the meaning varies.) For some distilleries the "master" distiller is simply the head distiller, or the person in charge of the distillation process. At others, such as ones with long traditions, the title is an honorific bestowed upon someone who has apprenticed and been working at the distillery for a long time. Tuthilltown does not use the term. As Ralph puts it, "To me, it's an honorific, and you don't take on that by yourself. You become a master when others recognize it, not when you decide you're a master." As Joel explains, "People who say that they're master distillers sometimes only make one product, so how can they say that they're a master of distilling?" He prefers the title "chief distiller" because "it implies authority without implying mastery."

2. When I returned to the distillery six years later, the waxing system was still in use, despite significant improvements in efficiency in other steps in the process. See the epilogue.

3. As I show in chapter 4, many butchers also work for wholesale meat companies (that is, meatpacking plants), who sell to retailers, and butchers at retail shops like supermarkets do not always interact with customers. However, butchers at whole-animal butcher shops interact with customers as part of their jobs and in accordance with the philosophy of the shop.

4. Scott (2006) refers to it as "neo-artisan manufacturing," while Moretti (2012) refers to it as "hipster manufacturing."

5. See Carroll and Swaminathan (2000) on the rise and transformation of the microbrewery movement. And see Borer (2010) for a discussion of the importance of "craft" in "craft beer."

6. I get most of the points in this paragraph from Heying and colleagues (2010), who refer to this groundswell as the "artisan economy," or an "urban economy that has broadly embraced the artisan approach to living and working" (17). They attribute its rise to the new sets of economic and institutional relationships of the "new economy," such as decentralized and more network-based organizations, a knowledge-based economy, and flexible specialization. Finally, they understand the artisan economy as being driven by a resistance movement, or a group of workers fighting against the products and methods of corporatized mass-production and the working conditions, relationships, and lifestyles such systems influence.

My own findings on craft distillers do not support this last argument. Many of the distillers and owners I studied do not represent a resistance movement, nor did a call to resistance compel them to start or join businesses in the artisan economy.

7. See Brown-Saracino (2009); Grazian (2003; 2008); Johnston and Baumann (2010).

8. For an exception see Dudley's (2014) research on how guitar makers understand their work.

9. Copper conducts heat evenly and well, and compared to other metals is most effective at stripping the sulfurs emitted by the yeast from the alcohol during distillation, resulting in a cleaner- (or at least distinctive-) tasting spirit. This latter fact partially explains why distillers must clean the inside of a copper pot still after each distillation.

10. The words "alembic" and "alcohol" both have Arabic origins.

11. An eau de vie is a colorless (that is, unaged) type of fruit brandy, which includes Applejack (an aged American spirit made from distilling apples), Calvados (similar to Applejack, except French), and Rakia (a popular aged or unaged spirit made from several different fruits in eastern European countries).

12. See Wondrich (2010, 9).

13. I get the history in these last two paragraphs from Forbes (1970); Wilson (2006); and Wondrich (2010).

14. A New World spirit, rum's base ingredient is molasses, the industrial waste of sugar production, which took place in the colonized Caribbean and played no small role in the slave trade. See Curtis (2006).

15. Like most of the history of alcohol (including cocktails), much of the history of barreling and bourbon is shrouded in mystery. They are all cultural inventions whose specific origins are impossible to accurately trace. Aging a spirit by putting it in a barrel is likely one of history's happy accidents. After using barrels to store their spirits, European distillers around the fifteenth century probably noticed how aging changed them, adding flavor, darkening them, and rounding out their harsh taste. It is unclear whether distillers in Kentucky knew of barreling as Europeans practiced it (or how they would have come upon this knowledge if they did), why it began and spread in Kentucky and not elsewhere, or even where the word "bourbon" comes from to describe their aged product. In any case, there are several differences between aging brandy (or cognac, which is brandy from the Cognac region of France), scotch, and bourbon, such as the type of barrels that must be used (new French oak for cognac; new American oak for straight bourbon; any type of oak barrel for scotch, including barrels that were once filled with bourbon). See Veach (2013) and Wondrich (2010).

16. I get much of this history of whiskey in the United States from Veach (2013).

17. I obtained the first number from David Wondrich's brief history of Prohibition for the website of the Distilled Spirits Council of the United States (DISCUS), a trade group: www.prohibitionrepeal.com/history/beyond.asp (accessed December 29, 2015).

18. For this reason pharmacies were popular places for people to purchase alcohol illegally (Okrent 2010). And some wineries were also allowed to legally operate and make wines for religious purposes.

19. Some bootleggers would add food coloring to cheap (and unregulated) neutral grain spirits to pass off a bottle as whiskey.

20. See Curtis's (2006, 178–81) history of rum in the United States.

21. Heying (2010, 139–41) gives a brief overview of how Oregon's craft distilling industry grew, focusing on Portland.

22. Federal law also prohibits home distilling. By contrast, the federal government lifted the national ban on home-brewing in 1978, and by 2013 every state allowed it. This decision benefited the craft beer industry by allowing people to experiment on their own before starting a business. I met only two people who worked at craft distilleries who distilled (illegally) at home.

23. Taken from the *Economist*, September 8, 2012: www.economist.com/node/2156 2224 (accessed December 29, 2015).

24. The cost was $65,000, and is now $1,500 for the A-1. According to the Alcohol and Tobacco Tax and Trade Bureau (TTB), a proof gallon is one liquid gallon of spirits that is 50 percent alcohol at 60 degrees F. A spirit bottled at 80 proof, or 40 percent alcohol, would be 0.8 proof gallons, while one at 125 proof would be 1.25 proof gallons.

25. For a time, Tuthilltown could sell and provide tastings only for its bourbon, rye, four grain, and corn whiskeys and its vodkas, but not its single malt whiskey or rum, because the base ingredients for the latter two (malted barley and molasses) come from Canada and Louisiana, respectively, not New York State. However, a separate amendment to the state's farm winery license allowed its holders to sell New York State–branded products, including all of Tuthilltown's products. Since it could hold multiple distiller licenses, Tuthilltown applied for and received a farm winery license, so now they can sell and provide tastings of all of their products at the distillery.

26. See Heying (2010, 139–41). According to the American Distilling Institute (ADI), a trade group for craft distillers, there are 241 craft distilleries in the United States and 24 in New York State. They provide the following definition of a craft distillery on their website: "Less than 25% of the craft distillery (distilled spirits plant or DSP) is owned or controlled (or equivalent economic interest) by alcoholic beverage industry members who are not themselves craft distillers. . . .

Maximum annual sales are less than 100,000 proof gallons. . . . Craft distillers produce spirits that reflect the vision of their principal distillers using any combination of traditional or innovative techniques including fermenting, distilling, re-distilling, blending, infusing or warehousing." Available at http://distilling.com /resources/craft-certification/ (accessed February 29, 2016).

The ADI recognizes far more "craft distilled spirits" than distilleries, because distilleries often produce multiple spirits, including brands owned by people independent of the distillery. To have this label by the ADI, the spirit must be run through a still owned by a certified craft producer. Not every craft distiller, however, is a member of ADI, so the actual number of distilleries that manufacture small batches of spirits is higher, probably more than 1,000. There are also far more distilling licenses than distilleries, since in states like New York craft distilleries may have multiple licenses.

Another industry trade group, the Distilled Spirits Council of the United States (DISCUS), which is older, wealthier, and more influential than ADI, started a "small distiller" category in 2010 in response to the booming craft distillery industry. They define "small distiller" as one producing less than 100,000 proof gallons per year. Interestingly, DISCUS only has 15 member companies nationally, but 135 "small distiller affiliate members." The member companies, however, are such powerhouses in the liquor industry as Beam Suntory, Diageo, Moet Hennessy, and Pernod Ricard, and are responsible for the vast majority of spirits consumed in the United States.

27. While I focus most of this chapter on people and conditions in New York State, distillers, owners, and cocktail bartenders I spoke to from other places agree on the importance of their local cocktail movement in sparking craft distilling in their states.

28. See Tsui's (2011) *New York Times* article on the return of rye.

29. They all also follow a similar pattern in terms of how the occupation and industry expand in the second generation, as I will discuss in the epilogue.

30. The first generation of cocktail bar owners is somewhat of an exception. While most of them had worked in the nightlife industry, they didn't work in specialized cocktail bars.

31. The name of the book is *Making Pure Corn Whiskey: A Professional Guide for Amateurs and Professionals* (1999).

32. Many craft distillers and owners offered the same assessment of distilling as Ralph and Brian: it's not that hard. Or, the actual distilling is not that hard, if you follow the basic process. But making something "good," or distinct, is another matter. I offer an analysis of the relationship between the science and the art of distilling in chapter 6.

33. See Carroll and Swaminathan's (2000) analysis of the craft beer industry's rise.

34. When I made this point about vodka to John, Prohibition Distillery's co-owner, he conceded it, and agreed it didn't neatly fit the historical reference of their brand. But he argued that while vodka wasn't really in the country during Prohibition, people were surely making it illegally without knowing what it was; they were just making booze and didn't care what it was called. Fair enough. John also admitted they chose vodka to be their first product because it is the most marketable spirit—as the largest category in terms of sales—and because of its quick turnaround—you can bottle vodka right off the still and bring it to market, without waiting as it ages in a barrel.

35. This Manhattan Cocktail Classic took place in May 2010.

36. Domaine Select Wine & Spirits is a large, private wine and spirits import and wholesale distribution company.

37. By "fresh herbs," Joel doesn't mean fresh from the garden, but ones grown for the specific purpose of distillation and dried properly, instead of premilled commodity spices from a supermarket.

38. Tuthilltown distilled for them until 2014, when they moved into their own distillery in the town of Roscoe. They now make a gin and bourbon in addition to vodka.

39. See Heying (2011) and Johnston and Baumann (2010) for examples of studies in which "handmade" gets equated with "authentic," or of a finer quality compared to mass-produced items. In reference to the rise of omnivorous foodie culture, the latter study argues that an item's level of authenticity plays a role in the shifts that have occurred in the taste system surrounding food, as products that demonstrate high levels of authenticity (for example, originating from exotic locales or being simple and handmade) confer greater status than either packaged products or former elite foods (such as French cuisine, or, in the case of spirits, aged scotches and cognacs).

40. *Mondovino* is a documentary film from 2004 about the impact of globalization and influential critics on the wine industry and wine-producing regions. The filmmaker largely takes a critical stance toward what he feels is the homogenization of wine vis-à-vis its taste and production.

41. I haven't seen the film since it came out more than ten years ago. I don't know exactly who Joel is referring to here. I assume he means Robert Parker, a well-known wine critic, or Robert Mondavi, the winemaker and vineyard operator in California. The film features both prominently, and at the time of the film, both were heavily criticized by certain members of the wine industry who felt they were in part responsible for this homogenization.

42. Joel here is referring to the idea of "terroir," or local qualities that make products taste distinct. See Bowen (2015) and Trubek (2008) for academic analyses of this concept.

43. See Grazian (2003).

44. I discuss the importance of this dimension of time for each of these occupations in chapter 6.

Chapter 3. Working on Men

1. Kimmel (2012) makes these points in his cultural history of manhood in the United States.

2. See West's (2001) examination of leisure spaces for how men negotiate masculinity through drinking subcultures.

3. Kimmel (2012, 20).

4. I base the following discussion on West and Zimmerman's (1987) integral article on "doing gender."

5. See Connell's (2005) highly influential examination of the multiple "masculinities" men perform and their relationship with "hegemonic masculinity."

6. Two recent studies have also examined these contemporary threats to masculine performance in terms of clothing (de Casanova 2015) and hair, specifically men who go to women's hair salons to achieve a certain style (Barber 2008; 2016).

7. The iconic barber pole appeared during this time. Staff and patients would hold the pole itself during procedures. A bowl sat on top to hold leeches (for bloodletting) and blood. The pole's different colors indicated the barber's roles: a blue and white pole meant a barber only cut hair, while a red and white one meant a barber also performed medical and dental tasks. It could be the red stripes came from the bloody rags hanging on the pole to dry after procedures. After barbers stopped performing surgeries and providing medical treatments, the barber pole remained as a decorative item, with the slanted stripes sometimes being red and white and other times being red, white, and blue, and with a globe on top in place of the bowl for the leeches and blood.

8. I get most of this history of barbers and barbershops in this paragraph from Sherrow (2006). And see Abbott's (1988) work on the rise of professions.

9. Barlow (1993).

10. See Whyte's (1956) classic work *The Organization Man* on conformity and collectivism among white-collar workers during the industrial era. And see de Casanova's (2015) work on how today's white-collar men navigate masculinity through personal appearance.

11. See Barber (2016); Frank (2014); Luciano (2001); and Salzman et al. (2005) for studies on men who feel and succumb to this pressure of conducting beauty work on themselves.

12. See Boyle 2013.

13. Examples of academic and popular publications that have examined the notion of metrosexuals include Brumberg (1997); Coad (2008); and Simpson (1994; 2002), the journalist who is credited with coining the term.

14. Digging beneath the surface of the idea's humor, Dean (2014) provides an excellent examination of how metrosexual masculinities represent a contradictory hybrid of multiple patterns of masculinity, resulting in a "quasi-hegemonic masculine form" (187–217). Also see Sender (2006).

15. See Frank's (2014) research on the discourses surrounding men's body hair and the construction of what it means to be masculine.

16. I base the points in this paragraph on Barber's (2008; 2016) research on professional, white, straight, middle-class men who go to women's salons because of the pressure they feel to look a certain way.

17. Following from Connell's (2005) defining work on masculinities, see Lawson's (1999) work on dominant masculinity in men's barbershops.

18. Of the various types of barbershops, the African American shop has been discussed and studied by far the most, usually because of its role in African American neighborhoods as places for the safe discussion of black masculinity. See Alexander (2003); Harris-Lacewell (2006); Mills (2013); Nunley (2011); Williams (1993); and Wright (1998) for examples.

19. Lawson (1999) also explains the significance of physical environment in her work comparing barbershops, salons, and unisex shops.

20. This business arrangement existed during my fieldwork. I discuss how it changed in the epilogue.

21. The origins of the alley's name are obscure. There are a few such midblock alleys in downtown Manhattan. The Bowery Mission, a charitable organization and men's shelter that opened in 1879, is located just around the corner from Freemans. The line of men to get in for food, services, and a place to stay used to snake around onto Rivington Street and would end down Freeman Alley, probably at the entrance to what would one day be a pricey restaurant.

22. I once coincidentally ran into a cocktail bartender I had gotten to know while I was conducting fieldwork at Freemans. He was getting his hair cut and told me he used to go to the Blind Barber. But since they knew he worked at a prestigious cocktail bar, every time he went in they would bring him drinks they were working on to taste so he could offer feedback. "I don't want to start drinking cocktails at noon. I just want a haircut. I don't want to talk cocktails," he told me. They would also try to comp him his haircuts, which made him uncomfortable. "I would feel different if they came into the bar, so I could reciprocate. But they never do." Exchanging comps within and across industries is quite common among these workers (for example, a barber I met had such an exchange with a retailer of expensive boots—free haircut for discounted footwear, and another

got a discount on an expensive watch). But a one-way exchange creates an unbalanced equation and causes discomfort. The bartender switched barbers.

23. See Felder's (2015) *New York Times* article on the phenomenon.

24. In their research on beauty therapists Black and Sharma (2001) use these distinctions of women's bodies being perceived as "made up," or having to be so, and men's bodies being perceived as "natural," or not in need of any beauty therapy.

25. While they appear natural, skin fades are quite modern, since they're achievable only with electric clippers. Clippers essentially do what barbers do when they use their scissors over a comb, except they do it much closer to the skin and more uniformly.

26. I discuss such "upscaling" neighborhoods in my previous book (Ocejo 2014).

27. These basic demographics correspond to customers at cocktail bars, consumers of small-batch spirits, and customers at whole-animal butcher shops.

     Several barbers said they sometimes cut women's hair at the shop, and a few said they have women as regular clients. I only saw two women get haircuts during my fieldwork, one of whom I saw return twice more to the same barber. I occasionally saw Asian and Latino clients, who in general resembled white clients in terms of style (hair and clothing) and perceived social class. I only saw two African American clients at Freemans, and they both went to Miles, who is half African American and half Puerto Rican and the shop's only nonwhite male barber (its only regular woman barber during my fieldwork was Japanese).

28. They are like many cocktail bartenders and butchers in this regard. As mentioned, craft distillers rarely had prior experience distilling.

29. This distinction echoes Bourdieu's (1984) point about people rich in economic capital being distant from necessity, and thereby able to pursue and cultivate cultural tastes (that is, accumulate cultural capital).

30. Hochschild (1983) originally formulated this concept from her work on flight attendants. Also see Gimlin's (1996) use of the concept on hairdressers in women's salons. While emotional labor is present among cocktail bartenders and whole-animal butcher shop workers, it is most pronounced among barbers.

31. See Robinson et al.'s (2011) research on men who work as hairdressers and the challenge this work presents to their masculinity.

32. There are some technical differences. Barbers use clippers more for men, since most men wear their hair short, and more women than men wear their hair long. But the work with scissors on shaping and sectioning are more or less the same. "With the long hair for men, you're not going to give it that style, that finesse that women have," says Joey. "But the basic guides are almost the same." A barber skilled with scissors and with a sense of style can cut women's hair as easily as men's hair.

33. As I will discuss in chapter 7, barbers do not avoid emotional labor at upscale barbershops. See Black and Sharma's (2001) work on beauty therapists.

34. In this regard, these barbers resemble other workers who perform "aesthetic labor," or when employees get hired based on their looks—appearance, accent, style, and deportment—which are often based on conventional middle-class standards of race and gender (Besen-Cassino 2014; Mears 2014; Witz et al. 2003; Wolkowitz 2006). Like employees at upscale retail stores, these barbers have to "look good and sound right" (Williams and Connell 2010). But the work performance of these barbers and the other workers in this book requires more than meeting certain aesthetical standards.

35. See Fine (1992).

36. This point relates to note 34 from this chapter on aesthetic labor: to get hired, they have to "fit" and get along with the other barbers.

37. Gimlin (1996).

38. Black and Sharma (2001) and Sharma and Black (2001) also reach this finding in their work on beauty therapists, although the means by which these workers hide their emotional labor differs considerably from barbers.

39. Robinson et al. (2011); also see Ahmed (2006).

40. During my fieldwork barbers sometimes talked about contributions clients made to the review website Yelp. These posts occasionally referenced being offended by some of the topics in their group banter. In addition, two barbers I studied who usually worked at the other Freemans location in the West Village occasionally worked at the Lower East Side location, but preferred the former because they felt the group banter at the latter covered themes they did not care for or feel was professional, such as drugs. They attribute the discussion of certain themes and topics to the specific social dynamic of the barbers at the Lower East Side shop.

41. When confronted with verbal assaults (that is, "shit talk") from their fellow crew-members, Desmond (2007) shows how wildland firefighters have the options of "engagement, escalation, or inaction" (96).

42. See Goffman (1981).

43. See Desmond (2007).

44. See Desmond (2007).

45. For instance, Bird (1996) argues that, "Competition with other men provides a stage for establishing self both as an individual and as appropriately masculine" and "contributes to the perpetuation of male dominance" (127).

46. Bird (1996).

47. See Bird (1996, 129); and Lawson (1999).

48. Freemans employed another woman barber, a white and heavily tattooed woman in her early thirties named Amanda, who primarily worked at the shop in the West Village. She occasionally filled in at the Rivington shop when someone was off. I did not observe her engage in any group banter at the West Village shop, and she would not initiate group banter topics at the Rivington shop. But the

barbers sometimes would ask for her opinion "as a woman" on some topics they were discussing, which they didn't do with Coco. I suspect her race and personal style played a role in this difference (an example of "aesthetic labor" in the shop). I have continued going to Freemans as a regular client since I ended my field-work, and I have noticed that they have employed more women barbers over the years. It is unclear if the group banter dynamic has changed in this time, but it seems the pattern remains: one-on-one the barbers all get along and are even friends with the women barbers, but they largely stay out of group conversations.

Chapter 4. Show the Animal

Portions of chapter 4 have been published in "Show the Animal: Constructing and Communicating New Elite Food Tastes at Upscale Butcher Shops," *Poetics*, 47: 106–21, 2014.

1. To give an idea of scale, Double L has two employees working on the kill floor (including the owner's son and nephew), three butchers working in the cutting room (including the owner), and a couple of additional employees who engage in various tasks such as grinding meat and cleaning. On the day I visited, the kill floor workers slaughtered two cows and fifteen lambs, while the butchers broke down and packaged animals for special orders between the hours of 7 a.m. and 3 p.m. with about an hour-long lunch break, which is their normal working day. By contrast, the industrial slaughterhouse Pachirat (2011) studied employs over 800 people (managers and workers) to slaughter, process, and ship 2,500 cows per day in a highly regimented environment. As he documents, with low pay and harsh conditions, such facilities have nearly 100 percent annual turnover among workers directly involved in the process.

2. Dickson's gets its poultry from separate sources. They are raised in Pennsylvania and slaughtered in Queens, at an abattoir called Madani Halal, who delivers them three (and sometimes four) times a week—usually Mondays, Wednesdays, and Fridays.

3. See Ferguson (1998; 2004) and DeSoucey (2010).

4. See Johnston and Baumann (2010).

5. As mentioned in chapter 2, farmers also distilled corn into whiskey for the same reason.

6. I base most of this and the forthcoming discussion on the history of the meat industry on Ogle's (2013) work. I also refer to the work of Leonard (2014), who focuses more narrowly on the history of the chicken industry and Tyson Foods, one of the four largest agribusinesses in the United States.

7. Cronon (1992).

8. See Pollan (2007); Leonard (2014); Schell (1985); and Schlosser (2001) for popular critiques of caged animals and feedlots, or "Animal Feeding Operations" (AFOs), a legal designation used by the Environmental Protection Agency.

9. See Hughes's (1971) classic essay on work that societies see as physically and/or morally "dirty," or work that people would prefer to distance themselves from. See Ogle (2013) and Pachirat (2011) for discussions on the history of separating the "dirty work" of the meat industry from more populated environments.

10. In his ethnography of an industrial slaughterhouse, Pachirat (2011) carefully explains how the process works. He breaks it down into its minute details and highly repetitive tasks, such as standing and inspecting cow livers and putting them on hooks in a freezing cold room for ten hours a day.

11. As Pachirat (2011) shows, today "only four corporations (Tyson Foods-IBG, ConAgra Montfort, Cargill-Excel, and National Beef) control more than 80% of the US market in beef, and the level of concentration is similar in other meat markets," while "a mere fourteen slaughterhouses account for 56% of all cattle killed; twelve slaughterhouses for 55% of all pigs killed; six slaughterhouses for 56% of all calves killed; and four slaughterhouses for 67% of all sheep and lambs killed" (275–76).

12. Today only nine meatpacking companies remain in the district, not enough to make a noticeable smell of meat and blood in the streets, as the plants once did. They operate as a cooperative under the historical name Gansevoort Market Meat Center, a complex of bedraggled buildings with loading docks.

13. See Pachirat (2011).

14. In discussing the greenmarket at Union Square in New York City, Zukin (2010) calls the notion of shopping "local" as a form of urban authenticity into question, given the relativity of distance. (I take up this point later in this chapter.) Also see de la Pradelle's (2004) study on how people in a town in Provence, France, essentially agree to pretend their market day is an authentic experience, when in fact it is not.

15. See Kamp (2006) and Johnston et al. (2014) for discussions of food celebrity culture.

16. Marlow & Daughters is also a craft butcher shop in Brooklyn. I interviewed several people from the Meat Hook, and one of the founding butchers of Marlow & Daughters.

17. I discuss how people in the craft butcher community make sense of the relationship between these factors and actual taste (for example, to what degree does how an animal was raised and slaughtered impact how its meat tastes?) in chapter 6. See Schatzker (2011) for a discussion of the various influences on steak's gustatory taste.

18. This person is Dario Cecchini, a well-known traditional Italian butcher with whom author Bill Buford apprenticed for his best-selling book *Heat* (2006).

19. Lindy and Grundy was a butcher shop in Los Angeles. It closed in 2014.

20. The fact that it's so close to the Meatpacking District is a coincidence.

21. See Goffman's (1959) classic use of dramaturgical elements to explain social structure and social interaction, and Pachirat's (2011) discussion of the "politics of sight," or the use of power to conceal the repugnance and moral dubiousness of killing work in industrialized slaughterhouses. Whole-animal butcher shops mirror the trend toward greater transparency in the food industry, from food TV shows to open kitchens at restaurants.

22. I discuss the tensions that emerge from this dynamic in the shop and in similar situations in the other occupations in chapter 8.

23. Dickson's employed a sixth butcher, Jeff, who used to work at the Chelsea shop before I started working there, but worked at its newer, smaller shop in TriBeCa for several months from when it opened in mid-2012 during my research. I visited this shop, which was more of a stand in an open-plan specialty market (like a mini–Chelsea Market), called All Good Things, several times; worked there; and interviewed him. Jeff also became a butcher after switching career paths. Most employees took shifts working at the TriBeCa shop during my fieldwork. I also observed and interviewed Jocelyn, who became the head butcher after JM was fired (see epilogue), which was after my formal fieldwork ended. All six of the non-Mexican butchers at Dickson's, as well as the butchers I interviewed from other craft butcher shops, share having gone to college and switching career paths in common.

24. Given the type of work (dirty, low-status) and low pay of the porter job, the position had a lot of turnover during my fieldwork.

25. Other shops whose owners and workers I interviewed and observed only do half of the volume at Dickson's, at best. Some get only one steer and a handful of pigs and lambs per week. They cannot sell more while adhering to their philosophy for any of a number of reasons: they don't have the walk-in space to store any more animals or meat, they don't have a kitchen for turning cuts into other dishes (or it's not very big), they don't have or can't afford the staff (in terms of quantity and skill) to produce more, and/or they don't have enough clientele to sell more meat (that is, no lunch crowd or many daytime customers), which may be due to their location. All have grinding and sausage-making capabilities, which helps with their volume.

26. I discuss how butcher shop workers accomplish this goal in chapter 7.

27. See Fine (1992).

28. This fact distinguishes them from other examples of intermediating cultural workers and producers (see Mears 2010; Nixon 2003; Smith Maguire 2008). Also see Ocejo (2010; 2014).

29. The other three occupations feature a similar relationship between the workers and the organization. Cocktail bars have a "house recipe" for certain classic

drinks, such as Martinis, or a way they want their bartenders to make a drink every time unless the customer asks for something different. Barbershops have certain parameters they require their barbers to stick to, such as tapering the back of the head. Craft distilleries are a bit different in that the quality of the spirit can vary significantly depending in part on the decisions of the worker. But they also have guidelines on other aspects of the work, such as labeling and bottling.

30. In short, they use embodied knowledge learned through focused practice (Hancock 2013; Leschziner 2015; O'Connor 2005; Wacquant 2004).

31. See Fine's (1992) discussion of chefs and the temporal conditions that influence their work. I touch on temporality in chapter 6.

32. See Naccarato and LeBesco's (2012) work on "culinary capital," or the role that food and food practices play today in shaping people's identities and social lives.

Chapter 5. How Middle-Class Kids *Want* Working-Class Jobs

1. Resembling a doctor's bag, this $595 accessory is rather deep to fit especially tall bottles, such as Luxardo's maraschino liqueur, and, for an extra $195, comes with a roll-up for tools like spoons and muddlers.

2. A book publisher and serious cocktail enthusiast, Greg Boehm also collects vintage books on cocktails, spirits, and alchemy, as well as vintage barware. He own hundreds of volumes, and people in the cocktail community regularly visit his office, which serves as a library and museum, to conduct research on recipes and products. Greg also reprints and sells classic out-of-print cocktail books, makes a line of bitters, and imports Japanese barware like spoons, shakers, and mixing glasses.

3. I refer here to Arne Kalleberg's highly regarded work on the subject, specifically his 2011 book, *Good Jobs, Bad Jobs: The Rise of Polarized and Precarious Employment Systems in the United States, 1970s to 2000s*. In this and other work, Kalleberg examines how the combination of globalization and deregulation, the rise of knowledge-intensive work and technological innovations and expanded service industries, and an ideological shift from collective responsibility to individualism and personal accountability have led to greater job insecurity (that is, precarious work conditions), "24/7" work lives, and vast differences in job quality, as measured by security and stability, compensation, autonomy, and time spent on the job.

4. See the work of Neff and colleagues (2005) on the "cool" jobs of fashion models and new media workers.

5. The idea of "institutional charisma" has a long history in sociology. Max Weber, whose work is firmly entrenched in the classical theoretical canon of sociology,

describes "charismatic" as one of three ideal types of authority ("traditional" and "legal-rational," as in a bureaucracy, being the other two; Weber 1947). Charismatic leaders possess an unfathomably awe-inspiring attractiveness, and are capable of disrupting social orders. Their followers believe them to have an innate, supernatural power to which they are inexplicably drawn. A problem, of course, is the life span of the collective once the charismatic leader dies. Without the source of divine power, Weber claims that the group either morphs into a legal-rational bureaucracy to survive or disappears. While Weber's concept of charisma often applies to a leader, scholars have taken this concept and applied it to the institution. Shils (1965) claims institutions can distribute charisma throughout their "hierarchy of roles and rules" (205). Through her work on utopian communities, Kanter (1972) argues that institutional charisma, and not charismatic leadership, explains the deep commitment of members to the group. Biggart (1989) applied these interpretations of charisma in her study of direct selling organizations. She found that these businesses secure social order and worker commitment through institutionalized awe. Chen's (2012) work on *Burning Man* shows that even the routine tasks necessary for organizing this enchanting arts event get "charismatized," or provided meaning, by its devoted members through forms of storytelling. Finally, Frenette's (2013) work on interns in the music industry shows the daily oscillation they experience between the drudge work of stuffing envelopes, making copies, and fetching coffee that composes their daytime lives, and the fun work of going to shows and staying out late they get to do at night. He argues that the institutional charisma promoted by the music industry is enough to keep interns and employees alike devoted to working in the industry for at least a short time despite the highly precarious nature of their jobs.

6. Examples of "bad" jobs in "cool" industries include unpaid record company interns (Frenette 2013) and recording studio attendants (Siciliano 2016).

7. See Currid's (2007) examination of the overlapping of these and other cultural industries, and the significant economic role they play, in New York City.

8. See Leschziner's (2015) study on elite chefs for another example of manual labor jobs that have become popular.

9. The term "hipster" originated in the 1940s during the jazz age to denote people (usually white) who were "hip," or "in the know" in the music and art scene (see Hobsbawm 1959). (The origins for the word "hip" as a synonym of "cool" or "in the know" are far older and very obscure. Multiple interpretations exist.) Contemporary usage of the word "hipster" begins in the 1990s and refers to urban gentrifiers interested in indie music and art.

10. See Greif et al. (2010) for a general discussion (mostly negative) of hipsters. And see Perry (2013) for an analysis of hipsters' use of working-class culture in their sense of style and Schiermer (2013) for a theoretical treatment of hipsters and irony.

11. Writer Kurt Reighley's 2010 book *The United States of Americana: Backyard Chickens, Burlesque Beauties, and Handmade Bitters: A Field Guide to the New American Roots Movement*, which includes whole-animal butchery, cocktails and distilling, and men's grooming as examples, signifies the popular notion that these trades deliberately recall a lost past.

12. For theoretical discussions of nostalgia, see Davis (1979) and Wilson (2005). And for discussions of how people define and use nostalgia in a variety of social contexts, see Kasinitz and Hillyard (1995); Milligan (2003); and Ocejo (2010; 2014).

13. A vast scholarly literature exists on what motivates and influences people to pursue the careers they do. Some demonstrate the role that early education plays. Through her in-depth examination of upper-middle-class and working-class parents, Lareau (2003) discovers how the former try to cultivate certain skills, abilities, and interests in their children by enrolling them in various activities. She finds these efforts lacking among working-class parents (also see Rivera's work [2015] on how people get elite jobs). In his classic study of "how working class kids get working class jobs," Willis (1977) argues that working-class "counter-school" culture, embedded in and encouraged by the structure of educational institutions, prepares working-class "lads" for a lifetime of giving their labor power to low-status manual labor occupations. While these analyses focus on how young children from different social class backgrounds perform in school, Khan's (2010) argument that members of today's new social and economic elite embody and perform their privilege pushes the notion that the abilities (or habitus; Bourdieu 1984) developed in the family and encouraged in adolescence and teenage years play a role in the fields they choose to enter. Finally, Judge and Bretz (1992) find that college students seek jobs in organizations that match their own value orientation, with "values" measured by the opportunity for achievement, concern for others, and levels of honesty and fairness. These various mechanisms represent a small sample of the many factors that influence people to choose the careers they do.

14. See Besen-Cassino (2014); Gatta (2011); and Pettinger (2005). And see Misra and Walters (2016) for an alternative conclusion.

15. Sociologically, "meaning" refers to how people ascribe value to various aspects of their lives, or come to see various aspects of their lives as meaningful, as reflective of and/or influenced by social standpoints and cultural perspectives (Geertz 1974; Mead 1934). In a broad review of the meaning of work literature, Ross and colleagues (2010) identify two key issues that scholars have focused on: the sources of meaning of work—specifically the self, others, the work context, and spiritual life; and the mechanisms through which work is proposed to become meaningful—such as authenticity, self-efficacy, self-esteem, purpose,

belongingness, and transcendence, and other cultural and interpersonal sense-making. Other than the overtly religious sources and mechanisms (spiritual life and transcendence), the new elite workers in this book find meaning from and through each of these sources and mechanisms at various points in their career paths and at varying strengths.

16. Based on her research on young coffee shop workers, Besen-Cassino (2014) argues that these youth "consume work" as they do any product. They self-identify with the brand of the company they work for, and their lifestyles suit the nature of the work. Her work also exemplifies the symbolic interactionist approach of examining the perspectives of workers when making a full determination of whether a job is "good" or "bad," which is an approach I take in this book.

17. Building from the argument Robert Bellah and his research team took in their book *Habits of the Heart* (1985), Wrzesniewski and colleagues (1997) examine three relations people have toward their work: as jobs (provide people with material benefits with not much extra meaning); as careers (provide people with opportunity for advancement, which includes higher status and self-esteem in addition to material rewards); and as callings (provide people with intrinsic rewards and fulfillment from work that is inseparable from life). The notion of the "calling," of course, has religious origins, as Weber discusses (1958; 1963). Some people felt that God "called" them to pursue certain work. This divine intervention imbued work with moral significance. Wrzesniewski and her colleagues refer to a secular version of a calling, or work that is inherently meaningful and fulfilling. The gut feeling that work brings personal value, or, as I see it and argue in this chapter, the self-discovered charisma from working the job replaces the voice of God calling people to socially and morally important work. These relationships—job, career, and calling—are not mutually exclusive, nor do they depend on occupation. In other words, people may feel all three in one occupation, and the same occupation may be a job, a career, or a calling for different people. To repeat, not all people are free to pursue an occupation that provides them with opportunities to advance in material benefits and status, improve their self-esteem, or find fulfillment in their work in a way that is intertwined with who they are. The workers in this book are among those who are lucky enough to do so.

18. See Leschziner's (2015) analysis of elite chefs.

19. Lave and Wenger (1991) introduced this concept, primarily in reference to socializing newcomers, and Wenger (1998) later explored it in greater depth to refer to informal forms of learning. Also see Cox's (2005) review of how the concept has been used in the literature.

20. As mentioned in a footnote in chapter 3, most barbers attend a formal school to get a license. But they can also apprentice under a "master barber."

21. In short, Jason "looked the part," demonstrating aesthetic labor. See Warhurst et al. (2000); Warhurst and Nickson (2007); and Williams and Connell (2010).

22. Owner of the Flatiron Lounge (where Hal went on his date), Julie Reiner is an older and well-respected person in the cocktail community. As mentioned in chapter 1, Audrey Saunders owns Pegu Club and Sasha Petraske owned Milk and Honey.

23. For others, meat was always central to their food sensibilities, but with a different role. An interesting number of people at whole-animal butcher shops—interns, counter workers, butchers, and owners—were vegetarian and/or vegan at some point in their lives for reasons that range from personal health to the ethics of slaughtering animals for food. They began eating meat again for a variety of reasons, such as personal health (like Sarah) and because they realized there were alternatives, like whole-animal butcher shops, that did meat "right" and with serious ethical considerations, unlike the mainstream meat industry, which had turned them off meat in the first place. (The people at Dickson's told me they hired a woman who was still a vegetarian as an intern after I had left. She was apparently interested in learning more about meat.) In a sense, their interest in food stemmed from these decisions and prepared them to work at a whole-animal butcher shop where passion for and knowledge of food is important. The other three jobs don't have exact comparisons with people in the butcher shop world, especially since ethics has very little to do with them (specifically the ethics of killing). I met only one person from the craft cocktail and distilling worlds who didn't drink alcohol at one point in life. He said he stopped drinking for several years because he had a drinking problem, and only learned to drink properly when he heard about the craft cocktail world. I met several barbers who cut their own hair and/or never went to a barber, but not for any serious reasons besides they liked doing it themselves or had a friend do it for them.

24. The "small" slaughterhouse Giancarlo worked at slaughtered sixteen cows per day, along with some lambs and pigs. This production is more than the slaughterhouse that Dickson's uses, as discussed in chapter 4, but far smaller than industrial slaughterhouses (see Pachirat 2011).

25. Coincidentally, the owner of the slaughterhouse Dickson's uses taught in that same program some years back.

26. Zukin (1995) documents how immigrant dishwashers and kitchen workers have sometimes used their work experience to open their own restaurants.

27. Thomas (1980) provides a typology of people who change careers based on the pressure they feel from themselves to do so (that is, personal motivations) and pressure they feel from their environment (that is, company actions, occupational shifts, and economic climate) (also see Thomas et al. 1976; and Murray

et al. 1971). Of the four groups in Thomas's typology, the "Opt-outs"—people who did not face much external pressure, if any, but who were motivated to do something more in their careers— best represent the workers in this book who switched careers. They seek a better fit between their own values and needs and the work they do. But unlike today's new elite manual laborers, most "Opt-outs" return to formal education to pursue a new career. And most of the career changers in this book are still very young, under 35, and not in their "midlife" as most of the literature on career change examines (Barclay et al. 2011). Also see Feldman (2002) and Heppner et al. (1994) for studies on career changers.

28. The examples of both Nicole and Jeremy reveal how these paths are not mutually exclusive. They both had "good" jobs in popular industries in the new economy (architecture and advertising). The same could be said for Hal, who was also attracted to craft cocktail culture while working in a "good" job. I include Nicole and Jeremy in this section because they were not in their industries because they saw them as potential careers, while Hal (and Rob) were.

29. See Warhurst et al. (2000); Warhurst and Nickson (2007); and Williams and Connell (2010) for examples.

30. The restaurant closed, in 2010, after being open for only ten months, and 3rd Ward went out of business in 2013.

31. Meat Hook, the whole-animal butcher shop, is located inside Brooklyn Kitchen, a retail store that sells ordinary and specialty cooking items. It also has a teaching kitchen for a variety of food- and beverage-related classes, including butchery.

Chapter 6. The Science and the Art

1. The full title of the book is *Whole Beast Butchery: The Complete Visual Guide to Beef, Lamb, and Pork*, by Ryan Farr, a San Francisco-based chef, butcher, and entrepreneur. It was published in 2011.

2. Fine (1992) refers to an occupational aesthetic as a "sense of superior production" (1268) that workers have for the practices they engage in.

3. I will also show in the next chapter how important public validation is for their professional identity.

4. This point of doing something well for its own sake is the central aspect of Sennett's (2008) definition of craftsmanship.

5. Fine (1995) discusses this idea in relation to chefs.

6. As manufacturing businesses, craft distilleries are less influenced by consumer market forces. They try to operate the distilling process continuously throughout the year. Given their size, however, there are situations when they are forced to

speed up production, such as if they don't receive a delivery for an ingredient in time to begin their distillation and then have to catch up.

7. This data collection method is called "photo elicitation." The aim is to get participants to see themselves doing what they do and to see their contexts from different perspectives. See Harper (2002; 2003).

8. This quote is from his book *Official Mixers' Manual* (1934).

9. I get this argument from Faulkner and Becker's (2009) work on how musicians put the jazz repertoire into action. As they state, "The songs of the jazz repertoire . . . are, for the most part, formulaic, elaborate variations on a small number of templates. Someone who knows the basic forms can play thousands of songs in this great reservoir without much work" (24). And: "To some extent every performance involves elements of improvisation, although its degree varies according to period and place, and to some extent every improvisation rests on a series of conventions and implicit rules. . . . [J]azz players routinely play versions of songs they already know of whose form they can guess at, substituting melodies composed on the spot for the original, but always keeping in mind that those melodies ought to sound good against the (more or less) original harmonies of the song, which the other players will be (more or less) expecting to be the foundation of what they play together. Jazz improvisation, then (more or less), combines spontaneity and conformity to some sort of already given format" (27–28).

10. I provide an example of such a request in the following chapter.

11. All Good Things was a miniature version of Chelsea Market with small artisanal food stands in a large single room. Jake owned the shop at All Good Things for a year. He chose to close it in 2013, after their one-year lease was up, largely because of disagreements with the manager.

Chapter 7. Service Teaching

Portions of chapter 7 have been published in "Show the Animal: Constructing and Communicating New Elite Food Tastes at Upscale Butcher Shops," *Poetics*, 47: 106–21, 2014.

1. I omit craft distillers from this chapter, because they primarily engage in light manufacturing and not service and customer interaction. Although they increasingly also come face-to-face with customers through tours of their distilleries and consumer events, which I discussed in chapter 2, such interactions and the retail transactions are not the focus or main revenue generator of their businesses. And some craft distillers almost never see these "customers," whereas all cocktail bartenders, barbers, and butcher shop workers do all the time.

2. See Leidner (1993); Ritzer (2000); and Tilly (1955) for studies on unskilled service workers who follow an automated script. And see Besen-Cassino (2014) for an analysis for how workers make sense of these jobs.

3. See Ocejo (2012).

4. Because of this social requirement, Rose (2004) has argued for the high intellectual capacity of workers like waitresses and hairdressers, who are usually regarded only for their manual labor.

5. For studies on the consumption habits of cultural omnivores, see Atkinson (2011); Bryson (1996); DiMaggio and Mukhtar (2004); Fisher and Preece (2003); Friedman (2012); Kanazawa (2001); Rebers et al. (2006); Rossel et al. (2006); Van Eijck (1999; 2001); Van Eijck and Bargeman (2004); Van Wel et al. (2008). For an analysis on the role of advertising in the shift toward omnivorousness, see Taylor (2009). And see Johnston and Baumann (2007; 2010) and Johnston and Cairns (2015) for studies on media images and discourses.

6. One cocktail bartender I studied got a tattoo of "1-1-1" on his ankle. He also said he kept a large batch of the Negroni at all times in his refrigerator, so that when he got home late after working he could easily pour himself a nightcap before bed.

7. I discuss "functional flair" in chapter 4 and in an earlier article on whole-animal butchers (Ocejo 2014), which I refer to as "functional aesthetics." Also see Fine (1992).

8. Milk and Honey is unique for having a verbal menu. But even cocktail bartenders who work at bars with a print menu have the same interactions with customers who are either new to the bar and/or new to craft cocktails. The key difference is that the menu serves as a preliminary guide for customers to ask questions about drinks and for bartenders to get an idea of what customers want.

9. I discuss the notion of "gateway" drinks in an earlier article (Ocejo 2010).

10. See Elliott's (2016) work on the concept of "caring masculinities."

11. In this regard, as discussed in chapter 3, the "emotional" aspect of their "emotional labor" (Hochschild 1983) disappears within the professional practices of the work.

12. See Katovich and Reese (1987) and my first book (Ocejo 2014) for a discussion of being a regular at bars. See Oldenburg (1989) for a discussion of "third places," or public gathering spaces where people benefit from being a part of a community.

13. In this case Phil later tinkered with his recipe based on his regular's feedback. He also gave it a name, as he did for many of Phil's drinks. The Joy Division, a gin-based Martini variation, was on Death & Co.'s next menu.

14. In this case I did not find out if Mel had already been part of the taste community and adhered to the meat philosophies of the shop before it opened or if Lena and the other workers were instrumental in getting him interested in meat. Either

way, his rapport with Lena and trust in what she tells him is exactly how butcher shop workers talk with regulars.

15. These are the nonmonetary, intrinsic, or psychic rewards workers derive from their work. They are impossible to quantify but play an integral role in the satisfaction workers receive from their work, especially in nonlucrative jobs such as those in the culture industries. See Frenette (2016); Menger (1999); and Oakley (2009).

16. Fine (1992) makes this point in reference to chefs.

17. As my internship progressed I overheard many customers ask counter workers the "organic" question, and even fielded it a couple of times myself. Many of these interactions ended with the customer not buying anything.

18. Becker (1951); Grazian (2003).

19. I did not witness Thorin with this client, but many times I saw a barber steer a client away from a certain style, both one they saw in a photograph, like in a magazine, and one they described to the barber. For instance, on multiple occasions I saw Miles talk to the same regular client about the limits of what he could do because of his receding hairline (the client wanted a certain style and to hide the hairline, but the combination was incompatible), and Van talk to his regular client about his comb-over to hide how much he was balding (Van would suggest shaving and close-cropping it). Neither client would listen despite the barbers' best efforts. They became a bit of an ongoing joke among the barbers. "My comb-over was in yesterday," Van would say. Having seen him regularly, the other barbers would know who he meant and understandingly nod their heads.

20. During my fieldwork Van was the most vocal to clients about not using shampoo, but most of the other barbers agreed with him, to certain extents. Some would give similar advice to clients.

Chapter 8. *Getting* the Job

1. Not to confuse Freemans' apprenticeship program with the internship programs at Tuthilltown and Dickson's, Jason was a receptionist and an apprentice.

2. This expression—"looking good and sounding right"—which comes from Warhurst and Nickson's (2001) book on the subject, is often used to denote the concept of "aesthetic labor." Also see Mears (2014); Williams and Connell (2010); Witz et al. (2003); Wolkowitz (2006).

3. "Codes" in the social sciences generally refer to "codes of conduct," or social norms that prescribe and proscribe how one should or should not behave. Jimerson and Oware (2006) discuss the differences between how ethnographers and ethnomethodologists examine codes. Ethnographers, they show, tend to focus on

how codes, which are often implicit, shape people's behavior within specific settings. Elijah Anderson's well-known work, *The Code of the Street* (1999), about life in the inner city in which people learn dichotomous sets of rules behind what it means to be "decent" and "street" as well as how to "code-switch" (36) depending on the situation, best exemplifies this analytic tendency. Ethnomethodologists, however, tend to focus on how people use codes to account for their behaviors. Wieder's (1974a; 1974b) work on "telling the code" among convicts at a halfway house, which examines how residents and staff interpret and use the code to structure and explain their everyday activities, best exemplifies this research tradition. In their work on black male basketball players, Jimerson and Oware persuasively combine the two approaches. They argue that codes are both "repertoires of action" that create parameters for behavior and "vocabularies of motive" (26) that justify behavior, and use their approach to examine black men who play basketball "tell the code of the street."

I follow their approach in this chapter. I see the "workplace code" for these workers as both a set of implicit (and sometimes explicit) social norms that guide their behavior that they also "tell" as justifications for how they make sense of each other within a specific setting.

4. In his work on students at an exclusive prep school, Khan (2010) argues that new elites have shed the sense of entitlement that traditional elites took for granted because of their economic standing and today display "ease" in their privileged environment. Since democratization has made culture, taste, and knowledge more easily accessible to people from diverse social backgrounds, new elites maintain their high status by embodying ease in their everyday behaviors. Rather than merely "knowing" cultural phenomena, these teenaged members of the new elite learn how to think and act comfortably when confronted with all sorts of cultural material, and how to not act snobbish when discussing their own tastes. Despite being distant from necessity, they learn to act like they earned their achievements, just as, they contend, all people have the opportunity to do. Those who fail in their performances (that is, demonstrate traditional elitism or appear stressed in their efforts), do not "get it," or do not see the importance of confident doing over confident knowing. New elites learn to perform taste (and other behaviors) with ease in a world where access to taste has been expanded.

I borrow my notion of confidence in performing the workplace code from Khan's concept of ease. These workers neither "construct boundaries around knowledge and use such knowledge as a resource" (16) in regard to the cultural knowledge they possess nor base someone's inclusion into the workplace and occupational community on the sole possession of one element, whether it be cultural knowledge, technical skills, or work ethic. Rather, they base it on someone's ability to embody and perform the code confidently. But the workplace code I examine differs from the sense of privilege that elite students learn at their exclusive prep schools in the sense that it does not signify a totalizing worldview from the setting of a total institution.

5. In his research on wildland firefighters Desmond (2007) shows how people come to the job already in possession of "country masculinity" and a "country-masculine habitus" that "guides the firefighters' thoughts, tastes, and practices" (30). As country boys who grew up in the same or similar woods and wildland they work in, firefighters bring country knowledge, a country way of life, and a sense of what it means to be a man with them to work, which they practice and display in front of each other as "country competence" (43), such as demonstrating sawyering skills or knowing what a cotton pin is (44–52). They already have a feel for the game (to simplify Bourdieu's classic concept of "habitus"), which they use to distinguish themselves from others, such as "city boys" and "structure firefighters," and to achieve status within their group.

   Since they often come from more varied backgrounds and locations, these workers do not possess a common habitus that they can readily apply to their job. Rather, they learn it through work and interaction with their co-workers and display it through "workplace competence," or, as I refer to it based on how many of these workers define it, confidence.

6. He was even inspired by Death & Co.'s reference to Prohibition in having an inconspicuous entrance and in choosing the bar's name. The Franklin Mortgage & Investment Co. was the front for an underground alcohol ring based in Philadelphia.

7. For studies on how people acquire embodied knowledge through practice, see Hancock (2011); Leschziner (2015); O'Connor (2005); Wacquant (2004).

8. Sherman (2007) discusses how luxury hotel workers aim for similar feelings for guests.

9. I observed consistent inconsistency as a deliberately discussed practice in the craft distilleries more so than in the other workplaces. Only they taught it and placed value in it, but I observed it in the others insofar as handmade products and services will always vary to some degree given the amount of human error that is inherently involved, even if such differences are difficult to detect: degrees of coldness and dilution levels in cocktails, varying hair lengths, and subtle changes in the appearance of meat.

10. See Sennett's (2008) work on the role of the hand in craftsmanship.

11. Men barbers are also no better at shaving clients than women barbers for another reason. As I showed in chapter 7, experienced barbers can give a good haircut for a first-time client, but it takes them up to three haircuts to really understand a client's hair and be able to experiment. While barbers have many regular clients for haircuts, they rarely have a client who regularly gets a shave. Most clients get shaves as occasional luxuries and for special events, like a bachelor party or wed-

ding, and they may never return. Therefore, barbers never get to really learn a client's face, like the direction the hair goes in and any sensitive areas. In many ways the pomp and circumstance of the shaving process covers up a bad shave. As Van says, "[The client's] not getting the world's best shave. Because who is better than yourself? You can feel every little thing you do. It's just are you willing to do what I do [oils, towels, massages, and so on], every morning?" Plus, since they replace the disposable razors for every shave, the blade is always very sharp. (As many readers who are men can likely attest, it sometimes takes a few shaves to break in a blade.) A sensitive face with a brand-new razor blade will usually lead to cuts and irritation. Man or woman, there is nothing a barber can do about it. Finally, men usually judge a shave's quality by their face's level of smoothness afterward. Shaving technology has come a long way since the days of straight and safety razors. Multiblade cartridges can usually give a closer shave than straight razors and disposable blades.

12. The company that makes this product is Balcones Distillery, in Texas.

13. I discuss this transition in the epilogue.

14. Here JM refers to the first head butcher at Dickson's, mentioned in chapter 6. Adam and JM stayed in touch after he left, and both have enormous respect for each other.

Epilogue. Outcomes, Implications, and Concluding Thoughts

1. See Florida (2002); Lane (2011); and Neff (2012).

2. See Cornfield (2015).

3. See Cooper (2014); Sharone (2013); and Sennett (1998).

4. See Besen-Cassino's (2014) work on middle-class youth who enjoy working bad coffee shop jobs because they treat them as a lifestyle they consume.

5. I discussed this shop a bit in chapter 3.

6. Aldo and Jake told conflicting stories when I conducted follow-up interviews with them. Aldo said Jake called him, while Jake said Lena told Aldo to get in touch with him.

Methodological Appendix

1. I discuss this episode in my previous book (Ocejo 2014, 161, 176–79).

2. He later opened the café, without a liquor license, with the name Mercury Dime. It closed a few years later. I also discuss this episode in my previous book (2014,

117–19). Interestingly, an upscale men's barbershop opened in the space after Mercury Dime closed. I interviewed the owner and one of its barbers for this book.

3. I show my first visit to Milk and Honey in my previous book (2014, 119–24).
4. Glaser and Strauss (1967)
5. See Duneier (1999) and Jerolmack (2013), both of whom studied people from backgrounds different from their own (for example, race, age, nationality, social class), for a discussion of this argument. And see Contreras (2011) for another discussion of using a recorder in the field.
6. We can call this getting to see "backstage" (Goffman 1959).
7. I was paid a small amount for my internship, conveniently enough to pay for my bus rides upstate.
8. I could have forgone barber school and trained under one of the barbers, but that also would have been very time-consuming and would have shifted my concentration toward cutting hair and away from the social interactions in the shop.
9. See Harper (2002) for a discussion of this method, and see Harper (2003) for an example of it in action.
10. See Glaser and Strauss (1967).
11. See Katz (1982).
12. The only reason to do so would be if another researcher wanted to conduct a fixed sample longitudinal study based on another researcher's work and study that researcher's exact same participants after a certain amount of time had passed. I have never heard of such a study.

REFERENCES

Abbott, Andrew. 1988. *The System of Professions: An Essay on the Division of Expert Labor*. Chicago: University of Chicago Press.

Ahmed, S. M. Faizan. 2006. "Making Beautiful: Male Workers in Beauty Parlors." *Men and Masculinities* 9 (2): 168–85.

Alexander, Bryant Keith. 2003. "Fading, Twisting, and Weaving: An Interpretive Ethnography of the Black Barbershop as Cultural Space." *Qualitative Inquiry* 9 (1): 105–28.

Anderson, Benedict. 1991. *Imagined Communities: Reflections on the Origin and Spread of Nationalism*. London: Verso.

Anderson, Elijah. 1999. *Code of the Street: Decency, Violence, and the Moral Life of the Inner City*. New York: W. W. Norton.

Ashforth, Blake E., and Glen E. Kreiner. 1999. "'How Can You Do It?' Dirty Work and the Challenge of Constructing a Positive Identity." *Academy of Management Review* 24 (3): 413–34.

Atkinson, Will. 2011. "The Context and Genesis of Musical Tastes: Omnivorousness Debunked, Bourdieu Buttressed." *Poetics* 39: 169–86.

Barber, Kristen. 2008. "The Well-Coiffed Man: Class, Race and Heterosexual Masculinity in the Hair Salon." *Gender and Society* 22 (4): 455–76.

———. 2016. *Styling Masculinity: Gender, Class, and Inequality in the Men's Grooming Industry*. New Brunswick, NJ: Rutgers University Press.

Barclay, Susan R., Kevin B. Stoltz, and Y. Barry Chung. 2011. "Voluntary Midlife Career Change: Integrating the Transtheoretical Model and the Life-Span, Life-Space Approach." *Career Development Quarterly* 59: 386–99.

Barlow, Ronald S. 1993. *The Vanishing American Barber Shop: An Illustrated History of Tonsorial Art, 1860–1960*. London: Windmill.

Beck, Ulrich. 1992. *Risk Society: Towards a New Modernity*. London: Sage.

———. 2000. *The Brave New World of Work*. Cambridge: Cambridge University Press.

Becker, Howard S. 1951. "The Professional Dance Musician and His Audience." *American Journal of Sociology* 57 (2): 136–44.

———. 1996. "The Epistemology of Qualitative Research." In *Essays on Ethnography and Human Development*, ed. Richard Jessor, Anne Colby, and Richard A. Schweder. Chicago: University of Chicago Press.

Bellah, Robert N., Richard Madsen, William M. Sullivan, Ann Swidler, and Steven M. Tipton. 1985. *Habits of the Heart: Individualism and Commitment in American Life*. New York: Harper and Row.

Bensman, David, and Roberta Lynch. 1988. *Rusted Dreams: Hard Times in a Steel Community*. Berkeley: University of California Press.

Berman, Marshall. 1982. *All That Is Solid Melts into Air*. New York: Penguin Books.

Besen-Cassino, Yasemin. 2014. *Consuming Work: Youth Labor in America*. Philadelphia: Temple University Press.

Biggart, Nicole Woolsey. 1989. *Charismatic Capitalism: Direct Selling Organizations in America*. Chicago: University of Chicago Press.

Bird, Sharon. 1996. "Welcome to the Men's Club: Homosociality and the Maintenance of Hegemonic Masculinity. *Gender and Society* 10 (2): 120–32.

Black, Paula, and Ursula Sharma. 2001. "Men Are Real, Women Are 'Made Up': Beauty Therapy and the Construction of Femininity." *Sociological Review* 49 (1): 100–116.

Blumenthal, Ralph. 2001. *Stork Club: America's Most Famous Nightspot and the Lost World of Cafe Society*. Boston: Back Bay Books.

Borer, Michael Ian. 2015. "Consuming Craft." In *Popular Culture as Everyday Life*, ed. Dennis D. Waskul and Phillip Vannini. New York: Routledge.

Bourdieu, Pierre. 1984. *Distinction: A Social Critique of the Judgment of Taste*. Cambridge, MA: Harvard University Press.

———. 1993. *The Field of Cultural Production*. New York: Columbia University Press.

Bowen, Sarah. 2015. *Divided Spirits: Tequila, Mezcal, and the Politics of Production*. Berkeley: University of California Press.

Boyle, Matthew. 2013. "Yes, Real Men Drink Beer and Wear Skin Moisturizer." *Bloomberg Businessweek*, October 3. Available at http://www.businessweek.com/articles/2013-10-03/men-now-spend-more-on-toiletries-than-on-shaving-products (accessed November 25, 2014).

Braverman, Harry. 1974. *Labor and Monopoly Capital: The Degradation of Work in the Twentieth Century*. New York: Monthly Review Press.

Brown, Jared, and Anistatia Miller. 2009. *Spirituous Journey: A History of Drink, Book Two*. London: Mixellany.

Brown-Saracino, Japonica. 2009. *A Neighborhood That Never Changes: Gentrification, Social Preservation, and the Search for Authenticity*. Chicago: University of Chicago Press.

———. 2010. *The Gentrification Debates: A Reader*. New York: Routledge.

Brumberg, Joan Jacobs. 1997. *The Body Project: An Intimate History of American Girls*. New York: Random House.

Buss, Terry F., and Stevens F. Redburn. 1983. *Shutdown at Youngstown*. Albany: State University of New York Press.

Carroll, Glenn R., and Anand Swaminathan. 2000. "Why the Microbrewery Movement? Organizational Dynamics of Resource Partitioning in the U.S. Brewing Industry." *American Journal of Sociology* 106 (3): 715–62.

Castells, Manuel. 1996. *The Information Age: Economy, Society and Culture*. Vol. I: *The Rise of the Network Society*. Cambridge, MA/Oxford, UK: Blackwell.

———. 1997. *The Information Age: Economy, Society and Culture*. Vol. II: *The Power of Identity*. Cambridge, MA/Oxford, UK: Blackwell.

———. 1998. *The Information Age: Economy, Society and Culture*. Vol. III: *End of Millennium*. Cambridge, MA/Oxford, UK: Blackwell.

Chen, Katherine K. 2012. "Charismatizing the Routine: Storytelling for Meaning and Agency in the Burning Man Organization." *Qualitative Sociology* 35: 311–34.

Cherlin, Andrew J. 2014. *Labor's Love Lost: The Rise and Fall of the Working-Class Family in America*. New York: Russell Sage Foundation.

Coad, David. 2008. *The Metrosexual: Gender, Sexuality, and Sport*. Albany: State University of New York Press.

Connell, Raewyn. 2005. *Masculinities*. 2nd ed. Cambridge, UK: Polity.

Contreras, Randol. 2012. *The Stickup Kids: Race, Drugs, Violence, and the American Dream*. Berkeley: University of California Press.

Cooper, Marianne. 2014. *Cut Adrift: Families in Insecure Times*. Berkeley: University of California Press.

Cornfield, Daniel B. 2015. *Beyond the Beat: Musicians Building Community in Nashville*. Princeton, NJ: Princeton University Press.

Cox, Andrew. 2005. "What Are Communities of Practice? A Comparative Review of Four Seminal Works." *Journal of Information Science* 31 (6): 527–40.

Crawford, Matthew. 2009. *Shop Class as Soulcraft: An Inquiry into the Value of Work*. New York: Penguin Books.

Cronon, William. 1992. *Nature's Metropolis: Chicago and the Great West*. New York: W. W. Norton.

Currid, Elizabeth. 2008. *The Warhol Economy: How Fashion, Art, and Music Drive New York City*. Princeton, NJ: Princeton University Press.

Curtis, Wayne. 2006. *And a Bottle of Rum: A History of the New World in Ten Cocktails*. New York: Broadway Books.

Davis, Fred. 1979. *Yearning for Yesterday: A Sociology of Nostalgia*. New York: Free Press.

Dean, James Joseph. 2014. *Straights: Heterosexuality in Post-Closeted Culture*. New York: NYU Press.

DeGloma, Thomas. 2014. *Seeing the Light: The Social Logic of Personal Discovery*. Chicago: University of Chicago Press.

de Casanova, Erynn Masi. 2015. *Buttoned Up: Clothing, Conformity, and White-Collar Masculinity*. Ithaca, NY: ILR Press.

Defours, Christophe. 2011. "Work and Subjectivity: Towards a Philosophical Anthropology from the Psychopathology to the Psychodynamics of Work." *New Philosophies of Labour* 13: 207–50.

de la Pradelle, Michele. 2004. *Market Day in Provence*. Chicago: University of Chicago Press.

Desmond, Matthew. 2007. *On the Fireline: Living and Dying with Wildland Firefighters*. Chicago: University of Chicago Press.

DeSoucey, Michaela. 2010. "Gastronationalism: Food Traditions and Authenticity Politics in the European Union." *American Sociological Review* 75 (3): 432–55.

Dick, Penny. 2005. "Dirty Work Designations: How Police Officers Account for Their Use of Coercive Force." *Human Relations* 58 (11): 1363–90.

DiMaggio, Paul, and Toqir Mukhtar. 2004. "Arts Participation as Cultural Capital in the United States, 1982–2002: Signs of Decline?" *Poetics* 32 (2): 169–94.

Drake, St. Clair, and Horace Cayton. 1945. *Black Metropolis: A Study of Negro Life in a Northern City*. Chicago: University of Chicago Press.

Dudley, Kathryn Marie. 1994. *The End of the Line: Lost Jobs, New Lives in Postindustrial America*. Chicago: University of Chicago Press.

———. 2014. *Guitar Makers: The Endurance of Artisanal Values in North America*. Chicago: University of Chicago Press.

Duis, Perry. 1983. *The Saloon: Public Drinking in Chicago and Boston, 1880–1920*. Champaign: University of Illinois Press.

Duneier, Mitchell. 1999. *Sidewalk*. New York: Farrar, Straus and Giroux.

———. 2016. *Ghetto: The Invention of a Place, the History of an Idea*. New York: Farrar, Straus and Giroux.

Ehrenreich, Barbara. 2001. *Nickel and Dimed: On (Not) Getting By in America*. New York: Henry Holt.

Elliott, Karla. 2016. "Caring Masculinities: Theorizing an Emerging Concept." *Men and Masculinities* 19 (3): 240–59.

Faludi, Susan. 1999. *Stiffed: The Betrayal of the American Man*. New York: HarperCollins.

Faulkner, Robert R., and Howard S. Becker. 2009. *"Do You Know . . . ?" The Jazz Repertoire in Action*. Chicago: University of Chicago Press.

Felder, Rachel. 2015. "You Want a Cappuccino with That Haircut?" *New York Times*, June 5.

Feldman, Daniel. 2002. "Second Careers and Multiple Careers." In *The New World of Work*, ed. Cary L. Cooper and Ronald J. Burke. Oxford: Blackwell.

Ferguson, Priscilla Parkhurst. 1998. "A Cultural Field in the Making: Gastronomy in 19th-Century France." *American Journal of Sociology* 104 (3): 597–641.

———. 2004. *Accounting for Taste: The Triumph of French Cuisine*. Chicago: University of Chicago Press.

Fine, Gary Alan. 1992. "The Culture of Production: Aesthetic Choices and Constraints in Culinary Work." *American Journal of Sociology* 97: 1268–94.

———. 1995. *Kitchens: The Culture of Restaurant Work*. Berkeley: University of California Press.

Fisher, Timothy C. G., and Stephen B. Preece. 2003. "Evolution, Extinction, or Status Quo? Canadian Performing Arts Audiences in the 1990s." *Poetics* 31 (2): 69–86.

Florida, Richard. 2002. *The Rise of the Creative Class, and How It's Transforming Work, Leisure, Community, and Everyday Life*. New York: Basic Books.

Foner, Nancy. 2013. *One Out of Three: Immigrant New York in the 21st Century*. New York: Columbia University Press.

Forbes, Robert J. 1970. *A Short History of the Art of Distillation: From the Beginnings Up to the Death of Cellier Blumenthal*. Leiden: Brill.

Frank, Elena. 2014. "Groomers and Consumers: The Meaning of Male Body Depilation to a Modern Masculinity Body Project." *Men and Masculinities* 17 (3): 278–98.

Frenette, Alexandre. 2013. "Making the Intern Economy: Role and Career Challenges of the Music Industry Intern." *Work and Occupations* 40 (4): 364–97.

———. 2016. "'Working at the Candy Factory': The Limits of Nonmonetary Rewards in Record Industry Careers." In *The Production and Consumption of Music in the Digital Age*, ed. Brian J. Hracs, Michael Seman, and Tarek E. Virani. Abingdon, UK: Taylor and Francis.

Friedman, Sam. 2012. "Cultural Omnivores or Culturally Homeless? Exploring the Shifting Cultural Identities of the Upwardly Mobile." *Poetics* 40: 467–89.

Gans, Herbert. 1962. *The Urban Villagers: Group and Class in the Life of Italian-Americans*. New York: Free Press.

———. 1999. *Popular Culture and High Culture: An Analysis and Evaluation of Taste*. New York: Basic Books.

Gatta, Mary. 2011. "In the 'Blink' of an Eye: American High-End Small Retail Businesses and the Public Workforce System." In *Retail Work*, ed. Irena Grugulis and Ödul Bozkurt. London: Palgrave Macmillan.

Geertz, Clifford. 1973. *The Interpretation of Cultures*. New York: Basic Books.

Gimlin, Debra. 1996. "Pamela's Place: Power and Negotiation in the Hair Salon." *Gender and Society* 10 (5): 505–26.

Glaser, Barney G., and Anselm L. Strauss. 1967. *The Discovery of Grounded Theory: Strategies for Qualitative Research*. Chicago: Aldine.

Goffman, Erving. 1959. *The Presentation of Self in Everyday Life*. New York: Random House.

———. 1981. *Forms of Talk*. Philadelphia: University of Pennsylvania Press.

Gray, Christopher. 2005. "From Oreos and Mallomars to Today's Chelsea Market." *New York Times*, March 7.

Grazian, David. 2003. *Blue Chicago: The Search of Authenticity in Urban Blues Clubs*. Chicago: University of Chicago Press.

———. 2008. *On the Make: The Hustle of Urban Nightlife*. Chicago: University of Chicago Press.

Greif, Mark, Christian Lorentzen, Jace Clayton, Reid Pillifant, Rob Horning, Jennifer Baumgardner, Patrice Evans, Margo Jefferson, Rob Moor, Christopher Glazek, and Dayna Tortorici. 2010. *What Was the Hipster?: A Sociological Investigation*. New York: n + 1 Foundation.

Grimes, William. 2002. *Straight Up or On the Rocks: The Story of the American Cocktail*. New York: North Point Press.

Halle, David, and Elisabeth Tiso. 2014. *New York's New Edge: Contemporary Art, the High Line, Megaprojects, and Urban Growth*. Chicago: University of Chicago Press.

Hancock, Black Hawk. 2013. *American Allegory: Lindy Hop and the Racial Imagination*. Chicago: University of Chicago Press.

Hannerz, Ulf. 1969. *Soulside: Inquiries into Ghetto Culture and Community*. Chicago: University of Chicago Press.

Harper, Douglas. 1987. *Working Knowledge: Skill and Community in a Small Shop*. Chicago: University of Chicago Press.

———. 2002. "Talking about Pictures: A Case for Photo Elicitation." *Visual Studies* 17 (1): 13–26.

Harrington, Brooke. 2016. *Capital without Borders: Wealth Management and the One Percent*. Cambridge, MA: Harvard University Press.

Harris-Lacewell, Melissa Victoria. 2006. *Barbershops, Bibles, and BET: Everyday Talk and Black Political Thought*. Princeton, NJ: Princeton University Press.

Hatton, Erin. 2011. *The Temp Economy: From Kelly Girls to Permatemps in Postwar America*. Philadelphia: Temple University Press.

Heppner, Mary J., Karen D. Multon, and Joe A. Johnston. 1994. "Assessing Psychological Resources during Career Change: Development of the Career Transitions Inventory." *Journal of Vocational Behavior* 44: 55–74.

Heying, Charles. 2010. *Brews to Bikes: Portland's Artisan Economy*. Portland, OR: Ooligan Press.

Ho, Karen. 2009. *Liquidated: An Ethnography of Wall Street*. Durham, NC: Duke University Press.

Hobsbawm, Eric. 1959. *The Jazz Scene*. London: Faber and Faber.

Hochschild, Arlie Russell. 1982. *The Managed Heart: Commercialization of Human Feeling*. Berkeley: University of California Press.

Holt, Douglas B. 1997. "Distinction in America? Recovering Bourdieu's Theory of Tastes from Its Critics." *Poetics* 25 (2): 93–120.

Hughes, Everett Cherrington. 1958. *Men and Their Work*. London: Free Press of Glencoe.

———. 1971. *The Sociological Eye: Selected Papers*. Piscataway, NJ: Transaction Publishers.

Hum, Tarry. 2014. *Making a Global Immigrant Neighborhood: Brooklyn's Sunset Park*. Philadelphia: Temple University Press.

Indergaard, Michael. 2004. *Silicon Alley: The Rise and Fall of a New Media District*. New York: Routledge.

Jakob, Doreen. 2012. "Crafting Your Way Out of the Recession? New Craft Entrepreneurs and the Global Economic Downturn." *Cambridge Journal of Regions, Economy and Society* 6 (1): 3–21.

Jerolmack, Colin. 2013. *The Global Pigeon*. Chicago: University of Chicago Press.

Jimerson, Jason B., and Matthew K. Oware. 2006. "Telling the Code of the Street: An Ethnomethodological Ethnography." *Journal of Contemporary Ethnography* 35 (1): 24–50.

Johnston, Josée, and Shyon Baumann. 2007. "Democracy versus Distinction: A Study of Omnivorousness in Gourmet Food Writing." *American Journal of Sociology* 113 (1): 165–204.

———. 2010. *Foodies: Democracy and Distinction in the Gourmet Foodscape*. New York: Routledge.

Johnston, Josée, Alexandra Rodney, and Phillipa Chong. 2014. "Making Change in the Kitchen? A Study of Celebrity Cookbooks, Culinary Personas, and Inequality." *Poetics* 47: 1–22.

Judge, Timothy A., and Robert D. Bretz. 1992. "Effects of Work Values on Job Choice Decisions." *Journal of Applied Psychology* 77: 261–71.

Kalleberg, Arne L. 2011. *Good Jobs, Bad Jobs: The Rise of Polarized and Precarious Employment Systems in the United States, 1970s to 2000s*. New York: Russell Sage Foundation.

Kamp, David. 2006. *The United States of Arugula. How We Became a Gourmet Nation*. New York: Broadway Books.

Kanazawa, Satoshi. 2001. "De Gustibus Est Disputandum." *Social Forces* 79 (3): 1131–62.

Kanter, Rosabeth Moss. 1972. *Commitment and Community: Communes and Utopias in Sociological Perspective*. Cambridge, MA: Harvard University Press.

Kasinitz, Philip, and David Hillyard. 1995. "The Old-Timers' Tale: The Politics of Nostalgia on the Waterfront." *Journal of Contemporary Ethnography* 24 (2): 139–64.

Kasinitz, Philip, John H. Mollenkopf, and Mary C. Waters (eds.). 2004. *Becoming New Yorkers: Ethnographies of the New Second Generation*. New York: Russell Sage Foundation.

Kasinitz, Philip, Mary C. Waters, and Jennifer Holdaway. 2008. *Inheriting the City: The Children of Immigrants Come of Age*. New York: Russell Sage Foundation.

Katovich, Michael A., and William A. Reese II. 1987. "The Regular: Full-Time Identities and Memberships in an Urban Bar." *Journal of Contemporary Ethnography* 16 (3): 308–43.

Katz, Jack. 1982. *Poor People's Lawyers in Transition*. New Brunswick, NJ: Rutgers University Press.

Khan, Shamus Rahman. 2010. *Privilege: The Making of an Adolescent Elite at St. Paul's School*. Princeton, NJ: Princeton University Press.

Kimmel, Michael. 2011. *Manhood in America: A Cultural History*. New York: Oxford University Press.

Kornblum, William. 1974. *Blue Collar Community*. Chicago: University of Chicago Press.

Kriendler, H. Peter. 1999. *21: Every Day Was New Year's Eve*. New York: Taylor Trade Publishing.

Kuh, Patric. 2001. *The Last Days of Haute Cuisine: The Coming of Age of American Restaurants*. New York: Penguin Books.

Lamont, Michele. 1992. *Money, Morals, and Manners: The Culture of the French and the American Upper-Middle Class*. Chicago: University of Chicago Press.

Lane, Carrie. 2011. *A Company of One: Insecurity, Independence and the New World of White Collar Unemployment*. Ithaca, NY: ILR Press.

Lareau, Annette. 2003. *Unequal Childhoods: Class, Race, and Family Life*. Berkeley: University of California Press.

Lave, Jean, and Etienne Wenger. 1991. *Situated Learning: Legitimate Peripheral Participation*. Cambridge, UK: Cambridge University Press.

Lawson, Helene M. 1999. "Working on Hair." *Qualitative Sociology* 22 (3): 235–57.

Leidner, Robin. 1993. *Fast Food, Fast Talk: Service Work and the Routinization of Everyday Life*. Berkeley: University of California Press.

LeMasters, E. E. 1975. *Blue-Collar Aristocrats: Life-Styles at a Working-Class Tavern*. Madison: University of Wisconsin Press.

Leonard, Christopher. 2014. *The Meat Racket: The Secret Takeover of America's Food Business*. New York: Simon and Schuster.

Lerner, Michael A. 2011. *Dry Manhattan: Prohibition in New York City*. Cambridge, MA: Harvard University Press.

Leschziner, Vanina. 2015. *At the Chef's Table: Culinary Creativity in Elite Restaurants*. Palo Alto, CA: Stanford University Press.

Liebow, Elliot. 1967. *Tally's Corner: A Study of Negro Streetcorner Men*. New York: Rowman and Littlefield.

Lin, Jan. 1998. *Reconstructing Chinatown: Ethnic Enclave, Global Change*. Minneapolis: University of Minnesota Press.

———. 2010. *The Power of Urban Ethnic Places: Cultural Heritage and Community Life*. New York: Routledge.

Lindquist, Julie. 2002. *A Place to Stand: Politics and Persuasion in a Working Class Bar*. Oxford, UK: Oxford University Press.

Lizardo, Omar, and Sara Skiles. 2015. "After Omnivorousness: Is Bourdieu Still Relevant?" In *Handbook of the Sociology of Art and Culture*, ed. Laurie Hanquinet and Mike Savage. London: Routledge.

Lloyd, Richard. 2006. *Neo-Bohemia: Art and Commerce in the Postindustrial City*. New York: Routledge.

Luciano, Lynne. 2001. *Looking Good: Male Body Image in Modern America*. New York: Hill and Wang.

Lynd, Robert S., and Helen Merrell Lynd. 1929. *Middletown: A Study in Modern American Culture*. New York: Harcourt, Brace.

Marcuse, Peter. 1985. "Gentrification, Abandonment, and Displacement: Connections, Causes, and Policy Responses in New York City." *Washington University Journal of Urban and Contemporary Law* 28: 195–240.

Marshall, Helen M. 1976. "Structural Constraints on Learning: Butchers' Apprentices." In *Learning to Work*, ed. Blanche Geer. New York: Sage.

May, Ruben A. Buford. 2001. *Talking at Trena's: Everyday Conversations at an African American Tavern*. New York: New York University Press.

Mead, George Herbert. 1934. *Mind, Self, and Society: From the Standpoint of a Social Behaviorist*. Chicago: University of Chicago Press.

Mears, Ashley. 2010. "Size Zero High-End Ethnic: Cultural Production and the Reproduction of Culture in Fashion Modeling." *Poetics* 38: 21–46.

———. 2014. "Aesthetic Labor for the Sociologies of Work, Gender, and Beauty." *Sociology Compass* 8 (12): 1330–43.

Menger, Pierre-Michel. 1999. "Artistic Labor Markets and Careers." *Annual Review of Sociology* 25: 541–74.

Milligan, Melinda. 2003. "Displacement and Identity Discontinuity: The Role of Nostalgia in Establishing New Identity Categories." *Symbolic Interaction* 26 (3): 381–403.

Mills, C. Wright. 1951. *White Collar: The American Middle Classes*. New York: Oxford University Press.

Mills, Quincy T. 2013. *Cutting against the Color Line: Black Barbers and Barber Shops in America*. Philadelphia: University of Pennsylvania Press.

Misra, Joya, and Kyla Hays Walters. 2016. "All Fun and Cool Clothes? Youth Workers' Consumer Identity in Clothing Retail." *Work and Occupations* 44 (3): 294–325.

Moretti, Enrico. 2013. *The New Geography of Jobs*. New York: Mariner Books.

Mundy, Liza. 2012. *The Richer Sex: How the New Majority of Female Breadwinners Is Transforming Sex, Love, and Family*. New York: Simon and Schuster.

Murray, James R., Edward A. Powers, and Robert J. Havighurst. 1971. "Personal and Situational Factors Producing Flexible Careers." *Gerontologist* 11 (4: 2): 4–12.

Naccarato, Peter, and Kathleen LeBesco. 2012. *Culinary Capital*. New York: Bloomsbury Academic.

Neff, Gina. 2012. *Venture Labor: Work and the Burden of Risk in Innovative Industries*. Cambridge, MA: MIT Press.

Neff, Gina, Elizabeth Wissinger, and Sharon Zukin. 2005. "Entrepreneurial Labor among Cultural Producers: 'Cool' Jobs in 'Hot' Industries." *Social Semiotics* 15: 307–34.

Newman, Katherine. 1999. *No Shame in My Game: The Working Poor in the Inner City*. New York: Vintage.

Nixon, Sean. 2003. *Advertising Cultures: Gender, Commerce, Creativity*. London: Sage.

Nunley, Vorris L. 2011. *Keepin' It Hushed: The Barbershop and African American Hush Harbor Rhetoric*. Detroit: Wayne State University Press.

Oakley, Kate. 2009. "From Bohemia to Britart—Art Students over 50 Years." *Cultural Trends* 18 (4): 281–94.

Ocejo, Richard E. 2010. "What'll It Be? Cocktail Bartenders and the Redefinition of Service in the Creative Economy." *City, Culture and Society* 1 (4): 179–84.

———. 2011. "The Early Gentrifier: Weaving a Nostalgia Narrative on the Lower East Side." *City and Community* 10 (3): 285–310.

———. 2012. "At Your Service: The Meanings and Practices of Contemporary Bartenders." *European Journal of Cultural Studies* 15 (5): 642–48.

———. 2014a. "Show the Animal: Constructing and Communicating New Elite Food Tastes at Upscale Butcher Shops" *Poetics* 47: 106–21.

———. 2014b. *Upscaling Downtown: From Bowery Saloons to Cocktail Bars in New York City*. Princeton, NJ: Princeton University Press.

O'Connor, Erin. 2005. "Embodied Knowledge: Meaning and the Struggle towards Proficiency in Glassblowing." *Ethnography* 6 (2): 183–204.

Ogle, Maureen. 2013. *In Meat We Trust: An Unexpected History of Carnivore America*. New York: Houghton Mifflin Harcourt.

Okrent, Daniel. 2011. *Last Call: The Rise and Fall of Prohibition*. New York: Scribner.

Oldenburg, Ray. 1989. *The Great Good Place: Cafes, Coffee Shops, Bookstores, Bars, Hair Salons, and Other Hangouts at the Heart of a Community*. New York: Marlowe.

Oldstone-Moore, Christopher. 2015. *Of Beards and Men: The Revealing History of Facial Hair*. Chicago: University of Chicago Press.

Pachirat, Timothy. 2011. *Every Twelve Seconds: Industrialized Slaughter and the Politics of Sight*. New Haven, CT: Yale University Press.

Pappas, Gregory 1989. *Magic City: Unemployment in a Working-Class Community*. Ithaca, NY: Cornell University Press.

Park, Robert E. 1952. *Human Communities*. Glencoe, IL: Free Press.

Park, Robert E., Ernest W. Burgess, and Roderick Duncan McKenzie. 1925. *The City*. Chicago: University of Chicago Press.

Parsons, Brad Thomas. 2011. *Bitters: A Spirited History of a Classic Cure-All, with Cocktails, Recipes, and Formulas*. San Francisco: Ten Speed Press.

Patch, Jason. 2008. "Ladies and Gentrification: New Stores, Residents, and Relationships in Neighborhood Change." *Gender in an Urban World*, Research in Urban Sociology, vol. 9, ed. Judith N. DeSena and Ray Hutchinson. Bingley, UK: Emerald Group.

Peretti, Burton W. 2007. *Nightclub City Politics and Amusement in Manhattan*. Philadelphia: University of Pennsylvania Press.

Perry, Forrest. 2013. "The Class Dimension of Hip Rebellion." *Rethinking Marxism* 25 (2): 163–83.

Peterson, Richard A. 1992. "Understanding Audience Segmentation: From Elite and Mass to Omnivore and Univore." *Poetics* 21 (4): 243–58.

———. 1997. "The Rise and Fall of Highbrow Snobbery as a Status Marker." *Poetics* 25 (2): 75–92.

Peterson, Richard A., and Roger M. Kern. 1996. "Changing Highbrow Taste: From Snob to Omnivore." *American Sociological Review* 61 (5): 900–907.

Peterson, Richard A., and Albert Simkus. 1992. "How Musical Taste Groups Mark Occupational Status Groups." In *Cultivating Differences: Symbolic Boundaries and the Making of Inequality*, ed. M. Lamont and M. Fournier. Chicago: University of Chicago Press.

Pettinger, Lynne. 2005. "Gendered Work Meets Gendered Goods: Selling and Service in Clothing Retail." *Gender, Work and Organization* 12 (5): 460–78.

Pollan, Michael. 2007. *The Omnivore's Dilemma: A Natural History of Four Meals*. New York: Penguin.

Powers, Madelon. 1998. *Faces along the Bar: Lore and Order in the Workingman's Saloon, 1870–1920*. Chicago: University of Chicago Press.

Pugh, Allison J. 2015. *The Tumbleweed Society: Working and Caring in an Age of Precarity*. New York: Oxford University Press.

Rebers, Hans, Ruben Konig, and Henk Westerik. 2006. "Omnivore Behaviour? Cultural Capital and Television Programme Genres." *Mens en Maatschappij* 81 (4): 375–88.

Regan, Gary. 2003. *The Joy of Mixology: The Consummate Guide to the Bartender's Craft*. New York: Clarkson Potter.

Reighley, Kurt. 2010. *The United States of Americana: Backyard Chickens, Burlesque Beauties, and Handmade Bitters: A Field Guide to the New American Roots Movement*. New York: Harper Perennial.

Rimmer, Mark. 2012. "Beyond Omnivores and Univores: The Promise of a Concept of Musical Habitus." *Cultural Sociology* 6: 299–318.

Ritzer, George. 2000. *The McDonaldization of Society*. London: Sage.

Rivera, Lauren A. 2015. *Pedigree: How Elite Students Get Elite Jobs*. Princeton, NJ: Princeton University Press.

Robinson, Victoria, Alexandra Hall, and Jenny Hockey. 2011. "Masculinities, Sexualities, and the Limits of Subversion: Being a Man in Hairdressing." *Men and Masculinities* 14 (1): 31–50.

Rose, Mike. 2004. *The Mind at Work: Valuing the Intelligence of the American Worker*. New York: Penguin Books.

Rosin, Hanna. 2012. *The End of Men: And the Rise of Women*. New York: Riverhead Books.

Ross, Andrew. 2003. *No-Collar: The Humane Workplace and Its Hidden Costs*. Philadelphia: Temple University Press.

Rossel, Jorg. 2006. "Omnivores in the Cinema: Distinction through Cultural Variety in Germany." *Soziale Welt* 57 (3) 259–72.

Rosso, Brent D., Katherine H. Dekas, and Amy Wrzesniewski. 2010. "On the Meaning of Work: A Theoretical Integration and Review." *Research in Organizational Behavior* 30: 91–127.

Ryan, Bill. 1995. "'Smirnoff White Whiskey—No Smell, No Taste.'" *New York Times*, February 19.

Salzman, Marian, Ira Matathia, and Ann O'Reilly. 2005. *The Future of Men: The Rise of the Ubersexual and What He Means for Marketing Today*. New York: Palgrave MacMillan.

Schatzker, Mark. 2011. *Steak: One Man's Search for the World's Tastiest Piece of Beef*. New York: Penguin Books.

Schell, Orville. 1985. *Modern Meat: Antibiotics, Hormones, and the Pharmaceutical Farm*. New York: Random House.

Schiermer, Bjorn. 2013. "Late-modern Hipsters: New Tendencies in Popular Culture." *Acta Sociologica* 57 (2): 167–81.

Schlosser, Eric. 2001. *Fast Food Nation: The Dark Side of the All-American Meal*. New York: Houghton Mifflin Harcourt.

Schwalbe, Michael. 2010. "In Search of Craft." *Social Psychology Quarterly* 73: 107–11.

Scott, Allen J. 2006. "Creative Cities: Conceptual Issues and Policy Questions." *Journal of Urban Affairs* 28: 1–17.

Sender, Katherine. 2006. "Queens for a Day: *Queer Eye for the Straight Guy* and the Neoliberal Project." *Critical Studies in Media Communication* 23: 131–251.

Sennett, Richard. 1998. *The Corrosion of Character: The Personal Consequences of Work in the New Capitalism*. New York: W.W. Norton.

———. 2008. *The Craftsman*. New Haven, CT: Yale University Press.

Sennett, Richard, and Jonathan Cobb. 1972. *The Hidden Injuries of Class*. New York: W. W. Norton.

Sharma, Ursula, and Paula Black. 2001. "Look Good, Feel Better: Beauty Therapy as Emotional Labor. *Sociology* 35 (4): 913–31.

Sharone, Ofer. 2014. *Flawed System/Flawed Self: Job Searching and Unemployment Experiences.* Chicago: University of Chicago Press.

Sherman, Rachel. 2007. *Class Acts: Service and Inequality in Luxury Hotels.* Berkeley: University of California Press.

Sherrow, Victoria. 2006. *Encyclopedia of Hair: A Cultural History.* Westport, CT: Greenwood.

Shils, Edward. 1965. "Charisma, Order, and Status." *American Sociological Review* 30 (2): 199–213.

Siciliano, Michael. 2016. "Disappearing into the Object: Aesthetic Subjectivities and Organizational Control in Routine Cultural Work." *Organization Studies* 37 (5): 687–708.

Simpson, Mark. 1994. "Here Come the Mirror Men." *Independent*, November 15.

———. 2002. "Meet the Metrosexual." *Salon*, July 22. Available at http://www.salon.com/2002/07/22/metrosexual/ (accessed November 25, 2014).

Simpson, Ruth, Jason Hughes, Natasha Slutskaya, and Maria Balta. 2014. "Sacrifice and Distinction in Dirty Work: Men's Construction of Meaning in the Butcher Trade." *Work, Employment and Society* 28 (5): 754–70.

Smith, Vicki. 2002. *Crossing the Great Divide: Worker Risk and Opportunity in the New Economy.* Ithaca, NY: ILR Press.

Smith Maguire, Jennifer. 2008. "The Personal Is Professional: Personal Trainers as a Case Study of Cultural Intermediaries." *International Journal of Cultural Studies* 11 (2): 211–29.

Spradley, James P., and Brenda J. Mann. 1976. *The Cocktail Waitress: Woman's Work in a Man's World.* New York: John Wiley and Sons.

Stack, Carol. 1974. *All Our Kin: Strategies for Survival in a Black Community.* New York: Basic Books.

Standing, Guy. 2011. *The Precariat: The New Dangerous Class.* New York: Bloomsbury.

Suttles, Gerald D. 1969. *The Social Order of the Slum: Ethnicity and Territory in the Inner City.* Chicago: University of Chicago Press.

Swidler, Ann. 1986. "Culture in Action: Symbols and Strategies." *American Sociological Review* 51 (2): 273–86.

Taylor, Timothy D. 2009. "Advertising and the Conquest of Culture." *Social Semiotics* 19 (4): 405–25.

Thomas, L. Eugene. 1980. "A Typology of Mid-Life Career Changers." *Journal of Vocational Behavior* 16: 173–82.

Thomas, L. Eugene, Richard L. Mela, Paula I. Robbins, and David W. Harvey. 1976. "Corporate Drop-outs: A Preliminary Typology." *Vocational Guidance Quarterly* 24: 220–28.

Tilly, Chris. 1995. *Half a Job: Bad and Good Part-Time Jobs in a Changing Labor Market*. Philadelphia: Temple University Press.

Trubek, Amy B. 2008. *The Taste of Place: A Cultural Journey into Terroir*. Berkeley: University of California Press.

Tsui, Bonnie. 2011. "Rye Is Back, with Flavors of Americana." *New York Times*, December 22.

Van Eijck, Koen. 1999. "Jazzed Up, Brassed Off: Sociale Differentiatie in Patronen van Muzikale Genrevoorkeuren." *Mens en Maatschappij* 74 (1): 43–61.

———. 2001. "Social Differentiation in Musical Taste Patterns." *Social Forces* 79 (3): 1163–85.

Van Eijck, Koen, and Bertine Bargeman. 2004. "The Changing Impact of Social Background on Lifestyle: 'Culturalization' instead of Individualization?" *Poetics* 32: 439–61.

Van Maanen, John, and Stephen R. Barley. 1984. "Occupational Communities: Culture and Control in Organizations." *Research in Organizational Behavior* 6: 287–365.

Van Wel, Frits, Willemijn Maarsingh, Tom Ter Bogt, and Quinten Raaijmakers. 2008. "Youth Cultural Styles: From Snob to Pop." *Young* 16 (3): 325–40.

Veach, Michael R. 2013. *Kentucky Bourbon Whiskey: An American Heritage*. Lexington: University Press of Kentucky.

Veblen, Thorstein. 1899. *The Theory of the Leisure Class: An Economic Study of Institutions*. New York: Macmillan.

Venkatesh, Sudhir. 2000. *American Project: The Rise and Fall of a Modern Ghetto*. Cambridge, MA: Harvard University Press.

Wacquant, Loic. 2006. *Body & Soul: Notebooks of an Apprentice Boxer*. New York: Oxford University Press.

Warhurst, Chris, and Dennis Nickson. 2007. "Employee Experience of Aesthetic Labour in Retail and Hospitality." *Work, Employment and Society* 21 (1): 103–20.

Warhurst, Chris, Dennis Nickson, Anne Witz, and Anne Marie Cullen. 2000. "Aesthetic Labour in Interactive Service Work: Some Case Study Evidence from the 'New' Glasgow." *Service Industries Journal* 20 (3): 1–18.

Weber, Max. 1958. *The Protestant Ethic and the Spirit of Capitalism*. New York: Scribner.

———. 1963. *The Sociology of Religion*. Boston: Beacon.

———. 1968. "The Concept of Legitimate Order." In *Max Weber on Charisma and Institution Building*, ed. S. N. Eisenstadt. Chicago: University of Chicago.

Wenger, Etienne. 1998. *Communities of Practice: Learning, Meaning, and Identity*. Cambridge, UK: Cambridge University Press.

West, Candace, and Don Zimmerman. 1987. "Doing Gender." *Gender and Society* 1 (2): 125–51.

West, Lois A. 2001. "Negotiating Masculinities in American Drinking Subcultures." *Journal of Men's Studies* 9 (3): 371–92.

Whyte, William Foote. 1943. *Street Corner Society: The Social Structure of an Italian Slum*. Chicago: University of Chicago Press.

Whyte, William H. 1956. *The Organization Man*. New York: Simon and Schuster.

Wieder, D. Lawrence. 1974. *Language and Social Reality: The Case of Telling the Convict Code*. Berlin: De Gruyter Mouton.

Williams, Christine L., and Catherine Connell. 2010. "'Looking Good and Sounding Right': Aesthetic Labor and Social Inequality in the Retail Industry." *Work and Occupations* 37: 349–77.

Williams, Louis. 1993. "The Relationship between a Black Barbershop and the Community That Supports It." *Human Mosaic* 27: 29–33.

Willis, Paul. 1977. *Learning to Labor: How Working Class Kids Get Working Class Jobs*. New York: Columbia University Press.

Wilson, Anne. 2006. *Water of Life*. London: Prospect Books.

Wilson, Janelle L. 2005. *Nostalgia: Sanctuary of Meaning*. Lewisburg, PA: Bucknell University Press.

Wirth, Louis. 1938. "Urbanism as a Way of Life." *American Journal of Sociology* 44 (1): 1–24.

Witz, Anne. 1992. *Professions and Patriarchy*. London: Routledge.

Witz, Anne, Chris Warhurst, and Dennis Nickson. 2003. "The Labour of Aesthetics and the Aesthetic of Organization." *Organization* 10: 33–54.

Wolkowitz, Carol. 2006. *Bodies at Work*. London: Sage.

Wondrich, David. 2007. *Imbibe! Updated and Revised Edition: From Absinthe Cocktail to Whiskey Smash, a Salute in Stories and Drinks to "Professor" Jerry Thomas, Pioneer of the American Bar*. New York: TarcherPerigee.

———. 2010. *Punch: The Delights (and Dangers) of the Flowing Bowl*. New York: TarcherPerigee.

Wright, Earl II. 1998. "More than Just a Haircut: Sociability within the Urban African American Barbershop." *Journal of Research on African American Men* 9: 1–13.

Wrzesniewski, Amy. 2002. "'It's Not Just a Job': Shifting Meanings of Work in the Wake of 9/11." *Journal of Management Inquiry* 11 (2): 230–34.

Wrzesniewski, Amy, and Jane E. Dutton. 2001. "Crafting a Job: Revisioning Employees as Active Crafters of Their Work." *Academy of Management Review* 26 (2): 179–201.

Wrzesniewski, Amy, Clark McCauley, Paul Rozin, and Barry Schwartz. 1997. "Jobs, Careers, and Callings: People's Relations to Their Work." *Journal of Research in Personality* 31: 21–33.

Zukin, Sharon. 1983. *Loft Living: Culture and Capital in Urban Change*. New Brunswick, NJ: Rutgers University Press.

———. 1995. *The Cultures of Cities*. Oxford: Blackwell.

———. 2010. *Naked City: The Death and Life of Authentic Urban Places*. New York: Oxford University Press.

Zukin, Sharon, and Ervin Kosta. 2004. "Bourdieu Off-Broadway: Managing Distinction on a Shopping Block in the East Village." *City and Community* 3 (2): 101–14.

Zukin, Sharon, Valerie Trujillo, Peter Frase, Danielle Jackson, Tim Recuber, and Abraham Walker. 2009. "New Retail Capital and Neighborhood Change: Boutiques and Gentrification in New York City." *City and Community* 8 (1): 47–64.

INDEX